FOUNDATION/INTERMEDIATE
GNVQ
BUSINESS

RG Bywaters

JE Evans-Pritchard

AJ Glaser

EZ Mayer

Longman

Edinburgh Gate,
Harlow, Essex

Pearson Education Limited
Edinburgh Gate
Harlow
Essex
CM20 2JE
England and Associated Companies throughout the World

ISBN 0 582 40633 1

First published 2000
Second impression 2000

Printed in Singapore (KHL)

The Publisher's policy is to use paper manufactured from sustainable forests.

Acknowledgements

Liz Mayer and Tony Glaser wish to thank Andy Hamment, MD, Controls Division, Ultra Electronics and Anthony Young, Senior Partner, The Young Veterinary Partnership, for their help and assistance.

We are grateful to the following for permission to reproduce copyright material:

The Body Shop for pages 7–8; Oxfam for page 17; The Corus Group for page 25; The Prince's Trust for page 75; Prontaprint Ltd for page 81; Saffery Champness for page 206; News International Syndication Ltd for 'Employers miss out on golden age for workers' in *The Times* 14.8.99 and 'Japanese firms rewrite rules of employment' in *The Times* 2.8.99; the Office of National Statistics for figures 'UK population of working age', 'Labour force by gender and age', 'Average hours worked by full-time employees', 'Employees in temporary jobs', 'Employees with flexible work patterns' and 'Job-related training opportunities' and 'Employees in temporary jobs' in *Social Trends 1997* and 'Employers' provision of training' in *Regional Trends* 1998 © Crown Copyright 1997, 1998; Tate Temp Specialists for page 224; Progress Magazine NEBS Management No. 20, August 1998 for pages 250 and 251; Dixons Group plc for pages 269 and 291; Safeway plc for page page 318; WHSmith High Street for page 329.

We are grateful to the following for permission to reproduce copyright photographs:

Collections for page 100 (Geoff Howard/restaurant), 88 (Robert Pilgrim/silk mill), 98 (Select/miner), 79 (Clive Shenton/Co-Op); James Davis for page 122 (Houses of Parliament); Greg Evans International for page 82 (hospital), 265 (high street), 340 (security camera); Eye Ubiquitous for page 23 (P Thomson/lorry), 43 (S Passmore/telephone), 83 (P Seheult/sorting office), 194 (P Seheult/newsagents), 13 (M Stace/charity shop), 73 (P Bennett/window cleaner); Getty One Stone for page 203 (Z Kaluzny/factory), 317 (K Share/point of sale); Sally & Richard Greenhill for page 277 (shopping centre); Pictor International for page 33 (reception); Stock Market for page 43 (telephone), 281 (specialist shop).

CONTENTS

Preface

Why GNVQ?

The main difference between GNVQ and GCSE is in how you will learn about business. GCSE courses tend to study business from textbooks and teacher's notes. The final test of your knowledge and understanding is in an examination paper that tests how well you have learned what you have been taught and how well you have revised.

GNVQ does require knowledge of the basic terms and theories and an understanding of how business works, but the main method of learning is through first hand experience of what is going on in businesses. Each time you shop, any work experience you do, any job that you have, all of these will give you a real understanding of what goes on in business. The best way to understand what business is about is to work in business, and this is the approach that is taken in this book.

The right GNVQ approach

As part of your study of GNVQ Business you will need to learn and understand basic terms and facts. These are provided in this textbook. You will be tested on this through your assignments and the external tests.

The major part of your study, however, will be about the real world of business. You will need to be able to use your knowledge and understanding to deal with real business situations. In studying finance, for example, you will need to be able to fill out financial documents correctly and interpret what financial data means. When you explain why businesses locate in certain places or advertise on television you will be expected to give general answers but also to give examples from businesses you have studied personally.

This textbook has been written to help you to look at business in this way. It gives you the facts, basic terminologies, and details of how some businesses deal with all the pressures of competition and changing business environments. But it also gives you advice on how to study real businesses and how to use this to help you to gain high grades in your assignment work and in your external tests.

GNVQ is about the real world. This textbook will help you to use facts, terms, and theories so that you can explain what goes on in the real world. With the help of this textbook you will be able to:

- explain why businesses behave in the way that they do.

- suggest ways in which businesses can improve.

- recognise general business terms and procedures and be able to use them.

This will enable you to write high quality assignments and gain high marks in your external tests.

WHAT IS A BUSINESS?

Foundation and Intermediate

> Definition – a **business** is an organisation that has been specifically set up to provide some kind of product to its customers.

It may seem that answering the question 'What is a business?' should be a fairly easy task. There are, after all, many well-known businesses all around us which we can take as examples, such as Tesco, Shell, McDonald's and Coca-Cola. It may also seem obvious why these firms are **businesses**. They all sell things, e.g. groceries, petrol, hamburgers and fizzy drinks.

Unfortunately, saying exactly what the term '**a business**' means is more complicated.

- Is a school a business?
- Is the government running a business when it

provides services such as libraries or a police force?

- Is a charity, such as the Samaritans, a business when it sells nothing, but simply listens to people in difficulty and gives support and advice?

The answer is that they are all businesses and therefore any definition of the term 'business' must be wide enough to include companies selling goods and services for profit, the government providing services free to its citizens, and charities helping people in need.

At the same time, however, many other activities that seem very similar to these will not be called businesses.

- A mother providing a cooked meal for the family.
- An experienced amateur golfer offering advice to her friends on how to avoid slicing the ball.
- A woman who looks in on her elderly neighbour every day to see if she can collect anything for her from the local shops.

So our definition must be narrow enough to exclude these kinds of activities.

Basic characteristics of businesses

Various basic features distinguish business activities from non-business activities. These include:

- **Businesses are all owned.** It is the ownership of a business that determines what kind of business it is – whether it is a sole trader, partnership, company, co-operative, or owned by the state. This ownership creates certain rights and responsibilities.

> Desborough Co-operative Society Ltd of Northamptonshire is owned by its 2,500 members.

- **The rights and responsibilities of businesses are laid down and enforced by law.** If the amateur golfer gives the wrong advice to a friend she cannot be sued, but if a bank gives customers the wrong advice and they lose money because of this, they can take the bank to court.

> Under the **Health and Safety at Work Act** all employers are required to prepare a written statement of their general policy on health and safety.

- **Businesses need to be set up under certain rules.** Companies, for example, must complete two main documents, called the Articles of Association and the Memorandum of Association, before they are allowed to start trading.

> No business selling alcohol or running a betting office can start trading without a licence.

- **Businesses need to keep records of what they do.** Running a business involves people, costs, payments and, usually, receipts of money, so records need to be kept. These records allow the owners, employees, customers, the tax office to check that the business is handling its finances correctly and that it is not doing anything that it is not allowed to do.

> All companies must provide the Registrar of Companies with a copy of their financial accounts every year.

- **Businesses provide goods and services to other businesses or to the public.** Usually these goods and services are sold for a profit, as with a car manufacturer or a bank, but sometimes the goods and services are given free to the user, as with state-run education or charity.

> The Pepsi Company, best known for its cola drink, actually earns most of its revenue from selling snacks and from its fast food restaurants such as Kentucky Fried Chicken, Taco Bell and Pizza Hut.

- **Businesses have customers.** Customers are people who benefit from what businesses provide. Without customers businesses would not exist. Customers may be other firms or they may be the general public.

> The customers of British Airways plc include members of the general public who want holidays in foreign countries and businesses that need to send staff to conferences or goods to their customers.

Whilst the mother, the amateur golfer and the neighbour mentioned above may have some of these characteristics, they do not have all of them. They are, therefore, not businesses. On the other hand, all of the following are businesses:

Figure 1.1.1. Types of business

Classifying Business

There are many thousands of businesses in the UK and every business is different in some way from every other business. It would be impossible to study them all to find out how each of them works. Our understanding of business must, therefore, come from studying a few businesses and then looking for common characteristics. This will tell us how different types of businesses work.

Throughout this book you will find that businesses are classified in different ways. Each way of classifying a business identifies particular characteristics that are common to all businesses of that type. Examples of these common characteristics are given below.

- All banks deal with money.

- All companies have shareholders.

- All businesses in tertiary industry provide a service.

- All sole traders have unlimited liability.

- All retailers sell goods or services to consumers.

In this unit we will look at some of these classifications.

In **Chapter 1** we will look at the aims and objectives of businesses (**Intermediate level**).

In **Chapter 2** we will look at the major functions that are carried out by business, such as finance and marketing (**Foundation and Intermediate levels**).

In **Chapter 3** we will look at the structure of businesses and how the staff fit into these structures (**Intermediate level**).

In **Chapter 4** we will look at how people in businesses communicate with each other and how they communicate with people outside the business (**Foundation and Intermediate levels**).

CHAPTER 1

BUSINESS AIMS AND OBJECTIVES

Intermediate level

KEY TERMS:

aims and objectives

profit making businesses

non-profit making businesses

short- and long-run objectives

mission statements

not-for-profit businesses

business activities

In this chapter you will learn about why people run businesses.

Some owners of businesses do have 'profit' as their major aim. Many others have profit as one of their major aims, but they have other aims as well, such as job satisfaction, power to do what they want, and making products that are environmentally friendly.

Definition – an **aim** is the long-term objective of a business, e.g. becoming the supermarket with the largest market share. An **objective** is a short-term target which should help the business to meet its long-term aims, e.g. improve its product range so that more customers will come to the supermarket.

The aims and objectives of businesses also depend on what type of business they are.

- State-owned businesses should be trying to produce products that are of benefit to the general public.

- Charities will be thinking about what is best for the aims of the charity.

- Most companies should be making profits for their shareholders.

- A private tennis club should be trying to provide the best facilities that it can for its members and give value for money.

This chapter will look at the wide range of aims and objectives that businesses have and how they set about achieving these.

Identifying the Main Aims and Objectives

Sometimes the main aim of a business is fairly obvious.

- Schools have a clear aim of educating students so that they can pass examinations and gain qualifications.

- Oxfam has the clear aim of raising funds so that it can support its charity operations around the world.

- Banks have the clear aims of serving their customers and making profits for their shareholders.

With other businesses it is far more difficult to see what their aims and objectives are. Why have Tesco and Dixons become providers of free access to the internet? Why do shops have sales after Christmas? Why do farmers sell their products to supermarkets for a few pence when they could sell the same products direct to the public for pounds?

Even with businesses that have obvious main aims there are often other objectives that are nearly as important. Educating students is the obvious main aim for schools and colleges, but their ability to do this depends on how much money they have to spend on teachers, books and facilities. This, in turn, depends on how many students they have. They therefore dedicate a considerable amount of time and effort to competing with other schools and colleges to attract as many students as possible. This is time and money spent on advertising and promotion and not on educating.

BP Amoco plc

'BP Amoco's goal is to play a leading role in meeting the world's needs for energy from oil, gas, solar power and petrochemicals without damaging the environment.'

IBM (UK) Ltd

'At IBM, we strive to lead in the creation, development and manufacture of the industry's most advanced information technologies, including computer systems, software, networking systems, storage devices and microelectronics. We translate these advanced technologies into value for our customers through our professional solutions and services to businesses worldwide.'

Source: annual reports

Oxfam's main aim is to provide aid to needy causes around the world. To fund these activities it needs money and rather than rely on donations from well-meaning people Oxfam also sells goods in its many shops throughout the UK. These shops are, however, in competition with other shops and in order to compete and raise funds Oxfam needs to consider what prices will bring it the most profit. In running its shops Oxfam spends time and money competing with other firms and not directly on supporting good causes.

To find out what the real aims and objectives of a business are you can use the following approaches:

- Ask the managers, owners or employees of the business. This is fairly easy if the business is small.

- Observe how the business is run and what it does.

- Check details in the press or on the internet. In many cases someone else will already have found out what the main objectives are and they will be published somewhere.

- Check the literature that the business itself produces, such as annual reports, press releases and internet web sites.

> Definition – a **mission statement** identifies the stated objectives of a business.

Many businesses issue what are called **mission statements**. These state what the aims of the business are. You must, however, be careful with these statements because they often say what they want customers and the general public to believe, rather than what their actual main aim is. For example, very few mission statements say that the business wants to make as much profit as it can. The Body Shop recognises a wide range of stakeholders in its mission statement.

The Body Shop's Mission Statement

Our Reason For Being:
to dedicate our business to the pursuit of social and environmental change.
- To creatively balance the financial and human needs of our stakeholders: employees, customers, franchisees, suppliers and shareholders.
- To courageously ensure that our business is ecologically sustainable, meeting the needs of the present without compromising the future.

- To meaningfully contribute to local, national and international communities in which we trade, by adopting a code of conduct which ensures care, honesty, fairness and respect.
- To passionately campaign for the protection of the environment and human and civil rights, and against animal testing within the cosmetics and toiletries industry.
- To tirelessly work to narrow the gap between principle and practice, while making fun, passion and care part of our daily lives.

Common Aims and Objectives of Businesses

Below, we will look at some of the common aims and objectives of different businesses. It should, however, be remembered that businesses often have different long-term and short-term objectives. Shops that have sales after Christmas used to do this so that they could get rid of surplus old stock, especially in clothes shops and furniture shops, to leave space to display new designs and fashions for the spring and summer seasons or updated products. Many toys, such as *Star Wars* models or Furbys, will not sell well for more than one year and businesses need to get rid of their stocks before children start to want yo-yos or Buzz Lightyear.

In the short run these businesses need to clear their stock, so they put their prices down. In the long run, however, they wish to make high profits, so when the new products come out the prices are put up again.

Table 1.1.1 Examples of short-run and long-run objectives for businesses

Short-run objectives	Long-run objectives
A large business may put down its prices so that it can capture custom from smaller businesses in the same area. This is called **destroyer pricing**.	Once the small businesses have been forced to close, and customers have to buy from the large business, it will put its prices up again.
A new business may set its prices below the market price so that people will try the products. This is called **penetration pricing**.	Once the business is established it will put up its prices so that other businesses already in the market are not upset and do not start competing aggressively with it.
A business may spend money on sponsoring a local club with no direct increase in its sales.	This should make its name better known and it will be seen as supporting the local community. Both may help to increase sales in the long run.
Charities may use some of their money not for supporting disadvantaged people but for opening more shops in new situations.	This will eventually allow the charities to sell more goods and raise more money for the disadvantaged.
A business may spend more money on making sure that its packaging is environmentally friendly and this may put up prices and lose the business customers.	The environmental image of the business may encourage more customers who care about the environment and, in the long run, the business may sell more than it did before.

Making a Profit

Most businesses do not make as much profit as they could, but they do need to make some profit. Profit is very important to businesses. Without profit many businesses would simply stop producing, especially if they are actually making a loss. But profit is important for other reasons, as shown in Figure 1.1.1.

Figure 1.1.1 The importance of profit

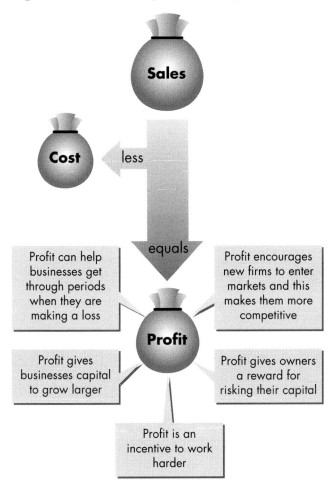

Profit is the difference between the amount of money gained from sales and the costs of producing the products that are being sold.

Profit = total sales − total costs

If a business wants to increase its profits it can do this in two ways:

1 by increasing its sales
2 by reducing its costs.

Many businesses try to increase sales or cut down on their costs in the short run because they know that in the long run this will make more profits for the business.

Increasing sales can be achieved by:

- finding new markets;

- making new products;

- advertising and promotion;

- competing against other firms and taking their customers;

- selling more of the same product to existing customers.

Reducing costs can be achieved by:

- finding cheaper supplies;

- buying in bulk and earning a discount;

- selling products direct to customers and cutting out the middlemen;

- reducing wage costs by paying less or reducing the number of staff;

- producing more efficiently so that more is produced from the same inputs.

If making more profit is the main long-term objective of the business then any, or even all, of the above may be the short-term objectives of the business. Many of the objectives that businesses seem to have, such as increasing market share or raising the image of the business, are simply short-term objectives that are designed to increase profits in the long term.

Other Aims and Objectives of Profit Making Businesses

Businesses that have a long-term objective of making a profit need to make certain that they run their businesses so that they *can* make profits. This often means that they must have other short-term objectives that keep their customers happy. Some of these objectives also apply to non-profit making organisations. These objectives include:

● producing competitive products;

● expanding the business;

● ensuring that the business survives.

1 Producing competitive products

All businesses provide goods or services, and often both, to their customers. Most businesses will try to provide the best goods and the best services that they can. This is the way that businesses keep their customers and, through this, meet their main objectives of making profit, providing charity, offering value for money.

Businesses should aim to provide customers with the goods or services that they want or need. How this is done will depend very much on the type of business involved and the characteristics of the customers. In a supermarket, for example, the following differences will occur:

Table 1.1.2 Customer wants and needs

Customer wants and needs:	**Met by:**
Customers with low incomes will want low prices and value for money.	Supermarkets provide a very low priced range of basic products such as toilet paper, pasta, bread, and tins of tomatoes.
Customers, often with good incomes, want quality and are prepared to pay for it.	Supermarkets provide a luxury range of goods with guaranteed quality.
Customers want to be able to choose from a wide range of different products.	All the larger supermarket branches offer in excess of 2,000 different products, and many types of product, such as cola, will come from different producers and in a variety of sizes, types and even flavours.
Customers want to be able to pay for their goods in different ways.	Supermarkets will accept cash, cheques, debit and credit cards and their own coupons.
Customers want a range of facilities that make shopping easier and more pleasurable.	Supermarkets offer credit, delivery, internet shopping, parking, restaurants and cafés, petrol stations, crèche facilities.

Most businesses are in competition with other businesses. If they do not produce products of a good enough quality and at a cheap enough price, their customers will simply go and buy what they want from someone else.

Case Study – The Virgin Group starts to produce cola

When the Virgin Group began the production of cola in 1994 through the newly formed Virgin Cola Company Ltd, it entered a highly competitive market, already dominated by Pepsi and Coke. It had the express aim of capturing 10% of the cola market in the UK. In order to achieve this aim it had to keep its prices lower than the prices for the Pepsi and Coke brands and carry out an extensive advertising campaign.

The Virgin Cola Company also had to find a major retailer which was prepared to stock the new brand. Sainsbury had launched its own brand of cola – Classic Cola – in competition with Pepsi and Coke, also at a lower price, therefore Sainsbury was not prepared to stock the Virgin brand. Virgin went to the other major supermarket chain, Tesco, which agreed to stock Virgin's range of colas.

In 1999 the cola market remained highly competitive, especially for relatively small companies like Virgin. Details of cola prices are given in the table below. Virgin had achieved its aim of breaking into the cola market, but in order to maintain its market share it still had to price its product below that of Pepsi and Coke.

Table 1.1.3 Prices of 6 cans of the leading cola products in supermarkets (1999)

Pepsi	£1.99
Coke	£1.99
Virgin	£1.80
Tesco	£1.59

2 Expanding the business

Most businesses trying to make profits have the aim of making higher and higher profits each year. Often the cost of making each product is much the same, so if the business can sell more it usually makes more profits. This expansion can take various forms:

- The business could sell more through its existing factory/shop.

- The business could open up new factories/shops.

- The business could sell in new markets, including abroad.

- The business could take over other businesses and run them as part of its own organisation.

- The business could start to produce different products and move into new markets.

Selfridges to open three new stores

In October 1999, following a rise in profits from £6.4 million to £8.3 million, Selfridges department store announced that it would open up three new stores in the UK. These will be located where there are high numbers of potential shoppers. Birmingham is a likely site and Glasgow is also being considered. The cost of opening these stores will be high, up to £30 million per store, and that may have a short-term effect on future profits. In the longer run, within five years, profits should be significantly ahead of those just reported.

Even very successful firms have to think about how they can expand. Often customers will buy only a certain amount of one particular product, even if the price is lowered. There are only so many bottles of tomato ketchup that a family will want to buy. Sales will reach a maximum as the market becomes 'saturated' and sales will then become steady, or may even begin to 'decline'. This effect is shown in what is called a product life cycle (Figure 1.1.2).

Figure 1.1.2 Product life cycle showing saturation and decline

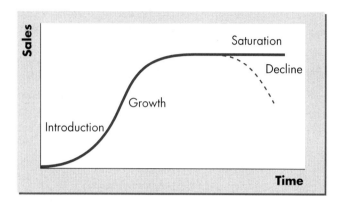

Advertising and promotion may keep the sales from declining (Heinz have been selling tomato ketchup since 1876), but if the firm wishes to expand it will have to find new customers or it will have to sell other products as well.

3 Ensuring that the business survives

Sometimes, when sales are falling or costs are rising, the main objective of the business becomes one of survival. If the business can survive in the bad times it may be able to recover and make profits in the future. Businesses can find themselves in this situation for any of the following reasons:

● Competitors take their customers.

● Costs rise and they cannot pass these on to their customers, or if they do pass them on they then lose sales.

● Their products have only a limited life span and they have moved into the decline stage of the product life cycle.

● The economy as a whole has moved into recession and the general public has less income to spend.

● The tastes of their customers change for some reason and so they decide not to buy the businesses' products.

Case Study – Marks & Spencer hits another low

Marks & Spencer, the retailing giant, which specialises in clothes and groceries, has just experienced two years of dramatic decline. Its supermarket sector has performed reasonably, but its clothes sector has fallen by nearly 20%.

As if that were not enough, Marks & Spencer announced on 12 January 2000 that Christmas sales had also fallen. Total sales were down by 3% and sales of clothing, footwear and gifts were down by 8% for the six weeks to 8 January. Peter Salisbury, the Chief Executive, had to admit that the new autumn range of clothes had not performed very well.

Plans for the spring collection make it look as though the firm is struggling to survive. Prices for the collection will be 5% lower than last year and some items will be priced 20% below last year's prices.

If profit is so important to businesses why do they not make as much as they can?

There are four main answers to this question.

1 Some organisations are not in business to make profits. Schools, hospitals and charities have other reasons for their work. They often provide their products free to users so they cannot make profits. They also do not need to make profits because their costs are being paid for by someone else, e.g. the state or through donations.

2 Some owners of businesses do not want to make

large amounts of profit. They are happy running a small business where there are limited pressures and they are their own bosses.

3 Some owners and managers want to make as much profit as possible but they are not able to run their businesses efficiently enough to achieve this.

4 Laws and government regulations may prevent businesses from making as much profit as they could. The privatised utilities, like the water and electricity companies, are not allowed to put their prices up beyond what the government regulators allow (see page 73).

Not-for-profit Businesses/Non-profit making Businesses

Some business are set up specifically not to make profit for their owners. These businesses are known as **not-for-profit businesses** or **non-profit making businesses**. Although these two sound as though they are the same type of business there are differences.

A **not-for-profit business**, such as Oxfam, may make a profit when it sells clothes and craft items in its shops, but it does not use these profits for the benefit of the owners or any shareholders. It uses them to support its charitable work. Many of these businesses are incorporated and operate in much the same way as other companies. They have directors and owners, but none of the funds that they earn goes to the owners. Everything they earn goes to support the causes or to pay for employing staff, renting the building, and so on.

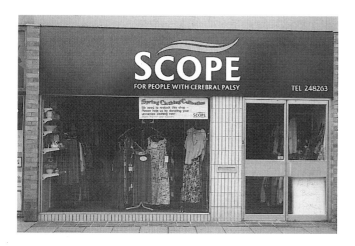

A **non-profit making business** is a business that makes no profit at all and has not been set up to make profits. The most common examples are local sports clubs and interest groups. Members will pay subscriptions to be part of the club and these funds will be used to buy and maintain any buildings or equipment that are needed and to pay for necessary administrative staff. Often the administration is carried out by members who work for nothing.

Definition – **charities** are organisations set up to help those in need or to promote good causes.

There are vast numbers of both not-for-profit and non-profit making businesses in the UK. Many of them are well-known national charities, such as Oxfam, Help The Aged, the NSPCC (National Society for the Prevention of Cruelty to Children) and Greenpeace. Other organisations are less well known (see the details on Continental Drifts below) and support very specific causes.

At the local level most amateur sports clubs are set up solely to support local members, as are interest groups such as writers' clubs and youth clubs, choral societies and amateur dramatic societies. Nearly all schools have charitable status and all state schools provide their basic educational services free.

Continental Drifts is a not-for-profit organisation representing the finest in UK underground performing arts. Our aim is to export the best of the UK festival and performing arts culture to the world. The acts we represent can be described as from 'outside of the mainstream'. Nevertheless, much of what we have to offer has developed a large following from the high exposure received at countless summer festivals and gigs throughout the world.

Apart from music, we have the finest performers, circus acts, artists, and production crews available through us. We regularly organise events and festivals throughout Europe that reflect new and underground UK culture. Through years of grafting on these stages, we have had the best possible vantage point on the new and emerging artists of tomorrow.

The reason why charities do not wish to make profits for themselves is because the people who set them up feel that helping other people or supporting causes that they care about is more important than making more money for themselves.

The reason why sports clubs and interest groups do not make profits is that they are set up to bring people together who have common interests. Money is required to buy only what is needed to help these activities to take place.

Organisations such as schools or hospitals are non-profit making because their funds are mainly provided from government and the government has instructed them to provide health or education to the general public.

Case Study – Whitchurch Old Time Favourites

In December 1998 a local Whitchurch group put on two performances of an evening of old time music numbers. The performances were given at the parish hall and tickets were sold to people in the town. As well as providing entertainment and food and drink the performances raised over £1,000 for a new bell for the local church.

All the performers and stage staff gave their services free of charge, but there were costs that had to be met. These costs included:

- renting the hall for the performances and for rehearsals;
- materials for costumes;
- food and drink;
- cleaning of the hall after use;
- printing programmes.

There are also many examples of businesses whose main aim is to make profit providing services free or at reduced rates for those who are less well off or for charity. Every year when the Children in Need appeal is made, the major banks, building societies and post offices provide free services so that people can pay in donations. Many cinemas and sports centres will charge special low rates for people who are unemployed and for old age pensioners.

Providing Public Services

A very large sector of business is involved in providing services, and some goods, free to the general public. Part of this is done by charities such as the Samaritans and Childline. Other parts are provided by central and local government, as with education, health, defence and law and order. For all these service organisations the main aim is to provide the best service possible for the benefit of the public.

There are also profit making businesses that provide services to the general public, such as the bus and train services and private hospitals and schools. Providing good services to the public is an important objective for these private businesses because if these services are not provided their customers will go somewhere else or use the services provided free by the state. However, many of these private businesses also have shareholders who expect them to make profits, and this may conflict with the objective of providing the best possible service for the consumer.

Examples of public services provided by the state:

- state education;

- the National Health Service;

- the Post Office;

- the BBC;

- the road transport system.

Examples of public services provided by private businesses:

- public schools, e.g. Eton and Winchester;

- private health care provided by firms such as BUPA;

- private delivery services, e.g. TNT and DHL;

- independent television;

- rail transport services such as SouthWest Trains and Virgin Trains.

Case Study – The health of the nation

The Department of Health has the ultimate responsibility for ensuring that the UK is provided with sufficient services to meet the main needs of the population. Its stated aim is to improve the health and well-being of the people of Britain by:

- supporting activity at a national level that will help to (i) protect (ii) promote and (iii) improve the nation's health;

- ensuring that comprehensive, high quality health care is provided to everyone who needs it, regardless of their ability to pay or where they live;

- ensuring that responsive social care and child protection is provided for those who cannot provide it for themselves.

Other Business Aims and Objectives

Today a great many people who own and run businesses believe that just making as much profit as possible is not the main reason for being in business. They believe that people who run businesses also have a social responsibility to run their businesses in a way that will help to improve society rather than just taking what they can from it for their own personal benefit.

These social objectives include:

- protecting the environment;

- providing their workers with good conditions and fair pay;

- supporting the local community of which they are part.

1 Protecting the environment

Protecting the environment has become very important to many people, and even if businesses do not see this as a priority, their customers may do. Most businesses now try to operate in a more environmentally friendly way, and they are also keen to tell their customers that they are doing this.

Protection of the environment is sometimes demanded by government and firms have to do what they are told. Examples of such laws include controls on vehicle emissions, noise from machinery, and how businesses are allowed to dispose of dangerous chemicals.

Other environmentally friendly actions are decided by the businesses themselves. Common examples include:

- making products and packaging that can be recycled;

- using recycled raw materials for making products or packaging;

- providing facilities for customers to recycle glass, paper and cans;

- using only raw materials which do not cause environmental damage.

Case Study – Reducing environmental pollution

Many businesses are now committed to reducing the negative environmental effects of their production processes. This is particularly important in the pharmaceutical and chemical industries, where dangerous drugs and chemicals can have a very damaging effect on animals and plants.

Akzo Nobel, maker of such products as Crown paint, is fully committed to reducing the environmental impact of its production. The business states that:

> "Concern for health, safety and the environment is an integral part of Akzo Nobel's business policy."

and that:

> "Akzo Nobel protects the environment by preventing or minimising the environmental impact of its activities and products through appropriate design, manufacturing, and disposal practices."

Its reduction of waste between 1995 and 1998 certainly supports these claims.

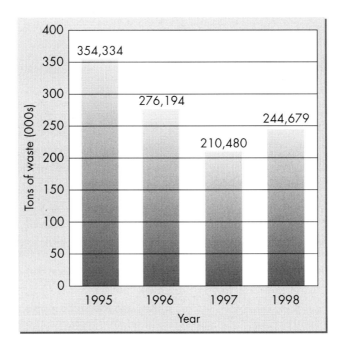

2 Providing workers with good conditions and fair pay

Some businesses have the reputation of exploiting their workers. Most businesses, however, treat their workers and staff with respect and pay them what is considered to be the going rate for the job. Yet other firms treat their workers particularly well because they believe that the benefits of running the company and making revenue and profit should be shared more equally among all the people who work in the business.

It is laid down by law that businesses must provide safe working conditions for their employees, and it is now also laid down that they must be paid a minimum wage (at least £3.70 per hour in October 2000). There are, however, many businesses which provide more than these minimum requirements. The kinds of additional benefits that firms may provide include:

- canteens for staff to use at lunch times and during other breaks;

OXFAM Oxfam operates a 'Fair Trade' policy which ensures that the producers of all the products it imports from developing countries receive a fair price and have decent working conditions. Originally this applied mainly to imported craft products but now Oxfam is selling a new range of food items, also covered by their Fair Trade policy.

Oxfam has also tried to persuade other businesses to follow suit. In May 1996, it launched the Clothes Code Campaign, calling on the top five UK high street clothing retailers to adopt a code of conduct which guarantees humane working conditions for the people who make their clothes.

- free leisure and sports facilities;

- private medical and pension cover;

- company cars;

- low interest loans for buying houses;

- shares in the company so that employees will receive part of the profits.

3 Supporting the local community

All businesses must be located somewhere. Some businesses are run by their owners from their own houses but many of them are located in premises in the local community. They usually employ people from the surrounding area and they often sell their products to the people who live in that area. When they transport their products or receive raw materials they use the local roads, and if they make a noise or create smoke, fumes or litter, it is the local community that is affected.

For all these reasons it is important that businesses keep on the right side of the local community and many businesses actively support local causes, sponsor local events or provide access to their own facilities for people who live nearby. Businesses also recognise that they owe a great deal to their staff, and if these people are local, supporting the local community is a way of giving something in return for their success.

Every November IBM at Hursley puts on a fireworks display to which the local village is invited as are friends and relatives of people who work there.

In many town centres McDonald's provide litter bins, not just for their own rubbish but for everyone using the centre.

Case Study – Supermarkets and the Council certainly not off their trolleys

As part of their efforts to keep Andover free of abandoned supermarket trolleys the local supermarkets and Test Valley Borough Council operate a trolleys hotline. Any members of the general public can use a Freephone service to report the location of trolleys that have been abandoned. The phones are answered by customer services in one of the supermarkets.

When the location is given, and the trolley is identified as one of Safeway's, Robert Greig's, Tesco's, Iceland's, Waitrose's or Marks & Spencer's, the supermarket is informed and arranges for the trolley to be picked up. The supermarkets get their trolleys back and the community gets rid of a possibly dangerous eyesore.

CHAPTER 2

DEPARTMENTS AND DEPARTMENTAL FUNCTIONS

Foundation and Intermediate

KEY TERMS:

departmental functions	production	marketing
human resources	finance	administration

In this chapter you will learn about:

- the functions that different departments carry out;

- the job roles that are commonly carried out within departments;

- how the roles and functions of different departments are connected and how they work together to achieve the aims and objectives of the business.

The Main Functions and Departments Found in Businesses

> Definition – a **function** is the job role carried out by an individual. Where a business divides these functions into different distinct sections the sections are called **departments**.

In business the term '**function**' means a main action that must be carried out if the business is to produce its goods or services. These functions include:

- bringing all the factors of production together so that the products can be made;

- actually producing the products;

- finding a market to sell the products in;

- persuading potential customers to buy the products;

- getting the products to the market;

- financing the production and advertising, and keeping records of all of the financial transactions;

- making certain that all the employees are trained, know what they have to do and work as they are expected to.

In small businesses most, if not all, of these functions may be carried out by one or two people. In large businesses these functions are often carried out by different departments. The common departments in a business are:

- production;
- distribution;
- human resources/personnel;
- finance;
- marketing.

For many businesses there may also be:

- sales;
- customer services;
- research and development.

Many businesses also have a separate department called 'Administration' but the activities that administration cover can be found in most departments. We will look at administration after we have looked at the other departments.

In business the term 'department' describes a separate part of the organisation which makes its own decisions about certain functions and has responsibility for carrying out these functions. Because the department must carry out certain functions it is sometimes called a **functional area**. This term is a little confusing and in most businesses the term 'department' is still used.

Production

> Definition – **production** is the process of combining factors so that a product is made. This product might be a good, such as a car, or a service, such as banking.

At the heart of all business is production. Without production there is nothing to sell. Normally, one thinks of production in terms of making goods out of raw materials, probably in a factory, e.g. making paper from trees in a paper mill, constructing cars from steel, glass, etc. in a car factory, and making paint from petroleum in an oil refinery and a chemical plant. In fact, all goods and all services need a production stage. This is shown for a range of products (goods and services) below.

The production process

In all businesses there will be a part of the production process where the product is changed in

some way. **Inputs** are changed to create **outputs**, which are then sold. *This is the function of production, to change inputs and make them ready for resale.*

Some of the main stages of the production processes for five very different products are shown below. Similar steps in production could be shown for any business.

> For a **dairy farmer:**
> - inputs (cattle feed, labour, straw, tractors) ➜ breeding cattle ➜ milking the cows ➜ supplying milk to the dairy.

> For **manufacturing pottery:**
> - inputs (clay, labour, electricity) ➜ making clay into plates, etc. ➜ painting and decorating pottery ➜ firing the pottery in kilns ➜ supplying pottery to wholesalers and retailers.

> For **building a house:**
> - inputs (wood, bricks, cement, cement mixers) ➜ digging out and making the foundations ➜ building the basic structure out of breeze blocks, bricks and wood ➜ fitting the floors and ceilings ➜ fitting the plumbing and electrics ➜ plastering, painting and decorating.

> For a **clothes retailer:**
> - inputs (labour, stocks of clothes) ➜ placing clothes on display ➜ serving customers.

> For **banking:**
> - inputs (labour, stationery, use of telephones, money transfer systems) ➜ providing services for saving and borrowing money ➜ allowing customers to pay in or take out money ➜ transferring money from one account to another ➜ advising customers of their bank balances ➜ providing a range of other financial services.

Figure 1.2.1 The basic production process

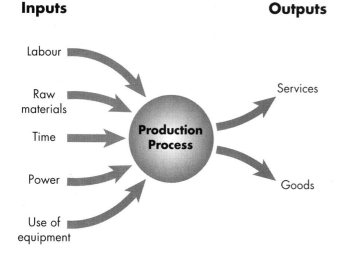

Included in the production process will be the design of the product and the packaging of the product.

Resources needed for production

For each production process the producer will need a wide range of resources before production is possible. These resources can be listed under four main headings.

- **Land and buildings**
  All production must take place somewhere and will therefore require some land. Most production also requires a building of some kind.

- **Equipment and furniture**
  Equipment will include **machines** such as computers and cement mixers, **vehicles** such as lorries and fork-lift trucks, and **tools** such as spades and rulers. Furniture will include **fixtures and fittings,** such as shelving in shops.

- **People**
  At some point in the production process people are needed to run machines, sell products to customers or give advice.

- **Materials**
  These are the materials that are needed to produce goods and services. For manufacturing firms these will be the raw materials that are turned into new products. For retailers these are the goods that are bought in and then resold. For service businesses, such as travel agents, the materials will be holiday brochures, paper, and possibly even tea and coffee for their staff and customers.

Tables 1.2.1 and 1.2.2 show examples of the kind of resources that each of the five products shown on page 20 would need under the four main headings.

A careful study of any of these production processes would show that a great many different resources are needed for each of them.

Table 1.2.1 Some resources used in selected production processes

	Dairy farming	Pottery manufacturing	House building	Clothes retailing	Banking
Land and buildings	Farmland Milking sheds Barns	Factory site Factory Warehouse	Building sites Works depot	Land for shop and car park Shop	Land for bank Bank premises
Equipment and furniture	Tractors Milking equipment	Pottery wheels Benches	Lorries/JCBs/ dumper trucks Drills, saws, cement mixers Scaffolding	Cash tills, security cameras Shelving, display racks	Cash point machines Security glass Office furniture
People	Farm labourers Tractor drivers Farm manager	Supervisors Potters Painters	Bricklayers Carpenters Plasterers	Shop manager Sales staff Cleaners	Bank manager Financial advisers Cashiers
Materials	Straw and hay Silage and cow cakes	Clay Paint Electricity	Bricks and mortar Timber Glass and putty	Clothes for resale Carrier bags	Paying in slips, cheque books Information booklets on services

Research and development (R&D)

The production department is often also responsible for carrying out research on new products and then developing them. Finding out what customers might want is the job of the marketing department and the function of market research (see page 28), but actually making new products and seeing if they work is part of research and development.

Most manufactured products have a limited life span and will eventually need to be replaced with new products. The research and development department must time this replacement carefully so that the new product will have been developed and introduced to the market before the current product reaches the decline stage. This is shown in Figure 1.2.2.

Figure 1.2.2 Timing for the launch of a new product

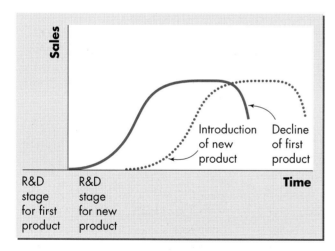

Quality control

> Definition – **quality control** is the process of ensuring that the quality of all products is of the required standard.

All businesses should ensure that their products are of high quality and quality control is an important function of all departments. The type of production will usually determine which department has the most responsibility for quality control.

- With manufactured products it is normally the production department that is responsible for the quality of the products that are produced.

- With retail services, like supermarkets or clothes shops, it is the sales staff who actually provide the service and the sales department, customer services department, or the human resources department are likely to be responsible for quality control.

- With smaller specialist businesses, such as dentists or solicitors, it will be the individual dentist or lawyer who is mainly responsible for the quality of his or her own work.

Distribution

Once goods have been produced in factories or on farms, they usually have to be transported to some other location where they will be sold. Sometimes manufacturing firms sell directly to the general public and then the goods may have to be delivered to them. Many shops also offer delivery services for their customers, as do businesses selling milk, building materials, coal and so on.

> Definition – **physical distribution** is the process of getting products to where the customers can see them and buy them.

All these businesses will need to provide the function of physical distribution. It is called 'physical' distribution because it deals with the actual movement of goods from one place to another. The distribution department will normally carry out all the following functions:

- preparing packing lists of the goods to be moved;

- packing the products into boxes or crates and then into lorries, vans;

- working out delivery schedules showing where and when goods are to be distributed;

- delivering the goods if the business has its own vehicles, or arranging for another firm to deliver them;

- receiving any returned goods and dealing with replacements.

Many large businesses, such as supermarket chains, collect goods from other producers and store them in a few large warehouses around the UK. These warehouses are called **regional distribution centres (RDCs)**. When individual stores need particular goods they will contact the RDC and the goods can be delivered immediately.

Retailers may also offer a delivery service to their customers. Most supermarkets now offer delivery to local households. Firms which sell large items, such as beds or sacks of coal, also offer delivery services. If the firm is large this may be organised by a separate distribution department.

Human Resources

> Definition – The **human resources/personnel department** is responsible for the management of the personnel in a business, with the aim of ensuring that they work as efficiently as possible.

People are at the heart of any business: managers, supervisors, clerical staff, machine operators, and so on. In large businesses recruiting, training and organising staff are major functions and are usually carried out by a separate human resources

department. The major functions of the human resources department include:

Recruitment, retention and dismissal of employees

Recruitment

Each individual department will know how many staff it needs and what jobs they will be required to do. The departments will then pass on these details to the human resources department. The human resources department will be responsible for recruiting new staff and will carry out all the following functions:

- making certain that a job specification and job description are created for each post;
- placing an advertisement in papers, trade magazines, at Job Centres, or contacting an agency or some other body that will be able to recommend suitable people;
- sending out details and an application form to people who wish to apply for the job;
- receiving applications and deciding who should be called for interview;
- conducting the interviews and appointing staff.

Retention

The human resources department is also responsible for making certain that good employees remain with the business. If employees leave, the businesses will have to go through the cost of recruiting more staff and training them. Retaining staff can be achieved through:

- paying higher wages than competitors;
- making the working environment pleasant, challenging, interesting, etc.;
- encouraging staff to buy shares in the business;
- providing good pension plans;
- offering promotion opportunities;
- providing interesting and valuable training.

Dismissal

There are a great many reasons why an employee may be dismissed, e.g. inability to do the job, stealing, racial discrimination towards other employees, too much time off work. The details will be recorded by the department in which the employee works, but it is the responsibility of the human resources department to discipline the staff, and if this does not work, to dismiss them.

Working conditions

The human resources department also has responsibility for general working conditions. These can be very wide but usually include:

- deciding rates of pay, bonuses, perks such as company cars and private health insurance cover;

- fixing the length, and possibly the timing, of holidays;

- deciding company pension provision;

- deciding redundancy conditions and payments;

- preparing the contract of employment and deciding about the conditions it contains;

- ensuring that the welfare of employees is monitored and supported;

- ensuring that staff and the business comply with health and safety regulations and legislation on discrimination (see below);

- providing a social aspect to the business, such as arranging works outings, social events, good canteen facilities, and so on.

Health and safety

All employees and their employer are responsible for ensuring that the workplace is a safe and healthy environment in which to work. Ensuring that this happens, and that the firm complies with the Health and Safety at Work Act, is the responsibility of the human resources department, as well as of the individual departments.

The details of what is involved are covered on page 244.

Training, development and promotion

All good businesses see staff both as a resource, which will help the business to achieve its aims and objectives, and as individuals who have their own aims and objectives. Very few individuals want to take a job at the age of 16 or 18 and then spend the rest of their lives doing that one job, especially if it is repetitive and boring. Good businesses will ensure that all staff are given training, opportunities of promotion and a personal plan that will help them to develop their skills and interests.

To ensure that all this is happening for every employee is a major task. That is why the human resources department is usually given the responsibility for seeing that all staff are being helped in this way.

Details of the way in which training is decided, and the types of training which businesses offer, are given on pages 249–256.

In the past, promotion was often almost automatic. The senior clerk retired, or died, and the junior clerk who had been with the firm for the most years was promoted. Today, promotion is generally based on who is the best person for the job. When a post becomes vacant, the human resources department will need to work out who is best for the job, and it will carry out the following procedures:

- identifying what job role needs to be filled, and what specification the applicant needs;

- checking the records of staff to see what skills they have and how they have done their jobs in the past;

- calling suitable staff for interview and appraisal and conducting the interview/appraisal so that the best member of staff will be appointed;

- appointing the member of staff to his or her new role;

- giving useful and supportive feedback to staff who have not been appointed.

Corus graduate recruitment and career development

corus The Corus Group believes in recruiting the most talented people for its graduate trainee programmes and helping them to develop into world-class managers.

Each trainee is given his/her own individually tailored career plan with support to help trainees to:
- develop their talents;
- work towards management positions;
- follow their own interests in a challenging way;
- learn by experience.

Graduates start their experience in one of the following functions but often experience a range of functions before they become managers:
- engineering
- manufacturing/operations management
- metallurgical and technical services
- research and development
- commercial
- customer technical services
- logistics
- supplies management
- finance
- human resources

Employee organisations and unions

> Definition – a **trade union** is an organisation of employees, or employers, which has been formed to achieve the common aims of the employees, or employers.

About 8 million people in the UK belong to trade unions. Most of these unions are formed to protect the rights and achieve the aims of employees, but there are also trade unions of employers which have been formed to achieve the common aims of employers. Employee trade unions usually have the following objectives:

- to ensure that their members are treated fairly in the workplace;

- to ensure that their members' jobs are secure;

- to improve working conditions, including rates of pay, length of working hours, holidays and pensions;

- to negotiate with management on behalf of their members;

- to support members when they are in dispute with the business, e.g. because of unfair treatment or unfair dismissal. This may include supporting them in legal action against the business.

Transport and General Workers Union

The Transport and General Workers Union (TGWU), the largest industrial trade union in the UK, has the following aim for its members.

'Our aim is to win the best possible terms and conditions for our members through improved competitive performance'.

It tries to achieve this by working in partnership with employers with:
- the common desire for competitive success in the workplace;
- flexibility with employee security;
- company growth through increased skills and personal development.

Many businesses, especially the newer businesses such as computer programming, have no employees who are members of trade unions. Many very small businesses also have no union members as employees. Other businesses, such as car manufacturing, farming, education, have a high percentage of employees who are members of trade unions. In these businesses the human resources department has the additional role of dealing and negotiating with trade union representatives.

Rights and responsibilities of employers and employees

When employers and employees work together they should consider the needs and rights of each other. If they do, the business is likely to run smoothly and employees, employers and customers will all benefit.

It is the function of the human resources department to see that these rights and responsibilities are carried out, both by the employees and by the employers.

Some responsibilities, such as helping employees to progress through the business, or not discriminating against people of different ages, are ones that the businesses and employees are *ethically* bound to meet. Other responsibilities, such as paying employees the same wage for the same work or not discriminating against people because of their gender or their race, are ones that the business and employees are *legally* bound to meet.

These rights and responsibilities are covered in full on pages 239 to 245. Details of four major acts are given on pages 40 to 42.

Finance

The finance function in business is more than just looking after money. The three main sections of finance are:

Management accounting – this deals with company budgets and strategic planning.
Management accountants:

● prepare business plans;

● monitor performance against set targets;

● suggest ways in which the financial performance of the business can be improved;

● give advice on how decisions in other departments, e.g. production or marketing, will affect the business financially.

Financial accounting – this deals with the keeping of the business's financial records. Financial accountants:

● keep records of all financial transactions in the business;

● monitor cash flow;

● ensure that the accounts are managed correctly;

● check that monies owed to and by the business are paid on time;

● check customers' credit positions if customers are being offered credit.

Internal auditing – this involves checking the finances of each department and how the departments are managing their finances.

Figure 1.2.3 Sources of finance

Finance will also cover other specialist services that involve the handling of money. These include:

● the payment of wages and salaries;

● calculation and payment of taxes, including income tax for employees, national insurance contributions for employees and the business, VAT and corporation tax;

● raising finance when the business needs additional funds.

Although the finance department has overall responsibility for the finances of a business, individual departments also make many financial decisions and handle money. When the marketing department advertises, it will decide where to advertise and it will consider which is the most cost-effective method of advertising. When the sales department in a business sells goods to consumers, its staff will take in the money, issue receipts and record what sales have been made.

The finance department will work closely with the other departments:

- providing them with finance;

- often deciding what budget they will be allowed to spend;

- receiving details of payments they have made and monies they have received;

- processing the financial documents that departments have created.

Marketing

The basic objective of marketing is to make sure that the right product is made and that potential customers are persuaded to buy it.

To make certain that this happens businesses must carry out a range of marketing functions. These include market research, advertising, pricing the product and selling the product. In small businesses these functions are likely to be carried out by one or two people, but in large businesses each function may be carried out by a different person. In some businesses the marketing functions are split into different departments, with advertising and promotion in a separate department from sales.

Figure 1.2.4 The four 'Ps'

The main functions of marketing are often referred to as the '4 Ps' – **price, promotion, place** and **product**.

- It is the job of the marketing department to decide what the **price** of products should be. The marketing staff will have researched the market and competitors' prices and will know what price is needed to get people to buy the products and make a profit.

- The marketing department is also responsible for **promoting** the product. This involves telling the customers about the product through advertising, sales literature, press releases, etc. It also involves persuading customers to buy the products through special offers, competitions, good advertising, and so on.

- The term **place** refers to where the product will be sold and how that will affect the way the business sells its products. We will look at this marketing function under the heading of 'channels of distribution' below.

- In marketing the term **product** does not refer to the actual production process, but to how the design of the product and the design of the packaging and advertising on the packaging will help to make the product sell.

Using the 4 Ps is a useful way of remembering what marketing involves but, unfortunately, there are functions of marketing, such as 'market research' and 'after sales services', that do not fit easily into these headings. We will therefore look at all the marketing functions separately, remembering that many textbooks will try to squeeze all of them into the 4 Ps.

Market research

In market research the business carries out research about its customers, about the competition, and about any factors that might affect the market into which it is putting its products. There will normally be a great deal of information that the business wants to find out about its **target population**. The target population is that group of people that the

Figure 1.2.5 Elements of marketing

business is trying to sell its products to. The kind of questions that the business hopes the market research will give answers to include:

- Where do these people live?

- What price are they prepared to pay for these kinds of products?

- How often do they buy them?

- Where do they buy them from?

- What qualities do they think are most important in these kinds of products?

- What similar products are they buying and why?

- What age and gender are they?

- What lifestyle and interests do they have?

If a business can find out exactly what its customers want it can then design, price and promote the product so that customers will actually buy it.

Pricing

Pricing is very important to a business. If the price is too high then the customers will not buy the product. If the price is too low then the business will lose profit that it could have made.

When businesses want to enter new markets they sell their products at a very low price to start with. This is called **penetration pricing**.

Many businesses simply check the price of competitors' products and charge the same price. This is called **competitor pricing**.

Many products are being upgraded all the time, e.g. computers. Other businesses regularly create new products all the time, e.g. books or computer games. For these products it is quite common to put the price very high to begin with. People who really want the new product will buy it, and then the business will lower the price and other people will now buy it. This is called **skimming**.

There are many other types of pricing and the marketing department must decide which would be best for its business and customers and for the actual product that is being sold.

Selling

Definition – a **consumer** is a person who buys a product for his or her own use or to give to other people for their own use, e.g. someone buying the weekly household shopping.

A **customer** is anyone who buys a product and this includes someone who is buying a product for a business to use, e.g. when a business buys office furniture or paper for its laser printer.

Consumers are always customers but some customers (businesses) are not consumers.

Selling takes place when a customer agrees to buy a product. With non-profit making organisations, such as charities where goods or services are given free, there is no selling process.

In shops the selling process is very easy to see. Goods are placed on display and sales staff help customers to choose clothes etc., wrap them up and take payment for them. Even with services such as hairdressing or banking it is easy to see who is doing the selling – the assistant who does your hair and then takes your money, or the financial adviser who arranges a loan.

With manufacturing firms it is more difficult to see the selling process. If producers want consumers to buy their products they will generally have to persuade shops to stock them first. Very few consumers will buy baked beans directly from Heinz. Instead, they will expect to find them in supermarkets and convenience stores. Here the manufacturers sell by sending **representatives** to the wholesalers and retailers, or by sending details of their products through the post or e-mail.

Some manufacturers will sell products directly to consumers, by telephone, through magazines and mail shots and, increasingly, through the internet. This is also a common method of selling financial services, holidays or entertainment. Here the selling function is being started by people on the end of a phone or by people explaining the product in magazines and brochures. The payment of money for the products may be by post, or with a credit or debit card. Unlike shopping, the selling process can take days, or even weeks, to complete.

Design

It is really the job of the production department to design products, but marketing needs to be involved.

> Definition – the **target population** is the customers that a product is aimed at.

Products should also be designed so that they appeal to the **target population**. Through its market research the marketing department should know what designs will be most appealing to its potential customers. The marketing department should therefore work closely with the design section of the production department to produce the best possible design.

Sensible businesses carefully research what their customers want, what other products are on the market, etc. and then produce products to meet the market demands. These businesses produce what are called **market orientated** products.

Other businesses can make products that are so good that they do not need to carry out market research. The product will 'sell itself'. These products are called **product orientated**.

Some firms are actually producing market orientated products which *do* require careful market research, but they think that their products are the best thing since sliced bread so they do not do the necessary research. The fairly inevitable result is that the products do not sell, and in some cases the business goes bankrupt.

Packaging

The physical process of packing up products is done either by the production department or the distribution department. The marketing department is involved in any advertising that comes with the packaging. Most goods that are found in supermarkets, for example, use the packaging around the goods to advertise. This will tell customers what the good is but it will also try to persuade the customers to buy the goods by using bright colours and bold writing, saying such things as 'special offer', 'new improved taste', etc.

The packaging will also contain a great deal of information about what the product is made of, what it can be used for, what the sell-by date is. Much of this information has to meet certain laws and regulations such as the Trade Descriptions Act, and it will normally be the marketing department which has to make certain that what is written on the packaging is legal and correct.

Channels of distribution

Channels of distribution show how products get from the original producers to the final customers. This is not the same as 'physical distribution' which, as we saw above, deals with how goods are transported from one place to another. The traditional channel of distribution is shown in Figure 1.2.6.

Figure 1.2.6 Traditional channel of distribution

This is still the most usual channel for producers of standard household goods which are sold through convenience stores and small supermarket chains. For large supermarkets and major chain stores selling clothes or electrical items, goods are often delivered directly from the producers to the retailers or to their regional distribution centres. The channel of distribution is shown in Figure 1.2.7.

Figure 1.2.7 – Modern channel of distribution

It is also possible for consumers to buy direct from the producers. Examples include farm gate sales, pick-your-own fruit and vegetables, factory sales and goods and services such as double glazing, hairdressing and some products bought through direct sales and mail order. Here the channel is:

Figure 1.2.8 Direct channel of distribution

It is the marketing department that must decide which of these channels of distribution would be best for the business's products. When it does this it will take into account the major functions of wholesalers and retailers.

The main functions of wholesalers are:

- to store goods and reduce the need for producers and retailers to store goods;

- to receive large deliveries from producers, which keeps costs down;

- to break up the large quantities received from producers so that the retailers can receive manageable quantities of goods;

- to provide retailers with credit facilities;

- to pass on information about new products to the retailers.

The main functions of retailers are:

- to display goods for consumers to see;

- to sell in small quantities, which is what consumers want;

- to pass on information about products to consumers;

- to provide consumers with additional services, such as a range of methods of payment, credit facilities, after sales service and deliveries.

Promotion

Promotion is that part of marketing which persuades customers to buy the product. Before customers can buy the product they must know that it exists and where it is being sold, etc. Promotion therefore has two parts: **information** and **persuasion**. All promotion will either be giving the customer information, as with a bus timetable displayed at a bus stop, or be persuading the customer to buy the product, as with advertisements for cola products on television.

Promotion is normally split into two sections, **advertising** and **other promotions**. There is a great deal of overlap between these two sections but other promotions would include sponsorship, competitions, special offers and press releases.

Figure 1.2.9 Methods of advertising

Figure 1.2.10 Forms of promotion

Advertising is essentially a process of communication where a message, usually designed to persuade people to buy products, is passed to the customers. It can be passed in a great many ways: spoken, written, with pictures. It can also be passed using a wide range of different methods of advertising. Some of these are shown in Figure 1.2.9. The marketing department will have to decide which method of communication will get the message across most clearly, and at a reasonable cost.

Other promotions are still trying to get a message across to the customers and still trying to persuade them to buy the products, but usually the message is less direct. If a business sponsors a local sports team it is not directly telling customers to buy its product. What it is doing, however, is to make certain that people in the area know the name of the business or the product and that they know that the business is willing to help the local community. Hopefully, this will also persuade people to buy the product.

Some promotions, such as special offers, are more direct and are clearly trying to persuade customers to buy the products. Examples of some main forms of promotion, including advertising, are given in Figure 1.2.10.

After sales service

Once products have been sold most firms will offer some form of after sales service and this will normally be part of the marketing department's responsibility. With some products, such as computers, cars, and televisions, the customers expect the products to last for some time and to continue to work. Firms that sell these products therefore usually give guarantees that the products will continue to work and that they will repair them, service them and, if necessary, replace them. But even firms selling perishable products like vegetables, or services like entertainment, are likely to offer some kind of after sales service.

> **Please keep your Receipt**
>
> *Roco is happy to exchange / credit note any perfect merchandise returned within 28 days of purchase upon production of your receipt.*
>
> This does not affect your statutory rights.

After sales service includes all of the following:

- guarantees and offers to repair or replace faulty products;

- servicing of products such as electrical equipment and cars;

- delivery of products, especially large items like furniture;

- credit facilities so that customers can pay for the products over a period of time;

- offering refunds for unwanted goods;

- information about new products, up-dates;

- answers to customers' queries about products they have already bought;

- dealing with customer complaints;

- follow-up communications to see that the customer is satisfied with the product.

Customer service

> Definition – **customer service** is any part of the service that customers receive from the staff of the business.

Customer service covers any service that the staff of a business provides to the customers as part of producing and selling a product. It also includes after sales service (see above).

Customer service is also dealt with under the heading of 'selling skills in retailing' (see Unit 5, Chapter 6, page 322). Here we will look at the general aspects of customer service.

Customer service will include all of the following functions:

Providing information

Staff must provide customers with information, otherwise they will not know what the business has for sale. But information is also provided about:

- the price;

- how customers can pay for the goods;

- what the product will do, how it works;

- what after sales services are provided, such as delivery, credit, refunds;

- when the shop or factory is open;

- address, directions, telephone number.

Giving advice

Customers often expect advice about the products that they are thinking of buying, especially if the products are technical or the customers know little about them. This is likely to happen with electrical appliances, cars or medicines.

It will also happen when one business buys goods or services from another business. When people buy machinery from engineering firms they expect to receive clear instructions and advice on how to operate and maintain the machinery. When a business or an individual goes to a solicitor, they expect that the solicitor will know a great deal about the law and that sound advice will be given.

Advice may be given on:

- what is the most suitable product, or action;

- what range of products will go well together;

- what is the best product within a certain price range;

- what is the cheapest way to pay for the product;

- how to use the product;

- whether or not it is compatible with the products the customer already has;

- how to store and look after the product.

Tailoring the product to what the customer wants

It is very important that staff make certain that customers get what they really want and are satisfied with the product. That is what will make them come back again. Staff must therefore work out very carefully what customers want and need. For retailing this has been covered on page 323.

> Definition – a product is **customised** when it is specially made or altered to meet the wants or needs of a specific customer.

Sometimes businesses will make products especially for their customers. This is called **customising** the product. Many pieces of machinery or equipment that manufacturers use need to be customised. Houses may be built to the specifications of the buyer. Tailors often still make suits to fit individual customers. Many takeaway sandwich bars will prepare sandwiches in the way that the customers want.

Providing credit facilities

Most businesses will accept payment in a variety of ways. This makes payment more convenient for the customers. Businesses may also allow customers credit, which means that they receive the products now but do not have to pay for them until later.

The types of credit offered by businesses are dealt with on pages 297 and 298.

Delivering goods

The cost of delivery will either have to be paid for by the customer or by the business. When the business offers to deliver products it usually charges for this service, either directly or by hiding the cost inside a higher price. Delivery is, however, a valuable customer service, even if the customer has to pay for it. This is because the customer often does not have the right kind of vehicle to collect the product.

If a consumer buys a washing machine or two dozen paving stones for the garden, a van or lorry may be

needed to deliver them. The business often already has such a vehicle, so it is easier and cheaper for it to deliver. (See also Unit 5, Chapter 3, page 298.)

After sales service

(See above and Retailing, Chapter 3, page 299.)

Administration

> Definition – **administration** is the management of services that help to support the smooth running of departments.

Administration is carried out by every department in a business. Sometimes a separate administration department is created to manage functions that are common to all departments or to the organisation as a whole. These general administration functions might include:

- staffing the **reception**, which will include greeting people visiting the business, checking who they are and who they will be visiting, and taking outside telephone calls and connecting people to the right departments;

- **handling** and **distributing mail** from outside;

- ensuring the **security** of the building, property and staff;

- supervising the **cleaning, maintenance** and **catering** staff, or arranging for outside contractors to carry out these jobs.

Administrative functions that might be carried out by a separate administration department, but are usually carried out by the departments themselves include:

- the **clerical work** of making records, managing records, **filing, photocopying;**

- **organising meetings, keeping minutes;**

- ensuring that **internal communications** (i.e. within the department) operate smoothly;

- ensuring the department staff arrive on time, have the facilities they need and have been paid.

Each department will operate in a slightly different way, so it is highly likely that different departments will have some administrative tasks that are unique to that department, e.g.:

- The finance department will have to ensure that all invoices are processed correctly, sent out at the right time, checked against orders, checked against payments, etc.

- The sales department in a retail store will have to ensure that all monies in the tills are checked at the end of the day and that the monies are locked away securely.

- The human resources department will have to ensure that it has a complete and accurate database of all employees, with contact addresses and telephone numbers.

CHAPTER 3

THE ORGANISATIONAL STRUCTURE OF BUSINESSES

Intermediate

KEY TERMS:

organisation charts	flat/tall structures
matrix structure	hierarchical/organic structures
project groups	quality circles

In this chapter you will learn how businesses are organised and which laws protect the employees in a business. You should also look at Unit 4 Chapter 1.

How Businesses are Structured

The structure of a business shows how the various jobs and responsibilities are divided in that business. Usually the structure is shown in the form of a diagram called an organisation chart which lists all the main roles and departments.

Organisations can be divided up in a number of ways:

- by departments and job responsibilities;

- by the kind of products that the business makes;

- by where the branches of the business are located.

In this chapter we will be concentrating on only the first of these divisions, but it may be important to know about the others when you look at the structure of individual businesses.

Organisational structures that are divided on the basis of department and job roles are classified in different ways. They may be:

- flat or tall;

- hierarchical (mechanistic) or organic (matrix).

These terms do overlap, and many businesses will have more than one of them operating at the same time. These points will become clear as you read through the rest of this section.

Flat or tall structures

As the name suggests, flat structures have very few layers of people involved in the business, whereas tall structures have many layers of people. The terms flat and tall are used because they describe what the structures look like. They do not actually show how the businesses are controlled.

Figure 1.3.1 Business structures

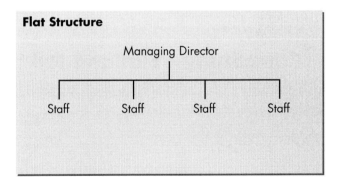

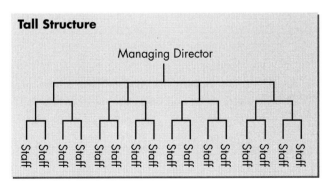

A flat structure shows that the manager is directly linked to the staff and, because of this, there are certain characteristics that flat structures are likely to have.

- The business is likely to be fairly small, otherwise it would be difficult for the manager to deal with everyone at the lower levels.

- Communications are likely to be good because the manager is in direct contact with the staff.

- The direct contact with management is likely to make control more friendly and less formal.

- The cost of management is likely to be fairly low because there is only one level of management.

- The burden of management falls on only one person.

A tall structure separates the senior managers from the staff at the bottom of the structure and this, again, will lead to certain characteristics.

- The business is likely to be fairly big, otherwise there is no point in creating many layers of management.

- Communications between one level and the next may be good because each person is likely to be dealing with only a few people below them. Communication from the top of the structure to the bottom can, however, be poor because of the number of layers involved.

- Control and decision making are likely to be very formal, with each person having clearly set out responsibilities and authority. This can lead to a less friendly working environment.

- The cost of management as a whole will be high because there are so many levels.

- Each person in the organisation will have a distinct role and this will allow people to specialise in what they are best at.

- There is usually a clear route for promotion and this may act as an incentive to work hard.

Case Study – Flat and tall organisational structures

Many small businesses have flat structures and local hairdressers are fairly typical. Below is the organisation chart for Focus on Hair in Whitchurch.

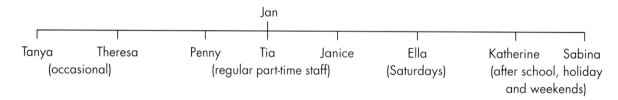

Jan is the manager and owner of the business. All the staff work closely with Jan, who is in charge of what they do, the hours they work, etc. Usually there are no more than three or four staff working at any one time. The staff all have equal status and help each other, although Ella, Katherine and Sabina are school students still learning about hairdressing.

Most secondary schools have tall organisational structures with the functions of the staff clearly defined and usually divided into (a) academic roles, e.g. teaching, and (b) pastoral roles, e.g. form tutors. The organisational chart below shows how this is divided for Tomlinscote School in Frimley.

Figure 1.3.2

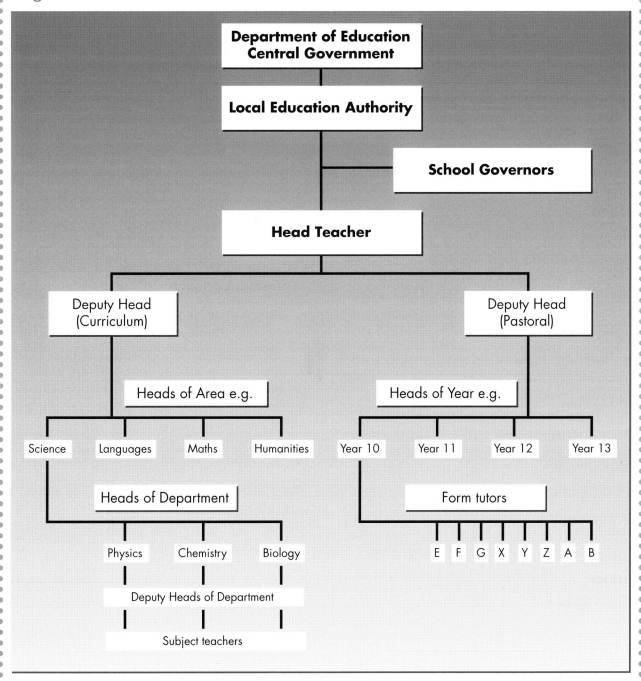

The chart shows only some of the subjects being taught and only some of the year groups. Each area, department, year head and year group has its own subdivision. In total, a full organisation chart for the school would show the positions of over 100 members of staff and this would include administrative and secretarial staff, technicians, maintenance and catering staff.

Hierarchical (mechanistic) and organic (matrix) structures

Hierarchical and organic structures describe how decisions are made in businesses.

With **hierarchical** (also known as **mechanistic**) organisations, people are placed in different grades, with the major decisions being made at the top and lesser decisions being made at lower levels. Most schools are typical hierarchical organisations, with decisions about what must be taught being dictated by government, decisions about who will be employed in the school being decided by governors and senior management, and decisions about which staff will teach which classes being decided by heads of department.

In companies ultimate control and decision making rest with the owners, but many large companies are actually run by **boards of directors**. Their job is to make certain that the senior managers are running the business in a way that is beneficial for the shareholders.

The day-to-day decisions and control rest with the senior managers in the company. Usually they have considerable power over what is actually done in terms of how products are produced and sold. Below the senior managers there will be managers who are responsible for different departments. Below this there are likely to be deputy managers, supervisors, staff and assistants.

The names of each of these job roles and the responsibilities that each person is given will vary considerably from one business to the next. The importance of the hierarchical structure is that:

- control comes from the top;

Figure 1.3.3 Lines of control

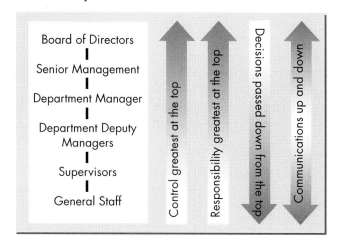

- the decisions that a person is allowed to make reflect the level that person is at;

- responsibility gets greater the further up the structure a person is;

- communications generally have to be passed up and down the lines shown on the organisation chart.

Organic (also known as **matrix**) structures allow decisions to be made across levels and the whole organisation is run in a much less rigid way. When decisions need to be made a group of people works together to decide what is best for the company.

Often these groups are formed to look after one particular product or section of the business. Such groups are know as **project groups**. An example of a project group is shown in Figure 1.3.4. Where the aim of the group is to look at the quality of the product and try to find ways of improving it, it is known as a **quality circle**.

Figure 1.3.4 – An organic structure at work planning a new product in a toy firm

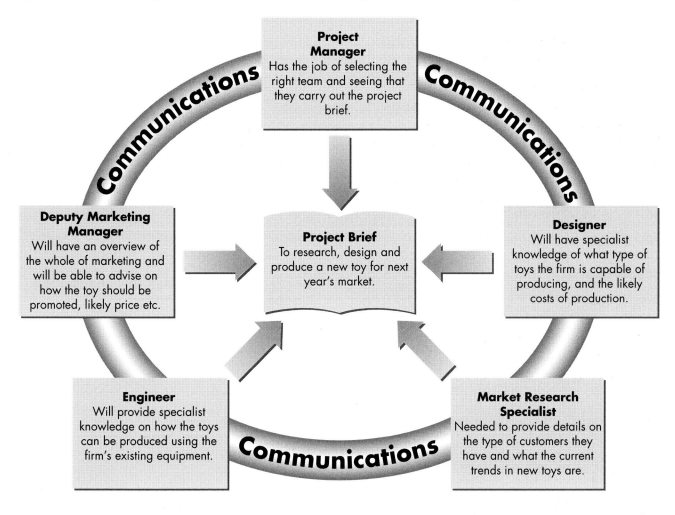

Organic/matrix structures tend to have the following characteristics:

- Although the main control still rests with senior management, many important decisions are made lower down the structure.

- Work is often carried out in teams, with members jointly making decisions.

- Decisions may take longer to be reached.

- Because all staff are involved in the making of important decisions the staff may be more motivated and may work harder for the business.

- Communication takes place directly between all levels in the business.

Legal Protection for Employees

A great many laws have been passed to protect employees. Details of some of the major acts are given below.

The Equal Pay Act 1970

The act deals with all details that would come into a contract of employment, such as rates of pay, holiday entitlements and hours of work. The act makes it illegal to treat employees of different sexes differently if they are doing similar work (or more accurately, like work, work of similar value or work which has been rated as being the same).

Examples:

1. If a factory made a contract that gave their female staff longer holiday periods so that they could look after their children but refused to allow the male employees the same holiday periods, this would be illegal.

2. If a school wanted to attract more men into the teaching profession and paid men higher rates of pay for teaching than women this would be illegal.

The Sex Discrimination Acts 1975 and 1986

The Equal Pay Act made it illegal to treat men and women differently in terms of whatever was written in their contracts of employment. The Sex Discrimination Acts make it illegal to treat men and women differently in term of their work when this is not covered by the contract of employment. It is, for example, illegal to have a policy where an estate agent would only employ men, or only employ women.

The 1975 Act made three forms of discrimination illegal:

- **direct discrimination**, e.g., when a person is refused a job because she is a woman or is married.

- **indirect discrimination**, e.g., when the rules of the business make it impossible for a woman or man to fulfil the job. An example would be if a bank insisted that all its counter staff had beards.

- victimisation after an employee has taken an employer to court under the Equal Pay Act or the Sex Discrimination Act. They might, for example, be passed over for promotion.

The 1986 Act added more actions by businesses that would be considered as discrimination between male and female employees. These included:

- treating men and women unequally in the recruitment process.

- offering men and women different conditions before the contract of employment was made.

- dismissing a person simply because he/she was male or female.

- offering training or promotion to only one sex.

Examples:

1. If a woman was asked, during an interview, who would look after her children while she worked, that would be illegal.

2. If a woman was offered less pay than a man for the same job that would be illegal.

3. If a man was dismissed because he allowed his hair to grow and there was no danger from having long hair, that would be illegal.

4. If only women in a college, which employed both men and women, were offered management training that would be illegal.

There are some circumstances where it is possible to employ one sex and not the other. These include:

- situations where the nature of the job requires a man or a women, as with fashion modelling, or a part in a play.

- situations where it would be considered indecent if a man or women was employed, e.g., measuring men or women in a tailor's shop or cleaning public toilets.

- jobs in single sex establishments such as a girls' boarding school or a men's prison.

- jobs such as housekeeper where the employee will need to live in and there are no separate sleeping or sanitary facilities.

The Race Relations Act 1976

The Race Relations Act is very similar to the Sex Discrimination Act. It makes it illegal to discriminate in the workplace on the grounds of race, colour, nationality or ethnic origin. The Race Relations Act covers both discrimination in the contract of employment and other acts of racial discrimination in the workplace.

Examples:
- If a car manufacturer refused to employ a black person that would be illegal.
- If a golf club advertised for a green keeper and said, "applicants must be English," that would be illegal.
- If a London banking business had a policy of never employing anyone from Brixton, that would be illegal because Brixton has a very much higher black population than the average for London.
- If employees in a business made jokes about other employees' turbans or head scarves, that would be illegal if the employees wore these because of their religious beliefs.

There are some circumstances when it is possible to discriminate. These include:

- employing people of a particular race so that what is being presented to the general public is authentic, e.g.:
  - employing only Chinese waiters and waitresses in a Chinese restaurant.
  - insisting that a black actor is employed to play the part of an Afro–Caribbean in a play.

The Disability Discrimination Act 1995

This act essentially put discrimination against disabled people on the same footing as discrimination on the basis of sex and race. However, it only applies to direct discrimination. Under this act it is illegal to discriminate against a disabled person in:

- the recruitment and selection process.
- the contract of employments and the conditions of pay, etc.
- provision of training and promotion opportunities.
- treatment within the workplace.

Examples:
- If a school refused to employ a history teacher because he only had one leg, that would be illegal.
- If a television programme dismissed a presenter because she had a lisp, that would be illegal.
- If a large company refused promotion to an employee in a wheelchair because that would mean working on the second floor and there was no lift, that would be illegal.

The act also requires that employers make changes to their premises so that disabled employees are not disadvantaged. This would include putting in ramps for wheelchair, lifts, good lighting for the partially sighted, special keyboards for blind people, etc.

There are two major exceptions to this act:

- It does not apply to businesses with less than 20 employees.
- Businesses will not be required to make adjustments to premises if the cost and inconvenience is very high.

The Employment Rights Act 1996

The Employment Rights Act established a wide range of rights that employees have when they are being employed. These are rights that are additional to the acts listed above. These rights include:

- The right to a statement of employment.
  - This must be given within two months of starting employment.
  - It must include:
    - names of the employee and the employer
    - date when employment began
    - rate of pay
    - when pay is due (weekly, monthly, etc.)

- details of the hours of work
- holiday entitlement
- sick pay (if any)
- pension arrangements
- length of notice required
- job title and brief details

- Protection against the employer deducting monies from pay without agreement.

- Guarantees that employees will be paid for the work that they have done.

- Protection for shop workers from being made to work on Sundays if they object.

- Allowing employees to take time off for certain activities, e.g.:
  - if they are members of local councils and need to do council work.
  - if they are school governors and need to attend meetings, etc.
  - if they are prison visitors and need to go to prisons.

- The right to take time off to look for a new job, e.g. attend interviews, and be paid.

- The right to maternity leave, both before the baby is born and afterwards. This can be for up to 29 weeks. Employers must keep the job open for the mother to return if she wants to.

- The right not to be unfairly dismissed.

- The right to be given the agreed period of notice by the employer.

- The right to redundancy payments if an employee is dismissed because the job is no longer available.

What action can employees take if these acts are broken?

In all cases of discrimination employees can take legal action against employers, or other employees, who break these acts. Any legal action will be taken to Industrial Tribunals, which will decide if the action did break the law. If the law was broken there are usually two remedies which will be considered:

- compensation for damages caused.

- making the business change their practices so that the discrimination no longer occurs.

CHAPTER 4

BUSINESS COMMUNICATION

Foundation and Intermediate

In this chapter you will learn about:

- why businesses need communication

- the main methods of communication

- which methods of communication are best for different circumstances

- how the size of the business affects communication.

What is Communication?

Definition – **communication** is the giving, receiving or exchanging of information.

Communication occurs when a message goes from a **sender** to a **receiver**. This may be direct, e.g. two people talking to each other face to face, or it may require some additional step, e.g. two people talking to each other on the telephone and being connected by wires or fibre optic cables through the telephone exchange. Each communication will have one or more methods of communication. In the photos below the sender and receiver are talking to each other using the telephone as a 'method'.

There are, in fact, a great many ways in which messages can be passed from senders to receivers, some of which do not even directly involve people. The main ways of communication are **spoken, written, visual,** and **electronic**. Common examples are given in Table 1.4.1.

Table 1.4.1 Main ways of communicating

Spoken	Written	Visual	Electronic
Meetings	Memos	Sign language	EPOS*
Speeches	Letters	Body language	BACS*
Interviews	Reports	Posters	Surveillance cameras
Talking to staff or customers	Notices	Photographs	

* EPOS stands for Electronic Point of Sale; BACS stands for Bankers' Automated Clearing Service

In today's world of advanced technology, there are fewer and fewer methods of communication that use just one of these ways of communicating. In business even the simple process of writing a letter may involve a manager recording the letter on tape and then a secretary listening to the tape in order to type it up using a computer and possibly sending it through the electronic mail (e-mail) system. Some common examples of how different ways of communication are combined in the business world are given below.

Table 1.4.2 Combinations of communication methods

Spoken and electronic	Written and electronic	Spoken and written	Visual and electronic	Written and visual
Telephone	Electronic mail	Dictation	Television	Logos
Tele-conferencing	Internet	Reading instructions out loud	Fax	Trade marks
Tannoy	Teletext		Digital cameras	

The Need for Good Communications

In any part of our lives good communications can be vital. Without them we get the wrong messages and come to the wrong conclusions. In our personal life that can be funny, annoying, and embarrassing, but in business it often leads to the wrong decisions being made and to increased costs, loss of customers, and probably a loss of profits.

Good communication occurs when the message that the sender is trying to get across is **received, fully understood** and **acted on** by the receiver. It is, therefore, very important that the communication system has some form of **feedback** from the receiver so that the sender can check that the message has been received and understood fully. A feedback process should be built into the communication system.

Figure 1.4.1 Circular communication

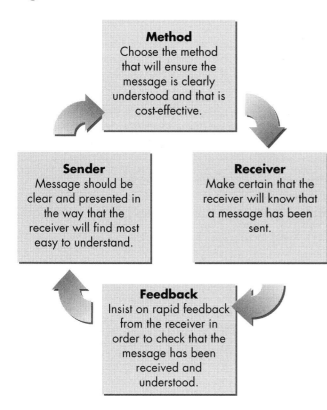

operates as efficiently as possible. When businesses practise good communications, staff will understand what they are expected to do, information will be accurate and clear, messages will be delivered quickly and time and money will be saved.

When communication is poor, mistakes will be made, staff will not understand what they are supposed to be doing and tempers are likely to become frayed. Important information will be lost, the wrong jobs will be done and the business will run inefficiently. In the end, staff will be unhappy, time will be lost and the firm will have higher costs, lower sales and a loss of revenue and profit.

With face-to-face and telephone conversations, it is usually fairly easy to check if people have understood what is being said because they can be asked directly or you can tell from their spoken reply or from their body language. With letters and faxes it is generally necessary to ask for replies in order to check whether the message has been understood. With memos and notices, it is often necessary to introduce some separate follow-up procedure to check that the message has been understood. If the memo is asking staff to attend a meeting, it is no use waiting until the time of the meeting to discover whether or not staff have received and understood the message.

Good communications have certain characteristics and these help to make certain that the business

Figure 1.4.2 Good communication

When deciding which method of communication is likely to be the best, the following checklist will help to ensure success.

Table 1.4.3 Which method of communication?

✓	**Access**	Do both sender and receiver have easy access to the method of communication, e.g. do they both have computers for e-mail?
✓	**Time**	How long does it take for the message to be sent and received? Is time important for the particular message being sent?
✓	**Understanding**	Is the message being set out and sent in a way that will be easily understood?
✓	**Ease of use**	How easy is it to use the method of communication?
✓	**Cost**	Is it the cheapest and most effective method?
✓	**Security**	Does it provide security in terms of confidentiality and in terms of information not being lost or stolen?
✓	**Accuracy**	How can the sender make certain that the information being sent is accurate and will provide the receiver with all the information required?
✓	**Record**	Does the method provide a record of the message and is this important?

Internal and External Communication

Definition – **internal communication** is communication between one part of the business and another part of the same business. **External communication** is communication between the business and people or organisations outside the business.

Businesses and their staff need to communicate with customers, suppliers, and tax offices such as the Inland Revenue and Customs and Excise. These are external to their businesses. They also need to communicate with their own staff, both on single sites and between sites. These communications are internal.

Examples of internal and external communications are given for a supermarket in the tables on the following pages.

Internal communications will take place in all of the following situations.

Table 1.4.4 Internal communication

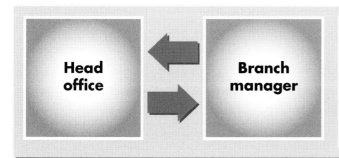

- When the branch manager attends regional meetings.
- When head office decides on a new range of products that will be stocked.
- In the weekly reports that are made to head office.
- When there is a major incident such as a serious fire.

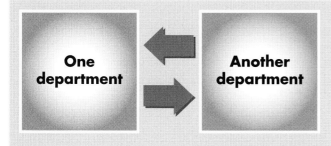

- When departments need new staff, they will have to tell human resources what they need.
- As goods are sold at the checkouts, details of what is sold will be recorded so that the purchases department will know when, and what, to reorder.
- When staff work, human resources will need to inform finance so that staff can be paid.

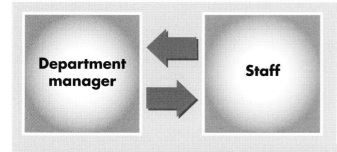

- When managers train new staff.
- When managers give instructions to staff on which shelves need to be refilled.
- When managers appraise staff.
- When staff need help and advice.

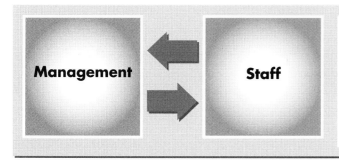

- When there is a dispute between staff and management.

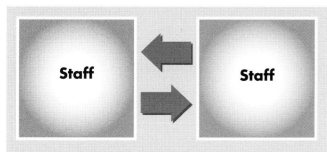

- When staff are working together serving at the delicatessen counter.
- When broken goods need to be cleaned up.
- As checkout staff replace each other.
- On lunch breaks in the staff canteen.

External communications will take place in all of the following situations.

Table 1.4.5 External communication

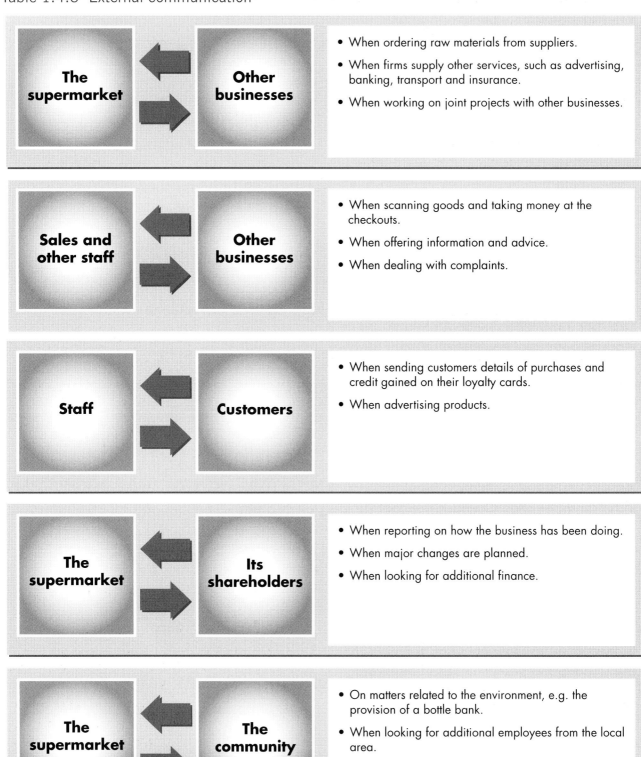

Case Study – Types of communication used at Jack's Fish and Chip Shop

Location: Bagshot, Hampshire
Researcher: Lee Collacott (Intermediate Business)

The business has 5 staff on weekdays and 8 to 9 staff on weekends, as well as one or two managers who are the owners. All of the following internal communications are to be found at Jack's:

Spoken: When the managers give instructions.
When special orders need to be given to the cooks.
When other staff need you to cover for them.
When the managers need to arrange for extra shifts.
When managers talk to staff in meetings.

Spoken communication is best for these situations because it is quick, things can be discussed and because we are all fairly close together in the shop. If the shop is very busy the messages can be misunderstood. Because there is no record of what was said, this can lead to misunderstandings and even disputes.

Written: Memos for meetings are put on the notice board.
Pay slips give written details of pay, hours, tax.

Written communication is best because it provides a record that can be referred to, and on the notice board everyone can read it. The writing does take time and often it is quicker just to talk to someone.

Electronic: When staff are ill they ring in. The telephone is also used to ask someone to be a replacement. Most orders are put in at the till and this automatically prints out the order where the cooks are so that they can start cooking it.

Electronic communications are very quick and therefore save staff time, but they are expensive and orders can be incorrectly entered.

The Main Forms of Business Communication

Large businesses use many different types of communication. The type of communication chosen will depend upon what message is being communicated, to whom it is being sent, how quickly it needs to get there and whether or not a hard copy is needed. The main forms of communication are given below and, with them, examples of when they would be used by a business and the advantages and disadvantages of each method.

Verbal communication

Verbal communication is still the most common form of giving and receiving information within a business. This is because businesses involve people and people normally communicate by speaking to each other. There are, in fact, a great many different ways in which people can talk to each other, as the list below demonstrates. Verbal communication has some general advantages and disadvantages which apply to all forms of spoken communication. When you look at individual forms of verbal communication, you should ask yourself if these general advantages and disadvantages apply.

General advantages

a) It is quick because sender and receiver are usually in direct contact with each other.

b) When something is not understood, questions can be asked.

General disadvantages

a) How well the message is put over will depend on how good a speaker the sender is.

b) Generally there is no record of spoken communication to refer back to in the future.

Face to face

Face-to-face communication, as the name suggests, occurs when people communicate with each other in the same place. One person may be telling another what to do, or reporting something to the other person. Alternatively, the sender and receiver may be talking to each other, discussing, socialising, or even arguing. It is used when one person is giving another person instructions, when people ask for advice or discuss problems and when people in the same office or workplace are simply talking to each other.

Advantages

a) Questions can be asked and answered.

b) Very quick if people are in the same place.

c) Usually there is no cost involved.

d) Facial reactions can be watched.

Disadvantages

a) There is usually no permanent record of what was said.

b) It can be used only when people are close together.

c) It may be difficult to keep the message confidential in a crowd.

Formal meetings

Some face-to-face communication is very structured. Business meetings are often formal and follow a set agenda. First, the minutes of the last meeting may be read out, and any follow-up points will be discussed. Then, each point of the agenda will be discussed in

turn with time for 'any other business' at the end. Meetings may have a chairperson who decides what will be discussed and who will talk. Often, each point on the agenda will be introduced by a specific person.

Advantages
a) Everyone knows what is going to be discussed in advance.
b) People will not talk at the same time.
c) A record of what is being said is usually recorded by the secretary.
d) Confidentiality can be achieved by inviting only certain people.

Disadvantages
a) Formal meetings take time to organise.
b) The formal procedure also means that meetings take a long time to get the points across.
c) These meetings work best with small groups of people and are not good for mass communication.

Interviews

Interviews are formal question-and-answer sessions. They take place in many different situations. They may, for example, be used when people are applying for jobs, when management is appraising staff, when management wants to find out what or who caused an accident, when management is disciplining staff and even when management is trying to find out why staff are leaving a business.

Interviews normally use face-to-face communication. Interviews for new employment tend to be very formal, often with a chairperson and a panel of interviewers. The order of questions will have been worked out in advance, and each member of the panel is likely to be asking questions about different points. The communication will be carried out mainly through questions and answers and the panel can learn a great deal about the interviewee in a relatively short period of time.

Advantages
a) Both sides can ask questions.
b) Detailed questions can be asked.
c) Information is given immediately.
d) Interviews are usually formal and they are a good way of testing how people react to formal communication.

Disadvantages
a) The information given is not always truthful.
b) Interviews do not really show if the applicant can do the job.
c) It is hard to put people at ease and they may not give the best answers that they could.

Speeches/lectures/general meetings/conferences
When many staff are being given the same message at the same time, one of the quickest and easiest methods of communication is to arrange a meeting

and talk to all of them at once. This may be done when staff are being trained, when news of some major change in the business is being explained, or simply when the managers wish to congratulate staff on how well they have done in the previous year. It is also one way in which businesses give details of important changes to their shareholders.

Advantages
a) The message can be given to a large number of people quickly.
b) Everyone is informed at the same time.
c) Points can be made without interruption.

Disadvantages
a) It often takes time to set up.
b) It is difficult for the audience to ask questions.
c) The speakers need to have good delivery in order to keep the attention of the audience.

Written communication

Written communication occurs when people write messages by hand or type messages on typewriters or word processors and then print out hard copy. Written communications will have some general advantages and disadvantages that apply to all forms of written communication.

Advantages
a) They provide a hard copy which can be kept for future reference.
b) They do not require the receiver to have specialist equipment (e.g. a fax machine or a computer).
c) Some forms of communication, e.g. contracts for the sale of land, must, by law, be written.

Disadvantages
a) The storage of written papers takes up a lot of space.
b) Many forms of written communication are slow.
c) If the receiver does not understand what has been written it usually takes time to ask questions and get replies.

Letters

Letters were, and sometimes still are, a very formal way of communication. For internal communication, they are used when businesses have branches in different parts of the country, or abroad, and when confidential information needs to be sent to other members of staff. Business letters still follow a fairly rigid format in which the layout and language used is considered important. As with many elements of

business, the format is becoming less important. In the past the two main ways of signing a letter were 'Yours faithfully' if you had started the letter 'Dear sir/madam', and 'Yours sincerely' if you had addressed the letter to a particular person, e.g. 'Dear Mrs Walker'. Today, letters may well be addressed in an informal way, e.g. 'Dear Jill', and signed something like 'Best wishes'. Letters will, however, still require names and addresses of senders and receivers, the date, reference codes if appropriate, and the conventional layout of a business letter.

Advantages
a) They are confidential.
b) They provide a hard copy.
c) The cost is still relatively low.

Disadvantages
a) It takes time to write letters and it takes time for them to arrive and for replies to be received.

Memorandum

A memorandum (memo) is simply a note from one person to another. In business it is often written in a rather formalised way. This helps to identify who sent it, to whom it was sent, why it was sent and when it was sent. It will be used when someone wishes to send a quick message to one or more people, to call a meeting, to send a reminder, etc. Today, many memos are written and sent using computers and the e-mail system.

Memorandum	
To: JJW	
From: RJS	26th May 2000
Re: The 486 Model – Second Stage	

We will need to meet to discuss Alan's proposals. Can you make it for 10.00 a.m. this Thursday? Please confirm with Jane.

Advantages
a) Very quick to write and send.
b) Can be kept as a record.
c) Only the most basic points are put down, so it is easy to understand.

Disadvantages
a) Can be read by people it is not intended for.
b) Not useful for long or complicated information.

Notices

Notices are used when a message needs to reach a number of other people. Frequently, the details are posted on notice boards where they can be seen by everyone. Notices may be formal, as with details of what to do if there is a fire or reports on how the company is performing. Often they are informal and give information about social events, such as a works outing to Alton Towers or encouraging staff to join the company football team.

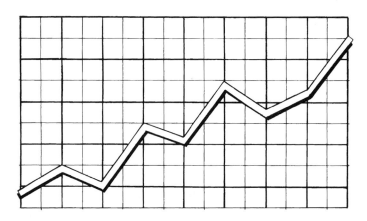

Monthly Sales Sept. 1990 to May 2000

Notices can also be 'posted' using computers. For internal notices, these are likely to be put on **bulletin boards** or possibly **web pages** on the internet. Web pages are, however, more commonly used for external communications.

Advantages

a) Everyone can see the message.

b) Many people can receive the message at the same time.

c) It can be left as a reminder.

Disadvantages

a) It is not confidential.

b) Some people may not bother to read the notice.

c) Old notices tend to be ignored.

Reports

In business, reports are used to give information about something that has been researched or investigated. They are used in a great many different situations and they can be presented in many different ways. It is even possible to give a spoken report, but normally reports are written and frequently they are expected to be set out in a particular way.

General reports will have:

- a front cover;

- a summary of what the report is about and what the original point of the research was;

- a contents page and introduction;

- each separate part of the report started with a new heading or new section;

- an appendix at the end with additional details, usually explaining where the data in the main report came from.

When reports are being written for a particular person, it is also normal to start the report with 'From: . . .' and 'To: . . .' or 'For the attention of: . . .'

All reports will have a date on them somewhere because the day on which the report was written is likely to be important. Where financial or numerical data is included, the writer of the report will often present the data as a table or graph. This makes sure that the data is presented in a clear and interesting way.

To: William Cross (Marketing Director)
From: John Drake (Marketing Manager)
Date: 14th June 2000

Summary

Initial research does confirm the general feeling that the nature of our customers has changed significantly over the last five to ten years. The major cause of this change seems to be the rapid growth of new housing to the North and East of Hamdown, with an influx of homeowners with much higher levels of income and expenditure than is normally found in Hamdown. The results of our market research strongly suggest that Cross Ltd should consider changing its image to appeal to this more up-market customer base.

Survey results

One hundred adults were asked to fill in our questionnaire over a two day period. Question 1 asked which garden centre people used. It is clear from the results that Cross Garden Centre does not have a large enough part of the market and that we are losing customers to our major competitors.

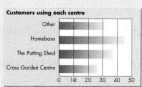

The Potting Shed has only been in business for six years and it has already overtaken us in terms of consumer preference. Homebase does sell a wide range of DIY items that we do not, and it is not really surprising that it has the major part of the market. Our real problem is how we can gain our market share back from The Potting Shed.

Advantages

a) The formal way of presenting reports means that the readers can easily follow the points being made.

b) They provide records that can be referred to in the future.

Disadvantages

a) They take a long time to research and write.

b) If conditions change they can go rapidly out of date.

Electronic communication

Electronic communications are, strictly speaking, communications that use electrical wiring. Nowadays, however, the term might be extended to include systems like television, mobile phones and satellite transmissions. All of these send the message by using waves that travel through the air, but at either end they are connected to terminals which convert the signals between waves and electricity. Many modern cable connections, like the main telephone cable under the Atlantic Ocean, are now fibre optical cables which send messages using light waves. As with written and spoken communications, there are some advantages and disadvantages that generally apply to all electronic/wave communication systems.

Advantages
a) Very quick, even over long distances, and allow quick replies.
b) Messages can be sent to individuals and/or many people.

Disadvantages
a) They require equipment that may be expensive.
b) If the sender or receiver does not have the equipment, the message cannot be transmitted.

Telephone
Telephones have been used in businesses for internal communications for over one hundred years. Their most obvious use is to contact staff who are away from the workplace and now that mobile phones allow telephoning without the need of fixed telephone points, this is a rapidly expanding form of internal communication. These general types of telephone system are provided by national and international telecommunication companies. Many businesses also provide their own internal telephone systems, where staff from one office can telephone staff in other offices. In many business there will be a much more restricted link between secretaries or receptionists and their bosses. Doctors will use an intercom to tell reception that they are ready for their next patient.

Advantages
a) Communication is very quick.
b) Telephones allow people to talk to each other and question anything that is not clear.
c) Conversations can be confidential.
d) With an answer phone, messages can be recorded when the office is closed.

Disadvantages
a) There is no written record, although telephone conversations can be recorded.
b) Telephone calls can, and often do, interrupt the work that people are doing.
c) Costs of mobile phones are very high.

Facsimile (Fax)
A facsimile (fax) machine converts pictures and text into electronic pulses which are then transmitted by telephone to another fax machine. The second machine converts the electronic impulses back into pictures and text and prints out a hard copy. This method of communication used to be very popular as a way of sending documents, maps and plans. It was almost as quick as using the telephone but it could transmit hard copy. Today fax machines are less popular because e-mail can be used instead which is even faster and has other benefits (see below).

Advantages

a) Communication is very quick.

b) Documents can be sent and received.

c) It can be used when no one is in the office at the other end.

Disadvantages

a) It is slow compared to e-mail.

b) Fax paper is not very permanent and the print fades if kept in sunlight.

c) Messages will not get through unless the fax machine is turned on at the other end.

Electronic mail (e-mail)

Electronic mail (e-mail) refers to the process of using computer networks as a postal system. Data is created on one computer and is then transmitted to another computer. Inside the same building, this is likely to be done by connecting the computers together into a network. If there is only local access, this is known as a LAN (local access network). If there is access to other centres, and even parts of the business in other countries, this is known as a WAN (wide access network). E-mail connections to parts of the business in other areas will generally use the telephone system and will require a **modem** to convert the data to electrical impulses that can be transmitted by the telephone, and a modem at the other end to turn the data back into what the computer can understand.

E-mail is a very fast method of communication because all the data is already saved in electronic form. Very large quantities of data can be transmitted in a very short time, so it also saves on telephone bills. At the other end, the data will arrive in the computer in the same form as it was sent, so it is possible to save the data on disk, print out hard copies, or pass that data on to other computers. One e-mail message can be sent to thousands of computers at the same time.

E-mail is very versatile and it allows businesses to send messages in many forms. Letters, memos, notices, reports, and even picture and video-recordings can all be sent using e-mail.

Advantages

a) It can be used to send a wide variety of types of message – written, visual, etc.

b) Very fast method of transmitting data, even large documents and pictures.

c) Saves on stationery and paper costs.

d) Data can be sent to many people at the same time.

e) Messages can be left for receivers to look at when they want to.

Disadvantages

a) Sender and receiver must have computers and software that are compatible.

b) Data is not secure if it is transmitted using the telephone system. It can be 'hacked into'.

c) Computer systems can go wrong and then communication is not possible.

Tele-conferencing

Many large businesses operate on different sites around the country and even in different countries. It is then very difficult to hold meetings, and it is also expensive and time consuming to get everyone to travel to one central meeting place. Tele-conferencing (or video-conferencing) allows meetings to take place when staff are in different places.

Centres are linked together using telephone, computer or video systems. The video-conferencing systems allow people to talk to each other and see each other because they are also being filmed.

Advantages

a) It is much quicker and usually cheaper than bringing people together at one centre.

b) Matters can be discussed as if in an ordinary meeting.

c) Video records of what was discussed can be made with video-conferencing.

Disadvantages

a) These systems are expensive to set up.

b) Meetings may be more difficult to control because people are in different places.

c) It is difficult for more than two or three centres to communicate together in this way because it becomes confusing.

Public address (PA) system/tannoy

In a supermarket, when additional staff are needed at the checkouts or to clean up something that has been spilled, the message will often be given over the public address system. This makes certain that the people being asked to go to the checkouts or clean up the mess will hear the message wherever they are in the building. PA systems are also used when a message is being given to everyone; when, for example, an emergency meeting of all staff is needed. PA systems may also be connected to alarm systems so that all staff can be warned of fires, bomb scares, etc.

Advantages

a) Staff can usually hear the message wherever they are in the building.

b) Many people can be given the message at the same time.

c) Very quick for getting messages to everyone, especially in an emergency.

Disadvantages

a) Messages are difficult to hear in noisy surroundings, e.g. a factory floor.

b) They cannot be used for confidential messages.

c) If they are used too often, staff will stop paying attention to them.

Promotion, advertising and public relations

> Definition – **promotion** is any form of communication that a business uses in order to communicate with customers in order to persuade them to buy its products.

When businesses want to give customers information about their products, or persuade them to buy the products, they will use some form of promotion. (See also page 31.) Promotion includes advertising, public relations, and other types of promotion such as competitions and special offers. All these are designed to communicate some message to the customers.

Advertising can be carried out in a great many different ways, including television, radio, newspapers and magazines, hoardings, signs on vehicles, point-of-sale displays, packaging and leaflets. The effectiveness of the advertising communication will depend on such features as:

- use of colour, pictures, sound, etc.;

- the size, length, positioning of the advert;

- sending the right messages to the target population;

- catching the attention of the target population.

Good advertising communication succeeds if it can get the customers' **attention**, make them **interested**, make them **desire** the product enough to want to buy it, and make them take **action** and actually go and buy the product.

Public relations helps to promote products by communicating a good image of the products or of the company. It includes press releases about the business or products, the business sponsoring events or sports teams and the business supporting good environmental practices.

Other methods of communication

Communication occurs every time a message is sent and received and there are, therefore, a huge number of possible ways of sending messages. The methods given above are important for most businesses, but there are many others that are also important for certain kinds of message. Examples of these are given in Table 1.4.6.

Table 1.4.6 Other methods of communication

Method	Example of when it is used
Sign language	• When there is too much noise to be heard. • When people are in sight but a long way away.
Videos	• When staff are being trained, these can be used to show how work should be done. • When the marketing department needs to see what a new television advertisement will look like.
House magazine	• This is often used to keep staff informed of what is happening in a business. • Can be used for staff to ask questions and have them answered.
Bleepers	• Used to tell people they are needed. They can then go to an internal phone and find out why.
Bells, hooters, sirens, etc.	• To indicate when work periods are starting or ending. • To warn people of some kind of danger.
Intercom	• When staff at the tills need to check prices with supervisors in an office in another part of the building. • When a doctor is calling through to reception to ask for the next patient.
Financial documents	• To record all orders, purchases, sales and deliveries. • To give details of profits, cash flow and what the business is worth.

Why Different Forms of Communication are Needed in Different Situations

Deciding which method of communication is best will always depend on the particular situation in hand. Large businesses can afford technology which small businesses might find useful but which they simply cannot afford. Noisy environments may make it impossible to use some forms of communication. Certain data, especially financial, must be written down. At horse racing courses, some bookies still use a special form of sign language,

called 'tic-tac', to tell each other what the betting odds for the horses should be. This method is even faster than a mobile phone because there is no need to dial numbers. It is also a great deal cheaper and it has the advantage that most outsiders have little idea what the bookies are telling each other.

When you examine actual businesses and see what forms of communication they are using you must also think carefully about why they have chosen them. In this section we will look at some of the different situations that will affect which methods of communication are chosen.

Figure 1.4.3 Factors influencing method of communication

How communication changes with the size of the business

As businesses grow larger, they will be able to afford more expensive methods of communication. Memos, letters, talking face to face and even telephones are relatively cheap. Computer networks and video-conferencing are expensive to set up.

Small businesses are often on single sites with few rooms and therefore complex forms of communication are not necessary. Many large businesses are on multiple sites, some of which may be in other countries. If rapid communication is required, then these firms must have access to telephones, faxes and e-mail.

In small businesses, the different functions of departments are often combined. The owner of the village shop may well carry out most, if not all, of the managing functions of marketing, finance, human resources, etc. The owner will not, therefore, need a special method of communication between departments. Large firms, on the other hand, will have their departments clearly separated and they will therefore need methods of communication between departments. They will also have far more staff and, probably, more levels in their organisational structure (see pages 35 and 199).

Case Study – Daily internal communications used by 'Jennings' village store

Inside the shop the manager, Mrs Jennings, gives instructions, answers questions and talks socially to her two members of staff face to face. Details of staff pay, tax, etc. and their contracts of employment are written. When staff are ill they use the telephone which is also used to find replacement staff.

The staff use the cash-till, which records all sales, and they also use a printed stock sheet which they have to update if they are taking stock out of the storeroom to fill shelves. The cash-till also has a bell which will ring in the flat above the shop if the staff need Mrs Jennings's help when she is not in the shop.

Large businesses will usually be dealing with much higher levels of sales, staffing, ordering and payments. It is much more convenient to store all this data on a computer. Staff who need to access the data will, therefore, also need computers. Once systems like this have been set up more and more communication begins to take place through the computers, with e-mail, bulletin boards, etc. Most small businesses do not have networked computers, so these forms of communication between staff are not possible.

How communications differ in different departments and businesses

In medium and large businesses, departments are usually separated, not only in terms of how they are staffed and run, but also in their physical location.

Where departments are close to each other, it is more likely that they will use face-to-face communication. Where they are on different floors or even in different buildings, they are more likely to use methods such as the telephone, fax and e-mail.

The departments themselves will have different methods of communication between their own staff because their functions tend to be different. The human resources department is responsible for recruitment, training, discipline, etc. and much of this is likely to be done with face-to-face communication, interviews, lectures. The finance department must keep records because these are required for tax purposes and for preparing the final accounts. Much of this department's communication will, therefore, be written.

The type of communication is also likely to change, depending on what stage a particular task has reached. When management is appraising staff, the following stages and communications might take place:

Figure 1.4.4 Communication methods at different stages of appraisal

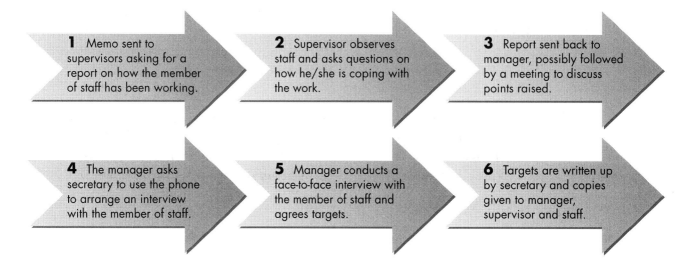

The main factor that will affect the type of communication used by departments is likely to be the nature of the business in which the firm is involved. This can be shown by comparing the sales department for a supermarket with, for example, the sales department for a local manufacturer of crisps. The sales staff will be doing completely different jobs and, therefore, the methods of communication needed will be quite different.

Case Study – Communication between sales staff in a supermarket

In a supermarket the sales staff will be stocking shelves, serving at the delicatessen counter, or working on the checkouts. Communication with other staff and supervisors will be face to face, using intercoms or buzzers, and possibly daily meetings to ensure that everyone knows what they should be doing. At the checkouts written lists of prices that change daily will be displayed.

When staff are to be replaced they will communicate face to face. If checkout staff have problems that they cannot deal with they will call for assistance using a buzzer, flashing light or intercom. When additional staff are required they may be called up using a PA system. Details of sales will be recorded automatically at the checkouts using the EPOS system.

Case Study – Communication for sales staff in a local crisps company

The main role of sales staff in this business will be to visit local shops and supermarkets to try to gain orders and inform customers of new products and new marketing campaigns. Most of their time will be spent away from the main building.

Communication will include weekly meetings to discuss new products, marketing campaigns, etc. with the marketing manager. Daily communication is likely to be by phone or by radio if their cars are fitted with these. Details of products and prices will be on written lists, as may be the names of the shops that they have to visit. Details of sales will be written down on order forms and taken back to the firm.

When individual firms and members of staff are compared the actual methods of communication may come down to personal preferences. Many people are still frightened by computers, others feel that face-to-face communication is best for good staff relations. Many forms of communication are used simply because they always have been. A study of these situations may well show that there are many businesses in which improvements to communications can be made.

How to approach your assignment

For your assignment you will need to choose one business and carry out research on what it does, how it is set up in terms of departments, what communications are used and how the customer services operate.

Choosing the right business

Before you decide which business to study you should consider the following points:

What information do I need?

- Carefully read the assignment you have been given.
- Check what information you need in order to do the assignment, e.g. details of what the business does, the work of different departments, etc.
- Make a list of all the information you will need.
- If any of this is unclear, check with your teacher or lecturer.

Deciding which business to study.

- You must choose a business which will allow you to collect all the information you need.
- The best businesses are likely to be:
  businesses that parents, close relations or friends are part of.
  businesses where you work, or have done work experience.
  businesses which publish a lot of information about themselves, especially on the internet.
  local businesses which want to support local schools and colleges and will, therefore, welcome and encourage students visiting and asking questions.
- Make certain, very early on, that you really can get all of the information that you will need from your chosen business. If there is any doubt you should consider choosing another business.

Contacting the business

- Remember that the business is providing you with the information that is going to help you gain your GNVQ.

- If you can, contact someone who knows you.
- Have a copy of your assignment and the Assessment Evidence ready to give to your contact. This will help them to understand what the assignment is about, and what information you will need.
- Think in advance about how much information you need, how many visit, interviews, etc., you are likely to need. For the business, "time is money".
- Discuss with the business when it would be best to collect the information, and then stick to the agreed times.

Before you start planning and researching you should have a copy of the **What you need to learn** section of the syllabus and the **Assessment Evidence**. It would also be very helpful if you had a copy of how the teachers will be expected to assess your work. This indicates very clearly what should be in your work for you to gain a **pass**, **merit** or **distinction** grade and how to meet each.

How to gain good grades for Foundation

For a **pass** grade you will need to describe various features of the business you have chosen to study. To do this well you should:

- Try to gather as much information as you can on all the functional areas.
- Choose the four functional areas that you have the best information for and give clear details of what tasks and activities are carried out in these areas.
- Choose one of these four functional areas where you have the clearest details of what is done and provide full details of what is done, by whom, whether it is a routine task done regularly or a non-routine task done in exceptional circumstances, e.g. Human Resources have to arrange training on a new set of computers that have been installed.
- Decide which roles in customer services are easiest to gain information about. Give a general outline of all the customer services but a detailed outline of these two.

- Check Chapter 4 and note the types of communication that are common. Most businesses will use a wide range of communications. Record as many forms of oral and written communications that the business uses as you can. For each work out why they are being used in terms of speed, ease of use, cost, whether they get the message across effectively, etc.

For a **merit** grade you need to:

- Note down and explain when and how departments work together, e.g., the sales department will pass copies of sales to the finance department so that it can either record the sale or send out an invoice asking for payment.
- Think carefully about any parts of the customer services that could be improved and suggest improvements, at the same time justifying why the changes would make the customer services better.
- For your section on communications you need to give more detail about why particular types of communication are being used and how they meet the needs of the business. For instance, if a business has sales reps who are travelling about the country a mobile phone would be the best way to contact them.

For a **distinction** grade you will need to give good detail of all the parts of the business that you have been studying.

- You also need to make it clear how the actions of the business and its departments affect and help customers and how they help the business to meet its aims.
- You need to think about one part of the business where you think there could be improvements. Explain what these improvements would be and why the change you have suggested would lead to the improvement.
- For each of the types of communication you have recorded provide a list, with explanations, of the advantages and disadvantages of the type of communication. Chapter 4 provides lists of advantages and disadvantages but you must apply these to the actual communication being used in the business.

How to gain good grades for Intermediate

Many of the points made for Foundation students above also apply to your assignment work. Read through them.

For your assignment you need to study a medium or large-scale business. It is particularly important that you know that you can collect all the data you need and a medium scale business is best, although it is acceptable to concentrate upon one branch of a large organisation, e.g. one branch of Sainsbury's.

To achieve good grades across the levels of pass, merit and distinction you must:

- Give clear details about the main activities of the business you have chosen and their main objectives. Usually larger businesses have stated published aims and objectives. You also need to give a clear outline of the functions of different departments, including Human Resources. As Human Resources must be included you must choose a business where you know you can get good details on this department (function).
- Show how the functions help the firm produce its goods or services and for the merit grade you must show how these functions work together to achieve the aims and objectives of the business. If a business wishes to expand its market share by attracting more customers you should be able to show how better marketing, better trained staff, finances to pay for advertising, training, etc., all work together to achieve the stated aim.

For a **distinction** you will need to be able to evaluate how the business is set up in terms of organisation and communications, what the strengths and weaknesses are and how they affect the ability of the business to achieve its aims and objectives.

The theme of aims and objectives flows through all parts of the assignment. Your ability to use details about the organisation of the business and to relate them to the aims and objectives will depend on how well you have researched the basic data. You must have full details on:
- the activities of the business.

- the departments (functions) of the business and what is done in each department.
- how the departments are organised, with a suitable organisation chart.
- what communications are used and how and why they are used.

In addition you will need information on:

- How employees are protected by legislation. You need clear details about the four listed acts, but you should also have examples of the kind of circumstances that employees are protected against. It is unlikely that you will find details of this from your business so you should use examples from textbooks, the press, the internet, etc.
- How customer services in the business you have studied meet customer expectations. You could find out what customer expectations are by carrying out a survey of customers and then matching these to the customer services provided by the business. As you will have to give an oral presentation of your study it is useful to have visual aids such as photographs, diagrams of, for instance, where the customer service desk is, and charts of customer responses. Your presentation should also suggest improvements.

CHAPTER 1

BUSINESS OWNERSHIP

Foundation and Intermediate

KEY TERMS:

ownership	sole trader	partnership
company	charity	franchise
shareholder	limited liability	co-operatives
the public sector	the private sector	public corporations

In this chapter you will learn about the different ways in which businesses are owned. You will also learn about how the type of ownership affects the way that businesses can operate.

This chapter will explain:

- what names are given to different types of firm;

- how you can recognise the different types of firm;

- why owners decide to set up as sole traders, partnerships or companies;

- how sole traders, partnerships and companies differ in terms of their main characteristics.

Introduction

Ownership actually decides how businesses are generally classified, e.g.:

- are they owned by the state or by private individuals?

- are they owned by one person or a group of people?

- what rights and responsibilities do they have?

You will learn what the classification of businesses means in terms of control, responsibilities, ownership and rights. You will study how these conditions are affected by whether the business is:

- in the private sector or the public sector;

- a sole trader, partnership, company, co-operative or franchise.

The Public and Private Sectors of Business

There are two main branches of business, the private sector and the public sector.

Definition – **private sector** businesses are owned by individuals or organisations which choose how they will be run. **Public sector** businesses are owned by the state (and therefore all of us) and the government and government departments choose how they are run.

Figure 2.1.1 Types of business

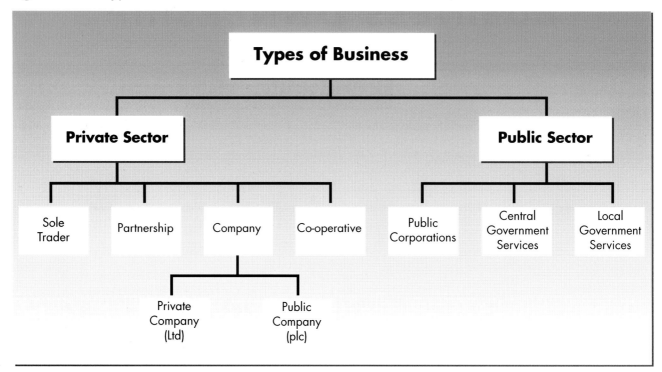

The **private sector** covers businesses that are owned by private individuals or organisations. In the case of companies they can be owned by other companies, but these other companies will eventually be owned by private individuals. There are some exceptions. When British Telecom was privatised the government did not sell all the shares at once, so it was still partly owned by the state.

Most charities and voluntary bodies will also be part of the private sector because they are owned and run by private individuals. Again there are some exceptions. In the UK the National Lottery is owned and run by a private company for profit, as well as giving money to charities, sporting bodies and other good causes. In other EU countries the lotteries are owned by the state, they are not run for profit, but charities etc. still receive some of the money.

The **public sector** is owned by the state or parts of the state, e.g. the local authorities. As all the citizens of the UK are the state, it is we who own the public sector. We own the state schools, the National Health Service, the Post Office and the BBC. The government does not own any of these. It simply controls or regulates them on our behalf.

Table 2.1.1 The owners of different businesses

Type of business	The owners
Sole trader	Single owner
Partnership	The partners
Private company	The shareholders
Public company	The shareholders
Co-operatives	The shareholders
Public sector organisations	The state
Charities Voluntary bodies	Can be single owners, partners, shareholders or the state

Note that **franchises** have not been included in Table 2.1.1. This is because franchises are not really types of ownership, they are special agreements between franchisers and franchisees (see page 80). They may be sole traders, partnerships or companies.

The characteristics of different types of ownership

Each type of business has its own special set of characteristics. These help to define whether it is in the public or the private sector and whether the business is a sole trader, partnership, company or public corporation.

The characteristics include:

- what rules have to be followed before businesses can start trading;
- what sources of capital are available to businesses;
- how businesses are controlled;
- how the profits are shared between the owners;
- whether or not the businesses have limited liability;
- how businesses must keep their accounts;
- who is allowed to buy shares in the businesses;
- what kind of taxation the businesses are liable for.

As we consider each type of business below we will be looking at these characteristics and how they differ between types of ownership.

Types of Business Ownership

The terms used to classify businesses by ownership suggest something about the ownership.

- **Sole traders** are called sole traders because there is only one owner of the business.

- **Partnerships** are called partnerships because two or more people own the business.

- **Companies** are called companies because the owners have agreed to own the business together under a set of legal constraints set down by the Companies Acts.

- **Co-operatives** are called co-operatives because the owners have agreed to co-operate together to sell products, make products, or market products, but not with the same strict controls that companies require.

- **Public corporations** are called 'public' because they are part of the public sector and we, the general public, own them. They are called 'corporations' because that means a group of people who act together as though they were one person.

Deciding which of these categories an actual business falls into can still be fairly difficult. The table below and the case studies should help you to decide what type of ownership a specific business has.

Table 2.1.2 gives examples of businesses that are typically found in each type of ownership. There are a great many other firms that do not fit into this simple pattern.

Table 2.1.2 Examples of businesses in each ownership category

Type of business	Typical examples	
Sole traders	Plumbers Gardeners Artists	Mobile hairdressers Window cleaners The self-employed
Partnerships	Doctors Solicitors Architects	Dentists Accountants Surveyors
Private companies	Building firms Local garages Printers	Engineers Furniture makers Hotels

Public companies	Car manufacturers Supermarkets Retail banks	Petrol producers Water firms Tobacco firms
Co-operatives	Retailers Workers owning and producing products	Service providers Farmers marketing produce
Public sector organisations	Postal services Health services Education	Regulatory bodies Local authority services Libraries
Charities Voluntary bodies	Helping the vulnerable Protecting the environment Schools	Sports clubs Social clubs Pressure groups

Case Study – Examples of types of ownership

Sole traders and partnerships

Many people operate businesses almost without knowing that they are doing so. The author has himself run a wide range of different businesses and a list of some of these should help to show the variety of businesses that come under the heading of sole trader and partnership.

Partnerships

Business	Partner	Nature of the business	Location
Chimera	Friends	Pop group	Oxford
J & D Decorators	Brother	Painting and decorating	Oxford
J & D Tree Felling	Brother	Tree felling, lopping and cutting timber	Oxford
E. P. Egg delivery	Wife	Egg delivery service	Crewe
The Teacher's Press	Wife	Educational publications	Whitchurch

Sole Trader

Sole Trader	Nature of the business	Location
Gardener	Gardener for private customers	Oxford
Freelance film critic	Contracted by *Oxford Journal*	Oxford
Leaflet distribution	Leaflet distribution to local homes	North Hampshire
E. P. Toys	Selling toys through toy parties	Basingstoke
Market stall holder	Selling toys	Andover
Author	Writing books for publication	From Whitchurch
Consultant	For educational boards	From Whitchurch

Most self-employed people are sole traders and work on their own. Many can be found in the construction industry. They are contracted by builders, private households or businesses to carry out particular jobs, and once the work is finished they move on to another job elsewhere. They include electricians, plumbers, carpenters, plasterers and painters.

Figure 2.1.2 shows the difference in the percentage of people employed directly by firms in the construction industry and those who are self-employed. The self-employed operate as sole traders. It also shows that there is a higher percentage of self-employed people in the primary sector than those employed by companies. This is because many farmers are also sole traders.

Figure 2.1.2 Percentage of employed and self-employed by sectors (UK 1997)

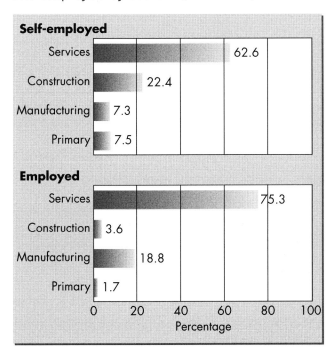

How to recognise different types of business

It is not always easy to know what type of business each individual firm is. Many owners of firms will simply give the business a name, such as The Camera Shop, and that will not tell you if it is a sole trader, partnership or company. There are, however, usually some clues.

Name:	Vernons Pools Ltd
Business:	Operating a football pools service
Name:	Times Computer Services Ltd
Business:	Selling computers by mail order
Name:	Barclays Bank plc
Business:	Banking services
Name:	Unilever plc
Business:	Soap powders, home and personal care and food products

- Nearly every firm that has 'Ltd' written after its name is a **private limited company**.

- Any firm that has 'plc' written after its name is a **public limited company**. These are also the businesses whose shares are listed in the newspapers.

- **Partnerships** will often call themselves 'partnerships', e.g. Doctor A.J. Austin & Partners of Farnham. Alternatively, they will call the firm by the names of the partners, e.g. Davies, Blunden & Evans (Solicitors) of Farnborough. There are, however, many firms that are named after people, e.g. Marks & Spencer, which are not partnerships but companies. The general rule is that if the business has 'Ltd' or 'plc' in its business name it is not a partnership.

- **Sole traders** are best recognised by what they do. Nearly all 'one man/woman' businesses are sole traders. They will not have 'Ltd' or 'plc' after their names and they will generally work on their own. Most self-employed people will be sole traders.

- **Charities** are often identified by their names which suggest that they have been set up to help disadvantaged people or promote particular causes, e.g. The National Society for the Prevention of Cruelty to Children (NSPCC) and Friends of the Earth.

Lists of major UK charities can be found on:
http://www.charitychoice.co.uk/default.htm
and on
http://www.waterlow.com/legalweb/charity/chasfram.html

- **Voluntary bodies** will normally be identified by their name, such as the Whitchurch Longmeadow Squash Club, but sometimes very similar sounding organisations, such as the Pine Ridge Golf Club in Frimley, Surrey, are profit making private companies.

- **Public sector organisations** are usually identified because they are so well known to the general public. Most schools and hospitals are in the public sector, and most people recognise the BBC as being a public service broadcaster. At the local level the provision of street lighting, library services and a fire service is recognised as being provided by the state.

These clues should help to identify the type of business you are looking at, but really the only way to be certain which type of ownership is involved is to ask the people who work there or who own it.

Limited liability

> Definition – **limited liability** means that if a business is in debt the owners are protected and will have to pay only that part of the debt that belongs to the business.

Owning and running a business can be risky. With most businesses it is necessary to spend money before the owners receive profits. Labour, raw materials, tools, equipment, rents, etc. all need to be paid for before the products can be made and sold.

Businesses can protect themselves against some risks by using insurance companies. They can insure against the dangers of fire, theft, accidents or the public being injured but very few insurance companies will cover the risk of the business making a loss.

For sole traders and partnerships the owners are usually directly involved in running the business. If they run it badly and go into debt, it seems fair that they should pay what is owed, otherwise someone else, say a firm supplying them with their raw

---

Bankrupt businesses for sale

Each year thousands of businesses go bankrupt. Many of them disappear and are never heard of again, but there is also a good trade in selling these businesses to people who think that they can turn them around and make them profitable. In November 1999 such businesses included:

Hallmark Narrowboats Ltd, offering a range of narrowboats for hire, some of which have already been booked, and a good reputation for quality in the market.

A. C. Edwards Ltd, a leading manufacturer of signs in the UK. Customers include major UK firms. Facilities include 60,000 sq. ft premises, 56 experienced staff and hi-tech plant.

P Van Zeist Ltd, distributors of houseplants and other goods. Facilities include a 16,500 sq. ft warehouse and an experienced workforce. Annual turnover is around £1.7 million with a secure customer base.

---

materials, will suffer. These firms have what is called **unlimited liability** for their debts. If they cannot pay from the money in their business the owners will have to pay by selling their cars, any shares they have in other firms, even their houses.

With many companies the shareholders are being asked to put money into the company but someone else often runs the business. The people running it may make bad decisions and put the company into debt. If the shareholders then had to sell their cars and houses etc. to pay the debt they would probably not risk investing in the first place. Large companies would therefore not exist.

Governments around the world have recognised this and they therefore give the owners of companies **limited liability**. When a company gets into debt the shareholders will lose what money they invested when they bought shares, but they will not be asked to pay any more. Their personal possessions, such as their houses, are safe.

Figure 2.1.3 Which businesses have limited liability and which do not?

Unlimited liability		**Limited liability**
• Sole traders		• Most companies
• Partnerships	?	• Limited partners
• Some unlimited companies		• Public corporations
• Co-operatives if they are sole traders or partnerships		• Co-operatives if they are companies
• Franchises if they are sole traders or partnerships		• Franchises if they are companies

Private Sector Businesses

Running a business in the private sector

A business cannot just set up and start trading. Trade involves other people. Certain rules and laws must be followed and contracts agreed. These rules, laws and contracts are required to ensure:

- that customers are protected against bad businesses;

- that customers will receive value for money;

- that owners know who has the right to make decisions about the way the business is run;

- that owners know how the profits of the business will be distributed;

- that suppliers to the business know what risks there are that they may not get paid;

- that the government can raise the taxation that it is entitled to;

- that the government can force businesses to act in a way that will protect the consumer, the environment and the community.

Many rules apply to all businesses, whatever type of business ownership they have, e.g.:

- Any businesses selling fresh unpacked food must have facilities for the staff who handle the food to wash their hands.

- All businesses selling alcohol, or running a betting office, must have a licence to do this.

- Any businesses employing staff must provide their employees with a written contract of employment.

Sole Traders, Partnerships and Companies

Setting up the business

> Definition – A **sole trader** is a firm that is owned by only one person.

Sole traders are still the most common form of business in the UK mainly because they are so easy to set up. There is no contract to be made with any other owner, no special documents that have to be filled out. Many sole traders are small businesses so limited capital is required, or they provide services such as gardening, plumbing, private tuition and no expensive equipment or premises is needed.

> Definition – A **partnership** is a firm that is owned by two or more people (usually up to 20) who have agreed to own and run a business together – but who are not forming a company or a co-operative.

Partnerships involve two or more people owning the business together and therefore a contract is needed between them. This can be very informal and may be a simple spoken agreement. Normally the agreement is written down in a formal document called the **Articles of Partnership**. This outlines the details of the partnership and how the control and profits of the business are to be divided between the owners.

> Definition – A **company** is a firm that is registered with the Registrar of Companies and involves two or more owners who have agreed to own and run a business together. (NB: see the box below about single member companies.)

Companies are given a special legal status. A company is treated by the law as though it is a person – it is **incorporated**. This gives the company special legal rights and responsibilities. It is therefore necessary for a company to be set up in a particular way. **Private companies** must fill out two documents, the **Articles of Association** and the **Memorandum of Association**. The first of these gives details of the internal set-up of the business, e.g.:

- the voting rights of shareholders;
- when annual general meetings will take place;
- how profits will be divided.

> ### Single member companies
>
> Since 1992 it has been possible to set up a company with only one shareholder. The business is known as a Single Member Private Limited Company. This allows someone who works completely on his/her own, such as a plumber or potter, to gain limited liability if the owner wants to. There are rules about how decisions must be made and recorded so the number of these companies is still small.

The memorandum gives details of how the business relates to everyone else, e.g.:

- the name and location of the registered office;
- what the business is allowed to produce;
- how many shares in total the business is allowed to issue.

These documents have to be sent to the **Registrar of Companies** with a fee for registration. If the Registrar is happy with the details he or she will issue a **Certificate of Incorporation** and a **Certificate of Trading**.

Public companies must complete all the stages that private companies need to complete but they must also be accepted by the Stock Exchange Council before they are allowed to be public limited companies. They need to send details of their company, and past trading histories if they are already in business, to the Council. The Council will examine the documents and decide if the business can be a plc. The business must then sell shares to the general public and ensure that the market makers in the Stock Exchange have shares. A business cannot become a plc unless it has more than £50,000 worth of capital.

All this is necessary because once the plc is set up, its shares will be quoted on the Stock Exchange and anyone who wishes to buy or sell shares must be able to do this through the Stock Exchange.

With private companies shares can only be sold privately, i.e. direct to other people. They cannot be offered to just anyone, and the company can restrict who the shares can be sold to.

Common sources of capital

The main sources of capital are explained on page 119. Many of these are available to all three types of business, but others are available only to specific types of business. Sources of capital include:

- savings
- loans from friends and relatives
- loans from banks
- loans and grants from government
- selling shares
- profit from previous sales.

Sole traders have the most limited sources of finance because they cannot bring in other owners and still remain sole traders. Public companies have the widest sources of capital because they can offer shares for sale to the general public.

Often sources of capital, like trade credit, loans from banks and debt factoring, are available to all businesses, but they are more likely to be offered to large rather than small firms. Sole traders can be large firms but they are usually small. Public companies can be small firms, but they are usually large.

Continuing success for the Prince's Trust

The Prince's Trust has now helped more than 40,000 people to set up their own businesses. This has been done by offering training, advice and financial support for the unemployed and for part-time workers who want to set up their own businesses. To qualify for 'Business Start-up' support you need to be between 18 and 30 years old, unemployed or part-time and willing to put in the work needed to succeed.

The Prince's Trust can provide a low interest loan of up to £5,000, and also offers grants to let you test your ideas in the market. Local business advisers provide specialist advice to help ensure that the right basic business decisions are made.

How Private Sector Businesses are Controlled

A **sole trader** is the only owner of the business and therefore decides exactly what will be done. He or she may employ other people but the final decisions will nearly always rest with the owner. The only exceptions will be when a lender of finance has insisted that the business will be run in a certain way, e.g. when the government offers a grant it may insist that the business is located in an area of high unemployment.

The control in **partnerships** depends on what agreement was made between the partners. Many partnerships have senior and junior partners, with the senior partners having more control and say in how the business will be run. There are also many partnerships where control is shared equally between the partners.

There are also special partnerships called **limited partnerships** where there are 'general partners' who are fully liable for any debts the partnership has and 'limited partners', also known as 'sleeping partners', who put money into the business but have no control over how it is run. At the same time they are not liable for the debts of the partnership beyond what they paid in.

Companies are ultimately controlled by their shareholders. Normally, shareholders are given one vote for each of their shares. If they have 100 shares they will get 100 votes. Major decisions will be made by holding meetings or writing to shareholders and asking them to vote. The majority vote wins.

In small businesses and especially in private companies the owners usually manage the business as well. Decisions about the day-to-day running of the business are made by the owners. In large businesses and especially in public companies the shareholders do not run the business and managers are employed to make day-to-day decisions.

With some shares there are no voting rights, but the owners of these shares do receive part of the profits.

How are the Profits of a Business Divided?

The profits of a business belong to the owners. How the profits are distributed, and how much each owner receives depends, to a great extent, on what type of ownership the business has.

- **Sole traders:** There is only one owner and he or she receives all the profits.

- **Partnerships:** The profits will be divided on the basis of what was agreed when the partnership was set up. Usually, if one partner puts in, say 40%, of the capital, that partner will receive 40% of the profits. Sleeping partners who take less risk (see page 75) often receive a lower percentage of the profits.

- **Companies:** When companies make profits they distribute them to their shareholders (unless they want to keep them for additional investments).

> Definition – A **dividend** is that part of the profits that each individual shareholder is paid.

The most common way of distributing these profits is to pay each shareholder a part of the total profits, a **dividend**. If a shareholder has 2,000 shares and there are 100,000 shares in the company, the shareholder would receive 2% of the total profits. With some shares, e.g. preference shares, a fixed dividend is paid for each share.

Special types of shares

Owners of **preference shares** are paid before other shareholders, but usually at a fixed rate (e.g. 5%). They may or may not have voting rights.

Owners of **'A' ordinary shares** receive the same dividends as ordinary shareholders but they have no voting rights and, therefore, no control over how the company is run.

Founders' shares are shares that the original owners of a company sometimes create in order to encourage potential owners to buy shares. These shares will receive a dividend only after all the other shareholders have been paid an agreed amount, say 7%.

Taxation of Profits

When businesses make profits, tax has to be paid on these profits. Two types of tax have to be paid.

> Definition – **income tax** is the tax paid on an individual's income.

The profits of sole traders and partnerships are treated as though they were the owner's income and therefore **income tax** has to be paid on these profits. The rate of tax will depend on how much income each owner has received over the year. In 1999/2000, if people had incomes below £4,335 the rate of tax was 0%. Owners with high incomes, over about £32,000, paid 40% on any additional income. In between, incomes were taxed at 10% and 23%. The tax rates change when the government chooses to change them.

> Definition – **corporation tax** is the tax paid on the profits of businesses that are incorporated.

Companies, corporations and most co-operatives are registered under the law as existing separately from their owners. The law and the Inland Revenue therefore treat them as though they were individuals. These businesses are taxed under a separate tax called **corporation tax**. In 1999 that was between 20% and 30% depending on how much profit the business was making, but, as with income tax, this can be changed by the government when it wants to. Full details of tax rates and how they work can be found at www.inlandrevenue.gov.uk/home.htm.

The profits of companies etc. will be taxed under corporation tax before the profits are paid to the shareholders. When the shareholders receive the profits this will be part of their income so they will have to pay income tax on this. Owners of shares in companies are therefore taxed twice.

The tax benefits of being a sole trader or partnership

Most sole traders and partnerships are fairly small but the savings on taxation compared to being a company can be considerable. Three examples are given below. For each example it has been assumed that the owner is one of two owners who have no other sources of income.

Owner's profit	£50,000	£150,000	£500,000
Partnership			
Corporation tax	0	0	0
Income	50,000	150,000	500,000
Income tax	13,056	53,056	193,056
Total tax on profits	**13,056**	**53,056**	**193,056**
Company			
Corporation tax	10,000	30,000	100,000
Income	40,000	120,000	400,000
Income tax	9,056	41,056	153,056
Total tax on profits	**19,056**	**71,056**	**253,056**
Extra tax paid by owner of company	**£6,000**	**£18,000**	**£60,000**

NB: The corporation tax has not taken into account the allowance for very small businesses, i.e. at £50,000.

Why Owners Choose to Become Sole Traders, Partnerships or Companies

When people decide to start a business, or change from one type of business to another, they will weigh up the advantages and disadvantages. Lists of these are given below for each main type of private sector business. There are, however, other general factors that will decide what type of business people set up, e.g.:

- If there is only one owner it is not possible to set up as a partnership or a public company.

- If the business has less than £50,000 worth of capital it is not possible to set up as a public company.

- A business cannot become a company unless it is approved by the Registrar of Companies, and it cannot become a public company unless it is approved by the Council of the Stock Exchange.

- Some businesses refuse to buy products from firms that do not have limited liability and if firms want to sell to them they will have to be companies.

Advantages and Disadvantages of Private Sector Businesses

Sole trader

Advantages
a) Easy and quick to set up and close down.
b) You are your own boss so there is no conflict; you have independence, and quick decisions can be made.
c) The owner gets all the profits.
d) Accounts do not need to be published, and they do not need to be set out in any particular way.
e) Only income tax is paid on the profits.

Disadvantages
a) Unlimited liability.
b) Limited access to capital.
c) All final responsibility falls on one person, which can be stressful.
d) There is no one who owns and really cares about the business who can step in when the owner is sick or on holiday.
e) Lack of continuity if the owner dies or retires.

Partnership

Advantages
a) Fairly easy to set up and requires no formal agreement (NB: many partnerships do write out a formal Partnership Deed of Agreement).
b) Additional capital can be gained by taking on additional partners.
c) Partners can be recruited with specialist skills.
d) Decision making is shared and is less stressful.
e) Partnerships have a good reputation and are thought to be respectable.

Disadvantages
a) Limited liability.
b) Partners are also responsible for the debts of other partners.
c) There can be disagreements between partners.

d) The total number of partners is limited so there may still be a lack of capital.
e) If partners die or retire it may be difficult to continue the partnership, and it will have to be dissolved and reformed.

Companies

Advantages
a) Limited liability.
b) More shareholders can bring in more capital.
c) Public companies can sell shares to the general public.
d) There is continuity of ownership; if one person dies or sells shares the company continues.
e) Public companies find it easier to borrow money from banks, etc.

Disadvantages
a) Fairly lengthy procedure to set up.
b) Accounts have to be kept in a certain way, and be audited, and copies must be sent to the Registrar of Companies.
c) Public companies must publish their accounts annually.
d) Private companies can sell shares only through private contacts.
e) Public companies can have their shares bought by hostile interest and may finish up being taken over.

Co-operatives

> Definition – a **co-operative** is a firm that has an agreement between its members to produce goods or services and share the profits.

Sole traders, partnerships and companies are easy to define. Co-operatives cause a problem because there are at least three types of business that call themselves co-operatives. Two of them are not actually co-operatives in terms of how they are owned. The three types of co-operative are:

● **Worker co-operatives,** where the people working in the business actually own it. Normally these businesses are private companies. All the workers are also owners and they therefore have a say in how the business is run.

Worker Co-operatives

The Wales Co-operative Centre has been set up to help worker co-operatives start their businesses in Wales. The businesses are registered as either private companies or industrial and provident societies. Some are formed by employee buyouts, others are completely new businesses.

Allsorts Childcare Services Ltd

This childcare co-operative was registered by the Wales Co-operative Centre in January 1995. It provides playcare services to families and children who live in the St Mellons area of Cardiff.

The service of child care helps parents to return to work, retrain or set up in business. The business now employs 23 full-time and part-time employees.

● **Marketing co-operatives,** where separate businesses agree to join together so that they can market their products. Usually these are fairly small businesses, and the co-operative agreement gives them the power and the cost benefits of big businesses.

Marketing Co-operatives

Fishing Co-operatives (UK) Ltd supplies protective clothing, gloves, boots, oilskins, filleting and gutting knives, etc., to commercial fishing, fish farming and processing industries.

● **Retail and wholesale co-operatives,** where members have set up a firm to sell goods to themselves and to anyone else who might wish to buy them. This may seem like a rather odd thing to do but when the members buy goods from their own stores they will then gain the profits from the store instead of the profit going to someone else.

When most textbooks and people talk about 'co-operatives' it is the retail co-operatives that they

Retail Co-operatives of different size

The Co-operative Wholesale Society Ltd
 – 5 million members
 – 31,300 staff
 – 2,255 branches
 – 164 supermarkets

Desborough Co-operative Society Ltd
 – 2,500 members
 – 60 staff
 – 12 branches
 – 1 supermarket

Highburton Industrial & Providential Society
 – 400 members
 – 1 branch

are referring to. These were first successfully established in Rochdale in 1844. By 1901 there were 1,438 co-operative societies with a total membership of over 3 million people.

These retail co-operatives were set up by poor working-class people to stop the rich owners of businesses from exploiting them. Since 1901 many of these co-operatives have joined together so that they can gain the benefits of being large firms. Many others have stopped trading because the supermarkets have made goods as cheap as, if not cheaper than, the old 'co-ops' could.

The other change that has occurred is that the co-operative movement as a whole has expanded into other types of production. Many retail co-operatives now have agreements with wholesalers, and even produce some of their own goods. They have also expanded into insurance and banking.

Retail co-operatives have the following characteristics:

- They are registered with the Registrar of Friendly Societies.

- They are owned by their customers who are called members.

- Members pay a nominal amount to be members, usually £1.

- Members have one vote each.

- The co-operatives are run by an elected Board of Directors, but members have the ultimate decision on what will be done.

- Individual members can invest capital in the business, on which they will receive profits on the basis of how many shares they have.

- Customers who are members also share in the profits on the basis of how much they buy.

- Nearly all retail co-operatives have limited liability.

There are still a large number of retail co-operatives around and details can be found in various trade directories including the *Retail Directory of the UK* by Healey & Baker (Newman Books, ISBN 0 7079 6994 8).

The Principles of the Co-operative Movement

1st Principle: Voluntary and open membership
Co-operatives are voluntary organisations which are open to everyone as long as they accept the responsibilities of membership.

2nd Principle: Democratic member control
Co-operatives are controlled by their members, generally on the basis of one person, one vote. Members act together to set policies and make decisions. Some co-operatives have other voting methods but they are all democratic.

3rd Principle: Members' economic participation
All members pay to be members and part of the benefits they receive is related to how much they have bought or sold to the co-operative.

4th Principle: Autonomy and independence
Co-operatives cannot be owned by other organisations and any agreements they make with other organisations must be made for the benefit of the members.

5th Principle: Education, training and information
Co-operatives provide education and training for their members, elected representatives, managers and employees, so they can contribute effectively to the development of their co-operatives. They also keep the general public informed about the nature and benefits of co-operation.

6th Principle: Co-operation among co-operatives
Co-operatives work with other co-operatives, locally, nationally and internationally, to help develop and strengthen the co-operative movement.

7th Principle: Concern for the community
Co-operatives work for their members but also for the benefit of the community.

Franchises

Definition – a **franchise** is an agreement between two businesses that allows one business (the franchisee) to use the name and reputation of the other business (the franchiser).

Franchises are not types of business ownership. They are special agreements between one business (the **franchiser**), which is willing to sell (or license) the use of its name, and another business (the **franchisee**) which wants to use the name. Many well-known businesses operating in the UK are franchises, e.g.:

- McDonald's
- Burger King
- Dyno-rod
- Sock Shop

- Perfect Pizza
- Kentucky Fried Chicken
- Avis Rent-A-Car
- Bonanza Travel
- BP retail outlets
- The Body Shop
- Prontaprint
- British School of Motoring

In 1999 the National Westminster Bank and the British Franchise Association completed a survey of UK franchises. The results of the survey included the following statistics:

- There were 596 franchises.

- Turnover of business related to franchise was £57.9 billion.

- Sales from firms that were franchised accounted for 29% of all retail sales in the UK.

- 606,600 people were directly and indirectly employed in the franchising sector.

The franchiser will allow the franchisee to use its name for a fee. Many franchises now cost between £10,000 and £20,000 although others can cost over £100,000. Details can be found at www.frainfo.co.uk and at www.franchisebusiness.co.uk.

When the franchisee buys the right to use the franchiser's name there will usually be fairly strict rules about how the business must be run, e.g. McDonald's will specify where the meat is bought from and will insist that all owners are trained by McDonald's. Most franchise agreements also insist that the franchisees pay part of the profits to the franchiser.

Advantages and disadvantages of franchising include:

Advantages
a) Usually the franchise name is very well known.
b) The success of one outlet helps all the others.
c) There is often joint national advertising and promotions.
d) Franchisers often provide financial help to the franchisees when they are setting up.

Disadvantages
a) A fee has to be paid for the right to use the name.
b) Part of the profits usually has to be paid to the franchiser.
c) Franchisees must run the business in the way the franchiser specifies.
d) Franchise agreements can be stopped and the franchisee will then be unable to trade.

The main benefits to the franchisers are that someone else runs the businesses for them, they receive payments for the name and profits, and they can spread their business name very quickly.

What is on offer with a Prontaprint franchise?

Prontaprint is the UK's largest network of franchised design, print and copy business service centres, with 220 outlets. It offers franchisees:

- training and other start-up support;
- innovative technology that allows the franchisee to be highly competitive;
- central marketing with advertising and promotion that ensure that the Prontaprint name is the leader in the field;
- central buying that allows outlets to keep their costs low;
- financial support in starting the business.

For an established business to become a Prontaprint franchisee, the following finances and terms are typical:

Total start-up costs		£100,000
Contribution paid by franchisee		£40,000
Royalties to be paid by franchisee		10%
Contract period		10 years
Typical turnover	1st year	£200,000
	2nd year	£250,000
Profits	1st year	£24,000
	2nd year	£45,000

The Public Sector

Many parts of production that used to be in the public sector are now in the private sector, e.g. British Steel, water supplies, train operating services and British Airways. Despite these changes the state remains a major producer of products and a major spender of money. Most health services, education, defence and law and order are provided by the state as well as smaller services such as the BBC, the Post Office and the Bank of England. Figure 2.1.5 shows how important the government sector still is.

Figure 2.1.5 General government expenditure as a percentage of total UK expenditure (1998)

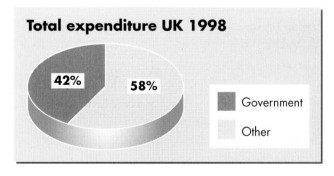

Government still spends a huge proportion of the total income of the UK. It therefore needs organisations and businesses to help it to manage this expenditure and to ensure that the public benefit. These are all part of the **public sector**.

The public sector is divided into three main parts.

Government departments

Government departments have the job of running the country for the benefit of the citizens. These departments include ministries for health, education and employment, transport and the environment, and defence. When government policies are made, such as the changes that have been introduced in the education system for the year 2000, the ministry will be responsible for ensuring that the policies are followed through. With education this is the responsibility of the Department for Education and Employment.

The money that is required to run the departments and to put the policies into effect comes mainly from taxation, although charges are made for some services, e.g. prescriptions for medicines, charges for borrowing tapes from libraries, charges for crossing the Severn Bridge.

The work of government departments is supervised by permanent staff but these staff are responsible to the minister and the minister will be responsible to the Cabinet, Parliament and, ultimately, to us, the electorate.

Public corporations

> Definition – A **public corporation** or **nationalised industry** is a business that is state-owned but sells a product to its customers.

Public corporations are businesses that are owned by the state and run as the government decides. They have a separate identity, like companies, and therefore have limited liability. They are managed by a board of directors which is responsible to a minister. The day-to-day running of these corporations is carried out by the managers.

There are no private shareholders because the public corporations are owned by the state and therefore by all of us.

They do sell their products, however, rather than giving them away free. The Post Office sells its delivery services by charging us for stamps. Through the TV licence the BBC charges us for the television programmes it provides. It also earns revenue by selling programmes to other stations, especially abroad. Because these businesses sell their products, their main source of capital is ploughed-back profits, although they also borrow from banks and from the government.

> Definition – **privatisation** is the selling of state-owned businesses to the private sector.

Many public corporations, often referred to as nationalised industries, have been privatised in the last 20 years. Some still remain, such as the Post Office, the BBC, the Atomic Energy Authority, the Bank of England and the Civil Aviation Authority.

Local authorities and local councils

Government also operates at a local level and manages a wide range of activities. As with central government, local government is responsible for seeing that its policies, and the policies of central government, are put in place. Councils have permanent staff but they are responsible to elected local councillors.

Much of the business of the local authority is, in fact, implementing the decisions of central government. The main expenditure of county councils is paying for the state education system.

The money to pay for the services that local authorities provide comes mainly from taxes collected by central government, but also from the Council Tax and from charges made for some services, such as the use of public swimming pools and sports centres.

As with all the other types of business there are advantages and disadvantages to public ownership. They include:

Advantages
a) They are owned by the state and can be run so that they are of benefit to the citizens.
b) They do not need to make profits so prices can be lower for customers.
c) Many services, e.g. education, are provided free to the users and are available for everyone.
d) Some businesses, e.g. atomic energy or defence, are safer under state control than under private control.

Disadvantages
a) Many are not run to make profits and that can make them inefficient.
b) Services like health and education have to be paid for out of our taxes and we have little control over what is provided.
c) Often decisions are made for political reasons rather than because they make good business sense.
d) There are many layers of control and this makes them expensive and inefficient to run.

CHAPTER 2

INDUSTRIAL SECTORS AND BUSINESS ACTIVITIES

Foundation and Intermediate

In this chapter you will learn how businesses are divided on the basis of what they produce. Five different ways of dividing businesses will be looked at:

- division between the production of goods or of services;

- division in terms of who receives the products. This divides businesses into producers of capital or consumer products;

- division in terms of what stage of production is being carried out. This divides businesses into primary, secondary or tertiary;

- division into different types of industry, e.g. the automobile industry, the clothes industry or the banking industry;

- division by what specific types of products the business produces, e.g. clothes shops, ski-wear shops, second-hand clothes shops.

This chapter will also look at how the types of business have changed over time.

Introduction

> Definition – **business activity** is the type of production that a business is involved in.

All businesses can be put into groups on the basis of what they produce. That is what we do when we describe firms as estate agents, publishing houses or car manufacturers. What they produce describes their **business activity**.

Sometimes businesses produce only one kind of product, as with Avondale Glass in Pembrokeshire which produces hand-blown glass products. Sometimes businesses are involved in producing a number of widely different products, as with Virgin Ltd which produces cola, records and hot air balloons, and provides train and air services, banking and financial services, and runs radio stations, hotels, travel services and even a modelling agency.

> Full details of the wide range of Virgin's products can be found on:
> **http://www.virgin.com**

All businesses will, however, fit into each of the five divisions of business covered below.

Goods and services

> Definition – **goods** are products that can be seen and touched; a **service** is a product that does something for the customer but it cannot be touched.

When businesses produce they produce either goods or services. A good is something that can be touched and passed from one person to another, such as a car, a television or a loaf of bread. A service is something that cannot be touched and cannot be passed on to someone else. Doctors, dentists, solicitors and teachers all provide services and whilst people can obviously touch the thermometer that the doctor uses or the books and paper provided by the teacher, they cannot actually touch the doctoring or teaching.

With many businesses it is easy to get confused about what is actually being provided. Supermarkets are an obvious example. When people go to the supermarkets to buy the weekly shopping they finish up with goods which they can touch, give to other people and take home and use. But the supermarkets themselves do not actually produce most of the goods. The goods are produced by Heinz, Kellogg,

Mars, etc. What the supermarkets are doing is unpacking them, putting them on the shelves and possibly advertising them. These are all services and, generally, that is all that supermarkets do – provide the service of retailing.

Even supermarket own brands are nearly always made for the supermarkets by other businesses, and it is the other businesses which are the producers of the goods. There are exceptions to this. When supermarkets bake their own bread on the premises they are producing the loaves of bread, so then they are producing goods.

Deciding exactly what a business does produce can be fairly difficult. A farmer who grows fruit and vegetables is clearly producing goods, but if he then sells them in his own farm shop he is actually providing a retailing service. Part of his production will be goods, and part will be services.

Figure 2.2.1 Goods and services businesses found in building and selling a house

Consumer Products and Capital Products

The terms 'capital' and 'consumer' are used to describe goods and services in terms of who finishes up using them.

> Definition – **capital goods and services** are products made by one business for other businesses to use.

Capital goods and services are used by businesses to help them produce other goods and services. Capital goods include:

- machines

- delivery vehicles
- factories
- furniture in offices

Capital services include:

- a service contract to repair and maintain machinery or vehicles;
- the telephone connections provided by BT or Mercury that allow businesses to talk to their suppliers and customers;
- the services of a security firm which provides regular checks through the night to ensure that offices and shops are not broken into.

Definition – **consumer goods and services** are products made by businesses for people who are not in business to use.

Consumer goods and services are those products which are received by the end user, the consumer. They are not being used to help produce anything else that will then be sold by a business. Consumer goods include:

- family cars;
- fruit and vegetables for personal consumption;
- home computers bought for use by an individual or a family.

Consumer services include:

- entertainment at a cinema;
- the retailing provided by shops;
- the service of your local GP or hospital.

Sometimes the same product can be both a capital product and a consumer product. It depends on who is receiving it. If a father buys a PC for his children, this will be a consumer good. If a business buys the same computer so that it can keep records of its customers and do its accounts more easily, the new computer will be a capital good.

Case Study – The Great Wall of China (Fish & Chip Shop and Chinese Takeaway)

The Great Wall of China serves takeaway meals every evening, providing its customers with **consumer goods** in the form of food and drinks. It also provides **consumer services** by cooking, serving and wrapping the food.

In order to provide these goods and services the Great Wall of China needs various capital goods and services.

The **capital goods** include the pot, pans, woks, spoons, spatulas, bowls, etc. needed to cook the food. They also include the ovens, grills, refrigerators and heated display cabinets. As customers wait for their food seats are provided and a slot machine, also capital goods. There is also the shop itself. Raw materials, the uncooked foods, spices, soft drinks, etc. are also capital goods when they are bought, but they will be used up fairly quickly and turned into the end product.

The **capital services** include the telephone link which allows customers to ring up and order meals, the insurance against fire and injury to customers and a contract with a firm that removes the dirty cooking oil, cleans it, and returns it to be used again.

Primary, Secondary and Tertiary Industry

Figure 2.2.2 Sectors of industry

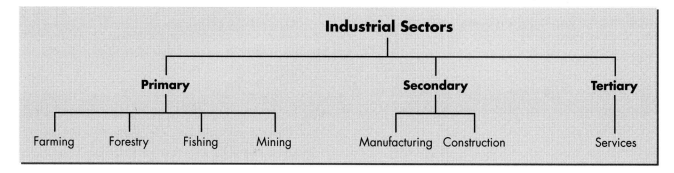

86

A very common way of dividing businesses is in terms of what stage of the production process the business is involved in. Most of the goods that we receive have gone through three distinct stages of production.

Figure 2.2.3 Stages of production

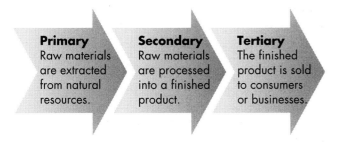

As the names themselves suggest, this division classifies business by the stage of production involved. Primary will come before secondary and then comes tertiary.

Primary

Primary industry covers the production of **farming, forestry, fishing** and **mining**. For many products, such as fish fingers, this will be the first stage of production. The fish will then be sold on for processing at the secondary stage.

- Fish are caught ready for making into fish fingers.
- Grapes are grown ready for making into wine.
- Iron ore is mined ready for making into steel.

Secondary

Secondary industry covers the **manufacturing** of goods such as steel, electricity, cars, televisions and tinned food. It also includes **construction** of factories, houses and roads. Secondary industry processes the goods that come from primary industry and turns them into something that people want.

- Fish ⇒ **processing factory** ⇒ fish fingers.
- Wood ⇒ **timber mill** ⇒ **furniture manufacturer** ⇒ tables.
- Clay ⇒ **brick manufacturer** ⇒ **builder** ⇒ houses.

Tertiary

Tertiary industry covers **services**. For example:

- Wholesaling, retailing, banking and insurance are all services which help businesses in the primary and secondary industries to sell their goods.
- Direct services are provided to the general public. Examples include hairdressing, hotels and restaurants.
- The government provides services such as health and education.

Sometimes a business can be producing in more than one sector (see the case study on Whitchurch Silk Mill below). With many larger businesses this is quite common because they are producing a range of different products, as in the case of Pepsi.

The Coca-Cola and Pepsi companies are both known primarily as manufacturers of cola and other soft drinks. As well as colas they produce Nestea (Coke), Lipton (Pepsi), Powderade (Coke), All Sport (Pepsi), Sprite (Coke) and 7Up (Pepsi).

In 1996 Coca-Cola sold £8.5 billion worth of soft drinks and £1.1 billion worth of juices and foods. All were manufactured by Coca-Cola and were part of **secondary** industry. The firm produced nothing else.

In 1996 Pepsi sold £6.4 billion worth of soft drinks and £5.9 billion worth of snack foods, both part of **secondary** industry. The highest part of Pepsi's sales, however, came from their fast food restaurants (Kentucky Fried Chicken, Taco Bell and Pizza Hut), which earned the company £6.9 billion of sales. These restaurants are part of **tertiary** industry.

Case Study – Whitchurch Silk Mill

Whitchurch Silk Mill in Hampshire has been manufacturing silk since the 1820s. It is now a working museum, producing high quality silks to order for theatrical costumes, interior decoration and historic houses. The silk thread, which is imported, is woven into cloth. It is then sold as rolls of cloth, or made into small items such as scarves and ties. This manufacturing of silk means that it is part of the **secondary** sector.

The business also runs a gift shop where customers can buy ties, scarves and small pieces of silk. The gift shop also sells a wide range of small gift items such as cards, local lavender items, and honey. These items have been bought from other producers and are resold in the shop. This retailing part of the business means that it is also part of the **tertiary** sector.

The Mill is very popular with tourists who can pay to walk around the buildings, see the silk cloth being woven, which is now done with electrically-driven machines, and look at how the weaving used to be done with water-driven machinery. The Mill runs a small tea room in the museum part of the building for tourists and any locals who want to go out for tea. The tea rooms are offering a service to customers and this is also part of the **tertiary** sector.

Businesses can be placed in the primary, secondary or tertiary sectors simply by finding out what they do and then matching this to one, or more, of the sectors. However, when it comes to working out what proportion of businesses in a country, town or local community are in each sector, there is an added problem. First one has to decide what measurement is being used. Four main measures are:

- How much is produced by each sector.

- How many people work in each sector.

- How many businesses there are in each sector.

- How many sites there are for each sector.

Measuring the size of the three sectors

For the UK as a whole the first two measures of output and number of employees are used. These are shown in Figure 2.2.4.

Figure 2.2.4 Division of UK industry by primary, secondary, tertiary (1998)

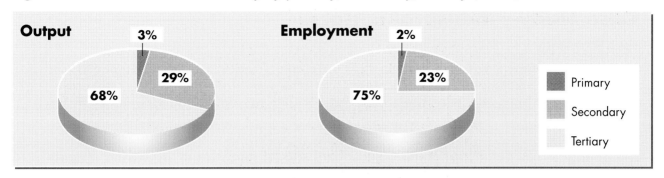

The output is measured by recording the sales revenue that all the businesses in the UK receive when they sell their products. All businesses have to declare their sales revenue to the Inland Revenue for taxation purposes, so it is fairly easy for the government to work out how much is produced in each sector.

The number of employees in each sector is also easy for the government to work out because it has records of all employees, both for income tax purposes and for payments of national insurance contributions.

When it comes to finding out how the local community is divided in terms of primary, secondary and tertiary production, it is usually very difficult to get details of how much each business produces, and it may also be difficult to find out how many employees each business has.

A simpler approach is to measure either how many businesses there are in each sector, or how many sites there are.

If you measure the number of businesses all you will need to do is to check the listed businesses in some form of trade directory. There are very few businesses that do not have phones, so you can find the businesses by checking *Yellow Pages* or a *Thomson Directory*.

Alternatively, business can be measured by the number of sites there are. Many businesses are parts of chains and have tens and even hundreds of sites around the country. Some businesses even have more than one site in the same community. In Andover Tesco has two supermarket sites, and in Winchester Sainsbury also has two sites. The number of sites in the UK owned by the Dixons Group is shown on page 269.

Case Study – Industrial Sectors

Figure 2.2.5 shows how many sites there are for primary, secondary and tertiary industry in the town of Whitchurch (Hampshire). It also shows how important it is to choose a representative area. The three pie charts show the result of recording the businesses that can be found within $\frac{1}{2}$ mile, 1 mile and $1\frac{1}{2}$ miles of the centre of the town. There are 90 businesses within $\frac{1}{2}$ mile, 150 businesses within 1 mile and and 156 businesses within $1\frac{1}{2}$ miles of the centre.

Figure 2.2.5 The number of primary, secondary and tertiary sites in Whitchurch (Hants) in 1999

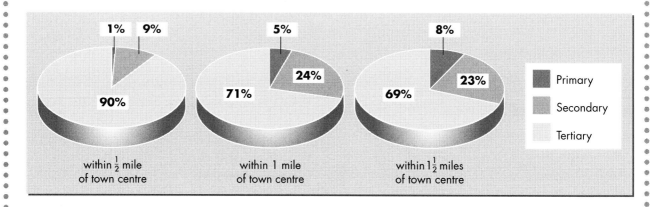

The centre of Whitchurch is essentially a shopping area. It has the usual small town retail shops, such as a supermarket, newsagent, grocer, butcher, and services, such as a bank, estate agent, doctor and dentist's surgery. It also has garages, public houses, restaurants and schools. All these are part of tertiary industry. The few firms in secondary industry are either small manufacturers or builders. The only primary industry which is within $\frac{1}{2}$ a mile of the centre is the Whitchurch Cress Beds. In built-up, residential areas large factories or farms are very unusual.

Within 1 mile of the centre, the small industrial estate on the outskirts of Whitchurch is included and the percentage of sites for secondary industry suddenly increases (from 9% to 24%). There are also now more farms so the percentage for primary sector sites also increases. As a result the percentage for the tertiary sector falls, even though more shops and services are included.

Moving further out to $1\frac{1}{2}$ miles brings in only six more businesses, five farms and a public house. The result is that the primary sector becomes larger still.

Classifying Businesses By What They Do

The division of businesses into primary, secondary and tertiary is a very broad way of classifying what businesses do. Even within that classification there are many subdivisions. In the primary sector there are four main subdivisions, and each of these can themselves be subdivided. This is shown in Figure 2.2.6 below.

Figure 2.2.6 Primary sector subdivisions

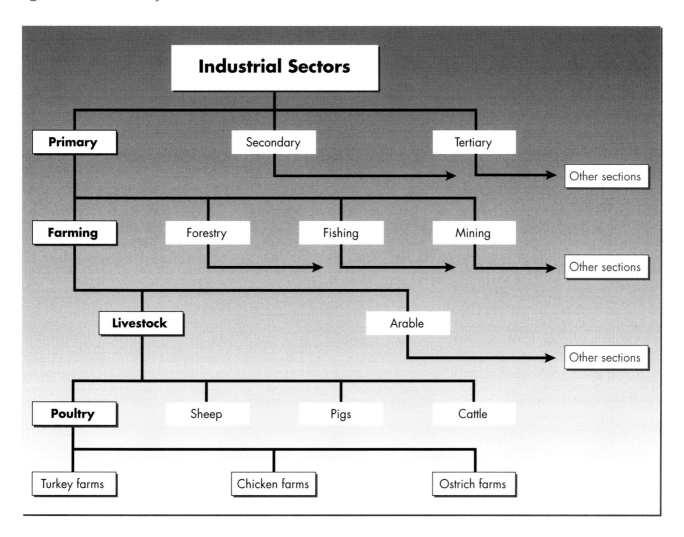

The same could be done for each of the sectors. In the end, a business will be classified by what it actually produces, e.g. turkeys, cars, hairdressing, banking.

The Standard Industrial Classification

In the UK, and in all European Union countries, businesses are classified by the government in terms of what they produce. In the UK this is called the Standard Industrial Classification or SIC.

The basic breakdown of industry by SIC is shown in Table 2.2.1. Some of these categories have headings that are not very easy to understand, but the examples should help to show what kinds of business are being covered in each section.

Table 2.2.1 The classification of business by the Standard Industrial Classification

	Type of industry involved	Examples in Guildford area	
A	Agriculture Hunting Forestry	Witley Park Farms Clinkard Beagle Kennels Commercial Woodlands Ltd	Wormley Bordon Headley Down
B	Fishing	Silkmill Fish Farms	Godalming
C	Mining Quarrying	Oxus Mining Ltd BFI Ltd (sand quarry)	Woking Shere
D	Manufacturing	Specialist Sports Car Ltd The Village Furniture Warehouse Dunlop Slazenger International Ltd	Woking Farnborough Camberley
E	Electricity, gas and water supply	Southern Water plc Southern Gas plc Southern Electric plc	Facilities are provided across the area
F	Construction	Alfred Charles Ltd (roads) Charles Church Ltd (houses)	Farnham Camberley
G	Wholesale trade Retail trade Repair of motor vehicles Repair of personal and household goods	Booker Cash & Carry Ltd W.H. Smith & Son Ltd Thompsons Garage Whirlpool (UK) Ltd	Basingstoke Aldershot Sandhurst Croydon
H	Hotel Restaurants	The Lismoyne Hotel Pizza Express	Fleet Basingstoke
I	Transport Storage Communication	DHL International (UK) Ltd Business Moves Ltd World Quest Networks UK Ltd	Camberley Farnborough Woking
J	Financial intermediation	Midland Bank plc American Express Europe Ltd Bi-Link Capital Market Ltd	Liphook Guildford Woking
K	Real esate, renting Business activities	County Property Management Ltd Aldershot Business Centre Ltd Wheeler & Co. (accountants)	Woking Aldershot Whitchurch
L	Public administration and defence Compulsory social security	Sandhurst Town Council Prince Philip barracks (army)	Sandhurst Bordon

M	Education	Basingstoke College of Technology	Basingstoke
N	Health and social work	King Street Dental Practice Mental After Care Association	Odiham Farnborough
O	Other community, social and personal service activities	Curtis Court Day Care Centre	Church Crookham
P	Private households with employed persons	These would include households employing cooks or housekeepers etc.	
Q	Extra-territorial organisations and bodies	These are organisations that operate outside their own country.	

Source: *Yellow Pages* (Guildford area)

These categories are still very wide and, in fact, each category is subdivided, so that nearly every type of business is eventually classified separately. Under 'wholesaling and retailing' there will be separate categories for clothes shops, sports shops, greengrocers and fishmongers. Food retailers are SIC No. 6410, retailers of household goods are SIC No. 6480 and retailers of footwear are SIC No. 6460.

Although the government uses the SIC categories it would be difficult for students to know exactly which category each type of business fits into. When you come to do your assignment, it will be much easier to use a simplified classification, e.g:

Figure 2.2.7 Simple classifications

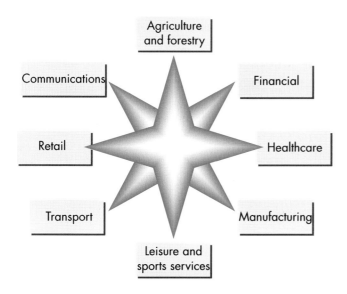

These are still fairly general categories. Many of these broad headings can be subdivided to give an even more accurate picture of what a business does. For example, retailing can be subdivided into a wide range of types of retail.

Figure 2.2.8 Types of retailing

With many businesses there is yet another possible level of subdivision, which shows what specific businesses specialise in. Usually that will also show how the businesses place limits on what they are prepared to produce. Women's clothes shops target their sales towards women, pig farmers concentrate on the rearing and fattening of pigs, video rental shops usually do no more than rent out videos and perhaps console games and make a few sales of these. Subdivisions for clothes retailers would include:

Figure 2.2.9 Examples of clothes shops

Some businesses concentrate on producing only one type of product. Most businesses produce a range of products and target them towards different people. Many clothes shops are now unisex, or have departments for men, women and children. Businesses like Marks and Spencer have clothes departments but also run an in-store supermarket. Department stores like Debenhams have cafés and restaurants, Toys-R-Us offers access to the internet, and Ford, Mars and British Nuclear Fuels offer educational visits to schools and the general public.

Case Study – Types of businesses

Whitchurch is essentially a residential town surrounded by farmland. There is, therefore, only a limited amount of secondary industry here. There are no natural resources for heavy industry so all the manufacturing tends to be light industry, where small items or components are made. There are some professional services aimed at industry, such as assessors and secretarial services, but most services, such as banks, doctors and garages, are provided for the general public. The same is true of the shops which provide the usual range of grocery items, newspapers, etc. Because this is essentially a residential town there is also a sizeable building industry and a range of service firms that are related to the building industry, such as plumbers, roofers, and electricians.

Table 2.2.2 shows how businesses are broken down into various sectors. The data shows the number of firms in each sector. It does not show the size of firm or the number of employees. All the firms within $1\frac{1}{2}$ miles of the centre of Whitchurch have been included.

Table 2.2.2 Types of Business (by sites) in Whitchurch in 1999

	No. of firms	Examples of types of business
Professional services	21	accountant, doctor, architect, vet
Specialist services	15	travel agent, bookmaker, hairdresser
Equipment manufacturers	13	electrical, floor maintenance
Specialist retailers	13	chemist, butcher, newsagent
Hotels/pubs/restaurants	13	
Farming	12	
Builders, construction	11	carpenters, plumbers, electricians
Building services	9	
Garages/petrol stations	8	
Component manufacturers	6	plastics, tiles, nuts & bolts
Engineering	5	
Business services	5	printers, secretarial
Transport/delivery	5	
Financial services	3	banks, building societies
Education	3	schools
Recreation/entertainment	3	sports centre
General stores/supermarket	3	
Police/fire/ambulance	3	
Libraries/museums	2	
Specialist housing	2	nursing home, medical care
Cloth manufacturers	1	silk mill
Total	156	

The breakdown shown in Table 2.2.2 suggests that professional services are the most important businesses in Whitchurch. This does not, however, consider how many people are employed in each of these businesses. The local dentist's surgery, for example, is normally run with only three people. On the other hand, the two main building firms employ 74 and 67 people and the local primary school employs 31 people.

When the number of employees is taken into account the table looks very different.

Table 2.2.3 Types of Business (by employees) in Whitchurch in 1999

	No. of employees
Builders, construction	237
Equipment manufacturers	214
Education	73
Farming	63
Component manufacturers	58
Hotels/pubs/restaurants	49
Engineering	48
Professional services	48
Garages/petrol stations	36
Specialist retailers	25
Cloth manufacturers	22
Business services	21
Building services	18
Transport/delivery	15
Specialist services	15
General stores/supermarket	12
Police/fire/ambulance	11
Specialist housing	10
Recreation/entertainment	10
Financial services	9
Libraries/museums	4
Total	998

The major employers are in the secondary sector and especially in the building industry. Education is also fairly high because that is a labour-intensive business. Specialist retailers and specialist services have dropped down the list because most of them operate with one, two or three people only.

How the Size of the Sectors Has Changed Over Time

For each sector described in this chapter there have been dramatically different rates of growth for different types of business. Some have grown rapidly, others have changed very little and yet others have seen very large falls in output and sales.

The decade from 1989 to 1999 shows a dramatic shift from secondary to tertiary industry. This is simply part of a continuing trend that has been going on since the early 1950s.

Figure 2.2.10 Changing output of UK production by sector (1989 and 1999)

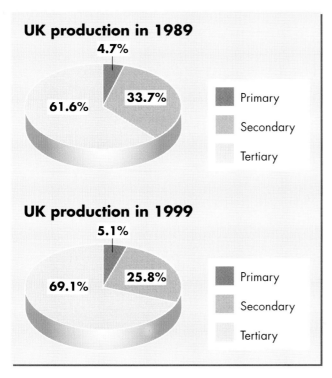

The charts above make it look as though output in the secondary sector has fallen very dramatically. In fact, between 1979 and 1989 it hardly fell at all, and between 1989 and 1999 it fell by only 3%. The output of the tertiary sector, however, has increased very dramatically indeed and that is why the percentages of secondary industry appear to have fallen so much.

If we look at the main sectors in primary and secondary we can see that most of them were growing in terms of their actual output. The exceptions are the agricultural, forestry and fishing sector, and construction.

Figure 2.2.11 Percentage change in major industrial sectors 1989 to 1997 (UK, real GDP)

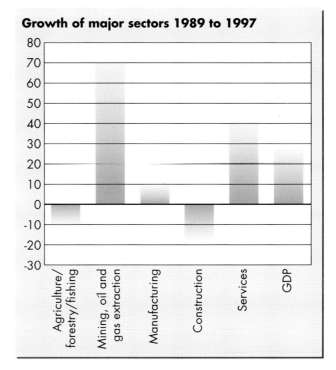

Agriculture, forestry and fishing have fallen because:

- There is growing competition for agricultural and fish products from abroad.

- Too much is being produced and this is causing prices to fall, so farmers earn less.

- For quite a long time British beef was banned from sale in many countries and this affected the demand for other agricultural products as well.

Construction has fallen because:

- There was a recession in 1991 and 1992 and people do not tend to buy new houses during recessions.

- In the past many houses were built by local authorities and now very few council houses are built.

- There has been a marked decline in road building programmes.

The **tertiary sector** has grown because:

- People's incomes have risen by over 20%. What people have decided to do with their extra income is to buy things like holidays, insurance and eating out (all of which are tertiary), rather than buy more food, clothes, etc. (which are primary and secondary).

- More of the secondary goods that we now buy, e.g. clothes and new cars, are imported and sold by retailers. This decreases UK secondary industry at the same time as increasing UK tertiary industry.

- There are more and more new tertiary products, such as adventure holidays, internet shopping, golf courses, theme parks and mobile phone services.

The **mining sector** seems to have increased a great deal but it was only 2.7% of total UK production to begin with. It has mainly increased because the world price of oil and gas has risen and this has made UK production more valuable.

Figure 2.2.12 The main movers in the primary sector (UK, 1989 to 1997)

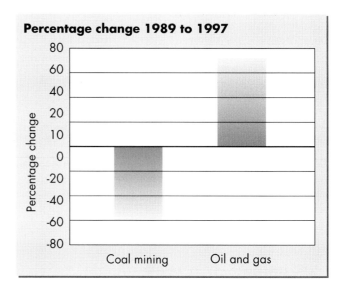

If the industrial sectors are broken down even further it becomes clear that some industries are doing very well and others are struggling.

The main reasons why these changes have occurred are:

- Oil and gas production has increased because the price of these products has increased.

- Coal mining has declined because many of the pits have been closed, and an increasing amount of the coal that we use is now being imported.

Figure 2.2.13 The main movers in the manufacturing sector (UK, 1989 to 1997)

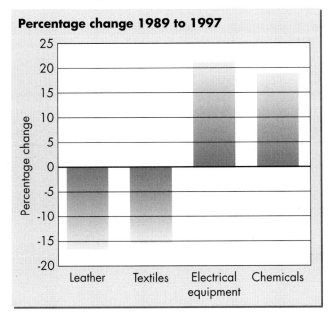

Figure 2.2.14 The main movers in the tertiary sector (UK, 1989 to 1997)·

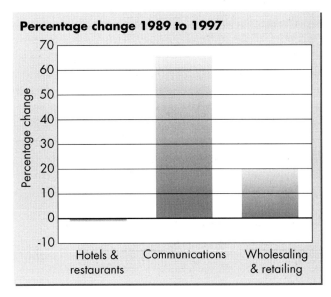

The main reasons why these changes have occurred are:

- More and more leather goods and clothes are now imported from abroad. There are two main reasons for this:
  i) The value of the pound is very high which makes imports cheaper;
  ii) UK producers find that labour costs are lower abroad so they have their clothes made abroad and then import them.

- Electrical equipment has increased because many more people want computers, hi-fis, microwave ovens and mobile phones, both in the home and in the workplace.

- The UK remains a major producer of chemicals for both the UK market and for export. Chemicals form the basis of many of our products, such as plastic goods, paint and medicines.

The main reasons why these changes have occurred are:

- In the hotel and restaurant sector it is the hotel part that has declined. This is in part due to the high value of the pound which discourages foreign tourists and encourages people in the UK to take holidays abroad. The restaurant sector has increased (see Figure 2.2.15 below).

- The communications sector has increased because of the rapid increase in the use of the internet and mobile phones.

- Wholesaling and retailing have increased because we now buy more of most of the things mentioned above, e.g. computers, mobile phones, fast food, cars, and so on.

If individual types of production are considered they will show even more distinct patterns. Details can be found in published government statistics such as *Social Trends* and the *Monthly Digest of Statistics*. They will also be found in trade magazines such as *Farmers' Weekly*, *The Builder* and *The Grocer*.

As well as looking at total production the importance of different businesses can be measured by the number of people employed. Figures 2.2.15 shows the general growth in employment in travel agents and restaurants and cafés.

Both sectors have increased considerably overall. In 1991 to 1993 there was a fall because the UK was in a recession and people tend to cut back on holidays and eating out during a recession.

Each type of business could be looked at in the following ways which would show how the business is likely to be affected by:

- changes in people's incomes – more money to spend on holidays and recreation;

- changes in people's tastes – wanting mobile phones, home computers, etc.;

- the competition between businesses – supermarkets driving small greengrocers and butchers out of business;

- how many people are working – after work they may wish to eat out rather than cook;

- the changing age structure of the population – there are now very many more people over the age of retirement, many of whom have good pensions but want smaller houses or sheltered accommodation.

Figure 2.2.15 The number of employees ('000) in travel agencies, restaurants and cafes (UK, 1988 to 1998)

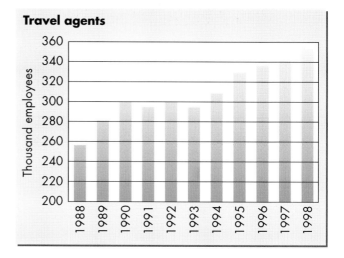

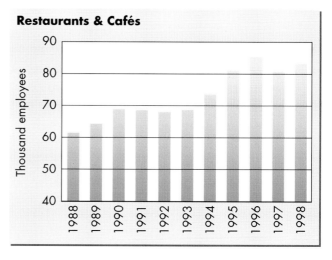

CHAPTER 3

FACTORS THAT AFFECT THE LOCATION OF BUSINESSES

Foundation and Intermediate

In this chapter you will learn about the factors that determine where a business locates. You will learn:

- what the main factors of location are;

- how different factors are important for different types of business.

Introduction

When owners decide where to locate they will take a great many factors into consideration. Most of these factors will relate to where their customers are, what costs are involved and what their personal preferences are.

Location of Primary, Secondary and Tertiary Businesses

There are some general rules about the location of major sectors of industry.

Primary industry has to be located where the raw materials are

Coal mining must take place where there are coal seams, and farmers growing wheat must grow their wheat where there is arable land. As always, there are some exceptions.

UK Fishing World lists 38 English counties that have commercial trout fisheries.

Figure 2.3.1 Factors of location

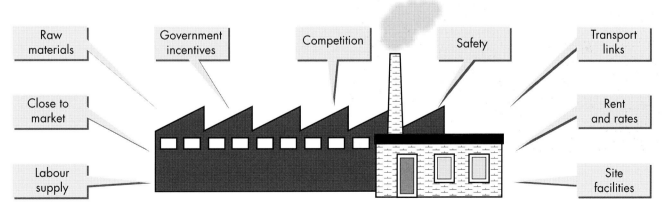

Raw materials · Government incentives · Competition · Safety · Transport links · Close to market · Rent and rates · Labour supply · Site facilities

- In the past nearly all fishing was done by going to where the fish were. Today, trout and salmon farming is done by breeding fish and rearing them in special areas, some of which never had trout or salmon naturally.

- Many crops, such as tomatoes, flowers, and lettuces, are grown in greenhouses, and the soil, manure and fertilisers can be brought in. These firms tend to be sited near their customers because of the cost of transporting the products.

The location of secondary industry is mainly dependent upon what is being produced and the scale of the production

Large-scale chemical factories need to be located where the raw materials and labour are available, but also away from where people live in case of pollution. Many small-scale craft manufacturers, such as potters, glass blowers and furniture makers, can be, and are, located right in the middle of retail shopping areas, even in residential areas. Exceptions include:

- Some of the older industries which were located in the centres of towns because, at that time, people did not worry about possible pollution. Some of these older firms still exist.

- The development of industrial estates which have lower rents and rates. These have encouraged some small manufacturers to set up away from their traditional customers.

> Avondale Glass, located north of Tenby in South Wales, is located on the junction of two main roads used by tourists. Here the owner has a ready source of passing customers.

Tertiary industry tends to be located near the customer

This is because the customer expects to find greengrocers, supermarkets, doctors, hairdressers, banks, etc. close to where they live or work. Again, there, are obvious exceptions.

- Mail order firms, such as Littlewoods and Next, which sell their products direct to consumers, do not need to be located near to their customers because customers do not need to visit the business in order to buy their products.

- The growth in the use of credit cards, and now telephone banking and insurance, means that these firms can locate anywhere as long as they can be easily contacted by post, telephone, fax or e-mail.

> Woolworth's location policy has always been to locate its stores in towns with a minimum number of residents. This was done to ensure that there would always be enough potential customers to sell to.

Businesses will normally locate where they can keep their cost/unit as low as possible and their profits as high as possible

Most businesses want to make as much profit as possible, and if a change in location can increase profits firms will often relocate. There are, however, many businesses that do not have 'making as much profit as they can' as their main objective.

- Many charities and voluntary bodies wish to maximise the service they can give to those people whom they are trying to help. This often means that they need to be located where they are needed and not where their costs are lowest.

- Many businesses, especially small businesses, are located where they are because that is where the owner wants to live and work. Making huge profits is of secondary importance.

The Main Location Factors

The location factors which affect particular businesses vary a great deal from one business to the next. Which factors are important depends on what the businesses do, and on the way that they do it. Certain location factors are particularly important for certain types of business. The main factors are given below, with examples of the kinds of business that are likely to be affected.

Proximity to raw materials/suppliers

This will include firms like oil refineries which locate near to the coast because their raw materials are imported. Examples include Fawley near Southampton and Milford Haven in South Wales. Generally, firms will locate near to their sources of raw materials or suppliers because this saves on the costs of transport.

Table 2.3.1 Closeness to supplies

Reasons for location	Examples of businesses
• All primary production must be located where the raw materials are because these are what they use for production.	• Fishing – Grimsby and Hull • Fruit farming – Kent and Evesham • Coal mining – Nottinghamshire
• Some manufacturing firms use up materials as they produce so it is cheaper to locate near the raw materials.	• Brewing – Burton-upon-Trent • Iron and steel – Sheffield, Port Talbot
• Some raw materials deteriorate if they are transported, especially agricultural crops.	• Fruit canning – Smedley in Dundee
• Often it is cheaper per unit to produce on a large scale rather than on a small scale. It therefore makes sense to produce in one place and deliver goods from there to a wide market.	• Car production – Ford at Dagenham • Processed bread – Rank Hovis produces at 11 sites in the UK but sells nationwide.

Closeness to the market/customers

All producers will eventually finish their production by selling their goods or services to their customers. There is, therefore, a strong incentive to locate close to the customers. This is especially true of retail firms because consumers expect to find shops, banks, etc. where they can reach them easily.

Table 2.3.2 Closeness to customers

Reasons for location	Examples of businesses
• Customers expect to find the businesses close by.	• Retailing – shops and supermarkets • Specialist services – doctors, lawyers • Business services – accountants, employment agencies
• Many firms provide components for other firms and are expected to be close by.	• Builders' merchants supplying the building industry.
• Some finished products deteriorate if they are transported over long distances.	• Market garden produce, e.g. lettuces and tomatoes.
• Some products cost more to transport after manufacture than before especially if they have become bulkier.	• Furniture manufacturing – High Wycombe
• Some products, such as houses, have to be located where they will finally be used.	• Building firms will actually work on the building site. • The same is true of road, rail, bridge, tunnel building, etc.

Figure 2.3.2 The location of Geest's ripening and distribution centres

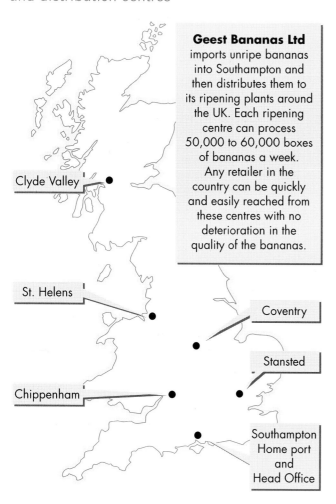

Geest Bananas Ltd imports unripe bananas into Southampton and then distributes them to its ripening plants around the UK. Each ripening centre can process 50,000 to 60,000 boxes of bananas a week. Any retailer in the country can be quickly and easily reached from these centres with no deterioration in the quality of the bananas.

Access to good transport systems

For many firms the choice between locating near the raw materials or the market is a question of transport costs. Nearly all goods have to be transported at some stage during their production process. Even a farmer running a 'pick-your-own' business will need to consider the costs of car fuel for the customers.

For some firms, choosing the right location in terms of transport is vital (see Figure 2.3.2 for the location of Geest).

Johnson Wax has only one production unit in the UK and Europe. This is located at Frimley in Surrey. A major location factor was the road and motorway links to the rest of the UK and to the ports of Dover

and Southampton. At Frimley there is quick and easy access to the M3 and to the rest of the motorway system. The details are shown on the map below.

Figure 2.3.3 Access to transport

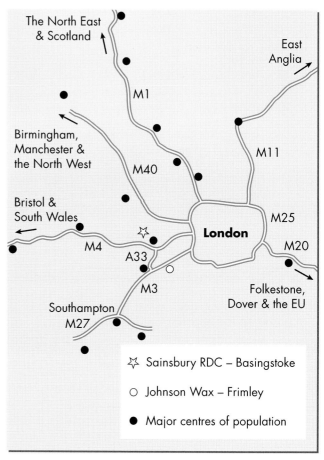

The closeness of the M3 and links to the M4 were the main reasons for locating the Sainsbury Regional Distribution Centre (RDC) at Basingstoke. From here Sainsbury can quickly restock all its supermarkets in the South and South East.

A skilled labour force

All businesses need some kind of labour, but this does not always mean that this is an important location factor. Businesses nearly always locate near people and if they require only unskilled workers they can locate near any centre of population. Sometimes, even when they require skilled workers, this is not a problem because the skilled workers will move to them. That is what normally happens in education, and with businesses like stockbroking.

With some businesses, however, the workers are not prepared to move without being paid a great deal more so it is cheaper to locate the business near the skilled workers.

> Glasgow is well known for its marine engineering skills and when the shipbuilding yards closed this meant that a great many skilled engineers were available for work. Many smaller engineering firms then set up in Glasgow.

> When Sir Clive Sinclair was deciding where to set up his computing business he chose Cambridge because he could then recruit the best graduates coming out of the university.

The effects of competition

Competition can affect business location in three ways.

1 If there is fierce competition between existing businesses it can cause the weaker businesses to lose sales and eventually have to close down. When this happens the community tends to become dominated by one or two large firms and no small producers are found in the area.

2 Some businesses will look very carefully at the location of existing firms before deciding where to locate. They will be very keen to avoid competition. For example, most people who want to buy fish and chips do not usually mind where they buy it. So if a fish and chip shop already exists in a local area, it would be foolish to try and set up another one near by, unless the new owner was going to try to put the existing firm out of business. With other types of fast food this is not the same, mainly because each business is trying to sell something that is slightly different.

3 In contrast to the example of fish and chip shops, a surprising number of types of business seem to want to locate close to each other. This is probably because the customers expect to find these sorts of businesses all in one place, and if a new firm decides to locate somewhere else it may find that it has very few customers. In some cases firms locate in the same area because they share common needs, such as the need for skilled labour.

Case Study – Whitchurch loses its shops

In the last 15 years the one remaining supermarket in Whitchurch has become dominant. The local Co-operative has closed, as have the only baker, two butchers, a grocer/general stores, and a greengrocer. All these firms have been forced out of business by the public's changed shopping habits and by the competition. In Whitchurch the battle was won by the local Somerfield supermarket. But even the Whitchurch Somerfield is under intense competitive pressure from the large out-of-town Tesco and Sainsbury at Winchester (12 miles away) and the Andover supermarkets of Safeway, Waitrose and two Tescos (7 miles away).

Case Study – Estate Agents in Winchester

In Winchester there are 15 estate agents but the vast majority of them are located within 400 yards of each other. This seems to reflect the fact that people who want to buy, sell or rent housing do not want to waste time finding the estate agents. When they find one, they expect another to be close by.

The map below shows where these businesses are located in Winchester, but most towns will have a similar pattern for their estate agents.

Figure 2.3.4 The concentration of estate agents in Winchester

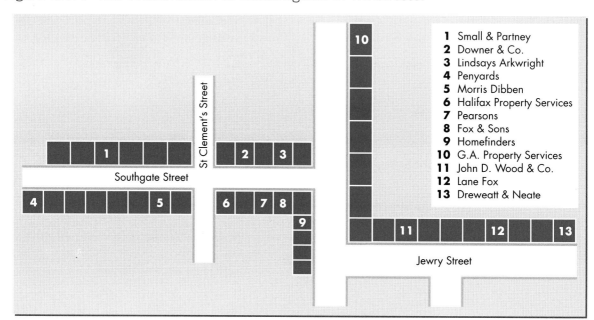

1 Small & Partney
2 Downer & Co.
3 Lindsays Arkwright
4 Penyards
5 Morris Dibben
6 Halifax Property Services
7 Pearsons
8 Fox & Sons
9 Homefinders
10 G.A. Property Services
11 John D. Wood & Co.
12 Lane Fox
13 Dreweatt & Neate

Government influences

Governments can affect where businesses locate by imposing restrictions on their location or by offering them incentives to move. These two approaches are often referred to as the 'carrot and the stick'.

'Carrots' will include grants, subsidies, reduced taxation, the provision of factory and office space at reduced rents and payment of relocation expenses. The government has designated certain assisted areas of the UK that will benefit from these incentives. These are called **development areas** and **intermediate areas**.

Many well-known foreign firms have located in the UK because of the generous incentives offered by the government. These include Nissan in Washington (Tyne & Wear), Sony in Bridgend (South Wales),

Regional Development Agencies

In 1998, eight Regional Development Agencies (RDAs) were set up, covering the English regions outside London. The London RDA was planned for 2000.

RDAs will take over the management of regional policy with the objectives of:
- managing rural regeneration programmes;
- co-ordinating inward investment in their own regions;
- developing the new Assisted Areas Map, which applied from 2000;
- encouraging business efficiency, investment and competitiveness;
- increasing levels of employment and the development of skills;
- ensuring sustainable development for the region.

Case Study – Attracting businesses to the old coal mining areas

In the late 1980s and early 1990s many of the traditional coalfields were closed, leaving areas of high local unemployment. The newly created Regional Development Agencies are continuing the task of getting the unemployed back to work.

A major part of this initiative has been to help the unemployed to set up their own businesses and to attract firms into these areas. To achieve this, training, good sites, good transport links and financial support are all needed. Enterprise zones have been established in East Durham, the Dearne Valley and the East Midlands, but it is felt that more assistance is needed.

Surveys of businesses show that, for them, good sites, trained labour and financial incentives are the most important location factors, but even more important is a strategic location with access to suppliers and customers.

Figure 2.3.5 Factors important to business when choosing location

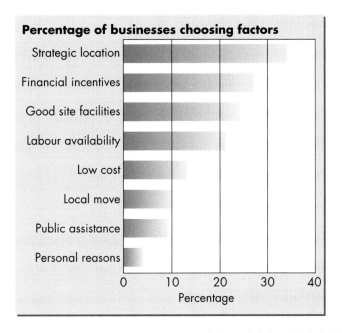

Toyota in Deeside (North Wales). Details can be found by checking the web sites for the regional areas, e.g. the Welsh Development Agency can be found at: **http://www.wda.co.uk/**.

The government has also given special benefits to what are called **enterprise zones**. These are local areas where there have been particular problems of industrial decline and unemployment, as in Docklands in the east of London. Businesses in these zones pay no rates, have few planning restrictions and receive other important financial incentives.

The European Union also provides funds for

Case Study – Nottinghamshire's assisted areas

Assisted Area: Nottinghamshire contains both kinds of assisted area: development and intermediate. As a result, it gives companies that locate there access to some of the UK's most generous grants.

Other kinds of financial assistance on offer: An attractive range of other incentives is also available, including Training Support Packages.

Enterprise zones: Some of the UK's newest enterprise zones are located in Nottinghamshire. They were established in 1996. The benefits they offer extend for a period of 10 years. They give companies locating in them capital cost allowances of 100% on buildings, and full exemption from property taxes (Uniform Business Rate) during the lifetime of the zone. Sites with enterprise zone status are at Sherwood Park, Annesley, Ashfield, Manton Wood near Worksop, Bassetlaw and Crown Farm Industrial Park at Mansfield.

developing regions and businesses. These come from:

- the European Development Fund;
- the European Social Fund;
- the European Agricultural Guidance and Guarantee Fund.

Local authorities also have the power to offer businesses special incentives to set up in their areas.

'**Sticks**' will include the need for planning permission, smokeless zones, and green belts. Those will all make it difficult, and sometimes impossible, for businesses to set up where the government or local authorities do not want them to set up.

Other Factors of Location

Each business has its own set of important location factors. Some are vital to that kind of business. For example, beer is over 90% water so a source of good water is vital to a brewery.

There are many other possible location factors. Some will be specific to one type of business; others will be factors that affect a range of quite different types of businesses. Water is one example. Different possible uses of water are given in Table 2.3.3.

Table 2.3.3 Water as a factor of location

Different uses	Types of products	Location	Water source
• For washing	textiles	Huddersfield	River Calder
• For cooling	power stations	Culham, Oxon	River Thames
• For recreation	sports	Thorpe Park	old gravel pits
• As a raw material	brewing	Burton-upon-Trent	River Trent
• As a source of power	hydro-electric power	Fort William	Glen Nevis
• For transport	oil refining (imported oil)	Milford Haven	Irish Sea
• For waste disposal	nuclear power stations	Sellafield	Irish Sea

Other possible factors of location include:

- The **flatness of the land** Airports need to be away from mountains. Flat land is needed for buildings.

- The **rents and rates** Rents in London can be four times higher than rents in Liverpool.

- The **site facilities** Most businesses require electricity, water, telephone lines, and sewerage, and others require gas and outside storage space. If these facilities are already there this is convenient and saves the cost of installation.

- **Climatic** conditions Growers of seed potatoes must have frosts in the winter to kill damaging aphids, so they locate in Scotland.

- **Personal choice** Many owners of businesses locate their businesses where they do simply because that is where they want to live and work. Morris Motors, which became British Leyland and then Rover, and now MG, was located first in Oxford because that is where William Morris was brought up and where his father's bicycle shop was located.

- **Industrial inertia** Some businesses set up in certain locations because the required factors are there to begin with but, over time, these factors disappear. The businesses do not move because it is too expensive to do so. The Whitchurch Silk Mill had water to run the mill and silk from silkworm bred in the town. Now the silk thread is imported and the weaving machines are run on electricity.

> Definition – a **footloose** business is one that can locate where it wants to and can move to a new location very easily.

There are many other businesses which do not require any particular location factors. These are known as 'footloose' businesses because they can locate almost anywhere they want to. Often the most important consideration is where the owners want to live and work.

Footloose firms include the following:

- mail order firms, because they send their products through the post;

- firms that provide services over the phone or internet, e.g. consultants and freelance journalists;

- firms with very low set-up costs, e.g. gardeners and window cleaners;

- firms with very low capital costs from plant and equipment, e.g. writers, photographers, and plumbers;

- firms that can be set up and closed down quickly. Many businesses set up simply to sell goods before Christmas and then close down immediately afterwards. Usually they will locate in vacant premises. Next year they will be located in some other vacant premises, often in another town.

CHAPTER 4

STAKEHOLDERS IN BUSINESS

Foundation and Intermediate

In this chapter you will learn about:

- what stakeholders are;

- how businesses affect stakeholders;

- how stakeholders affect businesses;

- how businesses change what they are doing in order to take the interests of their stakeholders into account;

- how the interests of stakeholders have changed over time.

Introduction

When businesses produce and sell goods and services they affect people in one way or another. The types of people or organisations that are affected include:

- the **owners** – who will receive more, or less, profit, depending on how well the business does;

- the **customers** – who have to pay for the products but also receive the benefits of having them;

- the **employees** – who help to make the products and receive wages and salaries for their work;

- the **suppliers** – who provide the business with raw materials, advertising, machinery, and need to be paid by the business for these;

- the **providers of finance** – who provide the business with the capital it needs to buy raw materials, pay staff, etc. and expect their loans to be repaid or to share in the profits;

- the **competitors** – who are trying to sell to the same customers and will therefore be affected by any action the business takes which encourages customers to buy from the business rather than from them;

- the **government** – which should have the wider interests of the general public at heart and will therefore control the business so that it benefits rather than harms the public;

- the **community** – which provides the employees, suffers the effects of pollution created by the business, and is affected in many other ways.

> Definition – **stakeholders** are individuals or groups who have an interest in what a business does and either are affected by what the business does or affect the business by what they do.

All these individuals or groups are stakeholders. All of them have a personal interest in the business. As stakeholders they will either be affected by what the business does or they will affect the way the business operates by what they do, e.g.:

Effect of the business on the stakeholder

- If a business is successful and makes a high level of profits, the employees may be given a bonus.
- If a business is successful it will make more profits and employ more people so the government will receive more corporation tax and income tax.

Effect of the stakeholder on the business

- If the employees work hard and produce quality products the business will make more profits.
- If the government gives a business a grant this will help it to set up, keep its costs and prices low and be able to compete in the market.

All types of stakeholders will be affected by the business, and can affect it. This means that all businesses have a great many individual stakeholders.

In this chapter we will look at the different types of stakeholders and how they affect, and are affected by, businesses. We will also see that in different businesses, and in different types of production, the importance of particular types of stakeholders varies.

Stakeholders fall into different categories, e.g. customers, shareholders, competitors, and each type of stakeholder tends to have a different effect on a business. The stakeholders are also affected in different ways by how the business acts. We will therefore look at each type of stakeholder separately.

Figure 2.4.1 Stakeholders in McDonald's

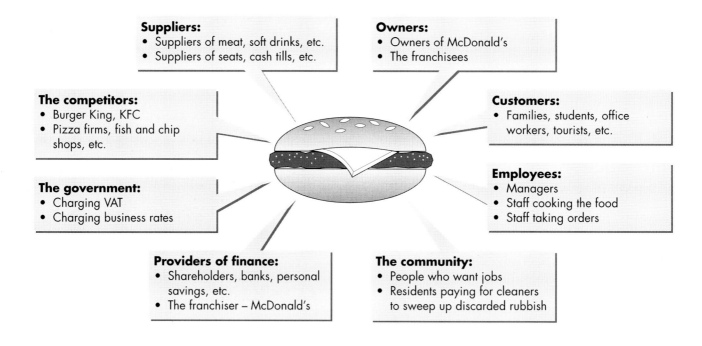

Suppliers:
- Suppliers of meat, soft drinks, etc.
- Suppliers of seats, cash tills, etc.

Owners:
- Owners of McDonald's
- The franchisees

The competitors:
- Burger King, KFC
- Pizza firms, fish and chip shops, etc.

Customers:
- Families, students, office workers, tourists, etc.

The government:
- Charging VAT
- Charging business rates

Employees:
- Managers
- Staff cooking the food
- Staff taking orders

Providers of finance:
- Shareholders, banks, personal savings, etc.
- The franchiser – McDonald's

The community:
- People who want jobs
- Residents paying for cleaners to sweep up discarded rubbish

The Owners/Shareholders

> Definition – **owners** are individuals or organisations to whom businesses belong.

Owners may be sole traders, partners, shareholders in companies or members of the general public who own public enterprises such as the BBC or the National Health Service (NHS). The type of ownership will affect how these stakeholders (a) affect the business, and (b) are affected by the way the business operates.

Privately-owned firms

a) In privately-owned firms the owners decide how the business will be run, what profits will be distributed to them and what profits will be kept in the business in order to increase future production. They will also decide what will be produced, when the business will be closed, what objectives the business should have, etc. Their power to control the business will, of course, depend on how many shares they have. The sole trader will have complete control. Small shareholders in a plc will have, essentially, no control.

b) If privately-owned firms are successful the owners will receive the profits. They will also own a more valuable firm which they could sell if they wanted to.

13% knocked off Unilever shares

Yesterday the price of Unilever shares fell by 13% knocking £4.9 million off its value in the market. The fall was caused, in part, by the announcement of a 3% fall in profits and no growth in overall revenue.

Sales in Europe had been poor in 1999 and top brands such as Prestige, Elisabeth Arden and Calvin Klein had not done as well as expected. There was also fierce competition from rivals Procter & Gamble, especially in Latin America.

6 November 1999

Publicly/state-owned firms

a) In state-owned businesses, such as the BBC, the owners, i.e. you and me, actually have very little control over the business. How the BBC ultimately operates is decided by the governors of the BBC and the government. We do, however, have the final control because state-owned businesses belong to the people. It was the British electorate that agreed to sell off the state-owned industries of British Gas, British Rail and British Telecom, but it is also the British electorate which is refusing to sell off the National Health Service and the Post Office.

b) State-owned businesses do affect us as stakeholders. If they make profits this goes to help pay for government expenditure. If they make losses we will have to pay through higher taxes.

How have the interests of owners changed over time?

Figure 2.4.2 UK businesses by type of ownership (percentage – 1998)

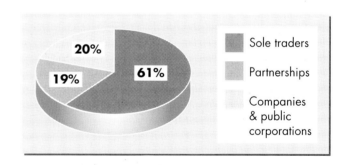

Source: *Labour Market Trends*

There have been three main changes to the ownership of businesses in the last 20 years and each has altered the relationship between the stakeholders and the businesses.

Table 2.4.1 Changes to business ownership

The change	The effects
There are now a great many more people who are self-employed and therefore work for themselves. Many also run their own businesses.	Because these owners work for themselves they will take the main decisions in the business and affect it directly. They will also be directly affected by anything that happens to the business.
There are now many more shareholders in the UK, partly because the government sold off the state-owned industries, such as British Telecom, very cheaply, especially to the general public, but also because people have higher incomes and understand the Stock Exchange better than they did.	Many shareholders have only a few shares and, therefore, no power to affect businesses. When businesses do well, or badly, however, a great many more people in the UK are now affected.
There are now many schemes, encouraged by the government, to get companies to give their employees shares, or allow them to buy shares in the company.	As the profits of these companies are now partly shared with the employees, the employees are directly affected if the company makes less profit so they tend to work hard to ensure that profits do not fall.

The Customers

Definition – a **customer** is any individual or organisation that receives the products of a business.

Customers are stakeholders because they receive the goods and services. Normally they also pay for the products, although with charities or education no charge may be made.

Customers may be positively and negatively affected by the way a business operates. A customer eating out in a restaurant may receive a really good meal at a low price and feel very satisfied with it. A customer in another restaurant may find the food overcooked, experience poor service and suffer from food poisoning.

Customers are the life blood of businesses because the customers provide the businesses with sales and hence with profits. Most businesses, therefore,

Figure 2.4.3 Some positive and negative effects on train passengers

Benefits
- Fast travel
- No traffic jams
- Cheap rates for students
- Can work as you travel
- Useful for people with no cars
- Safety is, on average, better than for road transport

Drawbacks
- Crowded trains
- Delays and late trains
- Prices rise above inflation
- Does not go door to door
- Only goes at certain times
- Some journeys require changes from one train to another

listen very carefully to what their customers want and try to provide this, as long as they feel that this will also help them to achieve their business objectives.

With charities the objective may be to reduce poverty, protect children or support young artists. With public services, such as education and the health service, the objective is to provide the best service possible. Usually the customers know what kind of help or service would be best for them and if charities, schools and hospitals want to achieve their objectives they must find out what their customers want and need.

It is generally true to say that if the customers of a business do not receive what they want, or need, the business has failed its most important stakeholders. Sometimes, however, businesses think that their owners are more important and that putting profits into the owners' pockets is the main objective. Frequently these businesses do not survive, although some do.

Table 2.4.2 Supermarkets adapt to customer needs

Supermarkets are listening to their customers	
As shopping habits change, the major supermarkets compete to stay ahead.	
• More people are out at work	– stores are open for longer hours and in the evenings
• Some people wish to shop from home	– internet shopping and home delivery are made available
• Mothers with young children use the supermarkets	– crèche facilities are made available
• Couples and families see shopping as a morning out	– restaurants and cafés are opened
• Customers want time to pay for their groceries	– credit and other banking facilities are offered
• Customers worry about how environmentally friendly products are	– organic foods, bottle banks, etc. are provided

How have the interests of customers changed over time?

The businesses that will survive and grow in the future are those businesses that can work out what the customers of the future will want and can then provide these products at a profit.

People's tastes are changing all the time. Real incomes are also rising – by over 20% every 10 years. As people become richer and have new experiences they demand new products from business. Sometimes it is the business that changes customers' buying habits through introducing them to new products and through advertising. Below are just a few examples of how customer interests are changing.

Figure 2.4.4 Household expenditure by category (1971 = 100) at constant prices

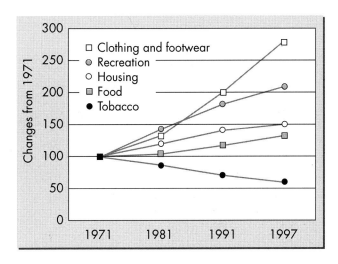

- More people now take foreign holidays on which they experience different lifestyles and, especially, different foods. When they return, they want the same products to be available at home, e.g. fresh pasta, baguettes and duvets.

- Many more students now have jobs and increased spending power. Some of this is spent in pubs and night clubs but it is also spent on fashion and many clothes shops now cater specifically for this age range.

- There has been a growing recognition that keeping fit improves health and lifestyle, so there has been a big increase in the demand for aerobics classes and exercise gyms.

- Most households in the UK now have home computers and more and more are getting connected to the internet. With this has come a huge increase in the demand, and supply, of on-line shopping, banking and investment.

- It is now clear that in the future the state will not be able to pay for pensions in the same way that it is doing now. All sensible people are therefore investing in pension schemes from the moment they start work.

Getting the students into the market

Students at universities and in higher education spend around £10 billion in the consumer goods market. Businesses are, understandably, very keen to make certain that it is their goods that the students are spending this money on.

Frontline, the magazine distributor of such covers as *FHM*, *Q*, *Select* and *Heat*, has recognised that this age group is a major potential customer. As well as tailoring many of its magazines for students, Frontline is now encouraging students to subscribe by offering them an attractive competition. The winners get 'free beer for a year'.

The Employees

Definition – an **employee** is any individual who has a contract of employment to work for a business.

Employees have their jobs because businesses need them to produce the goods and services they will sell. If a business does badly the employees may lose their jobs or, at least, receive lower pay. If it does well they may earn more income, gain promotion and receive shares.

In the UK there are over 6,600 businesses that have more than 250 employees, and nearly 25,000 businesses that have between 50 and 250 employees. When these businesses make decisions about rates of pay, working conditions or new products that may or may not be a success, a very large number of employee stakeholders is affected.

Fears of job losses

As orders for new aircraft have fallen, the aero-engines manufacturer, Rolls-Royce, has announced that it will need to cut staff. Trade unions in the Derby plant fear that as many as 400 jobs will go, or about 10% of the workforce.

6 November 1999

On the other hand, the actions of the employees also have a great effect on businesses. Employees carry out the production in a business and the standard of their work will determine how successful the business is. Products need to be produced at the right time, to the right quality and at the right cost. The way that employees approach their work will have a major impact on all these factors.

The businesses and their employers are clearly very closely related and influence each other greatly.

Figure 2.4.5 How restaurant employees and the business can affect each other

Effects of the business on the employees

- What rates of pay they are offered
- Which hours have to be worked
- Perks such as free meals
- When holidays can be taken
- Safe working conditions
- Training in restaurant duties, cooking, etc.

How employees can affect business

- Cooking, serving, cleaning done
- Ensure quality of food, service, etc.
- Suggesting new dishes, new promotions
- Working well or poorly
- Absences from work
- Interacting well or poorly with customers

How employees' interests have changed over time

Many businesses still see their employees as simply units of labour and just another cost that should be kept as low as possible so that they can make more profits. The nature of employment has changed considerably in the last 20 years, especially in terms of the type of employment businesses now want.

- There are now many more **part-time workers**. This helps the businesses because there is always someone there to work. It may also help the employees as it can fit in with running a home, looking after children when they are not at school, and providing students with employment opportunities out of school hours.

Zero-time contracts

One of the most recent methods employers have created for reducing labour costs is the 'zero-time contract'. Employees have a contract to work a basic week of **zero hours**, but they may be required, by their contract, to work additional hours when the business wants them.

This allows the business to insist that employees turn up for work when they want them, but it can also lay the employees off, with no commitment to pay them, when sales are slack.

- There are now many more **people who work from home**, connected by a telephone, modem and computer. These 'teleworkers' do not need to be in an office and this saves the business money.

- There are more **people who have short-term contracts**, because this allows businesses to get rid of these people easily when they do not want them.

There are, however, also many firms that recognise the need to get employees more involved in the business so that the employees do not simply see the factory, shop or office as just somewhere to earn money. Changes here include:

- giving employees shares and **letting them share in the profits** with profit-related bonuses. This encourages employees to work harder because the more profits the business makes the more they benefit personally;

- employees are now often a **part of the decision making process**, through quality circles, taking on management roles, etc. This motivates employees because they feel more involved;

- there is now **more flexible working** through job-rotation, job-sharing, multi-skilling. All of these can help to reduce boredom, meet individuals' job requirements and make employees feel valuable members of the team.

- In many businesses, e.g. computer software, the **employees know far more about the products than either the managers or the owners.** This gives the employees considerable power and they are often able to get very high salaries for their work.

The Suppliers

> Definition – a **supplier** is a business that provides another business with the goods or services that it needs for its production.

Suppliers provide businesses with all the goods and services that they need in order to produce. Suppliers will include producers of raw materials, tools, equipment, furniture and a wide range of other goods. They will also include providers of services such as finance (see below), advertising, insurance, transport, legal advice, telephone connections and garage services for repairing vehicles.

If the customer, say a sportswear shop, sells more trainers, tennis racquets, jogging suits, etc. then the suppliers of these items are likely to sell more of their products. If the sportswear shop goes out of business, the suppliers will lose sales.

A supplier may also lose out simply because a business customer decides to buy its raw materials or services elsewhere (see the example on clothing manufacturing in Leicestershire).

Clothing manufacturers lose a major customer

Clothing suppliers in Leicestershire have been shocked to hear that Marks & Spencer has decided to have its clothes made by cheaper suppliers outside the UK. Leicestershire firms have already had to lay off more than 6,000 workers and things look set to get worse.

November 1999

Many suppliers also allow businesses to buy products on credit (see page 297). When this happens, the supplier is owed money and may not receive it if the customers go bankrupt before they have paid.

So suppliers are affected to a great extent by their customers. The reverse is also true. Suppliers often affect their customers. Examples would include:

- the **quality** of the product that the suppliers produce. This will affect the business customers and their ability to sell their products to the consumers;

- the **cost** of the product that the suppliers produce. This will affect how much profit the business customers can make when they sell their products to the consumers;

- how **promptly** products are delivered. If there is any delay in the delivery from the supplier, and the consumers cannot get what they want, they will go elsewhere.

Figure 2.4.6 The suppliers of a market stall selling toys

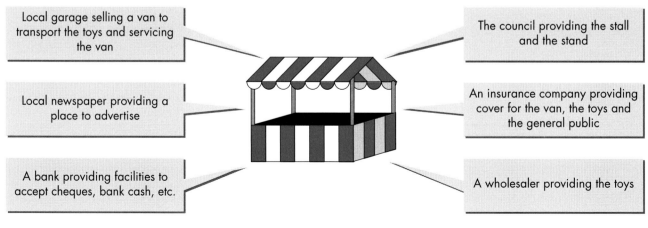

Local garage selling a van to transport the toys and servicing the van

Local newspaper providing a place to advertise

A bank providing facilities to accept cheques, bank cash, etc.

The council providing the stall and the stand

An insurance company providing cover for the van, the toys and the general public

A wholesaler providing the toys

How suppliers have changed over time

The way in which products are supplied to customers has changed a great deal over the last 20 or 30 years. In many cases producers have merged or been taken over and the suppliers have become very powerful. This power allows them to dictate to the businesses that want their products – to fix prices, insist on payments with little credit and, in some cases, decide who they are going to sell to.

At the same time there are some sectors of industry, especially in services, where many new firms are competing and this helps to keep prices down and allows the business to choose which supplier is best for them.

The other main change has been the growth of the power of certain businesses over their suppliers. Here the businesses can decide who they will buy goods and services from and the suppliers are forced to accept the prices that their customers dictate.

Providers of Finance

> Definition – **providers of finance** are individuals or organisations which provide a business with money which it can use to help it produce or invest.

Providers of finance are specialist types of suppliers because they give businesses the money they need to start their businesses and to keep them running. More importantly, however, they expect the businesses to act in certain ways. There are many possible providers of finance and they often expect different things from the businesses.

- **Banks** lend money to businesses and expect the money to be returned and interest to be paid.

- **Shareholders** provide finance by buying new shares and they expect to benefit by sharing in the profits.

- **Governments** provide grants to businesses setting up in areas of high unemployment and they expect the businesses to employ local people and reduce unemployment.

- **Suppliers** provide finance by giving businesses credit and they expect that this will encourage the businesses to continue to use them as suppliers.

Providers of finance will benefit if the businesses do well but will suffer, and probably lose money, if the businesses do badly.

Providers of finance can also affect businesses by what they do, e.g:

- Banks can raise/lower interest rates and therefore increase/decrease the costs of borrowing for the business.

- Shareholders can vote to pay themselves more/less of the profits of the business and this will affect how much money is left over for new investment or expansion.

- Governments can attach special conditions to their grants, for example by insisting that grants will be given only if businesses locate in certain regions.

- Suppliers can increase/decrease the length of the credit that they are prepared to offer to businesses.

Lennox Lewis's College KOd!

Lennox Lewis, the best British heavyweight boxer of the 1990s, and now undisputed world heavyweight champion, has reached the peak of his profession. As he rose to his position of the best in the world he did not forget his roots and how difficult it was for a black working-class child to succeed. He therefore used his hard-earned wealth to support others who were less fortunate than himself. He set up a college to support children who had been rejected by the education system. This college gave individual teaching, support and advice to the students and helped them to achieve qualifications and practical experience that would help them to get jobs. But the college needed additional finance and the government and other bodies were not prepared to support the project. The facts were reported, again, in *The Big Issue* (November 8-14 1999):

'Four years ago, the fighter set up Lennox Lewis College in Hackney, east London, investing millions of pounds of his own cash. The purpose was to provide vocational education for youngsters who had been excluded from school ... Students at the college were offered what Lewis called 'rehabilitation through education'. It was starting to see results, but foundered after failing to win financial support from the National Lottery, the Government and the local councils. Lewis, however, remains determined to resurrect the project.'

How the interests of providers of finance have changed over time

Many providers of finance, such as banks, will lend money to businesses when they set up. When the businesses are successful and have paid back their loans, the banks will no longer be stakeholders, although the businesses may borrow again to finance the purchase of new capital goods or if they are planning to expand.

As businesses grow they will buy more raw materials and will expect more credit from their suppliers.

Over time businesses often change their ownership and when this happens their sources of finance (and stakeholders) often change, e.g. if a business goes from being a sole trader to a private company, it will gain a new set of stakeholders in the shareholders.

At any particular point in time a business is likely to have a different group of stakeholders providing finance than at another point in time.

The Competitors

Definition – a **competitor** is any business that is trying to sell products to the same customers as another business.

If a business is a monopoly it may have no competitors, but there are very few real monopolies around. Practically every business in the UK has a competitor, and in many industries competition is very fierce.

There are many well-known examples of goods and services that are in close competition with each other:

- Coke, Pepsi, Virgin cola;

- Whiskas, Felix, Arthur's, supermarket own brands;

- Going Places, Lunn Poly, Thomas Cook, Toucan Travel;

- Barclays, HSBC, Abbey National, Royal Bank of Scotland.

The competitors of a business will be affected by what a business does because its actions affect their customers. If Coke lowers its prices the customers of Pepsi or Virgin cola may decide to buy Coke instead of Pepsi or Virgin. Competitors will be affected by all of the following actions by their competitors:

- changing the price of the products;

- marketing the products through advertising, special offers, competitions;

- changing the quality, design or packaging of the product;

- where firms compete internationally, import and export barriers may affect competition.

Each firm that has competitors affects them by what it does, but at the same time it is also affected by what its competitors do. If Lunn Poly lowers the prices of its holidays, this affects the demand for holidays from Thomas Cook and Toucan Travel. On the other hand, if one of their competitors decided to lower its prices or offer special bargains – 'One week for £250 and a **free** second week' – this would affect Lunn Poly.

How has competition changed over time?

Competition has always existed in business. The only thing that changes over time is how much competition there is.

Increasing competition for PC

When Clive Sinclair produced the first home computer in 1980 there were no other companies selling computers specifically for the millions of households in the UK. When firms like Commodore, Acorn and Amstrad saw the success of Sinclair's Spectrum computer they started to compete.

At that time IBM, the biggest producer of computers in the world, made only mainframe and large computers for businesses. IBM has also seen the potential of desktop computers and is now a major player in the PC market.

Less competition from butchers

In the last 40 years supermarkets have grown larger and chains like Tesco, Sainsbury and Safeway now cover the country. At the same time the small chains and independents have found it harder and harder to compete. It used to be common to find half a dozen butcher's shops all competing to supply fresh meat, pies, etc. to the public.

Today many towns have only one butcher's shop and many have none at all. Where they do survive they are in direct competition with the powerful supermarkets and their prices are dictated by what the supermarkets are doing.

The Government

Definition – as a stakeholder the **government** is any part of the state-owned administration which controls and regulates business.

As a stakeholder the government covers many areas, e.g:

- central and local government (councils) – making laws and seeing that they are obeyed;

- the organisations that enforce and judge the law – the police and the courts;

- ministries in charge of specific sectors of the economy, e.g. health, transport and the environment;

- organisations that operate specific government policy, e.g. the Competitions Agency;

- organisations that collect tax for the government, e.g. the Inland Revenue and Customs and Excise.

Figure 2.4.7 The government as stakeholder

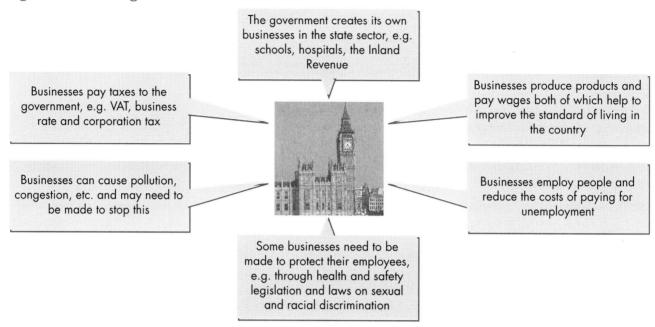

The government creates its own businesses in the state sector, e.g. schools, hospitals, the Inland Revenue

Businesses pay taxes to the government, e.g. VAT, business rate and corporation tax

Businesses produce products and pay wages both of which help to improve the standard of living in the country

Businesses can cause pollution, congestion, etc. and may need to be made to stop this

Businesses employ people and reduce the costs of paying for unemployment

Some businesses need to be made to protect their employees, e.g. through health and safety legislation and laws on sexual and racial discrimination

How the government is affected by what businesses do

The government's interest in business is very wide (see the diagram above). Businesses provide the government with most of the taxes that it needs to pay for health, education, etc. Businesses provide taxes directly because they pay VAT, but they also provide taxes because they pay incomes and their employees have to pay income tax. When businesses sell fewer goods and services, as in a recession, the government receives less tax revenue.

The government is also interested in how businesses are doing because it wants to have full employment and raise the standard of living of people in the UK. The main objective of government should be to make the life of the people in the country better. This should happen if people have jobs and money to spend and there are more products to spend the money on.

How the government affects what businesses do

The governments affects businesses in a great many ways – through taxes, laws, providing finance.

Very often the government affects businesses through laws and regulations because it knows that

if it does not make businesses operate in ways that are good for their customers, employees and the community, the businesses will do only what is best for them. Examples include:

- The **minimum wage** of £3.60 per hour was introduced because some firms were quite happy to pay their employees wages that they could hardly live on.

- The **sex** and **race discrimination laws** are needed because some employers think that women are inferior to men and dislike people of a different colour or ethnic background.

- The **Trade Descriptions Act** was introduced because some businesses were prepared to pretend that their products were better than they really were just to get more profit for themselves.

- The **Health and Safety at Work Act** was introduced because some businesses were not prepared to spend money, or to take the time, to ensure that their employees were not injured at work.

The government also has direct effects on particular industries, e.g. the car industry.

Figure 2.4.8 Examples of legislation affecting the car industry

Drivers must have a valid driving licence

Must have a horn, windscreen wipers, a silencer ...

Owners must have insurance

New cars must be able to run on unleaded petrol

Owners must have paid the road fund licence

Tyres must have a minimum depth of tread

New cars must have a catalytic converter

Must have an MOT every year if it is over three years old

How government interests in business have changed over time

Each year more regulations and laws are introduced by the government and by the European Union. Businesses have to take these laws on board and change the way they are operating. If they do not they may be fined, sued, or even forced to stop producing.

In some sectors of industry the government has less influence and control than before. Many state-owned businesses, such as British Steel, British Gas and British Rail, have been sold off and now belong to private shareholders. The stakeholding of the state has changed from being the owner (and receiving all the profits), to being a tax collector (and receiving part of the profits) and to being the guardian of the customer and the community (and ensuring that businesses operate fairly and without causing harm).

The Community

> Definition – **the community** is the society, and the people, where the business is located and carries out its production.

All businesses are located in particular communities and they therefore affect that community. At the same time, the community is usually able to affect the business.

The community will be affected by businesses because:

- businesses provide members of the community with jobs;

- businesses pay wages and salaries that will be spent in the community. When these are spent they will become someone else's income and the whole community will benefit;

- if businesses close down they may leave the community with fewer jobs, lower income;

- businesses can cause pollution and congestion or build ugly factories, all of which damage the standard of living of people in the community;

- businesses may bring in employees from outside the area and affect the social make-up of the community;

- businesses may support community activities through sponsorship of local organisations.

When a business does something which damages the community, but does not pay for this damage, e.g. causing congestion with its slow moving lorries, this is an **external cost**. Where it does something that the community benefits from and does not have to pay for, as with sponsorship or providing jobs, this is called an **external benefit**.

Winners and losers!

Now that the Newbury bypass has been built the traffic in the centre of Newbury is less congested and people living in the town can get to work more quickly. Drivers using the A34 to get from the South up to Oxford and the Midlands can now travel from Southampton to the M40 on dual carriageway all the way.

But inside the town some businesses, especially those on the old A34 route, now find that they have fewer customers. And outside the town the new A34 runs through countryside that was once unspoilt forest and farmland.

The community can also have a significant effect on how a businesses operates. In the final analysis, if a community as a whole does not approve of the ways in which a business operates it will not buy its products and it will not provide the workers to carry out the production. The community can have an effect on business by:

- lobbying the businesses to try to persuade them to change the way they produce, or to change the product itself;

- lobbying government to get it to make the businesses change what they do;

- refusing to buy the products or supply the labour;

- taking firms to court if the community feels they have broken the law or have caused damage to the community.

How the interests of the community have changed over time

Communities have always taken an interest in what businesses in their area do. When businesses change what they are doing, or new businesses come into the area, the interest of the community may change. In the last 20 years or so there have been two main changes to communities that have tended to cancel each other out.

- People tend to move their jobs and homes much more frequently now. When they do this they move away from the community they know into a new community of which they are not immediately a part. The sense of community and how it works together is therefore weakened.

- The general public is now much more aware of issues like pollution or animal welfare, and people are often more willing to get involved in trying to stop businesses causing external costs and in making them improve their production.

The GM debate is affecting how the producers can market their goods

After considerable debate about genetically modified (GM) foods the government has agreed to further restrictions on GM foods.

- The commercial growing of GM crops will be banned for three more years. Crops will not be allowed to be sold for profit.
- Any GM crops that might be used for animal feed and could therefore enter the human food chain will have to be traced, and the final foods will have to be labelled as containing GM material.

These changes have been forced on the industry by the general public's opposition to GM foods. A spokesman for one firm heavily committed to GM crops stated:

'I don't think anyone ever underestimated the ability of opponents to generate public concern. What did catch us out was the ferocity of the campaign.'

November 1999

How to approach your assignment

For your assignment you will need to choose two businesses. One must be a sole trader or a partnership and the other must be a company, a co-operative, a publicly owned business or a franchise. You have been asked to choose businesses from two different sectors because they have different characteristics, e.g. generally only sole traders and partnerships have limited liability. If you choose to study a franchise you should make certain that it is not a sole trader or a partnership.

Choosing the right businesses

General comments about choosing the right businesses were made at the end of Unit 1 on page 62. You should read through these before you decide which businesses to study.

In addition to those points you should note that you will need details on:

- two businesses and their features of ownerships such as, how many owners there are, whether they have limited liability, how they are controlled, how the profits are shared.
- what their main activities are.
- where they are located and why.
- who the main competitors are, so you will also need access to information on these competitors.
- who the stakeholders are and how they affect the businesses, so you will need to be able to find information about their customers, owners (shareholders), employees and how the local community and the government affect the business through legislation, pressure groups, etc.

At Intermediate level you will also have to provide details about how the industrial sectors the businesses are in, and the specific activity (e.g. window cleaning, or supermarket retailing) have changed over time. You must make certain when you choose your businesses that this additional data will be easy to find.

Before you start planning and researching you should have a copy of the **What you need to learn** section of the syllabus and the **Assessment**

Evidence. It would also be very helpful if you had a copy of how the teachers will be expected to assess your work. This indicates very clearly what should be in your work for you to gain a pass, merit or distinction grade and how to meet each listed point on the assessment grid.

How to gain good grades for Foundation

1   To gain a **pass** grade you will need to be able to describe a wide range of features about the two businesses. You must say what type of businesses it is, sole trader, company, etc., and describe all the usual features such as number of owners and limited/unlimited liability.

- Check the characteristics of different types of ownership given on page 69 and try to find which relate to each business you are studying.
- Decide what activity the business is involved in and describe it clearly.
- For a **merit** you will need to explain how the type of ownerships affects the businesses' main activities. For example:

    If the business was involved in building roads and paying out large sums of money to buy machinery, equipment and skilled employees, it could lose a great deal of money. It would, therefore, be sensible to be a company, with limited liability. Being a company would also make it easier to raise additional capital by selling shares.

2   For a **pass** you will also need to give reasons why the business is located where it is. Check Chapter 3. The owners/managers should be able to tell you which location factors were, and are, important but you will need to give added details, e.g.

    If transport links are important you should provide a map showing the main road/rail, etc., links, and the location of customers and suppliers. If competitors affect the location you should say who the competitors are and where they are located (preferably with a map).

This added detail will help you to push your grade up to a **merit** level. This higher level expects you to think about how particular location features will affect the business, e.g.:

> If a local village store is located on a main road through the village how will this help it to sell goods to people in the village and to people passing through?

3 For a **pass** grade you will need to identify the businesses' competitors. Sometimes this is obvious. If you are studying an estate agent any other estate agent in the area will be in competition. But all businesses are in competition, even ones that appear to have no competition. If there is only one pub in a village, the competition will come from the shops that sell cans of beer and bottles of wine, and from the video shop which rents out videos for people to take home and watch rather than going out to the pub.

For a **distinction** grade you will need to consider how these other businesses affect the business you are studying. You will need to explain, for example, why taking a video home is in competition with the local pub.

4 For a **pass** you must identify the stakeholders and be able to explain why they are important to the business. You should try to identify all stakeholders, even ones not listed. Examples of stakeholders for a window cleaner who is a sole trader could include:

- customers who need their windows cleaned, and pay for this, providing income and profits.
- an employee who helps to clean larger buildings or steps in when the owner is on holiday.
- no shareholders, but a loan from the bank which receives interest and thus helps to increase the bank's profits.
- a local community which now has clean looking houses, encouraging people to live there.
- suppliers who provide the window cleaner with

a ladder, a van, and washing materials, and therefore make sales that give them revenue and profits.
- the government which receives income tax on the income that the window cleaner has earned.

How to gain good grades for Intermediate

As an Intermediate level student you will be expected to able to produce all the work that a Foundation level student could produce but in greater detail. All of the points made for Foundation students above apply to your assignment work, but you should include all of these point simply to gain a pass grade. Read through the points made above and make certain that you have included all of them somewhere in your assignment.

To gain the **pass** grade you will also need to describe the industrial sector(s) that your businesses are in. They may be in more than one (see page 86). You will also need to identify the trend for the sector and for the particular industry in which your business is operating. To do this effectively you need to consider the following points, before you choose your business:

- Can you find data for at least the last ten years? The data for primary, secondary and tertiary products is easily available from government publications. What is more difficult is to find data, and trends, for specific industries, e.g. chicken farming, hairdressing, supermarket retailing or bicycle manufacturing. Government statistics are available and there are useful internet sites, but the safest approach is to check that you can get the data before you decide on your business.
- To gain a **merit** grade you will need to explain how the trends you have already identified are likely to affect or compare to one of the businesses that you have chosen to study. For instance, if you have chosen to study a business that produces leisure goods, you should compare the general growth in this industry with the growth for the business you are studying. To be able to do this you must make certain that you can find out (a) what the growth has been for the industry in general and (b) how your business has grown in the same period.

For good grades at this level you will need to make a full study of the stakeholders and how they affect the businesses.Nearly every business will have all of the stakeholders given in Chapter 4. You need to describe exactly who they are, and why they are stakeholders.

For instance, the community will be a stakeholder in a fast-food restaurant because the community provides the labour and will be affected by how many people go to the restaurant, what time of night it stays open to, if it creates a litter problem, etc.

For a **merit** you will need to explain why stakeholders in one of the businesses that you are studying affect the business differently than in the other business.

For instance, if you are studying a market stall holder selling books and a farmer selling eggs you might find that the customers buying the books expect that they are priced below the price in local bookshops and that the

customers buying the eggs expect them to be fresh, free range and carefully packed into boxes. The stall-holder will need to keep his prices low, the farmer will need to make certain that the quality of the eggs is what the customers demand.

For a **distinction** you will need to show that you understand that different stakeholders in one of your businesses can have interests that conflict with those of other stakeholders, e.g. shareholders want more profits, customers want lower prices.

You will also need to compare the two businesses. In order to do this you will need to decide on what basis you will compare them. There will be obvious facts, for example one is in the primary sector, and one is in the secondary sector, but there will also be less obvious ways of comparing them, e.g. why one is located near its competitors and one is located away from competitors. For each comparison you will need to explain why the businesses are different.

CHAPTER 1

BUSINESS DOCUMENTS

Foundation and Intermediate

In this chapter you will learn how to complete the business documents used when businesses buy or sell goods or services.

Completing Business Documents

In order to help you to understand which documents are completed and in which order, imagine that a retail shop, which we will call 'Office Shop', is going to buy some goods from a supplier which we will call 'Universal Office Supplies Ltd'.

Seller:	Universal Office Supplies Ltd
Buyer:	Office Shop Ltd

Products Requirement

Suppose Office Shop Ltd wants to buy from Universal Office Supplies Ltd the following goods:

> 2 computer monitors
> 4 computer keyboards

How does Office Shop Ltd let Universal Office Supplies Ltd know that it wants this computer equipment?

It could telephone, but Universal Office Supplies Ltd might not copy the message down properly and this might result in Office Shop getting the wrong goods. To make sure that mistakes are less likely, Office Shop fills in a document called a **purchase order**.

The Purchase Order

> Definition – a **purchase order** is completed by a customer and sent to a supplier to request the supply of goods or services.

The purchase order (see Figure 3.1.1) shows:

- the type of goods wanted;
- the number of goods wanted;
- the address to which the goods should be sent;
- the date when the goods are wanted;
- the price of the goods;
- the reference or catalogue numbers of the goods wanted.

Note that the purchase order has the name of Office Shop on the top. This lets Universal Office Supplies know who is ordering the goods so that it knows who to send them to. Office Shop also puts a special number (12540) on the purchase order so that both Office Shop and Universal Office Supplies can refer to the order easily when they need to. This is called the **purchase order number**. This is useful because Office Shop may have sent more than one purchase order to Universal Office Supplies and without a purchase order number, Office Shop and Universal Office Supplies might get the orders mixed up.

Figure 3.1.1 Purchase order

Office Shop

Shop 5, Lee Retail Park,
Roystam, Staffs, RO4 8PY

TEL: 0987541
FAX: 0987547
E-MAIL:OS@YNET.ORG
WEB: WWW.OSP.COM

PURCHASE ORDER

To

| Universal Office Supplies Ltd
35 High St.
Stanford
Herts
EN4 7RY | | Order No: | 12540 |
| | | Date: | 28/05/2000 |

Quantity	Description	Item Reference	Unit Price £
2	14" computer monitors	CM 17	105.00
4	keyboards	KO 3	10.00

Delivery: Immediate   **Authorised by:** *J.Lyon*

VAT Registration Number 2934781

If Universal Office Supplies wants to do business with Office Shop and has the goods in stock, it will arrange for the goods to be sent to Office Shop. Universal Office Supplies now fills out a **sales invoice**.

The Sales Invoice

Definition – a **sales invoice** is completed by a supplier and sent to a customer to indicate goods or services sold and the amount to be paid.

The sales invoice shows:

- the description of the goods being sold;

- the number of goods being sold;

- the address to which the invoice should be sent;

- the address to which the goods should be sent;

- the price of the goods;

- any discounts that Universal Office Supplies is offering to Office Shop;

Figure 3.1.2 Sales invoice

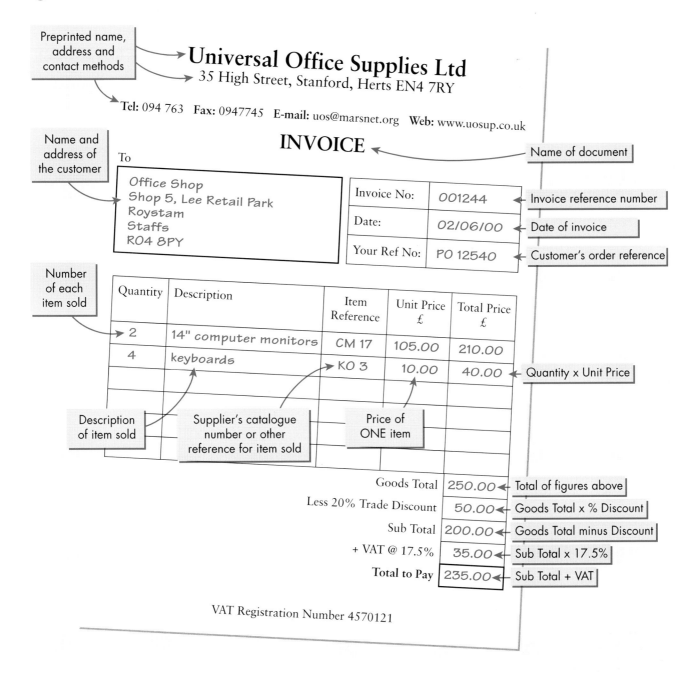

- the amount of VAT to pay on the goods being sold;

- the total amount that Office Shop has to pay to Universal Office Supplies;

- the reference or catalogue numbers of the goods being sold.

Note that the invoice also has a special number (001244) on it called the **invoice number** so that both Office Shop and Universal Office Supplies can refer to the invoice easily if there are any problems or queries.

Universal Office Supplies keeps one copy for itself so that it can update its own records and knows how much Office Shop owes. Another copy is posted to Office Shop so that Office Shop knows how much money it needs to pay Universal Office Supplies for the computer equipment.

When the computer equipment has been packed it is sent to Office Shop with a document called a **delivery note**.

Figure 3.1.3 Delivery note

The Delivery Note

Definition – a **delivery note** is completed by a supplier and sent with goods (not services) to show goods being delivered to a customer.

A delivery note can be:

- posted to the customer; or
- it can travel with the goods.

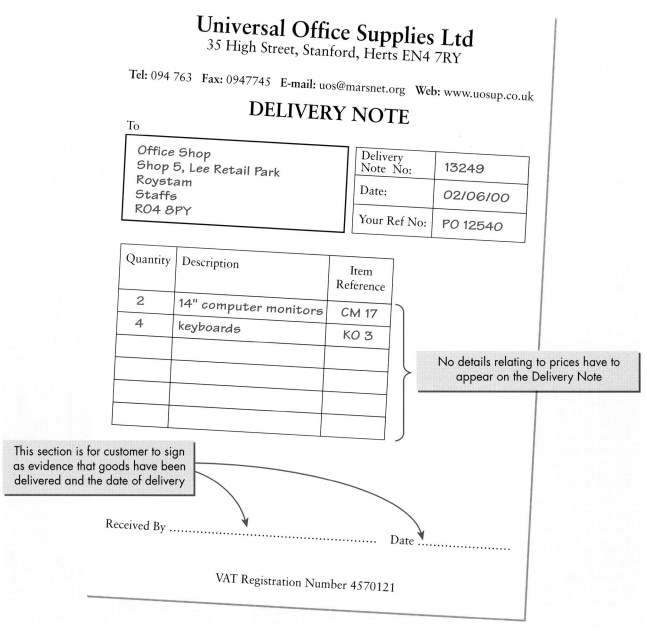

Universal Office Supplies Ltd
35 High Street, Stanford, Herts EN4 7RY

Tel: 094 763 **Fax:** 0947745 **E-mail:** uos@marsnet.org **Web:** www.uosup.co.uk

DELIVERY NOTE

To

Office Shop
Shop 5, Lee Retail Park
Roystam
Staffs
RO4 8PY

Delivery Note No:	13249
Date:	02/06/00
Your Ref No:	PO 12540

Quantity	Description	Item Reference
2	14" computer monitors	CM 17
4	keyboards	KO 3

No details relating to prices have to appear on the Delivery Note

This section is for customer to sign as evidence that goods have been delivered and the date of delivery

Received By .... Date ....

VAT Registration Number 4570121

The delivery note shows all the same details that would appear on the invoice but any details relating to the price of the goods or the amount to pay are blanked out.

When the goods arrive Office Shop will use the delivery note to check that it matches the contents of the packages.

If the delivery note travels with the goods, the person delivering the goods will ask the person who receives the goods to sign the delivery note as evidence that they have been delivered. If the goods described on the delivery note do not match the contents of the packages, then Office Shop should write on the delivery note the differences or details of any damaged goods before signing it.

One copy of the delivery note is left with the customer and the second copy is taken back to the supplier's office as proof that the goods were delivered.

When the computer equipment is delivered the customer will complete a **goods received note**.

The Goods Received Note

(Intermediate level only)

> Definition – a **goods received note** is completed by a customer to record goods (not services) received and their condition.

Figure 3.1.4 Goods received note

Office Shop — GOODS RECEIVED NOTE

Name and Address of Supplier

Universal Office Supplies Ltd
35 High St.
Stanford
Herts
EN4 7RY

G.R.N. Number:	23344
Delivery Note Number:	13249
Purchase Order No	12540

Quantity	Description	Item Reference	Condition of Goods
2	14" computer monitors	CM 17	satisfactory
4	keyboards	KO 3	2 damaged

Received by: R. Binks

Date: 4th June 2000

This is an internal document, which means that it stays on the customer's premises. It is not sent to the supplier.

The goods received note shows:

- the quantity and type of all the goods that have been received (even those that were not ordered!);

- if any goods were received in a damaged condition.

Figure 3.1.5 Credit note

Office Shop will only pay for goods it can use so it will return to Universal Office Supplies any damaged goods. If Universal Office Supplies agrees that some goods are damaged it will post to Office Shop a **credit note**.

The Credit Note

Definition – a **credit note** is sent by a supplier to a customer to reduce the amount owed by the customer.

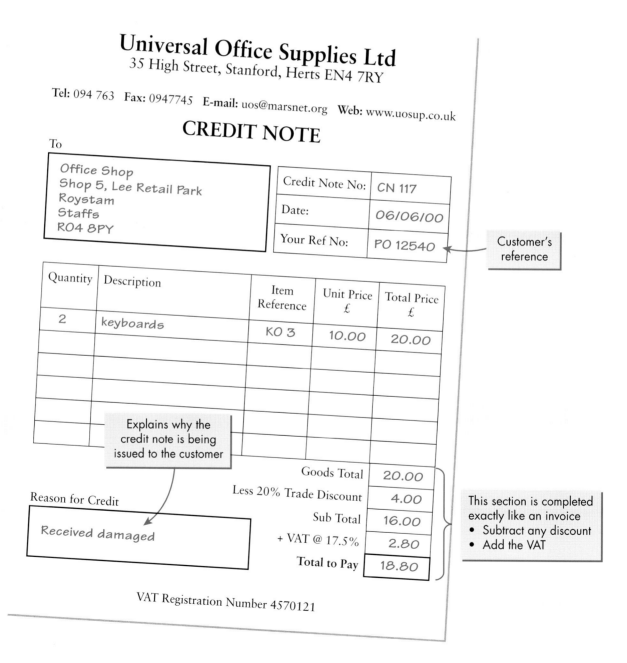

Universal Office Supplies Ltd
35 High Street, Stanford, Herts EN4 7RY

Tel: 094 763 Fax: 0947745 E-mail: uos@marsnet.org Web: www.uosup.co.uk

CREDIT NOTE

To

Office Shop
Shop 5, Lee Retail Park
Roystam
Staffs
RO4 8PY

Credit Note No:	CN 117
Date:	06/06/00
Your Ref No:	PO 12540

Customer's reference

Quantity	Description	Item Reference	Unit Price £	Total Price £
2	keyboards	KO 3	10.00	20.00

Explains why the credit note is being issued to the customer

Reason for Credit

Received damaged

Goods Total	20.00
Less 20% Trade Discount	4.00
Sub Total	16.00
+ VAT @ 17.5%	2.80
Total to Pay	18.80

This section is completed exactly like an invoice
- Subtract any discount
- Add the VAT

VAT Registration Number 4570121

The credit note shows the same details as shown on an invoice (for the returned goods only) and all the calculations are worked out in the same way – discount is still **subtracted** and VAT is still **added**.

The two main differences are:

- it has the words 'credit note' printed on it;

- it reduces the amount owed by the customer, whereas an invoice increases the amount owed by the customer.

It may also contain an entry which explains why the credit note is being sent.

Note that the credit note also has a special number (CN117) on it called the **credit note number** so that both Office Shop and Universal Office Supplies can refer to the credit note easily if there are any problems or queries.

Universal Office Supplies keeps one copy for itself so that it can record how much less Office Shop owes, and sends one copy to Office Shop. Office Shop can now update its own records to show that it owes Universal Office Supplies less than it did before receipt of the credit note.

Note: A credit note is not the same as a refund of money. The supplier does not send money to the customer when a credit note is issued. The credit note allows the customer to pay a lower amount by reducing the overall amount that is owed to the supplier.

When customers pay invoices they will often send with the payment a remittance advice slip.

The Remittance Advice Slip

Definition – a **remittance advice slip** is sent to a supplier with payment to indicate which invoices are being paid.

When Office Shop pays any invoices it encloses a cheque for the correct amount and a remittance advice slip.

The remittance advice slip shows:

- which invoices are being paid off;

- any credit notes being used to reduce the amount owed.

Office Shop does not need to send a remittance advice slip but it helps Universal Office Supplies to match up the amount on the cheque with the invoices being paid off. This is particularly helpful if the cheque is paying off more than one invoice. A common payment method is by **cheque**.

Figure 3.1.6 Remittance advice slip

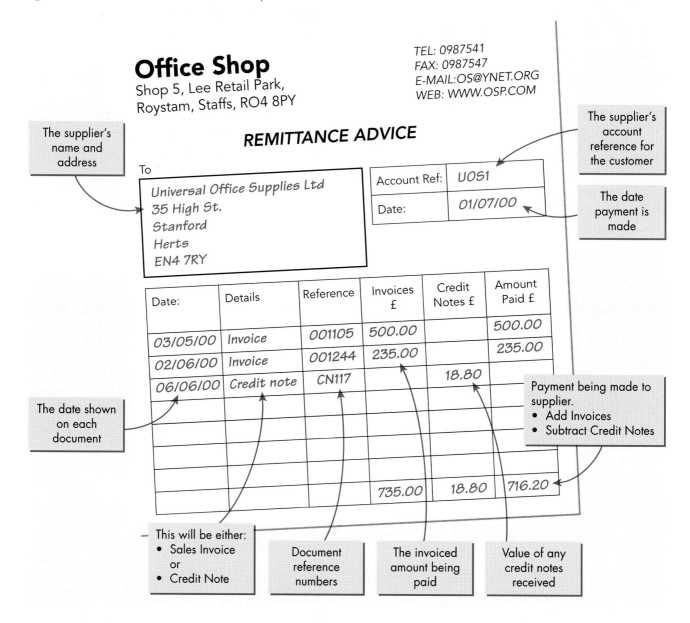

The supplier's name and address

The supplier's account reference for the customer

The date payment is made

Office Shop
Shop 5, Lee Retail Park,
Roystam, Staffs, RO4 8PY

TEL: 0987541
FAX: 0987547
E-MAIL:OS@YNET.ORG
WEB: WWW.OSP.COM

REMITTANCE ADVICE

To

Universal Office Supplies Ltd
35 High St.
Stanford
Herts
EN4 7RY

| Account Ref: | UOS1 |
| Date: | 01/07/00 |

Date:	Details	Reference	Invoices £	Credit Notes £	Amount Paid £
03/05/00	Invoice	001105	500.00		500.00
02/06/00	Invoice	001244	235.00		235.00
06/06/00	Credit note	CN117		18.80	
			735.00	18.80	716.20

The date shown on each document

Payment being made to supplier.
• Add Invoices
• Subtract Credit Notes

This will be either:
• Sales Invoice
or
• Credit Note

Document reference numbers

The invoiced amount being paid

Value of any credit notes received

The Cheque

Definition – a **cheque** is a manual method of payment which allows money to be transferred from the customer's bank account to the supplier's bank account.

Rather than paying off invoices by sending notes and coins through the post, Office Shop can write out a cheque for the required amount. This cheque is posted to Universal Office Supplies which pays it into its bank. The cheque then passes through a system called 'clearing' which usually takes three days.

Figure 3.1.7 Cheque

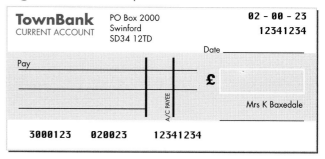

The Cheque Clearing System

This is a system run by all the banks to arrange for the transfer of money from one bank account to another. Once Universal Office Supplies' bank has received the cheque it arranges for the amount stated on the cheque to be transferred from Office Shop's bank account into Universal Office Supplies' bank account.

Paying off invoices by cheque is safer than sending money as thieves are less likely to steal cheques. It is also easier and more convenient than having to keep lots of different notes and coins.

At the end of every month Universal Office Supplies sends out to its **credit customers** a **statement of account**.

The Statement of Account

Definition – a **statement of account** is sent to credit customers to show them the transactions which have affected their account and to encourage them to pay their invoices within the agreed credit period.

Figure 3.1.8 Statement fo account

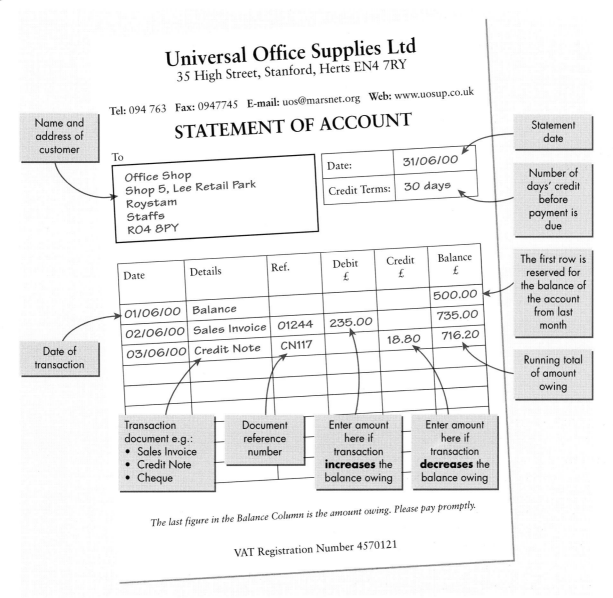

If Office Shop regularly buys goods from Universal Office Supplies it will probably have a credit account. This means that Office Shop does not have to pay for the computer equipment immediately but can pay after an agreed period of time. The usual credit terms are 30 days. In other words, the customer is expected to pay the invoice amount not more than 30 days after it was sent. Some customers may get 60 or even 90 days' credit.

The statement of account shows:

- the amount owed by the customer at the beginning of the month (based on previous months' transactions);

- any transactions during the month which increased the amount owed, e.g. issue of a sales invoice;

- any transactions during the month which reduced the amount owed, e.g. issue of a credit note or receipt of money from customers;

- the amount owed by the customer at the end of the month.

The Receipt

> Definition – a **receipt** is given to 'cash customers' as evidence that a payment has been made.

Figure 3.1.9 Receipt

Universal Office Supplies Ltd
35 High Street, Stanford, Herts EN4 7RY

Tel: 094 763   Fax: 0947745   E-mail: uos@marsnet.org   Web: www.uosup.co.uk

RECEIPT

Customer

R. Pato

| Receipt No: | **457** |
| Date: | 02/08/00 |

	£
5 staplers @ £2.00 each	10.00
6 packs staples @ £0.40 per pack	2.40
Sub-total	12.40
VAT	2.17
TOTAL	14.57

VAT Registration Number 4570121

A **receipt** is not usually given to 'credit customers' as the invoice acts as proof of the transaction. Customers who pay for goods or services immediately (cash customers) will not receive an invoice, however, and these customers often request a receipt to prove that a transaction has taken place.

Note that 'cash customers' can pay by cash, cheque, debit card or credit card – not just by cash.

The Petty Cash Voucher

Definition – a **petty cash voucher** is completed when a small payment in notes or coins is required.

Figure 3.1.10 Petty cash voucher

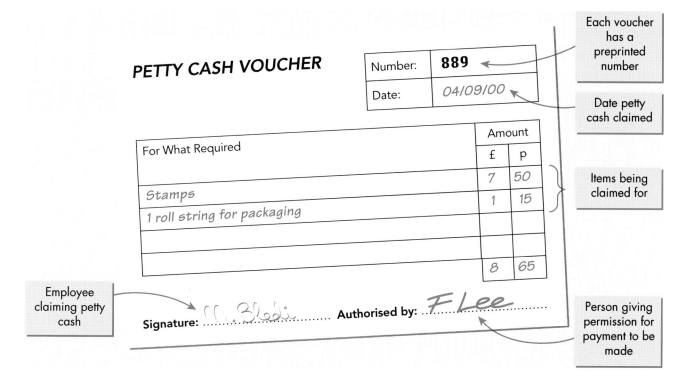

A petty cash voucher is an internal document. This means that it is completed for use within a business by employees of that business. It is not sent to any other businesses. It is usually used for making small payments to employees of the business who have bought items for use in the business with their own money and want to be paid back. Payments are usually made for such things as:

- taxi, bus or train fares incurred on business;
- stamps for business letters;
- tea and coffee for staff refreshments.

A 'float' of notes and coins, known as the 'imprest' amount, is kept in a lockable petty cash box. A petty cash payment is made by taking out notes and coins and replacing them with a completed petty cash voucher for the same amount. This allows the cashier to check for theft or errors since the value of the vouchers in the box plus the value of the notes and coins should always add up to the imprest amount. Every week the imprest amount is topped up to its original level by replacing these completed vouchers with the equivalent value of notes and coins.

Checking the petty cash

In these examples assume that a weekly imprest (float) amount has been set at £100.

Figure 3.1.11 Petty cash

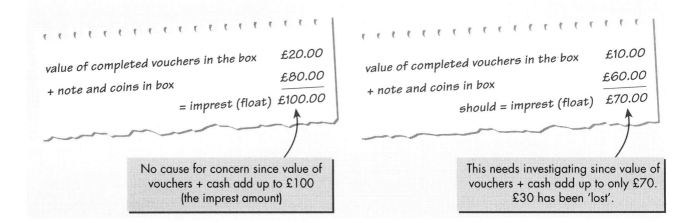

Checking Documents Before Paying Invoices

(Intermediate level only)
To make sure that only goods which have been ordered and received are paid for, the customer needs to check the three documents used in the transaction.

Table 3.1.1 Checking the transaction details

Purchase Order	Sales Invoice	Goods Received Note
Question:	**Check the:**	**With the:**
Have we received the goods we ordered?	Purchase order	Goods received note
Have we been charged the agreed price?	Purchase order	Sales invoice

Office Shop checks that the quantity and description of the goods shown on the invoice it received from Universal Office Supplies are the same as on the purchase order and the goods received note.

It also checks that the prices and amounts shown on the purchase order match those on the invoice.

If it didn't check these three documents together it might pay for goods that it didn't order or that it hadn't received. It might also pay too much or too little for the goods.

Figure 3.1.12 Cross-checking the documents

Office Shop

PURCHASE ORDER

To

| Universal Office Supplies Ltd
35 High St.
Stanford
Herts
EN4 7RY | | Order No: | 12540 |
| | | Date: | 28/05/2000 |

Quantity	Description	Item Reference	Unit Price £
2	14" computer monitors	CM 17	105.00
4	keyboards	KO 3	10.00

Office Shop

GOODS RECEIVED NOTE

Quantity	Description	Item Reference	Condition of Goods
2	14" computer monitors	CM 17	satisfactory
4	keyboards	KO 3	2 damaged

Universal Office Supplies Ltd
35 High Street, Stanford, Herts EN4 7RY

Tel: 094 763 **Fax:** 0947745 **E-mail:** uos@marsnet.org **Web:** www.uosup.co.uk

INVOICE

To

Office Shop Shop 5, Lee Retail Park Roystam Staffs RO4 8PY		Invoice No:	001244
		Date:	02/06/00
		Your Ref No:	PO 12540

Quantity	Description	Item Reference	Unit Price £	Total Price £
2	14" computer monitors	CM 17	105.00	210.00
4	keyboards	KO 3	10.00	40.00

CHECK BEFORE PAYING INVOICE

1 Have the goods ordered been received? (Check GRN and P.O.)

2 Does the Unit Price charged match the price agreed? (Check Invoice and P.O.)

Revision

Questions

1   When are the following documents used:
    a) purchase order;
    b) delivery note;
    c) remittance advice slip?   (3 marks)

2   What document would a supplier send to a customer if the customer returned
    unwanted goods?   (1 mark)

3   What checks should a customer make before paying an invoice from a supplier?   (2 marks)

4   Put the following documents in the order in which they would be completed for a transaction:
    a) cheque
    b) purchase order
    c) invoice
    d) statement of account
    e) delivery note
    f) remittance advice slip   (1 mark)

5   Complete the following invoice extensions by filling in the grey boxes.

Quantity	Description	Price per Item	Total Price
2	disk boxes	£3.00	
3	scanners	£52.54	
5	printer cartridges	£62.18	

                                                                                  (1 mark)

6   Copy out and complete the following invoice section by filling in the grey boxes.

Quantity	Description	Catalogue Ref.	Price per Item	Total Price
6	mouse mats	mm 3	4.50	27.00
4	screen guards	sg2	3.21	12.84
2	printers	p5	320.18	640.36
			Goods Total	
			less 20% trade discount	
			Sub total	
			+VAT @ 17.5%	
			Total to Pay	

                                                                                  (3 marks)

7 Two screen guards priced at £3.21 have been returned to the supplier because they were the wrong size.
Complete the credit note that would be sent to the customer assuming that the customer was originally given 20% trade discount on the purchase.   (3 marks)

8 Copy out and complete the statement extract **in date order** from the information given below:

Balance of the account on 1st May 2000: £1000.00

Invoices sent to customer:			Cheques received from customer			Credit notes issued to customer		
Date	Invoice No.	Amount	Date	Cheque No.	Amount	Date	Credit Note No.	Amount
3/5/00	12457	250.00	11/5/00	564	800.00	18/5/00	cn2864	20.00
25/5/00	12884	50.00	28/5/00	578	100.00			

Statement of Account (extract)

Date	Details	Ref	Debit	Credit	Balance

(3 marks)

9 Check the following invoice for errors and recalculate the correct figures.

Quantity	Description	Item Reference	Unit Price £	Total Price £
3	14" computer monitors	CM 17	105.00	315.00
4	keyboards	KO 3	10.00	40.00
			Goods Total	345.00
			Less 20% Trade Discount	69.00
			Sub Total	276.00
			+ VAT @ 17.5%	48.30
			Total to Pay	324.30

(3 marks)

10 Check the following invoice for errors and recalculate the correct figures.

Quantity	Description	Item Reference	Unit Price £	Total Price £
4	14″ computer monitors	CM 17	105.00	420.00
6	keyboards	KO 3	10.00	60.00
			Goods Total	480.00
			Less 20% Trade Discount	96.00
			Sub Total	576.00
			+ VAT @ 17.5%	100.80
			Total to Pay	676.80

(3 marks)

CHAPTER 2

COSTS INVOLVED IN A NEW BUSINESS

Foundation and Intermediate

In this chapter you will learn which costs are involved in starting up and running a new business. You will also learn that different types of business have different costs and revenues.

KEY TERMS:

start-up costs   running costs   revenue

Covering the Costs of a New Business

When businesses are planning to produce new products they must work out the costs involved and the likely **revenue** they will make from selling the new products.

Definition – **start-up costs** are costs which need to be met *before* a business can start selling new products.

These costs will include:

- the cost of buying a workshop or other buildings in which to make the products;

- market research costs to find out what customers want or to find out if customers will buy the new products;

- the cost of buying machinery to make the new products;

- the cost of buying and installing computers, filing cabinets and other office equipment.

Depending on the type of product or service, businesses may have other start-up costs as well.

Definition – **running costs** are costs which the business will have to meet as part of the *ongoing* process of producing and selling the product.

These will be regular costs that may have to be paid daily, weekly, monthly or yearly throughout the life of the business.

Running costs will include things like:

- advertising costs;

- paying rent on the factory or other buildings;

- paying business rates to the local council;

- paying wages and salaries to employees;

- paying bills for electricity, gas and water;

- paying suppliers;

- the cost of buying goods to resell (if they are retailers);

- the cost of buying raw materials (if they are manufacturers) from which to make their own products.

Definition – **revenue** is money coming into a business as a result of selling goods or services.

When a business sells goods or services it will receive money from its customers. The money coming into the business in this way is called **sales revenue** or sometimes just **revenue**.

Types of Business

Different types of business will have different costs and sources of revenue. Examples of the different costs and revenues associated with different types of businesses are shown below.

Type of business: manufacturing

Example	Start-up costs	Running costs	Revenue from selling
Vehicle manufacturer	• machinery to move vehicles on the assembly line • purchase of specialist equipment to build the vehicles	• cost of raw materials to make the cars, such as paint, plastic and metal • power to run the machinery	• cars • vans • spare parts • accessories

Type of business: retailer

Example	Start-up costs	Running costs	Revenue from selling
Supermarket	• building costs of constructing the supermarket • shelving on which to stack food products for sale	• cost of food bought from suppliers • wages of the checkout cashiers	• food • drink • household products • magazines

Type of business: service industry

Example	Start-up costs	Running costs	Revenue from selling
Tennis instructor	• cost of video equipment to record learners' strokes	• cost of tennis balls	• lessons

Revision

Questions

1 Classify items in the list below into 'start-up costs' and 'running costs'.
   a) factory machinery;
   b) stock of raw materials;
   c) factory rates;
   d) purchase of factory buildings;
   e) wages.   (2 marks)

2 (i) In each case below identify whether the revenue is derived from selling goods or selling services.
   a) solicitor;
   b) car mechanic;
   c) golf teacher;
   d) greengrocer;
   e) estate agent;
   f) burger bar.   (6 marks)

   (ii) Identify examples of the kind of costs you would associate with each type of business.
                                                                             (6 marks)

   (iii) Identify examples of the sources of revenue you would associate with each type of business.
                                                                             (6 marks)

CHAPTER 3

METHODS OF MAKING AND RECEIVING PAYMENTS

Foundation level

In this chapter you will learn about different methods of making and receiving payments. You will also learn the costs, advantages and disadvantages of each method.

KEY TERMS:

cash payment   EFTPOS   cheque payment

overdraft   credit card payment

debit card payment

Cash

This is the simplest method of payment.

Definition – a **cash payment** is made by giving notes and coins to the supplier of the goods or services.

Advantages of payment by cash

For the buyer	• simple – no need to open a bank account.
For the seller	• simple; • immediate use of the money, e.g. for paying bills, buying stock; • cash can be deposited in the bank to earn interest immediately; or • it can reduce bank charges if customer has a bank **overdraft**.

Definition – an **overdraft** is a means of borrowing money from a bank. Interest is charged only when the account balance goes below zero. Customers may borrow only up to a limit agreed by their bank.

Costs and disadvantages of payment by cash

For the buyer	• need to have cash available in a range of denominations (different notes and coins); • greater possibility of theft or robbery since cash is difficult to trace once stolen; • may need to pay for additional security if large sums of money need to be kept for paying suppliers. This may include increased insurance premiums; • no credit period from supplier so cash withdrawn from bank is not earning interest; • if buyer becomes overdrawn (has an **overdraft**) at the bank, interest will be charged to the buyer's bank account – increasing costs.
For the seller	• greater possibility of theft or robbery since cash is difficult to trace once stolen;

- may need to pay for additional security if large sums of money have to be received and stored before being taken to the bank;
- costs of cash handling and administration.

Cheque

This is a common method of paying for goods and services.

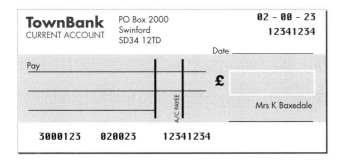

TownBank
CURRENT ACCOUNT
PO Box 2000
Swinford
SD34 12TD
02 - 00 - 23
12341234
Date _____
Pay _____
£
A/C PAYEE
Mrs K Baxedale
3000123   020023   12341234

Definition – a **cheque** is a written instruction to a bank to pay a sum of money to a named person or business.

Advantages of payment by cheque

For the buyer	• three-day credit period as the cheque passes through the **cheque clearing system** (money stays in buyer's bank account earning interest or reducing overdraft charges); • no need to hold large amounts of cash; • some banks will pay interest on some cheque accounts.
For the seller	• completed cheques are not as attractive to thieves since stolen cheques are difficult to turn into cash – reduced cost of security; • easy to handle.

Costs and disadvantages of payment by cheque

For the buyer	• banks charge businesses when a cheque passes through the buyer's account; • many businesses pay to have their cheques pre-printed with their business name and logo. These cheques are a cost.
For the seller	• banks charge businesses when cheques pass through the seller's account; • money cannot be used until the cheque has been deposited in the bank and passed through the cheque clearing system.

Debit Card

Definition – a **debit card** is a method of transferring money from the buyer's bank account to the seller's bank account using EFTPOS.
EFTPOS stands for Electronic Funds Transfer at Point Of Sale.

A debit card operates in a similar way to a cheque but without the need to carry a cheque book.

The debit card is 'swiped' through an EFTPOS computer terminal by the seller and the amount is automatically transferred from the customer's bank account to the seller's bank account.

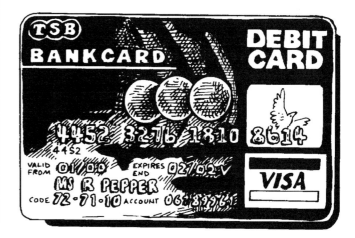

Advantages of payment by debit card

For the buyer	• simple and convenient – one card is all that is required to make payments; • no need to hold amounts of cash or cheques; • a debit card is small and can be carried by the user more easily than cash or cheques; • some banks will pay interest on some cheque accounts.
For the seller	• automatic receipt of money through electronic terminal; • no cash or cheque deposit administration required.

Costs and disadvantages of payment by debit card

For the buyer	• banks charge businesses for debit card transactions; • not all businesses accept debit cards; • no credit period; • money has to be in the bank to support the transaction otherwise the customer will become overdrawn and incur interest charges.
For the seller	• banks charge businesses for debit card transactions.

Credit Card

> Definition – a **credit card** is a method of obtaining goods on credit, using EFTPOS, which allows payment to be made at a later date.

Goods and services can be obtained for use by presenting a credit card for payment. If used to buy goods or services in a shop, the credit card is swiped through an EFTPOS electronic card reader at the till where it is automatically checked for validity by the credit card company's computer. If the card is valid a credit card slip is issued by the terminal for the customer to sign.

Once a month a statement will be sent to the card holder showing:

- all the purchases made on the card;

- any payments to the credit card company by the cardholder;

- any interest charged by the credit card company;

- the balance of the account – the amount owed to the credit card company.

This balance does not have to be paid off in full but if it isn't then the card holder will be charged interest on any unpaid balance remaining at the end of the free credit period. In all cases, however, the cardholder must pay off at least 5% of the total balance shown on the statement.

> If the total balance shown on the statement is £200 then the minimum payment which must be made is £200 × 5% = £10.

All credit cards have a spending limit which the cardholder is not allowed to exceed. This limit is shown on the customer's monthly statement. The credit card companies (e.g. VISA, MasterCard) set different limits for different cardholders but cardholders can apply to have their limit increased or decreased.

The card can also be used to order goods using the telephone, e-mail, the internet or by mail order.

The buyer gives the supplier:

- the cardholder's name;
- the credit card number;
- the expiry date.

In these circumstances the credit card slip is often marked 'cardholder not present' as the credit card slip cannot be signed by the cardholder.

Advantages of payment by credit card

For the buyer	• simple and convenient – goods or services can be paid for without leaving the buyer's premises; • no need to hold amounts of cash or cheques; • a credit card is small and can be carried by the user more easily than cash or cheques; • the credit period allows purchases to be made even if the seller has no money available; • goods and services may be obtained without having to pay for them immediately; • some credit cards give additional benefits such as free insurance on purchases; • there is a free credit period from the date the card is used to the date when minimum repayment is due; • no need to carry cash so risk of robbery is reduced; • payments can be spread over many months, since only the minimum repayment amount is required every month; • greater security since the contract is with the credit card company not the seller.
For the seller	• automatic receipt of money through EFTPOS; • no cash or cheque deposit administration required; • automatic verification of validity through a computer terminal. Time is not spent telephoning the credit card company for authorisation.

Costs and disadvantages of payment by credit card

For the buyer	• not all businesses accept credit cards; • use of the card needs careful control since it is possible to spend up to the card limit; • if the card is stolen, the cardholder is liable for all the purchases made on it until the credit card company is informed of the theft.
For the seller	• businesses which accept credit cards in payment for goods or services have to pay a fee to the credit card company. Typically this is 2% of the value of the transaction.

Cost to seller of receiving payment by credit card		
Cost of music system	=	£300.00
Credit card fee £300 × 2%	=	£6.00

Revision

Questions

1 Name the method of payment which can be sent through the post to a supplier in settlement of a debt:
   a) credit card
   b) debit card
   c) cheque
   d) standing order   (4 marks)

2 An agreement between a bank and a business to borrow money from the bank only when the account goes below zero is called:
   a) an overdraft
   b) an account
   c) a direct debit
   d) a bank loan   (4 marks)

3 What is the *financial* advantage to a buyer of paying a supplier by credit card?   (1 mark)

4 What is the main disadvantage to a seller of accepting a credit card in payment for goods or services?   (1 mark)

5 Which payment method allows automatic transfer of funds between the buyer's and seller's bank accounts using EFTPOS?   (1 mark)

6 Which other method of payment uses the EFTPOS system?   (1 mark)

7 Which payment method allows goods to be bought now and paid for later?   (1 mark)

8 Why do most businesses not use cash as a payment method?   (1 mark)

CHAPTER 4

BREAK-EVEN

In this chapter you will learn how to obtain a break-even point by calculation and by plotting a graph. You will learn how to interpret a break-even chart and to explain the effects of changes in fixed and variable costs on the break-even point and level of profit.

> ### KEY TERMS:
>
> | | | |
> |---|---|---|
> | level of activity | break-even point | profit |
> | margin of safety | revenue | loss |
> | fixed costs | variable costs | |

Break-even analysis is concerned with estimating costs, revenues and profits at different **levels of activity** and finding the level of activity at which the business breaks even.

> Definition – the **break-even point** is where neither a profit nor a loss is made. At this point the money flowing *out* of the business is matched exactly by the amount of money flowing *into* the business.
>
> ### TOTAL COSTS = REVENUES
>
> The **level of activity** is the number of units of products or services sold.

Typical examples of levels of activity are:

- goods sold
- tickets sold
- hours of service
- lessons

Importance of the Break-even Point

Few businesses will want to operate at the break-even point of activity but it is an important factor because it shows the minimum level of activity required for the business to survive. A business using a break-even chart has to decide if the level of activity shown by the chart to be necessary to achieve a desired profit is possible.

> If a break-even chart for a business giving tennis instruction showed that the instructor had to work 180 hours a week in order to make a profit of £2 it is unlikely that this business would start as there are only 168 hours available in a week.

If a business finds the **level of activity** required to achieve a desired level of profit is too high, it has three options:
1 reduce fixed or variable costs (or both);
2 increase the revenue by increasing the price charged to customers (but remember – an increase in the price may reduce the number of customers willing to pay the higher price);
3 don't start the business!

The advantage of determining the break-even point before producing a new product is that a decision to start can be made before any major costs have been incurred.

Before calculating the break-even point the **revenue** has to be identified and the costs have to be split into **fixed** and **variable** costs.

> **revenue** is income from selling products:
> = (selling price of one unit × number of units sold)

> Definition – **fixed costs** are those costs which *stay the same* whatever the level of activity.
>
> **variable costs** are those costs which *increase* or *decrease* as the level of activity rises or falls.

How do I know if a cost is fixed or variable?

To find out if a cost is fixed or variable ask yourself the following question:

Figure 3.4.1 Fixed or variable?

If more items are made or sold would the costs increase or stay the same?

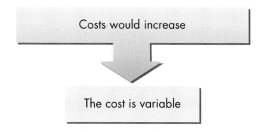

Costs would increase

The cost is variable

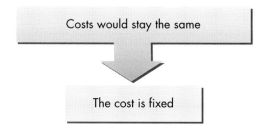

Costs would stay the same

The cost is fixed

Examples of Fixed Costs

Rent

Suppose the rent of a workshop producing garden sheds is £1,000 per week. This is payable even if no sheds are produced or sold but will still be £1,000 even if 500 sheds are sold. This cost is therefore a fixed cost.

Office staff wages

Suppose the wages bill for the office staff is £500 per week. Office staff are not paid according to how many sheds are made or sold. This bill will stay the same whatever the level of activity. This cost is therefore a fixed cost.

Examples of Variable Costs

Raw materials

Suppose £5 worth of raw materials (wood, nails and roofing felt) are used to make one shed. If more products are made and sold then more raw materials will need to be bought to replace those used in manufacture. If two products are made then the raw material cost will be 2 × £5 = £10. Raw material costs will therefore increase or decrease as production increases or decreases. This cost is therefore a variable cost.

Commission-only salespeople

If salespeople are paid only when they sell the sheds this is known as 'paying on commission'. Suppose salespeople get paid £40 every time they sell one shed. If they sell two sheds they will earn 2 × £40 = £80 and so on. For the business, this commission increases or decreases their costs (because they have to pay the salespeople) depending on the number of sheds sold. Commission is therefore a variable cost.

Calculating the Break-even Point

A formula is used to calculate the break-even point:

$$\text{Break-even point} = \frac{\text{fixed costs}}{(\text{selling price per unit less variable cost per unit})}$$

Worked example

Suppose a business selling a new product has fixed costs of £500 per week and variable costs of £15 per product sold. The product is sold to customers for £25.

$$\text{Break-even point} = \frac{\text{fixed costs}}{(\text{selling price per unit minus variable cost per unit})}$$

Replace the words in the formula with the actual figures to get:

$$\text{Break-even point} = \frac{500}{(25-15)}$$

Now do the calculation in the brackets or you will get the wrong answer!

$$\text{Break-even point} = \frac{500}{10}$$

$$\text{Break-even point} = 50 \text{ units}$$

To break even the business must sell 50 units. The break-even point is not £50.

Note: The break-even point is always stated in terms of level of activity – never as £.

The Margin of Safety

Most businesses will want to achieve sales above the break-even level as this will bring them profits. The extent to which they exceed the break-even point can be expressed in terms of the **margin of safety**.

Definition – the **margin of safety** is the forecast level of activity minus the break-even level of activity.

In the example above the break-even level of activity was 50 units per week. Suppose the business forecasts (expects) sales of 80 units per week:

Margin of safety	=	forecast level	–	break-even level
Margin of safety	=	80	–	50
Margin of safety	=	30 units		

The margin of safety allows managers to know by how much sales can fall before the business starts to make a loss. The larger the margin of safety the more certain they can be that the business will make a profit.

Activity

The following data is for a business which will produce and sell table lamps.

Copy out and fill in the shaded boxes:

Fixed costs (FC):   £500.00 per **month**

Variable costs (VC):   £20.00 per **lamp**

Selling price: £70.00 per **lamp**

1 Calculate the break-even point

This business will break even when [   ] lamps are sold during the month.

<u>At this level of sales:</u>

Fixed costs (FC) **for the month** will be: £ [   ]

Variable costs (VC) **for the month** will be: £ [   ]

Total costs (FC+VC) **for the month** will be: £ [   ]

Sales revenue **for the month** will be: £ [   ]

2 Calculate the margin of safety (if expected level of sales is 12 table lamps per month)

This business's margin of safety is [   ] table lamps per month.

Construction of a Break-even Chart (Line Graph)

An alternative method of finding the break-even point is to construct a graph. Three lines are drawn on the graph:

- The fixed costs line;

- The total costs lines (fixed costs + variable costs);

- The sales revenue line.

Constructing a break-even chart does not mean that sales will definitely reach a desired level or that a profit must be made. For it to succeed, the product needs to be of the appropriate quality and price and there needs to be a market for the product.

The break-even chart will show the business the level of activity (usually how many sales) it needs to make to achieve a desired level of profit.

Since break-even occurs when **total costs** are the same as **sales revenue**, the break-even point is where these two lines cross each other. At this point the outgoing costs exactly match the incoming revenues and no profit or loss is made.

Activity table

In order to generate the line points on the graph, an activity table has to be completed on which to enter the appropriate costs and revenues at different levels of activity.

Figure 3.4.2 Break-even activity table

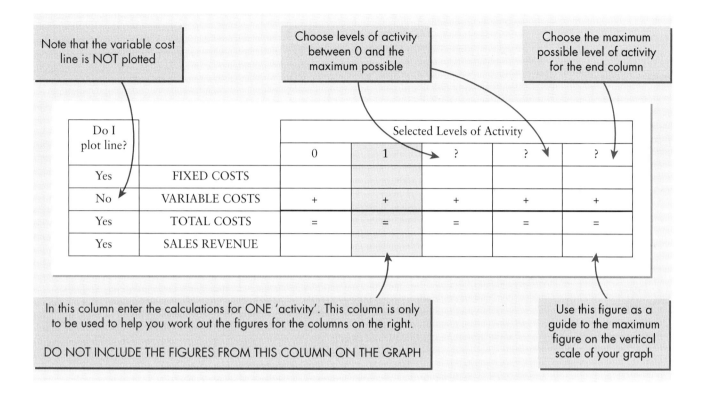

Note that the variable cost line is NOT plotted

Choose levels of activity between 0 and the maximum possible

Choose the maximum possible level of activity for the end column

Do I plot line?		Selected Levels of Activity				
		0	1	?	?	?
Yes	FIXED COSTS					
No	VARIABLE COSTS	+	+	+	+	+
Yes	TOTAL COSTS	=	=	=	=	=
Yes	SALES REVENUE					

In this column enter the calculations for ONE 'activity'. This column is only to be used to help you work out the figures for the columns on the right.

DO NOT INCLUDE THE FIGURES FROM THIS COLUMN ON THE GRAPH

Use this figure as a guide to the maximum figure on the vertical scale of your graph

To reduce the chance of error it is better to plot three or four points for each of the three lines required to create the break-even chart.

If the points are entered on the graph correctly it should be possible to draw a straight line through each set of them. If the points do not form a straight line an error has been made. If only one point fails to line up, this point is likely to be incorrect and should be checked.

Drawing points on the graph

Use a sharp pencil to draw an X to mark points on the graph. The line you draw can be accurately drawn through the centre of the X (as shown in the worked example). If you draw a ● to mark points you are more likely to plot the line inaccurately and this will lead to false readings from your graph.

You may lose marks in the external test if your graph is not accurately drawn.

Worked example

Paul Hone is a self-employed tennis coach at the local sports centre. He has the following costs:

- He has to pay the sports centre a **centre fee** of £50 every week for the use of the facilities.

- He has to pay himself £100 every week to cover his **personal expenses**.

- He has to pay the centre £2.00 each time he books a court (**court fee**).

- He has to pay £0.50 per lesson for **tennis balls**.

He charges clients £10 per lesson (the selling price).

Currently he gives 80 lessons per week.

Solution

Firstly, you must identify the fixed costs and the variable costs and total them as in the table below:

Fixed Costs

	Description	Amount £
1	Centre Fee	50.00
2	Personal Expenses	100.00
	Fixed Costs =	150.00

Then draw up the level of activity table.

Remember: the fixed costs are the same at all levels of activity.

Variable Costs

	Description	Amount £
1	Court Fee	2.00
2	Tennis Balls	0.50
	Variable Costs =	2.50

Plot Line?		Level of Activity				
		0 lessons	1 lesson	40 lessons	100 lessons	140 lessons
Yes	Fixed Costs	£150	£150	£150	£150	£150
No	Variable Costs	+£0	+£2.50	+£100	+£250	+£350
Yes	Total Costs	=£150	=152.50	=£250	=£400	=£500
Yes	Sales Revenue	£0	£10	£400	£1000	£1400

Figure 3.4.3 Break-even graph

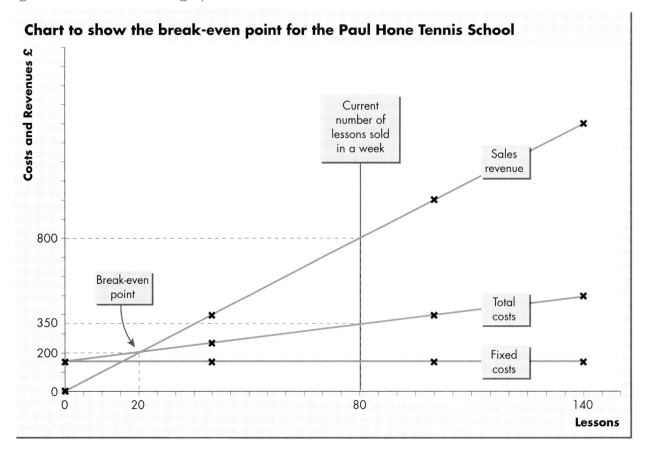

By referring to the graph:

Break-even point

The total costs and sales revenues are the same (lines cross) at

£200

Therefore the break-even point occurs when he has taught

20 lessons

Margin of safety   If Paul Hone currently teaches 80 lessons per week:

The current level of activity is:

80 lessons per week

The break-even level of activity is:

20 lessons per week

Therefore the **Margin of Safety** is:

60 lessons per week

Profit or loss

The sales revenue at the current level of activity (80 lessons) is:

£800 per week

The total cost at the current level of activity is:

£350 per week

Therefore the profit is (the difference):

£450 per week

Interpreting a Break-even Chart

A company has drawn up a break-even chart based on a forecast of 90,000 units produced and sold during the coming year. This is shown by point Q1 on the chart.

Figure 3.4.4 Break-even diagram

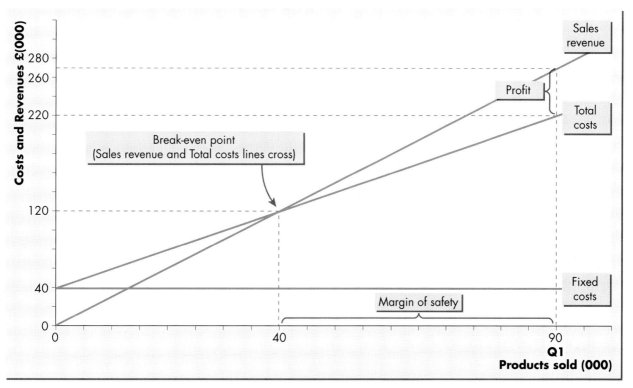

When interpreting the chart most answers can be obtained by looking at the two axes. The horizontal axis is labelled 'Products sold' and the vertical axis has shared labelling allowing both 'Costs' and 'Revenues' to be read.

Q How many products need to be sold for the business to break even?

A The break-even level of 'Products sold' is where the total costs and revenues are the same. The total costs and revenues are the same at only one point on the graph – where the two lines cross. Look down to the horizontal axis and read off the number of products sold at this point.

The break-even level of production is 40,000 units.

Q What are the total costs and revenues at the break-even level of 'Products sold'?

A Look for the break-even point and note the total costs and revenues at this point by referring to the vertical axis. At the break-even level the total costs line and the revenue line cross each other.

The total costs are £120,000 and the revenues are also £120,000.

Q What is the margin of safety at the Q1 level of 'Products sold'?

A The margin of safety is the difference between the actual or estimated level of products sold (90,000 units) and the break-even level of products sold (40,000 units).

The margin of safety is 50,000 units.

Q What is the profit or loss at the Q1 level of 'Products sold'?

A Profit or loss at the Q1 level of 'Products sold' is the difference between the total costs at Q1 and the revenue at Q1.

The revenue (£270,000) is higher than the total costs (£220,000).

Profit at Q1 = £50,000

(**Note:** *A loss would occur if the total costs were higher than the revenues. This would occur at any point of 'Products sold' below the break-even point.*)

Activity

THE COACH TRIP

A tour operator runs weekly trips to Paris.
For each trip the costs are as follows:

> Wages of driver and tour rep: £500
> Fuel for coach: £400
> Fixed administrative costs: £100 per week
> Accommodation and meals: £200 per passenger

The operator is selling each holiday to tourists for £250 for the week-long trip.

1 List and total the fixed costs of the trip.
2 List and total the variable costs of the trip.
3 Prepare a break-even activity table to show values for 0, 1, 10, 20, 40 clients.
4 Draw a fully labelled graph showing the break-even point.

By referring to your graph:

(*Assume that the tour operator expects to sell 50 holidays per week.*)

Break-even
5 How many holidays does the tour operator need to sell to break even?
6 What are the values of the total costs and sales revenues at the break-even point?

Margin of safety
7 What is the expected level of activity?
8 What is the break-even level of activity?
9 What is the expected margin of safety?

Profit or loss
10 What is the sales revenue if 50 holidays are sold?
11 What are the total costs if 50 holidays are sold?
12 What is the profit or loss if 50 holidays are sold?

Q **What price is the product sold for?**

A Choose any point on the graph where a gridline intersection is cut by the revenue line. In examinations, you can usually use the break-even point since this point is usually on a gridline intersection.

If 40 units are sold for £120 the price per unit is
£120 ÷ 40 = £3.00

The product is sold for £3.00.

Effects of Changes

If fixed costs, variable costs or prices change then the break-even point and level of profit will change.

To maintain the same level of profit

- If costs increase:
- If price of the product decreases:

→ the level of activity will need to increase.

- If costs decrease:
- If the price of the product increases:

→ the level of activity can be decreased.

If the business decides to decrease costs by buying cheaper raw materials this may result in a lower quality product. This may then result in either an overall increase in costs – as some customers may return faulty goods – or lower sales – as the product gets a reputation for poor quality.

The business cannot increase the price of the new product without this having some effect on the level of sales. Generally, the higher the price the lower the level of sales. The business may even find that as the price is increased beyond a certain level the revenue actually drops as more customers decide not to buy the product because it has become too expensive.

Effect of changes in fixed costs

Suppose **fixed costs** rise by £150 per week due to either a Sports Centre fee increase or an increase in Paul Hone's personal expenditure. His new fixed costs are now £300 per week. What are the effects of this change?

It is necessary to replot the fixed cost line, as shown in the table below. Note that the total cost row also has to be recalculated.

	Lessons (level of activity)				
	0	1	40	100	140
Fixed Costs	**£300**	**£300**	**£300**	**£300**	**£300**
Variable Costs	£0	**£2.50**	£100	£250	£350
Total Costs	**£300**	**£302.50**	**£400**	**£550**	**£650**
Sales Revenue	£0	**£10**	£400	£1000	£1400

Figure 3.4.5 Break-even point (increased fixed costs)

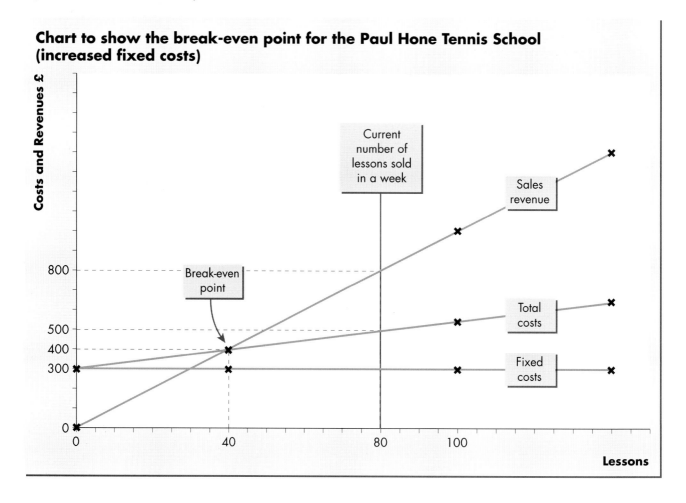

Effect of changes in variable costs

Suppose variable costs rise by £5.00 per week due to either a court fee increase or an increase in tennis ball costs. Paul's variable costs are now £7.50 per lesson. What is the effect of this change?

It is necessary to replot the variable cost line, as shown in the table below. Note that the total cost row also has to be recalculated.

	Lessons (level of activity)				
	0	1	40	100	140
Fixed Costs	£300	£300	£300	£300	£300
Variable Costs	**£0**	**£7.50**	**£300**	**£750**	**£1050**
Total Costs	**£300**	**£307.50**	**£600**	**£1050**	**£1350**
Sales Revenue	£0	£10	£400	£1000	£1400

Figure 3.4.6 Break-even point (increased variable costs)

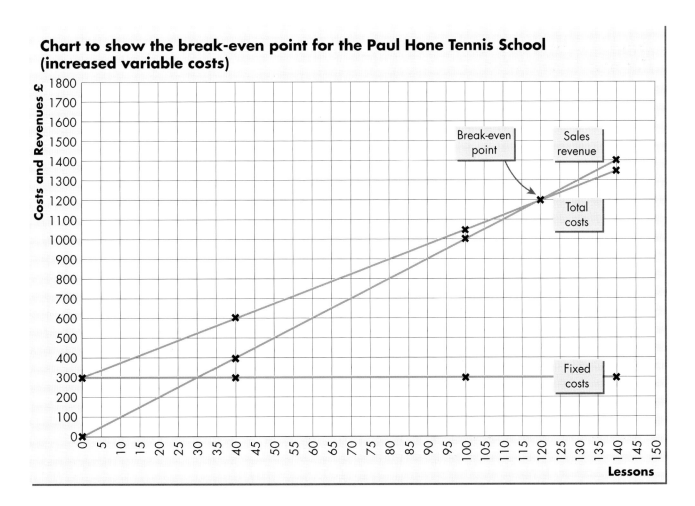

Effect of changes in selling price

Suppose Paul raises the price of his lessons so that clients are now paying £12.50 per lesson. What is the effect of this change?

It is necessary to replot the sales revenue line, as shown in the table below.

	Lessons (level of activity)				
	0	1	40	100	140
Fixed Costs	£300	£300	£300	£300	£300
Variable Costs	**£0**	**£7.50**	**£300**	**£750**	**£1050**
Total Costs	**£300**	**£307.50**	**£600**	**£1050**	**£1350**
Sales Revenue	£0	£12.50	£500	£1250	£1750

Figure 3.4.7 Break-even point (increased price)

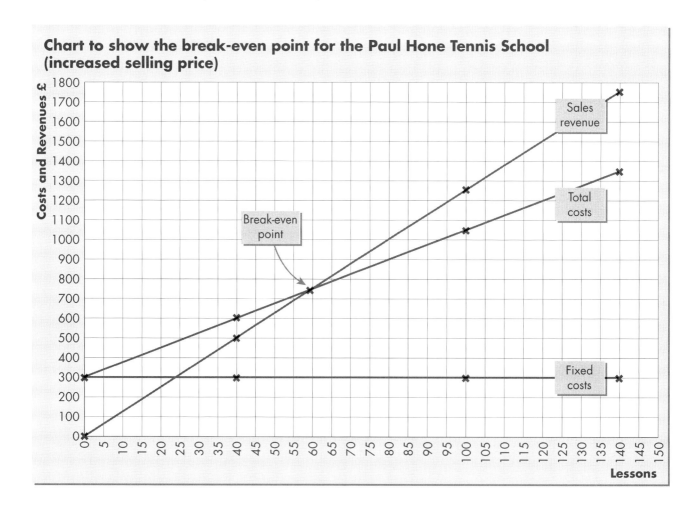

Revision

Questions

1. Classify these costs of a car manufacturer into fixed costs and variable costs:
   business rates
   metal sheeting
   managers' salaries
   wheels and tyres
   lighting and heating costs
   engines
   factory heating costs
   office salaries
   oil and petrol   (2 marks)

2. A business has fixed costs of £900 per week and variable costs of £30 per item made and sold. The product sells for £90.
   How many products need to be sold every week for this business to break even?   (1 mark)

3. A sandwich bar has the following costs:

bread	£0.20 per sandwich
sandwich fillings	£0.30 per sandwich
rent	£500.00 per week
wages	£250.00 per week
heating and lighting	£10.00 per week

   Each sandwich is sold for £2.50.

   a) Classify the costs into fixed and variable costs.   (2 marks)
   b) Calculate how many sandwiches need to be sold every week for the sandwich bar to break even.   (1 mark)

4 A company has drawn up a break-even chart based on a forecast of 90,000 units produced and sold during the coming year. This is shown by point Q2 on the chart.

Figure 3.4.8 Break-even chart (revision)

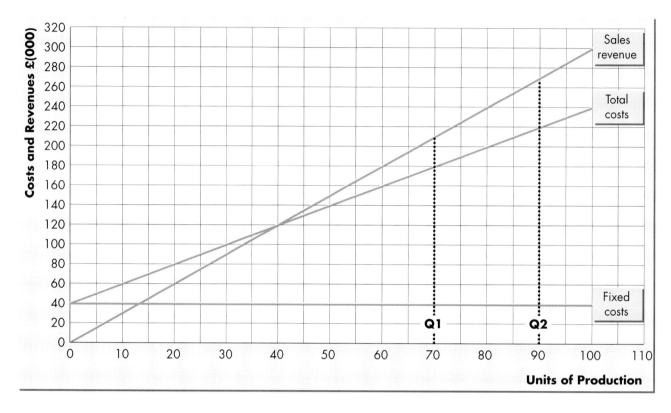

a) What is the break-even level of production? (1 mark)
b) What is the margin of safety? (1 mark)
c) How much profit will the company make if it decides to reduce the output to point Q1 on the chart? (1 mark)
d) What is the selling price per unit? (1 mark)
e) What are the fixed costs at the Q1 level of production? (1 mark)

CHAPTER 5

CASH FLOW FORECAST

Foundation and Intermediate

In this chapter you will learn how to construct a cash flow forecast. This will involve identifying the cash inflows and outflows associated with running a business. You will also learn how to check your cash flow forecast for accuracy.

> **KEY TERMS:**
>
> | | | |
> |---|---|---|
> | inflows | outflows | bank balance |
> | credit period | initial capital | bank loan |

All businesses need to make sure that they have enough money to meet both the **start-up costs** and the regular **running costs**.

A cash flow forecast is useful for a new business because it shows the estimated revenues and costs for a future time period, usually a year ahead.

> Definition – **initial capital** is the amount of money used to start a business (usually put into the new business's bank account).

If the **initial capital** is known, then future **bank** balances can be estimated to see if the business has enough money to make payments when they are due. If the cash flow forecast shows **bank balances** regularly below zero then it may be better:

- to try to increase revenue;

- to try to decrease costs; or

- not to produce the new product or service at all.

If the cash flow forecast shows occasional times when the **bank balance** becomes **overdrawn** it may be possible to arrange an **overdraft** for this period or to take out a **bank loan**.

> Definition – a **bank balance** is the amount of money in the business's bank account.

The bank will, however, charge interest on both an overdraft and a bank loan and these costs will add to the existing outflows.

> Definition – a **bank loan** is money borrowed from a bank.

A Cash Flow Forecast

Figure 3.5.1 Bank statement

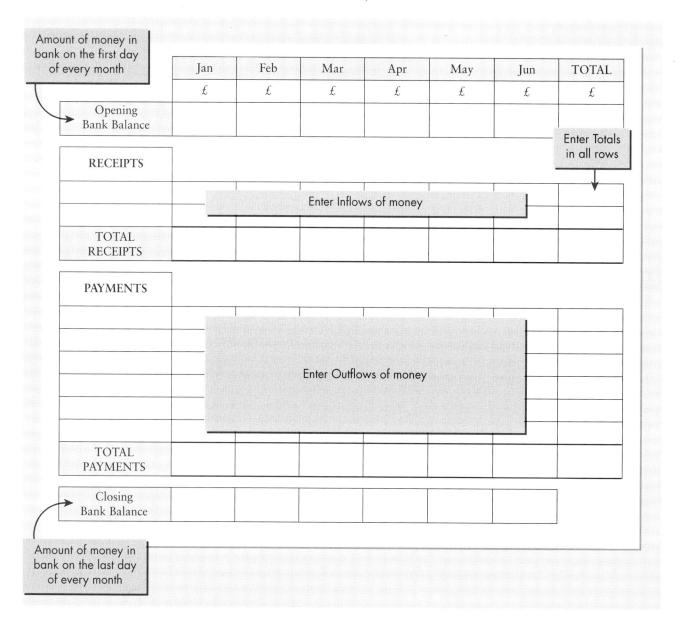

The importance of the cash flow forecast

Although it is called a *cash* flow forecast it does not record just the flows of coins and banknotes. The cash flow forecast will record any flows that will affect the bank account. Cheques received and paid out will also be recorded on the cash flow forecast.

A cash flow forecast will tell the business:

- when in the year money will be required;

- the amount of money that will be required.

The business can then take action to ensure that money is available to make payments when they are required.

Effects of incorrect forecasting

If the cash flow is not completed accurately, decisions based on this incorrect information may create problems for employees, customers, suppliers, providers of finance (e.g. banks) and the owners.

For example:

- Money may be borrowed from a lender when it is not required. This will involve unnecessary costs to the business in the form of interest payments to the lender.

- The business may unexpectedly run out of money. In this situation the bank may:
  - refuse to 'honour' cheques already issued (not make the payment to the supplier)
  - allow these cheques to be processed (make payments to the supplier) but charge a penal (extra high) rate of interest on the amount overdrawn because an overdraft had not been arranged beforehand.
  - write a letter to the business asking funds to be placed in the bank to cover the amount overdrawn. This will create an additional cost to the business since many banks will charge at least £15 for sending the letter.

If the business has insufficient money to pay suppliers, these suppliers may:

- withhold existing orders of goods until outstanding invoices have been paid.

- refuse to accept new orders from the business.

If suppliers stop supplying then the business has no products to sell and without sales profits cannot be made. Poor forecasting can, in some cases, lead to the failure of the business.

Calculating the 'Opening Bank Balance' and 'Closing Bank Balance'

The closing bank balance shows only how much money is in the bank. Money in the bank and profit are not the same thing.

Profit figures can be found only by constructing a **profit and loss statement**.

> ## The Closing Bank Balance is not the Profit!

Entering amounts when a credit period is given

Amounts are entered in the cash flow forecast only in the month in which they are received or *due to be* paid. In most cases it is a simple matter of entering payments or receipts in the month for which you have data. For example, if the wages for January are £3,000 then £3,000 would be entered in the January column where it meets the 'Wages' row.

Customers and suppliers, however, often give periods of credit which allow goods or services to be obtained, but not paid for, until one, two or even three months later.

> Definition – a **credit period** is the length of time between buying products and having to pay for them.

In these cases you must take care to enter the inflows or outflows only when the money is paid out to suppliers or due to be received from customers.

> Definition – **inflow** is a receipt of money ('money coming in').
>
> **outflow** is a payment of money ('money going out').

Figure 3.5.2 Inflows and outflows

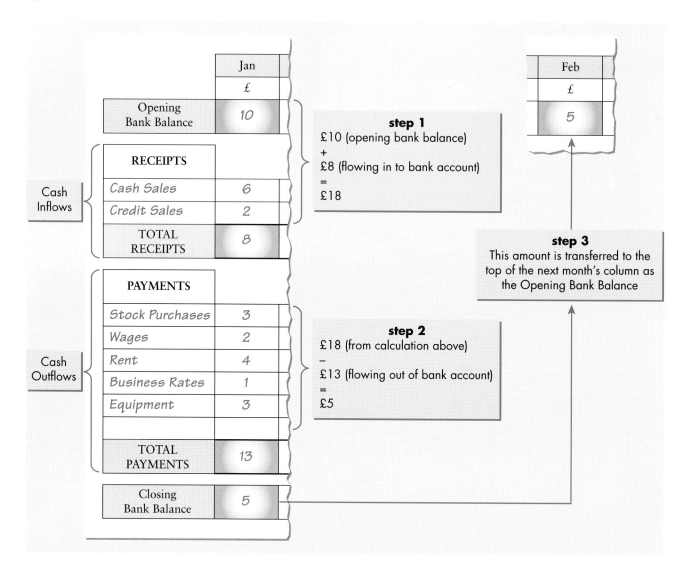

Figure 3.5.3 Credit sales/purchases

Worked Example 1

Customers are given 2 months' credit.

Question
If customers are sold £500 worth of goods in February,
when will the money from these sales actually be received?

Answer
Two months later – in April.

	Jan	Feb	Mar	Apr	May	Jun	TOTAL
	£	£	£	£	£	£	£
RECEIPTS		Goods sold in Feb		Customers pay in April			
Credit Sales				500			
TOTAL RECEIPTS							

Worked Example 2

Suppliers give 1 month's credit.

Stock purchases are as follows:

Jan	Feb	Mar	Apr	May	Jun
£100	£200	£300	£400	£500	£600

Question
When will these purchases have to be paid for?

Answer
In each case, payment will be made in the next month.

	Jan	Feb	Mar	Apr	May	Jun	TOTAL
	£	£	£	£	£	£	£
PAYMENTS							
Stock Purchases		100	200	300	400	500	
TOTAL PAYMENTS							

Note that the June purchases (£600) will not be paid for until July.
They do not, therefore, appear on the cash flow forecast.

Checking the Accuracy of the Cash Flow Forecast

When the cash flow forecast has been finished it can be checked for accuracy by looking at the final bank balance at the end of the last month of the cash flow forecast. This figure should be the same as the figure worked out from the calculation below and shown in Figure 3.5.4.

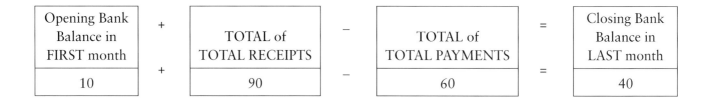

Opening Bank Balance in FIRST month	+	TOTAL of TOTAL RECEIPTS	−	TOTAL of TOTAL PAYMENTS	=	Closing Bank Balance in LAST month
10	+	90	−	60	=	40

Figure 3.5.4 Final bank balance

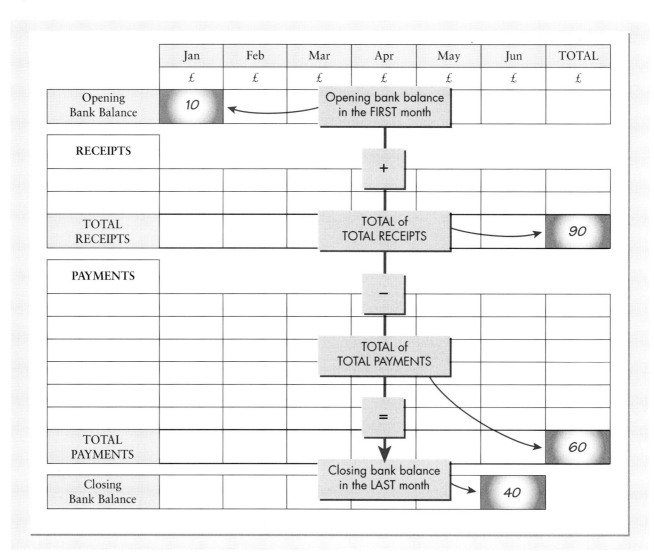

If the figure you calculate is not the same as the final bank balance showing in your completed cash flow forecast then the cash flow forecast contains an error.

1 Check each section by adding their totals both down and across. Again the totals should be the same.

2 Make sure that you have calculated the closing bank balance correctly for each month as described in Figure 3.5.4.

3 Check that you have transferred the closing bank balance at the end of every month to its corresponding position as the opening bank balance at the beginning of each following month.

Revision

Questions

1 Parvez Hussein plans to commence trading on 1st January 2002. He has initial capital of £15 000 which he puts into the business bank account.

- He estimates Sales to be as follows:

Jan.	Feb.	March	April
£800	£1600	£1800	£2000

- He estimates Purchases of Stock to be as follows:

Jan.	Feb.	March	April
£400	£800	£900	£1000

- Parvez will spend £60 each month on advertising.
- He has ordered a 'fire safe' for delivery in April. This will cost £400 and has to be paid for in March.
- Various running expenses are expected to be £100 for the first two months and thereafter about £200 per month.
- Parvez needs to buy and pay for office equipment in January at a cost of £8500.
- He intends to pay himself cash drawings of £200 per month.

Complete the cash flow forecast for Parvez Hussein.   (9 marks)

	JAN.	FEB.	MAR.	APR.	TOTAL
	£	£	£	£	£
Opening Balance at Bank					
RECEIPTS					
TOTAL RECEIPTS					
PAYMENTS					
TOTAL PAYMENTS					
Closing Balance at Bank					

2 Complete the entries in the boxes which allow you to check the cash flow forecast (above) for accuracy. (2 marks)

Opening Bank Balance in January	+		−		=	Closing Bank Balance in April
£						£

3 The following cash flow forecast is a summary of 6 months trading.

Note: All customers receive 2 months credit.

	JAN.	FEB.	MAR.	APR.	MAY	JUN.	TOTAL
Opening Balance at Bank	30 000	16 000	1 000	0	3 000	7 000	
Total Receipts	0	0	11 000	15 000	17 000	18 000	61 000
Total Payments	14 000	15 000	12 000	12 000	13 000	14 000	80 000
Closing Balance at Bank	16 000	1 000	0	3 000	7 000	11 000	

a) Check this cash flow forecast for accuracy by entering the appropriate 'checking totals' in the boxes below.

£	plus	£	minus	£	=	£

(2 marks)

b) Why should action be taken even though the cash flow forecast does not indicate an overdrawn balance? (1 mark)

c) Explain the action you would recommend. (1 mark)

d) What are the disadvantages of taking any action you propose in (c)? (1 mark)

e) Why are there no receipts of money in January or February, even though Sales were made to customers in these months? (1 mark)

f) The business received £18 000 in June from customers. In which month were goods sold to these customers? (1 mark)

g) How is the closing bank balance calculated at the end of each month? (1 mark)

h) How is the opening bank balance obtained in each of the months from February to June? (1 mark)

i) What is the advantage of using a spreadsheet to create a cash flow forecast? (1 mark)

CHAPTER 6

PROFIT AND LOSS STATEMENT

Foundation and Intermediate

In this chapter you will learn about the main elements of a profit and loss statement. In addition you will learn how to put these elements in the correct order, perform appropriate calculations and create a profit and loss statement.

> ### KEY TERMS:
>
> | | | | |
> |---|---|---|---|
> | cost of sales | expenses | gross profit | loss |
> | net profit | sales | | |

Most businesses operate in order to make profits for their owners. The profit and loss statement is designed to show the amount of profit or loss a business has made over a specified period of time. Most businesses will construct profit and loss statements at least once a year but they can be prepared more frequently.

The profit and loss statement lists the expected running costs and revenues (from selling goods or services) over a stated time period.

If the sales revenues are greater than the costs a profit will be made; if not, a loss will be incurred.

The profit and loss statement is concerned only with the running costs and revenues related to the buying and selling of goods or services. It does not consider, for example, the initial costs of buying vehicles or machinery since these items are not bought to sell to customers for profit but to use within the business.

Model Layout

A basic model of a profit and loss statement is shown on the next page. The values are small so that you can see the calculations easily.

> Definition – **gross profit** = sales – cost of goods sold.
>
> **sales** is the selling price of one unit × number of units sold.
>
> The **cost of goods sold** is the cost of stock or raw materials bought from suppliers which has been sold.
>
> > Note: the 'cost of goods sold' is also known as the 'cost of sales' or the 'cost of stock sold'.
>
> **net profit** is gross profit less expenses.
>
> > Note: if expenses are higher than gross profit then a 'net loss' will occur.
>
> **expenses** are regular ongoing costs which a business has in order to buy and sell products.

Figure 3.6.1 Profit and loss account

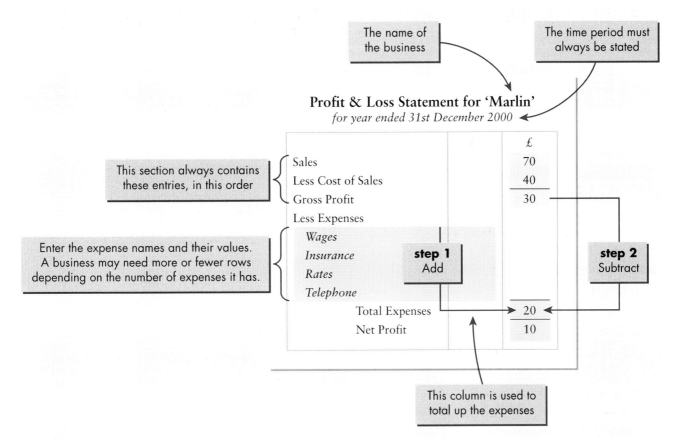

The name of the business

The time period must always be stated

Profit & Loss Statement for 'Marlin'
for year ended 31st December 2000

This section always contains these entries, in this order

Enter the expense names and their values. A business may need more or fewer rows depending on the number of expenses it has.

	£
Sales	70
Less Cost of Sales	40
Gross Profit	30
Less Expenses	
Wages	
Insurance	
Rates	
Telephone	
Total Expenses	20
Net Profit	10

step 1 Add

step 2 Subtract

This column is used to total up the expenses

In Chapter 3 you were told about running costs. In the profit and loss statement the running costs are divided into two sections as shown in the diagram below:

Figure 3.6.2 Running costs

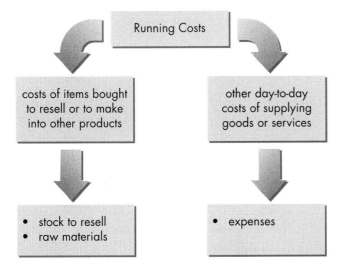

Running Costs

costs of items bought to resell or to make into other products

other day-to-day costs of supplying goods or services

- stock to resell
- raw materials

- expenses

Expenses

The list of expenses will vary between organisations but most will have some or all of the typical expenses listed below.

- rent
- rates
- wages
- salaries
- postage
- stationery
- fuel bills (gas, electricity, water)
- telephone charges
- advertising costs
- marketing costs
- insurance premiums
- interest on loans
- distribution costs
- administration costs

Calculating the Gross Profit

(refer to Marlin's profit and loss account)

If the goods bought from suppliers are sold to customers at a higher price, then a gross profit will be made.

Goods bought from suppliers for £40 were sold for £70

Sales	=	£70
Cost of sales	=	**£40**
Gross profit	=	£30

So gross profit is the difference between the value of sales made to customers and the cost of those products or services bought from suppliers.

Calculating the Net Profit

(refer to Marlin's profit and loss account)

In order to sell their products, businesses also incur other costs called expenses which will reduce this gross profit. Subtracting these other costs will leave the net profit.

Gross profit	=	£30
Expenses	=	**£20**
Net profit	=	£10

If the expenses are higher than the gross profit then the business will make a net loss.

If a business continues to make a loss it cannot survive.

Using Computers

All the documents mentioned in the previous chapters can be prepared by hand using a calculator and a pen. They are, however, more easily and accurately prepared using a spreadsheet program found on most business computers.

Advantages

- 'What if' situations can be examined. This means that you can change a cell of a spreadsheet to see the effect this change has on other cells of the spreadsheet. For example, you could change the forecast receipts of a cash flow forecast to see the effect of this change on the bank balance at the end of the year.

- Alterations can be made without the need to recalculate figures manually.

- Access to updating of files is faster.

- Less storage space is required.

- Work can be password protected, thereby increasing security.

- Accounts and related records can be updated automatically.

- Calculations are likely to be more accurate if performed by the computer application.

- Several users at different locations/workstations can have shared access to information.

- Transmission of data is made easier via network links.

- Financial documents can be prepared automatically, saving time and making errors less likely.

- Reduces the need to copy transactions manually into related records.

- Management information is always readily available.

Disadvantages

- Time consuming to set up.

- There is usually a need to keep manual and computerised record systems running together when the computerised system is first installed in case of computer problems.

- Lack of staff expertise.

- Need for staff training.

- Cost of new system.

- Cost of staff training.

Revision

Questions

1 Which of the following items are expenses?
   a) stationery
   b) sales
   c) electricity
   d) stock of goods
   e) stamps
   (1 mark)

2 What is the correct heading for a profit and loss statement for Halco covering the period 1st December 1999 to 30th November 2000?
   a) Profit and loss statement for Halco for period ending 30th November 2000.
   b) Profit and loss statement for Halco for year ending 30th November 2000.
   c) Profit and loss statement for Halco as at 30th November 2000.
   d) Profit and loss statement for Halco for year as at 30th November 2000.
   (1 mark)

3 Grogan bought goods for £50 and sold them for £90.
   What were the sales?
   What was the cost of sales?
   What was the gross profit?
   (1 mark)

4 Portcal made a gross profit of £200 and incurred expenses covering the same period of £40. What was the net profit?
   (1 mark)

5 (i) Which of the following items will not appear in the profit and loss statement?
      a) gas charges
      b) office equipment
      c) cost of goods sold
      d) insurance premiums
      (1 mark)

   (ii) Explain why the item you chose will not appear.
      (1 mark)

6   The following table relates to information available to Fendale on December 2000 at the end of a financial year.

	£
Salaries	15000
Heating and lighting costs	2000
Insurance premiums	1800
Interest on loans	500
Advertising costs	1200
Stock purchase costs	30000
Sales of goods	90000

Copy out and complete the profit and loss statement for Fendale by filling in the boxes.   (5 marks)

Profit and loss statement for

	£	£
Sales		
Cost of sales		
Gross profit		
Less expenses		
Net profit		

7   The following table relates to information for the financial year available to Rombical on November 30th 2000.

	£
Wages	1200
Rates	700
Telephone charges	500
Sales	8000
Marketing costs	600
Distribution expenses	400
Stock purchased	5000

Construct the profit and loss statement for Rombical.   (5 marks)

Revision Test

1 Laramco is a business which sells a range of products and services to the public and expects, in its first year, to receive the following revenues from its activities:

Food sales	£14 million
Household goods	£16 million
Insurance	£6 million
Legal advice	£2 million

How much revenue does it expect to get from selling **products**?   (1 mark)

2 Some of the costs for a new business are listed below.

Wages and salaries
Delivery vans purchase costs
Business rates
Office equipment
Stocks of goods to resell
Electricity bills
Insurance bills
Machinery purchase costs

Select from the above those costs which are usually known as 'start-up' costs .   (3 marks)

3 A manufacturing company has some costs as listed below.

Bank interest
Business rates
Raw materials
Wages and salaries
Advertising

State the cost which would apply only to a manufacturing business.   (1 mark)

4 Carmen Din plans to commence trading on 1st January 2001. She has initial capital of £2,500 which she puts into the business bank account.

(i) Carmen estimates sales of stock to be as follows:

January	February	March	April
£800	£1600	£1800	£2000

(ii) She estimates purchases of stock to be as follows:

January	February	March	April
£400	£800	£900	£1000

(iii) Carmen estimates spending £100 each month on telephone charges.

(iv) She has ordered a photocopier costing £800 which will be delivered in April. The photocopy company expect payment in March.

(v) Various general expenses are expected to be £300 for the first month and thereafter about £200 per month.

(vi) Office equipment will be bought and paid for in January at a cost of £1,000.

(vii) She will pay wages to a part-time employee of £200 per month.

Construct a cash flow forecast for this business for the period January–April. (9 marks)

5 The following cash flow forecast is a summary of six months' trading for Ramato. All customers receive one month's credit.

	Jan	Feb	Mar	Apr	May	Jun	Total
Opening balance at bank	4000	1975	(1250)	25	800	2075	7625
Total receipts	0	1000	6000	5500	5000	6000	23500
Total payments	2025	4225	4725	4725	3725	3725	23150
Closing balance at bank	1975	(1250)	25	800	2075	4350	

a) Check this cash flow forecast for accuracy by entering the appropriate figures in the boxes below.

$$\boxed{} \quad + \quad \boxed{} \quad - \quad \boxed{} \quad = \quad £4,350$$

(2 marks)

b) In which month may Ramato not be able to pay its debts? (1 mark)
c) Why may Ramato be wise to arrange an overdraft in that month? (1 mark)
d) Explain any effects of incorrect forecasting. (3 marks)
e) Although the business is due to start trading in January no income will be received until February. Why is this? (1 mark)

6 Spreadsheets are often used to create cash flow forecasts. Explain two advantages of linking the cells of the spreadsheet by formulas. (2 marks)

Questions 7–9 relate to Framlin, a business that will be set up to make and sell Christmas crackers.

7 Read through the following text which contains details of some of the costs of the business.

• The crackers will be made by people working at home. They will be paid according to how many crackers they produce.
• Raw materials bought to make the crackers include paper, explosive 'snaps', card and plastic toys.
• Office staff will be paid a regular salary.
• Salespeople will be recruited to sell the crackers to corner shops and their wages will depend on how many crackers they sell.
• Business rates will have to be paid to the council.

Classify each of the accounts from the text above as either a fixed cost or a variable cost by placing a tick √ in the appropriate column of the Cost Classification Sheet below:

Cost Classification Sheet

Summary of accounts to be classified	Fixed costs	Variable costs
Cracker makers wages		
Office salaries		
Business rates		
Raw materials		
Salespeople's wages		

(2 marks)

8   The costs of the business have been estimated as follows:
Fixed costs per week: £300;
Variable costs: £0.60 per cracker.
Each cracker is expected to sell for £1.00.

$$\text{Break-even point} = \frac{\text{fixed costs}}{\text{(selling price less variable cost per unit)}}$$

a) Using the formula above, substitute the appropriate amounts.   (1 mark)

$$\text{Break-even point} = \frac{£}{£ \qquad \text{less} \qquad £}$$

b) Calculate the number of crackers that need to be sold per week for the business to break even. (You must attach the correct units to your answer.)   (1 mark)

9   If the price of the crackers was increased to £1.10:
a) How many crackers per week would need to be sold for the business to break even? (1 mark)
b) State the profit or loss if 400 crackers per week are sold.   (1 mark)

10 The table below shows the expected costs and revenues at different sales levels for Amathist – a business producing garden benches.

	Number of benches sold			
	0	25	50	100
Fixed costs	6,000	6,000	6,000	6,000
Variable costs	0	500	1,000	2,000
Total costs	6,000	6,500	7,000	8,000
Sales revenue	0	2,500	5,000	10,000

Use the data given in the table to:

a) plot the fixed cost line and label it;

b) plot the total cost line and label it;

c) plot the sales revenue line and label it. (4 marks)

d) Identify the break-even point and label it. (1 mark)

11 Jonto has drawn up a break-even chart based on a forecast of 80,000 units produced and sold during the coming year. This is shown by point Q2 on the chart.

Figure 3.6.3 Break-even chart for Jonto

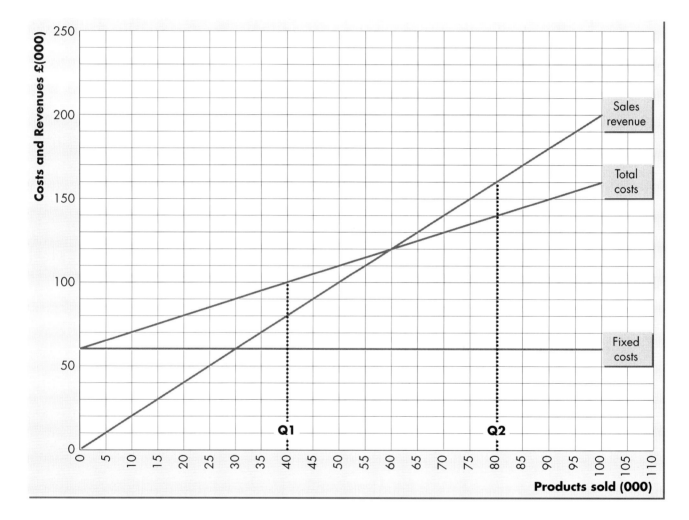

a) What are the costs and revenues at the break-even level of products sold? (1 mark)

b) What profit does the company expect to make in the coming year? (1 mark)

c) What is the margin of safety? (1 mark)

d) How much profit or loss would the company make if the level of products sold reached point Q1? (1 mark)

e) What is the selling price of one product? (1 mark)

f) How many products are sold when fixed costs and total costs are the same? (1 mark)

12 Barra has drawn up an estimate of costs and revenues for the year ended 31st December 1999.

	£
Wages	50,000
Heating and lighting costs	2,000
Telephone charges	3,000
Insurance costs	4,000
Stock purchase costs	40,000
Sales of goods	160,000

Complete the profit and loss statement for Barra by filling in the boxes.   (5 marks)

Profit and loss statement for

	£	£
Sales		
Cost of sales		
Gross profit		
Less expenses		
Net profit		

13 Documents will flow between buyer and seller.

Identify the name of the missing document.   (7 marks)

a) A . . . . ? . . . . is sent to a supplier to order goods or services.

b) A . . . . ? . . . . is packed with the goods to be sent to a customer.

c) The customer fills in a . . . . ? . . . . to record the condition of the goods sent by the supplier.

d) If faulty goods are returned to the supplier the customer will expect to receive a . . . . ? . . . . from the supplier.

e) A . . . . ? . . . . is sent to the customer at the end of every month listing all transactions affecting the account and reminding the customer of the balance of the account to be paid.

f) A . . . . ? . . . . is completed, signed and posted to a supplier in payment for goods or services.

g) A . . . . ? . . . . is enclosed with payment to show which invoices are being paid.

14 a) Why should the purchase order, invoice and goods received note be checked against each other before the accounts department pays an invoice? (3 marks)

15 Bramcote has received the following purchase order from Langto Ltd:

PURCHASE ORDER No 45781	
Langto Ltd 47 Low Street, Pim, Lerts LU47 4RE Tel 01137856954	
To Bramcote Unit 6, Muss Industrial Est Greens, Brops BR3 7TY	
Please supply	Catalogue Reference
2 typist chairs @ agreed price of £24.50 each 3 footrests @ agreed price of £3.95 each Delivery: As soon as possible	TC047 FO16

Complete the invoice which would be prepared for Langto based on the information given in the purchase order. (4 marks)

SALES INVOICE   No: 001274

Bramcote Unit 6, Muss Industrial Est Greens, Brops BR3 7TY

Tel: 0119873 547581
VAT Registration No 76 346 24378652

To:

Your Purchase Order No:

Quantity	Description	Catalogue Ref	Price per Item	Total Price
			+VAT @ 17.5%	
			Total to Pay	

16 If Langto receives some unordered, unwanted goods from Bramcote:
   a) Which document will be incorrect?
   b) What action will Bramcote take to correct the error?   (1 mark)

17 Explain three advantages of using a computerised system to generate accounting
   documents and records.   (3 marks)

18 Explain the disadvantages of replacing a manual accounting system with a
   computerised accounting system.   (3 marks)

UNIT 4

PEOPLE IN BUSINESS

CHAPTER 1

WHO ARE THESE PEOPLE?

Foundation and Intermediate

In this chapter you will learn about different jobs in different kinds of organisations, and about the skills and experience needed to do these jobs, as well as about the importance of job roles in a business.

Introduction

You already know that there are many different kinds of businesses, the vast majority of which are privately owned. Some are very large and employ thousands of people.

An example of a large business organisation is Marks & Spencer, a retail firm in the private service sector. Today, Marks & Spencer sells a variety of goods, including household goods and a large range of food, but in its early days it sold only clothing. This **diversification** is quite common. The large food supermarket chain Asda even has its own designer clothes – label George – and most of the other big supermarkets also sell many items which, strictly speaking, do not belong in food stores.

Definition – **diversification** is the introduction of new goods produced, or sold, by a business organisation.

Another example of a large business is the petrol giant British Petroleum (BP), which is also a private business. British Petroleum operates in all three **industrial sectors**: primary, secondary and tertiary (see Unit 2 Chapter 2).

Figure 4.1.1   The three industrial sectors

In the public sector, there is the British Broadcasting Corporation (BBC). It is financed by television licence fees, and has many thousands of employees.

On the other hand, many businesses are much smaller. Some have only a few employees, or even just one. The window cleaner who comes to your house every few weeks is often a 'one man' business – a **sole trader**. This type of business is described in Unit 2 Chapter 1.

In a small business, such as a newsagent or a greengrocer, one person, the owner, usually has to do several jobs personally, even if there are other people working in the business.

Let us look at the various jobs which the person who runs the local newsagent's is likely to have to do:

- place regular orders for newspapers and magazines;

- order other items sold in the shop, such as ice cream, chocolates, soft drinks and stationery;

- get up and open the shop around 5.30 in the morning to sort the newspapers into piles ready for delivery;

- make sure that each paper boy and girl has the right papers;

- if one of them does not arrive, the owner might have to do the delivery himself, rather than upset the customers;

- serve behind the counter all day every day;

- deal with sales representatives;

- after closing time, check the stock and work on day-to-day accounts.

We can see that the owner of such a shop must be a Jack or Jill of all trades, and be able to carry out a number of different tasks. Also, nowadays most such shops are open seven days a week, and many do not close till 6 or 7 in the evening.

Activity

Do you know someone who runs his or her own small business? Find out how many hours per week they spend working, and make a list of all the things which they must do, then compare it with the jobs of the newsagent listed above.

Case Study: the Young Veterinary Partnership

In 1950, Mr Michael Young bought an existing practice, situated in the residential centre of Ealing, West London. Today, the Young Partnership is well established, and has four clinics; in addition to the original one, there are two others, serving other West London locations, as well as a franchise in a PETsMART Store, acquired in 1992.

After the retirement of the founder, the practice was taken over by his son, Mr Anthony Young. Recently, he has taken on a partner, and changed the status of the practice into a partnership, with himself as senior partner. The practice deals mainly with small domestic animals and is required to provide 24-hour cover in case of emergencies. This means that the veterinary surgeons work weekend and night rotas.

Management

The running of the practice is divided equally between the two partners, who rely on regular meetings as a means of efficient communication. One of the partners is in charge of staff recruitment, while the other looks after the financial and administrative side of the business.

The Head Nurse line-manages the veterinary nurses, and the Head Receptionist is in charge of the reception staff. Their line manager is the junior partner.

Employees

- 6 veterinary surgeons (this includes both the partners)
- 11 nurses (4 fully qualified)
- 5 receptionists (full-time)
- 2 receptionists (part-time)
- 1 administrative manager
- 2 Saturday helpers

In addition, holiday locums are employed when needed and some administrative and receptionist duties are carried out by the wives of the partners, as is quite often the case in family businesses.

Hours and conditions of work

Because of the requirement to provide round-the-clock service, all staff work rotating shifts. The nurses work a 37.5-hour week, as do the full-time receptionists, with part-time workers being employed on a pro-rata basis. As already mentioned, both the partners also work as veterinary surgeons and this, together with their other duties, brings their average work load to about 56–65 hours a week.

All staff are paid their salaries by bank transfer, and the holiday entitlement for full-time employees is 4 weeks a year.

Training and job opportunities

- Partly qualified nurses receive on-the-job training in the practice, and also attend Berkshire College of Agriculture on a day release basis.
- Qualified nurses can gain additional qualifications, such as surgical nurse, and can become practice managers.
- Veterinary surgeons can progress through specialisation.

Advertising and publicity

The partnership does advertise in the *Yellow Pages*, but mostly it relies on word of mouth. Its steady growth can be explained by its well-established reputation in the West London area.

Difficulties and future plans

The main difficulty is, as already mentioned, the restraint on growth because of the need to provide 24-hour cover. Very strict COSHH (Control of Substances Hazardous to Health) regulations apply to the practice and are exceedingly time consuming. The practice is well regarded and doing well in its present size and structure. The partners hope that in the future they will be able to bring in more specialisms, in addition to the generalist service now provided.

We have mentioned very large businesses and have looked in some detail at small ones. There are, of course, a number of business organisations which are neither tiny nor huge. These are called medium-sized firms, and can employ from about 50 to 100 workers.

Medium-sized businesses cannot be run like the very small ones. The bigger the business, the more necessary it becomes for different people to do different jobs, and for the business to have a clear **management structure**, so that everyone knows who is responsible for what, and also to whom each person is answerable.

> Definition – **a management structure** is the framework of inter-connecting management job roles in a business organisation.

In a large organisation the management structure is more formal and each person has a clearly defined job that needs special qualifications, experience and training.

Case Study: Ultra Electronics

Ultra Electronics is an international group of businesses specialising in the design and manufacture of products for aerospace markets worldwide, as well as providing specialist equipment for ships and submarines, and for land fighting vehicles.

Ultra was founded in 1920, and has gone through many changes over the years. In 1977, Ultra was bought by Dowty which was itself acquired by the TI Group in 1992.

In 1993, as a result of a management buy-out, Ultra Electronics Ltd was formed and, thanks to good management, has since gone from strength to strength.

Ultra Electronics Holdings plc was floated on the Stock Exchange in 1996 and in the same year the company was awarded the Queen's Award for Technology.

The company has been growing steadily over the last few years, and now has businesses in Canada and the USA, as well as the UK. Currently, Ultra has 13 sites and employs over 2000 people. Of these 823 work in Engineering, 861 in Production, while Administration and Sales account for the rest.

Both sales and profits increased in the years 1994–1998.

Among its customers are such very important organisations as Airbus Industries, the Ministry of Defence, British Aerospace and Rolls Royce.

The management structure of the Ultra Group is a flat one, with Head Office consisting of only 8 people. Authority and responsibility are given to the divisions, one of which is described below.

Figure 4.1.3 Pyramid structure of Ultra Electronics

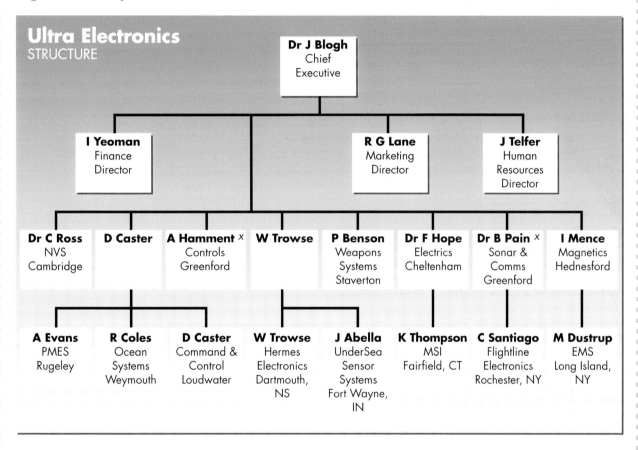

The Controls Division

The Controls Division, situated in Greenford, West London, is not typical of Ultra as a whole, because it is concerned with Civil Aerospace products, rather than Defence Electronics.

The Managing Director is in charge of the division and runs it with little interference from Head Office. He has to work in accordance with the agreed strategy and to an agreed budget, and the aim of the division is always to 'meet or beat' the budget.

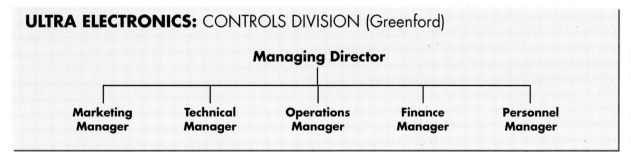

The MD's role

- to win new business (this involves a lot of travel)
- to develop new products (in this industry, this takes 4–5 years)
- to ensure support for existing products (repairs, spares)
- to ensure the high level of quality control which is vital in Ultra's business
- working with his five heads of departments

ULTRA ELECTRONICS: Functions and responsibilities

Managing Director

- Strategy
- Top level financial performance
- Organising the top team

Marketing Manager	**Technical Manager**	**Operations Manager**	**Finance Manager**	**Personnel Manager**
• New business • Existing business Time scale: Typically – 12 to 18 months	• New product development Time scale: Typically – 4 to 5 months	• Existing products "keep wheels turning" Time scale: Typically – 40 years	• Financial and Management Accounts and Systems	• Staff – people issues

---

The MD ensures that he is in regular contact with all his workers, which contributes to employees' interest and loyalty.

Workforce

The Controls Division is organised into a **manufacturing cells structure**.

The workers used to be allocated to separate sections. Now the manufacturing cells system means that workers can be shifted from one cell to another. This gives them more interest in the job, and leads to job enrichment. Working closely together, workers learn from each other, and they acquire additional skills. This leads to greater flexibility.

About 95% of the workers are full-time. All undergo a three-month trial period, and have six-monthly reviews. Training and retraining are carried out as required, and are the responsibility of managers and supervisors, supported by the division's Personnel Manager. In 1999 the training budget was set at £160,000. This means an average of $3\frac{1}{2}$ days training per person, apart from the engineers who each receive on average 5 days' training.

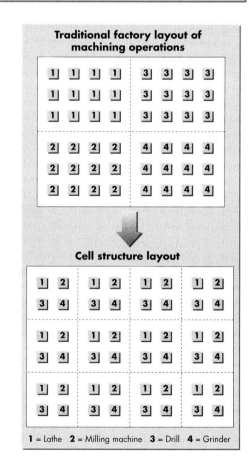

Traditional factory layout of machining operations

Cell structure layout

1 = Lathe   **2** = Milling machine   **3** = Drill   **4** = Grinder

Because many production processes are semi-automated, the division no longer needs to have workers on regular round-the-clock shifts but workers do additional shifts when required. All employees are willing to be flexible with respect to working patterns when customer demand requires it.

The division, as is normal within Ultra Group, is not unionised. It has a very low worker turnover, indicating good management–worker relationships.

Payments
All workers are paid a monthly salary by direct debit. Depending on the division's financial performance, all employees qualify for an annual bonus. They also receive free shares in the company and have an option to join a share save scheme in which additional shares can be bought at below market price.

Roles in Different Types of Organisations

Just as there are many different kinds of businesses, there are also many different kinds and levels of jobs within each business organisation. **Job roles** make it clear what individual people do. For example, every business has a **manager** but while a small business might have only one, who will certainly have to know how to do a bit of everything, a large one will have a number of people in managerial positions.

> Definition – a **manager** is a person who directs or controls an organisation, e.g. a company, or a department of a company. There are junior, middle and senior managers.

The word 'manager' does not have to appear in the job title of a person who carries out the duties of a manager. Some business organisations actually avoid using this term, and call those who do the job 'team leaders' or 'executive officers'. On the other hand, there might be those with the word 'manager' in their job title who do not carry out the functions of a manager. It is important to remember that it is the content of the job that makes a person a manager, not simply the job title. A little later in this chapter we shall be looking more closely at what a manager does.

In a manufacturing firm such as Ultra Electronics, the company in our case study on page 190, a person with junior management responsibilities is called a **supervisor**.

Supervisors manage a group of **operatives** who carry out the **production** of a business. In some factories there are also **foremen** or **charge hands** who manage small groups of operatives, and who themselves are managed by the supervisor.

> Definition – **production** used to mean the making of goods in a factory but today it also includes the provision of services.

A business also needs **general staff**, such as secretaries, warehouse staff and drivers, without whom it could not function.

For a business to be successful, whatever its size, the separate departments must work smoothly and efficiently together. This is why, in order to understand how such an organisation works, we must investigate all its parts in detail. We need to know the **function** of each department and how it is linked to the other parts of the organisation. (This topic was dealt with in detail in Unit 2.)

The best way to see how the different departments are linked is by an **organisational chart**. In some businesses the structure is **flat** (in other words, there are very few levels of management); in others it is **tall** (with more management levels).

A tall organisation

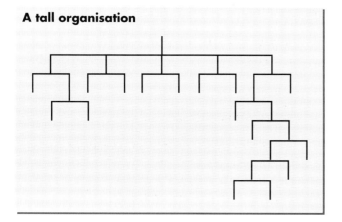

A flat organisation

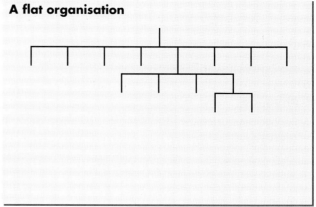

Page 197 shows five departments, each controlled by a manager who has responsibility for one area, or function, of the business. All departments work towards achieving the company's common objective of making and selling goods. It is the **managing** director's duty to see that this is done as profitably as possible. The **board of directors** is collectively answerable to the **shareholders** (who are the owners of the business) for the continuing **profitability** and success of the business.

Case Study: Better Buildings Ltd

Better Buildings Ltd was started 12 years ago by two brothers, David and Eddy Small. They shared the work between them, and specialised in high quality conversions, residential and domestic.

Because of the good quality of their work, the brothers found that they did not have to advertise – new work came their way by word of mouth.

Two years ago, they decided to try and expand their business. They also changed its legal status from a partnership to a private limited company.

David and Eddy became directors of the new company, and several members of their family bought shares in the new business.

Recently, the brothers have taken on several new jobs, and have found that the lack of a proper management structure means that, while both of them are working very hard, they are often duplicating each other's duties. In addition, since they now employ about 50 people, it is impossible for them to supervise everyone personally.

The time has come, they have decided, to draw up a management structure which will establish precisely the job roles of:

- each of the directors;
- support staff (they employ an administrative assistant, a secretary and two drivers);
- people in charge of teams of operatives (the firm employs electricians, plumbers, tilers, painters and decorators).

General Job Roles

Broadly speaking, the main roles in an organisation can be illustrated as follows:

It does not matter whether the business is in the primary, secondary or tertiary sector, the same divisions still apply.

Directors

In the private sector, the chief executive (the person at the very top of the business) is referred to as the **managing director**. He or she has overall control of the company. It is his or her job to make decisions and to ensure that these decisions are carried out with the support of a team of senior executives who normally are members of a **board of directors**.

> Definition – a **board of directors** is a group of senior directors who run a private or a public limited company.

Among other duties, the managing director's job involves:

- the day-to-day running of all aspects of the business;

- planning for the future;

- dealing with customers and staff;

- chairing meetings, mainly with heads of departments;

- dealing with any unexpected problems as they occur;

- acting as a referee between the demands of the various departments, which are often in conflict.

In the public sector, the structure is similar. In a school or college, for example, the head teacher or the principal acts as a managing director, and is helped and assisted in his or her various duties and responsibilities by the heads of departments and the board of governors.

It is the managing director, the head teacher or the principal who will decide, together with the heads of departments, on **strategic** issues.

> Definition – **strategic** means concerned with a long-term plan of action in a business organisation. Those senior managers who are engaged in strategic planning are not usually involved in the day-to-day running of the business.

The board of directors has a **chairperson** who is chosen by the other directors. In smaller companies, the managing director often fills this position.

Under the leadership of a managing director, directors are those people charged with the overall control of a private company. They decide the company goals, and how those goals should be achieved. In particular, they have the responsibility for ensuring that the company is profitable.

To become more profitable, the business should:

- sell more goods/services;
- earn a larger profit on sales;
- save money and reduce wastage;
- increase productivity;
- recruit well-motivated and efficient staff;
- provide staff with adequate conditions and training;
- keep customers and clients happy.

The above objectives are all long-term ones and have to be decided by top management. They are called **strategic** objectives. Once the strategic objectives have been set, the ways in which they can be achieved are decided. Each departmental head will know what his or her department should be doing in the next period, usually one **financial** year. These aims are called **operational** objectives, and managers must work with their teams, and also in co-operation with other departments, to try and put them into practice.

Definition – **operational** means carrying out the objectives of a business plan.

A **team** is a group of people who are organised to work together to achieve an objective, e.g. a production team or a sales team.

Managers

Managers work under the general direction of directors.

A manager is the person in charge of a part of a business. Here are two quotations which describe the role of a manager (they could just as well apply to directors who are, in reality, senior managers):

'Deciding what should be done and then getting other people to do it.' (Rosemary Stewart)

'Deciding what to do, and then getting it done through effective use of resources.' (Michael Armstrong)

It is clear from these quotations that managers make plans about what the business has to do, and also make decisions about the present and future direction of the business. This is done within their particular area of control. They organise the **resources** of the business. Every business has resources, and one of these resources is people. This is generally recognised as the most important resource, because no business could function without people, but it is not the only one. Other **resources** controlled by managers are money (capital) and materials.

When we look at Ultra Electronics (see page 190), which is, as you know, a manufacturing company, we see that it has four resources:

- people – all those working for Ultra;
- capital – which it needs to carry out its business;
- materials – in this case, metals, plastics and electronic components which are assembled to make the finished products;
- machinery, equipment and buildings.

On the other hand, the Young Veterinary Partnership does not manufacture anything but provides a service for its clients. The partnership has the following resources:

- people;
- capital;
- equipment, etc.

but not materials.

You will see from the organisational chart on page 197 that managers often have different titles and do different jobs.

- A **general manager** looks after the whole business and, in most firms, is answerable to the managing director.
- A **departmental manager**, e.g. a production manager, is responsible for a part or section of the business. Later in this chapter we will examine the duties and responsibilities of a production manager in more detail.

In a large business, which has several departments, there might be six or seven managers.

For example, Ultra Electronics Ltd has a number of managers (see the chart on page 197). Each manager is responsible for the work of the department and for the people who work in it.

It is important, of course, that all the managers work well together as a **team**. They have to meet regularly and understand exactly what information they must get from the other departments, and what information they must pass on to the **supervisors** and **operatives**. This is more difficult in a large business, such as Ultra, than in a smaller one like the Young Veterinary Partnership which has only two partners who are also managers.

The Production Manager

In a manufacturing company such as Ultra Electronics, the production manager is responsible for organising the most efficient use of the production operatives and machines that, together, make the company's products. Assisted by production-line supervisors and others, the

production manager oversees the processing of raw materials and components into finished products to be sold to the company's customers. He or she is responsible to the production director.

Why is proper maintenance of machines of great importance in a manufacturing firm?

Here are some of the production manager's many duties:

- meeting production targets on time;
- consistently achieving quality standards;
- making efficient use of staff, machinery and materials by planning working arrangements;
- making sure that production machinery is maintained in good order;
- supervising production staff, such as:
  production engineers
  jig and tool makers
  maintenance engineers
  quality control engineers and line inspectors
  production supervisors and charge-hands
  production operatives

The Marketing Manager

AND TOP OF
THE CHARTS
THIS WEEK
IS.........

The marketing manager is in charge of the marketing department and the people who work there. In a large company, the marketing manager will be responsible to a marketing director; in a smaller company, to the managing director.

The main function of the marketing department is to find out the customers' current needs and wants, and to satisfy them. This might not seem very complicated but it is difficult, particularly as other marketing departments in firms with which the company is in competition are all trying to do this too.

In addition, the marketing department is also expected to **predict** the needs and wants of its existing customers and potential customers. This means trying to forecast what is going to happen in the future. It is of very great importance to try and get these predictions right most of the time. Failure to do so might mean great losses to the business, sometimes even leading to its closure.

A successful marketing prediction

The Marketing Department of B Sky B was right when it predicted that British TV viewers would happily pay to watch big sporting occasions and new films on television. Perhaps the BBC's marketing executives have not been quite so smart on this occasion. The result is that the size of BBC audiences is falling, while B Sky B's audiences are increasing.   .

The marketing manager is responsible for:

- the sales and marketing of the organisation's products or services;

- the strategic marketing plans;

- the organisation's market research programmes and information database;

- the organisation's promotion and sales campaigns;

- the budget of the department.

The people for whom the manager is responsible will include:

- sales manager(s);

- market researchers and research analysts (the researchers provide the information while the analysts examine it carefully and draw conclusions from their findings);

- product brand executives (in large companies there is a person in charge of each separate product or group of products);

- sales representatives;

- advertising manager.

Figure 4.1.4 Marketing manager advertisement

GLOBAL MARKETING MANAGER

Supplying the Paper Industry

c. £45,000 + Incentivised package   Flexible location

Rare opportunity created by the merger of two global market leaders generating a unique product range with the potential to dominate world markets.

➤ THE POSITION

- Devising and driving strategy for growth. Capitalising on freshly created opportunity to enhance product portfolio and supply right product to right market.
- Grasping ownership of the challenge. Introducing newly merged business to its markets.
- Migrating from regional to global marketing. Abandoning product push in favour of market pull.
- Working closely with colleagues and customers. Refining products and approach. Travelling widely to major global markets.

➤ THE CANDIDATE

- Highly organised, confident marketeer. In-depth knowledge of paper manufacturing process and industry.
- Exceptional relationship builder. Able to lead, influence and persuade others.
- Experience of global marketing. Culturally aware. Scandinavian or German languages an advantage.
- Analytical with technical understanding and wider business acumen. Perhaps a Masters in Marketing or MBA.

Please reply in writing quoting reference number B905/ST enclosing a copy of your CV and giving full salary details to the address below:

Hanover Fox International,
160 Aztec West,
Bristol BS32 4TG.

HANOVER FOX
INTERNATIONAL

Tel: (01454) 617555
Fax: (01454) 618222
hanoverfox.brstl@dial.pipex.com

Executive Search & Selection

The above advertisement shows the experience and qualities required of candidates for the position of global marketing manager.

Activity

Work with a friend. This task will be easier for you if you like watching commercial television, and do not switch off or go away during the breaks! Make a list of the commercials that you have seen on television in the last two weeks. Choose one group of commercials (e.g. all those advertising hair care products, cleaning materials, or food).

How many of the advertisements in your chosen group:

i) are for a new product?

ii) advertise a well-established product?

iii) would encourage you to buy the new product because of the commercial?

The accounts/finance manager

The manager of this department supervises all matters concerning the financial affairs of the business. The department is usually split into two sections.

1 Financial accounts

The person in charge of this section is the **financial accounting manager**. The section which he or she manages monitors and records all the incoming and outgoing cash and credit transactions of the business. At the end of each **financial year** an outside firm of chartered accountants will audit (check) the accounts produced by this section. From these accounts, the chartered accountant will produce a **profit and loss account** and a **balance sheet**. The first is a statement of how well the business has done in the past year, in other words, it gives the amount of profit or loss made. The second informs the owners of the business how much it would be worth if, for example, it were to be sold.

2 Management accounts

The **management accounts manager** is in charge of the section that concentrates on analysing figures provided by the various departments of the business. The section is also responsible for making sure that up-to-date financial data is always available to the management team. This information is essential in helping managers to make decisions concerning the running of the business. Directors and shareholders also need to be able to see this information.

Among the management accounts manager's responsibilities are:

- calculating product costs for the marketing and production departments;
- monitoring the financial performance of the production department;
- developing costing systems for all departments;
- setting, together with other departmental managers, budgets and forecasts for their departments;
- supervising personnel in the accounts office

(these will include specialist accountants, credit controllers and accounts and payroll clerks).

The department is also legally responsible for keeping accurate accounts of all the tax, national insurance and pension deductions handled by the business on behalf of the government.

This advertisement shows the qualifications, experience and qualities that a successful candidate for the position of finance manager must have.

Figure 4.1.5 Finance manager advertisement

Finance Manager - Internet Software

- **Circa £32k**   Slough
- Generous benefits including car or car allowance
- Quarterly bonus scheme and Stock options

BroadVision is the leading worldwide supplier of one-to-one business applications for extended relationship management. Its worldwide HQ is in California. World wide revenues rose from $11m in 1996 to $51m in 1998 and in Q2/99 the revenues increased to $23.5m. Assets rose from $27m to $102m over the period 1996 - 98. Founded in 1993 its progress to profitability has been exceptional in the internet software business.

The UK subsidiary is responsible for UK sales and EMEA-post sales support and also provides some training-services on a European basis. Current staffing is around 20 people in the UK with 100 projected within 1-3 years.

The Finance Manager will manage all the day to day financial issues of the company, including cash flow, bank liaison, purchasing, shipping, planning and forecasting and contract supervision. The individual will pull together their results and ensure all other financial records are kept. This will include checking and processing expense accounts, purchase invoices, supplier invoices and sales invoices. Initially the position will carry out bookkeeping functions personally, but he or she will be expected to recruit and manage an assistant focussing on the invoice processing and bookkeeping functions.

The individual must have at least four years relevant experience. He or she would ideally have worked in a IT software or hardware company.

We would prefer an ACA / ACCA / CIMA or equivalent, with a relevant degree.

Employment prospects are extremely good, with the company possessing ambitious expansion plans in which the finance manager is expected to play a key role.

Please write by 24 August to Jon Young: Saffery Champness. Fairfax House. Fulwood Place. Gray's Inn. London. WC1V 6UB Tel: 0171 405 2828 Fax: 0171 405 7887 E-mail: jyoung@saffery.com

Saffery Champness CONSULTANCY SERVICES

Supervisors

In large organisations the management structure is usually divided into junior, middle and senior managers. A supervisor is a junior manager (sometimes called a first line manager) who works with, and leads, a small team, and is involved in making straightforward, simple, day-to-day decisions. The role of the supervisor is essential to the efficiency of the business. Decisions made by middle and senior management involve more planning and have longer-term effects on the organisation.

In the 1990s all companies became more and more concerned with cutting costs. This has resulted in organisations becoming **leaner**, a way of organising a business learnt from the Japanese. A 'lean' business has a flat structure. This can be achieved only by getting rid of one or more levels of managers. In many cases, this has led companies to phase out middle managers. Although there are still organisations where middle managers are the link between senior managers and supervisors, in firms where middle managers have been removed the supervisors are now expected to take more decisions. They now have to do more than just supervise their teams of operatives. Increasingly, supervisors must take responsibility for the **quality** of the products, and it is expected that they will make suggestions about improving methods of working and the efficiency of the operatives. The **cell structure** of the production process at Ultra helps to encourage this particular development (see page 198).

> Definition – a **lean business** is a Japanese method of working, now adopted by Western companies. It involves the removing of 'unnecessary' levels of management, which is intended to bring about a more efficient operation.

A **cell structure** is groups of workers organised into separate but closely co-operating teams. Workers can move between the cells. This motivates them to learn new skills.

quality is the achievement of high standards in products and services.

In addition to a reduction in costs due to fewer management positions, many people believe that a 'flat' structure makes communication in the firm easier and quicker.

Operatives

In a manufacturing company production operatives make the goods. In a service industry, such as a dry cleaner's, the operative's job is to load the clothes into the dry-cleaning solution, run the machine and then retrieve and pack the clean clothes.

The job of an operative is frequently repetitive, routine and boring. In addition, many people doing such jobs feel that there is no way in which they can advance, and no promotion prospects. This is why a sensible management will try to introduce variety into an operative's working day, perhaps by varying the tasks to be done if that is possible but, best of all, by training in new skills. This is often not possible in small firms. Repetitive work, as carried out by operatives, is the easiest work to automate.

General staff

Clerks, telephonists, receptionists and drivers are known as general or support staff, and can be found in all types of business organisations. You will note, though, that people working in different businesses often have the same job titles but their jobs might differ a great deal, depending on the firm's business and size. If you look at the Ultra case study, you will see that there are a number of people working in administration. In the Young Veterinary Partnership, however, there is only one administrator. The work of the administrative staff in Ultra deals with suppliers, visitors, clients and the products of a large, specialised manufacturing organisation. At the

Young Partnership, on the other hand, the administrator deals with patients and their owners, and looks after staff.

The same is true of reception staff. In the Young Veterinary Partnership the receptionists must know and understand the services offered by the practice, and be able to deal with worried people and their sick animals which are often distressed. Reception work in an organisation such as Ultra is quite different, and the receptionists there must be able to deal with calls, visits and appointments of customers, suppliers and outside visitors.

We have now looked at different people doing different jobs in different business organisations. The bigger the organisation, the more complicated is its structure. As you will remember, a sole trader must be a bit of a 'Jack or Jill of all trades', and carry out a number of different tasks in order to make his or her business a success. In a business the size of the Young Veterinary Partnership we find people with quite different qualifications and experience as line managers. However, the partnership is still small enough to be run by two partners. In contrast, a large organisation such as Ultra Electronics needs a formal structure of departments and departmental heads, as well as a clear line of management within each department.

Activity

You have been asked by your supervisor to write a job description for a junior assistant in the office. As you are a junior assistant yourself, you know that the person must:

- have a good standard of English;
- be able to answer the telephone correctly;
- have some keyboarding skills;
- be well organised;
- pay attention to detail;
- carry out everyday office tasks such as photocopying.

Write out the job description. You can add other details which you think should be included.

Activity

For this task you have to work with a friend.

One of you will be the interviewer and the other the candidate for the job of junior office assistant.

The **interviewer** should prepare questions to ask the candidate, and also a list of additional information, such as hours of work, holidays and method of payment.

The **candidate** should be ready to answer the interviewer's questions, and should also prepare some questions to ask.

Revision

Questions

1   Why does the owner of a small business have to carry out a number of different jobs?   (2 marks)

2   What is the difference in the ownership of Marks & Spencer and the BBC?   (1 mark)

3   BP operates in all three sectors of production. What does this mean?   (4 marks)

4   Why must all departments in a large business work well together?   (3 marks)

5   What is the meaning of the term 'function'?   (1 mark)

6   Explain the difference between a 'flat' and a 'tall' organisational structure.   (4 marks)

7   Why is it necessary in large businesses for people to have very clearly defined job roles?   (4 marks)

8   Who is in overall control of a private company?   (1 mark)

9   What is meant by 'chairing' meetings?   (1 mark)

10   Why might there be disagreements between various departments?   (2 marks)

11   What are strategic objectives?   (1 mark)

12   Who decides on the strategic objectives of a business?   (1 mark)

13   A board of directors is described as a 'team' of senior executives. Why is such a team necessary to run a business?   (4 marks)

14   Why is up-to-date financial information so important, and why must not only managers, but also the shareholders, have access to it?   (5 marks)

15   The office manager of a large company has been instructed to try and find out how wastage can be reduced. She has discovered that some of her assistants always run off more copies than needed, and that some use good quality paper for scrap. Can you think of other ways in which an office can waste money?   (6 marks)

16   Explain what is meant by a financial year.   (1 mark)

17   What is a transaction? Give two examples.   (3 marks)

18   Why is it necessary to record all transactions?   (1 mark)

19   Why is an audit done by an outside specialist firm?   (2 marks)

20   What is meant by 'production' in a business?   (1 mark)

21   List and explain the differences between the job of a manager and the job of a supervisor.   (4 marks)

22   Who are the operatives, and what do they do?   (2 marks)

23   Who are the shareholders of a company?   (1 mark)

24 What is the difference between a general manager and a departmental manager? (3 marks)

25 What are the functions of a managing director? (3 marks)

26 Name four departments in a large business, which might have a departmental manager. (2 marks)

27 All managers in a large business must work closely together and communicate regularly. Why is this necessary? (3 marks)

28 A sole trader has to work very hard and carry out many different jobs. Why do many people choose to run a sole trader business, in spite of the difficulties? (4 marks)

29 Explain why job descriptions are necessary. (2 marks)

WORKING ARRANGEMENTS

Foundation and Intermediate

CHAPTER 2

> **KEY TERMS:**
>
> | statistics | life expectancy | workforce |
> | short list | flexible | freelance |
> | scarce resources | | |

In this chapter you will learn about the different patterns of employment and the reasons why some are preferred by employers and employees. You will also learn how the British workforce is changing.

Much of the information in this chapter will be presented in the form of figures, tables and graphs. If you understand percentages and fractions reasonably well, you will not have any difficulty in understanding the **statistics** (check this word among the Key Terms, if you are not sure of its meaning). If you are not confident in your understanding of percentages and fractions, ask your teacher to run through them before you begin working through this section.

> Definition – **statistics** are information shown as figures and percentages, rather than described in words.

You already know that different businesses have different needs, and not everybody works eight hours a day, five days a week. In Ultra Electronics there used to be night shifts. Due to automation, these are no longer necessary but workers do, when required, work additional hours or weekends. The Young Veterinary Partnership employees have to work in the evenings, and some must work round the clock to deal with emergency cases.

There are also many people who want to work but who cannot work every day or from 8 a.m. to 6 p.m. Mothers with children at nursery or school are a good example. Many of them are valuable workers, but they can take only a part-time job, perhaps from 9 a.m. to 3 p.m. Often they cannot work during school holidays.

In the past, most workers worked all week. Today this has changed. Different working patterns have developed because of the changing needs of businesses and of the people who work in business.

Many people now work from home. This has been made possible by advances in information technology. Others want temporary jobs, either because they are waiting for another job, or because they like frequent changes. Some prefer night work or working at weekends for a variety of personal reasons.

Business organisations also have different needs. Some need to take on additional staff when there is a lot of work to be done. Some, like the Young Veterinary Partnership, need to have somebody on duty 24 hours a day, every day, and do need workers who are flexible and prepared to work shifts. Others take on new workers on short contracts to try them out before they are offered permanent employment. Workers who can work at home are often useful to businesses short of office space.

> Definition – **flexible** workers are able and willing to carry out a variety of tasks and can adjust to new situations in the workplace.

After finishing their education, the majority of the population become part of the country's labour force. For most people this will continue, with occasional breaks, for the rest of their working lives. This country's labour force consists of people aged between 16 and retirement age. Retirement age in the UK is still 60 for women and 65 for men, but this is going to change in the near future to 65 for everybody. Quite a number of people, however, now take early retirement and finish working when they reach 55.

Over the past 25 years, the make-up of the UK labour force has changed greatly. For example, many more women have entered paid employment, particularly part-time work, and have also returned to work after having children.

> In 1996 in the UK there were 35.5 million people of working age out of a population of 58 million.
> (Source: *Labour Force Survey*, Office for National Statistics, in *Social Trends*)

However, not everyone of working age is either working or looking for work. Some are in full-time education, some stay at home looking after young children or old or disabled members of the family, while others cannot work because of ill health.

In recent years, the number of people over retirement age has grown considerably in line with the increase in **life expectancy**. There are now more than three-quarters of a million people in the labour force who are above the state retirement age. Some companies are very keen to employ these people. For example, over the past few years, B&Q, the DIY retailing chain, has introduced a policy of taking on older people. The company claims that older workers are more knowledgeable about DIY products, more reliable and more loyal than people in younger age groups.

> Definition – **life expectancy** is the average number of years a person is expected to live.

Figure 4.2.1 Article from *The Times* 14 August 1999

Employers miss out on golden age for workers

BY ALEXANDRA FREAN, SOCIAL AFFAIRS CORRESPONDENT

EMPLOYERS are missing a golden opportunity to improve their image and boost their profits by failing to recognise the enormous value of workers in their fifties, research has shown.

A report published yesterday by the Institute for Employment Studies found that although many firms judge the fifty-somethings in their workforce to be "over the hill", they actually represent some of the companies' most valuable assets.

While ambitious younger employees jump from employer to employer, workers aged 50 or more display greater loyalty and commitment. They are better time-keepers, less likely to take time off for illness and more skilful at dealing with customers.

Jenny Kodz, a research fellow with the institute who co-wrote the study, said that fifty-something workers were more reliable than their younger colleagues because they had the maturity to concentrate on the job, rather than worrying about their social lives. "Anecdotal evidence also suggests that there is no difference in productivity between older and younger workers," she said.

The study found that nearly three fifths of those aged 50 and over "do the best they can", with respect to their job, even if it interferes with the rest of their life, compared to less than two fifths of those aged 18 to 24. It also showed, however, that despite their value to employers, older workers were often denied access to training and development. In 1998, only 17 per cent of employees aged 50-plus had received recent training, compared with 29 per cent of those aged below 50.

The study also found that although there are a growing number of older people available for work, the number in employment is falling.

A report published earlier this year by the London School of Economics Centre for Analysis of Social Exclusion found that employment for men aged 50 and over has declined faster than for any other age group. Two fifths of men aged 55 to 65 are without work, compared with one fifth in 1979 — a loss of 600,000 jobs for that age group alone.

Despite the negative attitudes of many companies toward older workers, employers will be forced to rely more on them, whether they like it or not, Ms Kodz's study suggests.

By 2001, 35 per cent of the population will be aged over 55 and 18 per cent will be aged between 45 and 55. This, combined with the fact that pensions and early retirement packages are decreasing in value, means that more people will be working later in life.

On the other hand, some employers take the opposite point of view. They prefer to employ younger people whom they can train to fit in with the ways in which things are done in the company. Very young workers are also usually paid less as they have less experience.

Recruitment and Selection Procedures

All businesses need workers. Even a sole trader often employs other people to help in the running of the business. There are different ways in which businesses can find their employees. We must remember that it is important for all business organisations to **recruit** the best possible workers. This means finding people who have the right qualifications and skills, as well as the right experience, unless the firm is looking for young employees whom it will train.

You have probably seen job advertisements in local and national newspapers. This is one way of finding new employees. Employers can also use **Job Centres** and **employment agencies** which specialise in finding jobs for people and people for jobs. The procedure for finding suitable workers is quite complicated.

1 First of all, the management must decide which positions, and how many, must be filled.
2 In a big organisation, the details of the positions to be filled are passed to the human resources department by the manager of the department which needs the workers. (For example, the marketing manager would provide the details, including a job description, for the position of a marketing assistant).
3 The next decision is how to find the employees. This could be done through:
   i) the Job Centre;
   ii) an employment agency;
   iii) advertising (in the local papers, the national papers or perhaps, for highly skilled jobs, in specialist magazines and journals).

4 If the job is to be advertised, the advertisement must be put together, giving details taken from the job description and also exact information about how those interested should apply (they might be asked to telephone for further details, write a letter of application, or send in a CV and a completed application form).
5 When all the applications are received, they must be read, and a **short list** drawn up. This is a list of those applicants whom the manager wants to **interview**.
6 The short-listed applicants are asked to come for an interview. This means they must be informed of the exact date, time and place of the interview. Sometimes only one person interviews the candidates. More often, and particularly for more skilled jobs, there is a group or **panel** of interviewers, usually consisting of the head of department, the supervisor, a member of the human resources department and perhaps one or two others. For very senior management jobs, there might be two or even three interviews.
7 When all candidates have been interviewed, the decision must be made by those who have interviewed them as to who is the best candidate for the job.
8 The successful applicant must then be informed, and if he or she accepts the job, final details, such as the starting date, must be decided.

As you can see, the procedure is quite long and complicated. From the organisation's point of view, it is most important that the right candidate is chosen, otherwise the time and money spent on selection and recruitment will be wasted.

Figure 4.2.2 Advertisement for the job of secretary from *The Times* 20 July 1999

Figure 4.2.3 Advertisement for jobs in a property company from *The Times* 29 July 1999

SECRETARIES REQUIRED
£16,000 p.a.

Faron Sutaria are acknowledged to be a progressive, dynamic and forward thinking Estate Agent. We currently require secretaries with a minimum of 2 years' experience in a similar role for our busy London offices. Aged 25–40 years, you will need to have excellent communication skills both written and spoken with a minimum typing speed of 45 wpm.

Interested ?

Then call Sophie Lumba today for an interview on 0171 243 1444.

Work within
Chartered Surveyors,
Chartered Quantity Surveyors,
Architects, Construction
and Estate Agents

PROPERTY SPECIALISTS

RECEPTIONIST   **£18,000 + Dress Allowance + Grooming Allowance + Bonus + PRP + STS**

A Prestigious Mayfair Property Company are currently seeking to recruit a 1st Class experienced receptionist working within a plush reception area. Your daily duties will include meeting and greeting clients, organising name badges, booking meeting and dining rooms on Word 4 Windows and E Mail. You'll be immaculately groomed, well spoken and have a friendly personality.

JUNIOR PERSONAL ASSISTANT   **£18,000 + Superb Benefits**

This is an excellent opportunity to join a "Blue Chip" Organisation working within their Property Management Department, assisting the Surveyors, arranging meetings and taking minutes will be just part of your day, you will also be accompanying surveyors on site visits. The ideal candidate will have good secretarial and administrative skills coupled with a warm friendly disposition.

For further information and an interview, please telephone The Eclipse Organisation, 13 Maddox Street, London W1R 9LE.
0171 629 4060 or fax 0171 629 5493
We are open 8.30am till 6.00pm.

Activity

Choose one of the two job advertisements shown above. If you were applying for the job you have chosen, you would have to send in a **curriculum vitae** (CV). Refer to the sample CV and prepare a CV of your own.

Figure 4.2.4 Example of a curriculum vitae

CURRICULUM VITAE

Name:	Victor Trent
Date of birth:	14th March 1978
Nationality:	British
Address:	44 Cottage Close
	Hayes
	Middx UB10 4SJ
Tel. No:	020 8166 9870

Education:
1995 – 1997   Torrenton College for FE, Torrenton
1989 – 1995   Mirren High School, Hayes

Qualifications:
1997   GNVQ Advanced in Business
1995

GCSE	Grade
English	C
Maths	C
Geography	B
Business Studies	B
History	D

Employment:
1997 –   Trainee Manager, Happy Returns Ltd
1994 – 1997   Shop Assistant, M Shoes Ltd (part-time)

Interests:
Travel, learning foreign languages (currently studying Spanish), football and cricket. Holder of the Duke of Edinburgh Gold Award, and coach of the football team of his primary school, Benton Junior, in Hayes.

References:

Ms Ann Stone
Human Resources Manager
Happy Returns Ltd
Hayes Middx UB12 5YA

Mr Alan Chase
Head of Department
Torrenton College for FE
Torrenton Middx TO6 3BS

Case Study

John Metcalf runs a bookshop in the city centre. He and his partner, Mariko Li, specialise in old and rare books. They are now ready to expand the business and want to open another shop in the suburbs and also to start a mail-order section, as they receive many enquiries from potential customers in other parts of the country and abroad.

They are now looking to appoint:
- a person to take charge of the mail-order section;
- a manager of the new bookshop;
- two part-time workers for the bookshop.

They have advertised the vacancies and have had a number of applications. The following people seem to have most to offer:

i)   Kim New, aged 21, with a GNVQ qualification and two years' experience in retail, but no knowledge of the book trade;

ii) Amanda Gray, aged 56, recently retired; her last job for 16 years was as office manager of a medium-sized local newspaper;

iii) James Stowe, aged 47, an ex-librarian, who can now work only two days a week because he is the sole carer of his aged mother;

iv) Ted Wall, aged 17, still a student, looking for a part-time job to supplement his income. Ted is not interested in a career in books or in retail, but is hard-working and bright;

v)   Marianne Gill, aged 35, who is, in her own words, 'a great reader', and has office work experience; she hopes to return to full-time work as her children are now of school age.

John and Mariko cannot agree on the best candidates for the jobs which they must fill. Mariko is generally in favour of taking on people who already have experience, while John is not so sure.

Task: The partners have asked you to help them decide. Select the four people whom, in your opinion, they should employ. You must state which candidate should be offered which job, and give reasons for your choice. You should also explain why you have rejected the fifth candidate.

Your answer should be written in the form of a memo to John and Mariko.

Table 4.2.1 UK population of working age

UK population of working age by gender and employment status, Spring 1996

Millions

	Males	Females	All
Economically active			
Full-time employees	10.8	5.9	16.7
Part-time employees	0.8	4.5	5.3
All employees	11.6	10.4	22.0
Full-time self-employed	2.2	0.4	2.6
Part-time self-employed	0.2	0.4	0.5
All self-employed	2.4	0.7	3.1
Others in employment[1]	0.2	0.2	0.4
All in employment	14.2	11.3	25.4
ILO unemployed	1.5	0.8	2.3
All economically active	15.7	12.0	27.8
Economically inactive	2.9	4.9	7.8
Population by working age	18.6	17.0	35.5

Males aged 16 to 64, females aged 16 to 59.
[1]Those on government and training programmes and unpaid family workers.
Source: Labour Force Survey, Office for National Statistics, in *Social Trends 1997*

Here are some facts about the employment of men and women that you should know.

In 1996:

- 71% of women and 85% of men of working age had a job;

- for every woman who was **self-employed** there were three men;

- for every five women in **part-time** employment there was only one man.

This last fact tells us something about one of the most important changes which have taken place in the UK labour market in the twentieth century – the big increase in female employment, especially in part-time employment.

The following table tells us a great deal about the changes in the make-up of the labour force during the 25 years between 1971 and 1996.

Table 4.2.2 Labour force by gender and age

Labour force[1]: by gender and age

Great Britain							Millions
	16 – 24	25 – 44	45 – 54	55 – 59	60 – 64	65 and over	All aged 16 and over
Males							
1971	2.9	6.3	3.1	1.5	1.2	0.5	15.6
1981	3.1	7.0	2.9	1.4	0.9	0.3	15.7
1991	3.0	7.9	2.9	1.1	0.7	0.3	10.0
1996	2.4	7.9	3.3	1.1	0.6	0.3	15.6
2001	2.3	8.1	3.4	1.2	0.7	0.3	15.9
2006	2.4	7.8	3.4	1.3	0.7	0.3	16.0
Females							
1971	2.2	3.4	2.1	0.9	0.5	0.3	9.4
1981	2.6	4.4	2.1	0.9	0.4	0.2	10.6
1991	2.5	6.0	2.3	0.8	0.3	0.2	12.1
1996	2.0	6.2	2.8	0.8	0.3	0.2	12.3
2001	2.0	6.3	3.0	0.9	0.4	0.1	12.8
2006	2.1	6.3	3.1	1.1	0.5	0.2	13.3

[1]The former Great Britain civilian labour force definition of unemployment has been used to produce the estimates for 1971 and 1981; in later years the ILO definition has been used and members of the armed forces excluded. Data for 2001 and 2006 are Spring 1995-based projections.
Source: Census and Labour Force Survey, Office for National Statistics, in *Social Trends 1997*

Look at the figures for males in the last column of the table. Now look at the figures for females in the same column.

You probably realise that more young people now remain in full-time education; but did you know that in 1996 nearly 40% of 16–19-year-old full-time students also had jobs? As may be expected, most of these jobs were part-time or temporary.

Activity

If you now have, or have had in the past, a part-time or temporary job, answer the questions below. (If you have not had any jobs yourself, find out the answers from a friend who has.)

i) What was the job?

ii) Who did you work for?

iii) How many hours a week did you work?

iv) What were your days/hours of work?

v) What was the main reason for taking the job?

At the other end of the age scale, the reason for the decrease in the level of employment of older workers (those over 55) may have been the introduction of early retirement schemes. There was certainly a trend towards early retirement during the 1970s and 1980s, which continued, but more slowly, in the 1990s.

Case Study: Quickburger

Quickburger, a fast food chain with 20 outlets in the UK, but hoping to expand, has a policy of employing only young people. The average age of Quickburger counter assistants is 21, and their branch managers are rarely over 26. The management's policy to employ young people is based on the belief that they are easier to train and more ambitious. They also respond better to an award system introduced by Quickburger and, because of their age and lack of experience, they do not expect to be paid very high wages.

There are, however, some problems with such young staff. Many take the job as a stop-gap 'before something better crops up', and there are many students who want only to supplement their income. Few are interested in a career at Quickburger, and the management has now begun to rethink its employment policy.

Types of Employment

Self-employed

You already know from Unit 2 Chapter 1 that the most basic form of business organisation in the private sector is the sole trader who is self-employed. Put simply, the sole trader employs himself or herself and is his or her own boss. In a partnership, the partners are also self-employed.

A self-employed person, such as a plumber or a window cleaner, can work for a business, or may be called into a house to repair a burst pipe, or clean the windows, but he or she is not an employee of the organisation or the householder that uses the service. A self-employed person works on a **freelance** basis.

Among the self-employed, women are under-represented. In 1996 there were 3.3 million self-employed people in the UK. Of these, three-quarters were men. The number of self-employed increased throughout the 1980s and reached a peak of 3.6 million in 1990. In the early 1990s there was a **recession** and the numbers fell, but they are now increasing in line with a general improvement in the economy.

Definition – a **recession** is a temporary decline in economic activity or prosperity.

Self-employment is more common in some industries than in others. In 1996 almost half of the workers in agriculture, fishing and construction (building) were self-employed. Compare this with only 5% of those who worked in education, health and manufacturing.

One fact is true of the self-employed in any industry – they usually work longer hours than full-time employees do. The average per week for men is 52 hours, and 48 for women.

Workers who are hired by a company provide their labour in exchange for wages. Such workers are **employees** and the law treats them quite differently from those who are self-employed.

Why do you think a self-employed person is likely to work much longer hours than somebody who is an employee?

Full-time work

Full-time workers normally work a five-day week. Their weekly hours can officially be between 37.5 and 40 hours per week. Figure 4.2.5 shows some interesting differences between industries and between the hours worked by men and women in those industries.

Figure 4.2.5 Average hours worked by full-time employees

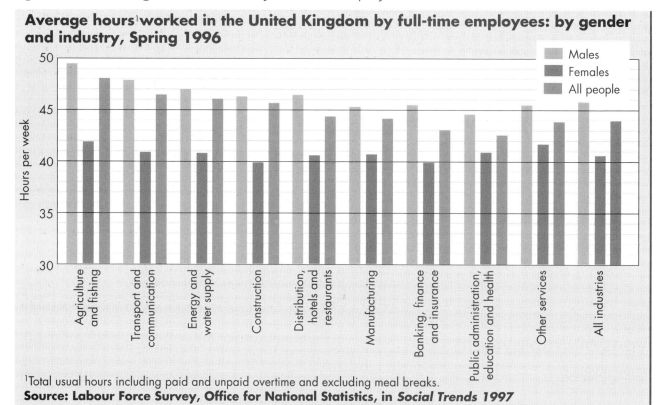

Average hours¹worked in the United Kingdom by full-time employees: by gender and industry, Spring 1996

¹Total usual hours including paid and unpaid overtime and excluding meal breaks.
Source: Labour Force Survey, Office for National Statistics, in *Social Trends 1997*

In common with part-time employees, full-time staff may be employed either permanently or temporarily. Those that are permanent are given special protection as workers by the:

● Employment Protection (Consolidation) Act 1978;

● Sex Discrimination Acts (1975 and 1986);

● Race Relations Act 1976;

● Employment Act 1989.

The protection provided by this legislation has been extended to cover part-time employees. Temporary full-time staff employed for short periods (e.g. for the Christmas rush) do not have to get a written job description. This is one of the reasons why this category of workers is not in a strong position when dealing with employers. When a temporary period of service is finished, the employer does not have to renew the contract of employment.

Activity

Your friend Sukhdev has been looking for a part-time job. He is a full-time student and can work only in the evenings or at weekends, as well as during college vacations. He has been reading advertisements in the local paper and in shop windows but has now become completely confused. He needs to know the difference between:

● a temporary job;
● a part-time job;
● being self-employed.

He needs the answers quickly. Write him a note explaining the differences. You should give at least two examples of each kind of job.

Part-time work

The Employment Protection Act (1978) defines a part-time employee as one who works fewer than sixteen hours a week. He or she may be employed on a permanent or a temporary basis.

If you are a part-time worker in the UK today, you are likely to be a female. In the 10 years from 1986, the number of women in part-time employment rose by nearly a fifth to 5.3 million. This amounted to almost 20% of the total labour force. Among men, the number of part-timers almost doubled, but was still only 1.2 million.

More facts you should know:

- about half of all female employees work part-time;

- less than 10% of men work part-time;

- in both sexes, it is the youngest and the oldest employees who are most likely to be in part-time work;

- the high proportion of part-timers among the young is explained by students taking part-time jobs.

Part-time working is more common in certain industries. For example, nearly half of all employees in distribution (shops, warehouses, etc.) work part-time, while over one third in public administration (civil service, local councils) do so.

If you look at the employment make-up of Ultra Electronics, you will find that there are no part-time workers there, while the Young Veterinary Partnership employs part-time receptionists.

People often imagine that all part-time workers would prefer full-time posts and only accept part-time work because they have no choice. While this is no doubt true of some sections of the workforce, there are many people who do not want to work full-time. In further education colleges, for instance, most part-time workers do not want full-time jobs. This is particularly true of women. Mothers with children at nursery or at school are a good example. Many are valuable workers, but can take only those jobs that fit in with their children's school or nursery day.

In most businesses there are jobs that require only a few hours of work to be done each day. For these, it is sensible for management to employ part-time staff. Examples include cleaners, canteen staff and caretakers. (You can probably think of others.) Part-time staff may also be taken on to meet unexpected and unplanned increases in demand. For example, in a heatwave there may be a sharp rise in the demand for ice cream, so the manufacturers have to produce more quickly.

From the employer's point of view, part-time workers are:

- cheaper to employ;

- more flexible;

- not entitled to the same employment protection as full-time staff.

Furthermore, they are much easier and cheaper to dismiss if the company no longer needs them or has to save money.

Permanent work

Permanent workers have a contract (a legal agreement) with their employer, which states that their jobs will last until they, or their employers, decide to end them. Thirty or forty years ago, this could have meant that a person remained in one job after leaving school or college until retirement. This is practically never the case nowadays. The demand from employers now is for **flexible** working, as this helps a business to be more competitive.

Figure 4.2.6 Article from *The Times*
2 August 1999

Japanese firms rewrite rules of employment

FROM ROBERT WHYMANT IN TOKYO

WHEN Toshiyuki Sakai was assigned to a desk in a windowless room at head office, with no outside telephone line and no work to do, he knew that his days with Sega Enterprises, the video-game maker, were numbered.

Workers were sent to this room — officially called the "persona room", but known to employees as the "company jail" — when Sega had no further need for them and wanted them to quit, according to Mr Sakai, a 35-year-old quality controller. A week or two idling in the room were enough to persuade most people to accept "voluntary" retirement.

However, Mr Sakai endured three months of "solitary" as he calls it, until Sega finally fired him in March for "insufficient work ability". He is suing the company for unfair dismissal.

Though news reports of these tactics surprised many Japanese, Mr Sakai's experience was hardly unique. Until a few years ago, most big Japanese companies shied away from making employees redundant. The so-called "jobs for life" system, rewarding loyalty with security, was sacrosanct. But the world's second largest economy is undergoing a quiet and painful social tranformation. Recession, falling profits and the struggle to remain globally competitive are forcing corporate Japan to rethink the tradition of employment for life. More and more big companies are biting the bullet, "restructuring" and cutting payrolls, making Western investors happy but driving up unemployment. The latest unemployment figure of 4.9 per cent is a postwar record.

For the Japanese worker, being cast out of the company womb is traumatic, all the more so as there is very little scope for changing jobs in mid-career and no provision for the long-term unemployed. The methods used to get workers to leave the company of their own accord often border on harassment. Unwanted employees are deprived of job title, desk and dignity — and Japan's docile "house unions" accept such abuses.

Munehiro Umemura, a Sega spokesman, acknowledged that seven employees sent to the "persona rooms" — there are three in all — had resigned, adding: "But most of them had already decided to leave anyway." People who cannot be found jobs were sent to the rooms on "standby". "The media have reported the rooms as if they were company jails. Sega has never done anything to drive those in the rooms to leave."

While others are hunting for a new job, Mr Sakai has taken Sega to court, bitter at the way he was treated by a company to which he devoted nine years of his life. "It was really like an isolation ward," he said. "When the personnel department ordered me to spend the whole day there, I was close to tears, thinking of all I'd done for the company."

You read about the business term 'competition' in an earlier chapter. It is worth repeating here that businesses which fail to be competitive will not survive in the long term. If they are not competitive, countries that depend heavily on exports, like the UK and Japan, will have problems providing their population with a good standard of living.

Nowadays, the term 'permanent employment' can be misleading. A contract of employment does not protect the permanent employee from **redundancy** (that is, being made unemployed when the company can no longer provide work and the employee lacks the skills to be transferred to another job within the business) or if the firm closes down.

Temporary Work

An employee on a temporary contract is employed for a fixed period. It may last one month, six months, a year, or more. When the contract expires, it may be renewed, but the employer is not obliged to do this.

Some people are employed temporarily in the UK, e.g.:

- sales assistants during the summer and winter sales;

- additional postmen taken on for the pre-Christmas period;

- office staff who provide short-term cover while permanent staff are on holiday, are sick or are on maternity leave.

Can you think of any other workers who are frequently employed on a temporary basis?

Case Study: Happy Returns Ltd

Happy Returns Ltd is a small manufacturer of greeting cards. It employs 20 full-time permanent staff, and also a number of temporary full-time and part-time workers during busy periods, such as the three months before Christmas and the weeks before Valentine's Day.

The firm is doing well, and the Managing Director, Mr Franco Malli, needs to take on extra staff if Happy Returns is to continue to compete successfully with other, often bigger, card makers. Mr Malli wants to employ five full-time permanent workers, but his accountant, Mr Ian McAndrew, is against the idea.

'Take on more part-timers,' advises Mr McAndrew. 'You can dismiss them quickly if you have to, and you don't have to give them contracts or bother with all the legal details. It will be cheaper and better in the long run.'

Mr Malli is not convinced but cannot quite put together the arguments for employing the additional people on a permanent, full-time basis.

Can you help him?

Make a list of **advantages** to a firm of having permanent workers.

Although more than nine out of 10 employees are currently in permanent jobs, more and more are considering a change to temporary employment because of family commitments and other personal reasons. It should, however, be remembered that around 20% of temporary workers, when asked, said that they took the temporary position because they could not find a permanent one.

Figure 4.2.7 Advertisement for temporary staff from *The Times* 29 July 1999

Table 4.2.3 Employees in temporary jobs

Percentage of employees with a temporary job: EU comparison[1], 1995			
United Kingdom			Percentages
	Males	**Females**	**All**
Spain	33	38	35
Finland	13	19	16
Sweden	10	14	12
France	11	13	12
Denmark	11	13	12
Netherlands	9	14	11
Germany	10	11	10
Irish Republic	9	12	10
Greece	9	11	10
Portugal	9	11	10
Italy	6	9	7
United Kingdom	6	8	7
Austria	6	6	6
Belgium	4	7	5
EU average	11	12	11

[1]Data for Luxembourg are not available.
Source: Labour Force Survey, Eurostat, in Social Trends 1997

Job sharing

Overall, one and a half million people – 7% of all employees in the UK – were in temporary jobs in 1995. This proportion is quite low when compared with other European Union (EU) countries (see Table 4.2.3).

It seems certain that in the future the number of workers in temporary jobs is set to increase. The overriding need for companies to be as competitive as possible ensures that this trend will be with us for the foreseeable future.

In recent years, job sharing has become popular. When a business needs an employee to work full-time, it is sometimes possible to have two people sharing one post, e.g. each working half a week. This is a very good solution for some workers who are trying to combine a career with raising a family, for example. However, it is only possible in certain types of job, and it requires the two sharers to work well together. It is particularly important that they communicate effectively. Nowadays, modern technology makes communication easy through the use of the telephone, fax machine and home computers with e-mail.

Each sharer would have a separate contract of employment, detailing duties, hours of work and salary. However, even when the arrangements are very carefully made, job sharing can be successful only if the two job holders 'work as one' and make sure that, even if some duties are allocated to one only, both know and understand all that the job requires.

Working from home

This working arrangement is not new. **Outworking,** as it is also called, used to be quite a common practice in manufacturing businesses but it has now declined in line with the decrease in the number of manufacturing firms. It worked this way: factories delivered partly prepared components to the outworkers' homes, where they would be put together at the kitchen table. When finished, they were collected by the factory and a new batch delivered. The outworker was then paid for the finished work.

This kind of work was usually repetitive and boring, and very poorly paid. The workers usually had no qualifications and were unable to spend time in the factory.

Today, working from home has completely changed in character. It is happening as a direct result of the growth and widespread use of information technology (IT) and telecommunications. As is the case with job sharing, its success depends on reliable and fast communication, provided by the telephone, fax and personal computer. Many people now working from home are those with jobs in the world of journalism, publicity and computer technology. Although they work at home, only going into the office from time to time, IT allows them to hold video-conferences with others on their team.

In 1995 three out of 10 employed men in the UK, and a quarter of all employed women, worked from home at least some of the time. These rates were higher than in any other EU country, and are growing.

There are benefits for both the employer and the employee. There are also benefits for society:

- fewer people travelling at peak times on our congested roads and railways;
- less pollution, as cars stay at home in the garage;
- reduced use of **scarce resources** – petrol etc;
- parents can be at home when children return from school.

Definition – **scarce resources** are those in short supply, not easily replaceable.

Mobile working

The continuous improvement and reduction in size of communication equipment has made it possible for managers and executives to have mobile offices in their cars, on trains and in aeroplanes. This is mobile working – working while on the move. The portable fax machine, the laptop computer and the mobile telephone enable the executive to work from almost anywhere in the world. Keeping in touch with the business is no longer a problem.

One of the first computers

A modern laptop

Shift working

The tradition of the 9 to 5 working day is no longer standard in many businesses. Factories especially want to avoid having non-automated, expensive machines standing idle outside 'normal' working hours. Shift work is the solution. It works in the following way: a third of the hourly paid workers will be starting their shifts as another third are finishing. The pattern of the working day will look something like this:

Day shift	8 a.m. to 4 p.m.
Evening shift	4 p.m. to 12 midnight
Night shift	12 midnight to 8 a.m.

The day shift workers, for example, might work in the above pattern for a month, then move on to the evening shift. After a month on 'evenings', they would spend the following month working 'nights'. The night shift workers are usually paid at a higher than standard hourly rate to compensate for the unsociable hours.

There are other reasons for organisations to adopt a shift-work system. The emergency services: police, fire brigade, ambulances and hospitals need to be open and staffed round the clock. The reasons for this are obvious.

In the early 1990s, when the Channel Tunnel was being constructed, the civil engineering contractors met to agree completion dates for the project. There were heavy financial penalties for finishing behind schedule, so shift work was a crucial part of the companies' planning strategy. It was also important for the companies to avoid having very expensive tunnel-boring equipment standing idle for long periods.

Table 4.2.4 Employees with flexible work patterns

Employees with flexible working patterns: by gender, Spring 1996

United Kingdom			Percentages
	Males	**Females**	**All employees**
Full-time employees			
Flexible working hours	8.6	13.2	10.2
Annualised working hours	3.7	4.2	3.9
Four and a half day week	2.7	2.4	2.6
Term-time working	1.0	4.7	2.3
Nine day fortnight	0.5	0.2	0.4
Any flexible working pattern	16.6	24.7	19.4
Part-time employees			
Flexible working hours	5.9	7.4	7.1
Annualised working hours	2.6	3.2	3.1
Term-time working	4.6	9.7	8.9
Job sharing	4.6	2.4	2.2
Any flexible working pattern	14.2	22.9	21.5

Source: Labour Force Survey, Office for National Statistics, in *Social Trends 1997*

Flexi-time

Flexi (flexible) time working arrangements have now become popular with workers in many businesses. Flexi-time, like shift work, does not rely on everyone clocking on and clocking off at the same time each day. This is how it works:

- Everyone has to work the same number of hours per week.

- Everyone has to be at work during 'core' hours (usually 11 a.m. – 4 p.m.).

- The rest of the hours can be worked either early in the morning or later in the evening.

- If a worker puts in more hours one week, he or she can work fewer hours the following week.

Flexi-time is most widely used in administrative and office work, and requires careful planning, monitoring and record-keeping.

Activity

Amelia works as a full-time librarian. For the last three years, she has worked a 37.5 hour week, from 9 a.m. to 5.30 p.m., Monday to Friday, with an hour off for lunch. The library now wants to introduce flexi-time but Amelia and the other librarians are not sure about this.

i) Make a list of the benefits of flexi-time to someone like Amelia who is married and has a six-year-old son.

ii) Prepare a sample fortnight's flexi-timetable for Amelia.

Activity
(Intermediate)

Ask five people who work to give you some information about their working arrangements. (They can be members of your family, friends or anyone you know who can spare the time to answer your questions.)

- Ask them about their pattern of work, hours they work and also what they like and dislike about the arrangements. (You should prepare a simple questionnaire before the interviews).

- Make notes of their answers.

- At the end of each interview, ask the person how he or she thinks the working arrangements in their firm could be improved.

- Write a short report on their answers, and give your own conclusions on the good and bad aspects of each working arrangement.

Revision

Questions

1 i) In which female group has the biggest increase in employment taken place? (1 mark)
   ii) What do you think is the reason for this increase? (2 marks)

2 For both males and females employment levels in the age group 16–24 have decreased. Why has this happened? (2 marks)

3 What does working 'freelance' mean? (1 mark)

4 Why do many young people work part-time? (2 marks)

5 Why do some companies like to employ older workers? (2 marks)

6 Why do some people prefer to have part-time work? (2 marks)

7 Look at Figure 4.2.5. In which industries do the men work the longest hours? In which do they work the shortest hours? (3 marks)

8 How do the hours worked by women in the above industries compare with the hours worked by men? (3 marks)

9 Why do you think men and women working in the same industries often work different hours? (2 marks)

10 Ultra Electronics is a large company but it does not employ thousands of people. What are the reasons for this? (4 marks)

11 Can you think what the benefits of working from home might be both for the employer and the employee? Fill in the grid below:

Advantages for the employer	Advantages for the employee

(10 marks)

12 Currently, what is the retirement age in the UK for:
    a) men;
    b) women? (1 mark)

13 What has been the most significant change in the composition of the UK labour force in the last 25 years? (3 marks)

14 Give two reasons why part-time work is predominantly a female occupation. (2 marks)

15 In 1996, the UK population was approximately 58 million. Of this number, nearly 36 million were of working age, yet there were only 27 million in employment. What were the other 9 million of working age doing? (6 marks)

16 Give three methods used by employers to recruit workers. (2 marks)

17 With reference to recruitment of staff, give two reasons for drawing up a short list. (2 marks)

18 Which members of staff are usually included on the interviewing panel when selecting candidates for a job? (2 marks)

19 Why is a panel of interviewers preferable to one person conducting an interview? (2 marks)

20 In 1996, 40% of 16–19-year-old full-time students had jobs. Why were the jobs mostly part-time? (1 mark)

21 What sorts of jobs did outworkers do in the past? (1 mark)

22 Why were the outworkers generally poorly paid? (2 marks)

23 Why is working from home now becoming popular? (2 marks)

24 One job which was often done at home in the past was addressing envelopes to a firm's customers. Why has this become unnecessary now? (1 mark)

25 Imagine that you have to address 500 envelopes to earn £1.89, and it takes you four hours to do so. How much would you earn if you worked 20 hours a week? (4 marks)

26 Select three Acts of Parliament which give protection to employees and:
    i) state the dates when they were passed; (1 mark)
    ii) explain why they are necessary; (2 marks)
    iii) give your opinion on the view that older workers, i.e. those over 50, should be given additional legal protection. (3 marks)

27 Which of the following statements are true? Which are false? Give reasons for your answers.
    i) Construction workers usually work from 8 a.m. to 5 p.m. and are full-time employees. (2 marks)
    ii) The self-employed work longer hours than the employed. (2 marks)
    iii) Employment laws apply equally to the employed and the self-employed. (2 marks)
    iv) If you are a part-time employee, you are a temporary employee. (4 marks)

When answering Questions 28 and 29, consider carefully the choices open to the employer, choose the one you think is best, and give reasons for your choice.

28 A soft drinks manufacturer employs 40 people full-time. In the off season, the employees often do not have enough to do to fill the working day but they cannot cope with the workload during the summer months. Should the firm:
    i) take on more full-time workers?
    ii) reduce full-time workers to 20, and employ additional staff on a temporary basis when needed?
    iii) bring in job-sharers? (12 marks)

29 Mrs Patel is a secretary with a large company. At present, she is on maternity leave. Her boss wants her back full-time as she is very good. Mrs Patel has asked if she can come back to work on a part-time basis. Should her boss:
    a) tell Mrs Patel she can come back only on a full-time basis?
    b) tell Mrs Patel to take extended leave, and then come back full-time?
    c) Offer the job to Mrs Patel and Mrs Joric, another employee currently on maternity leave, on a job-share basis? (10 marks)

PAY AND BENEFITS

Foundation and Intermediate

In this chapter you will learn how people are paid for their work, about the different methods of payment, and what additional benefits some workers can expect to get from their employers.

All people working in business are paid for doing their work. They can be paid in different ways, depending on the type of job and company policy. In addition to pay, many workers get benefits which are useful to have but are not actually money.

In the past, **manual workers** were paid **wages**, and **non-manual workers** were paid **salaries**. Today, many businesses have gone over to **single status** payments which make no distinction between workers in a company. Other employers still pay their workers by different methods.

> Definition – **manual workers** are those who work mainly with their hands, e.g. factory workers who operate machines.

Wages

- **Fixed time rate** – some workers are paid a fixed hourly or weekly rate which can be easily calculated. This method does not take into account the amount of work done, only the time that the employee spends on the job.

  In many jobs it would be impossible to work out exactly what and how much a worker has produced, and this payment method is the only one that can be used. Some people criticise this method because it means that everyone is paid the same whether they work hard and efficiently or not.

- **Piece rate** – this means getting paid a certain amount for every unit or 'piece' made. Piece rate pay can be used only where a product is manufactured, and where it is possible to count the number of products produced by each worker. Some factory jobs are like this. One advantage of piecework is said to be that every worker tries to earn as much as possible by working quickly and efficiently. On the other hand, this could be a disadvantage – workers want to produce more and more, and they might become careless and not do a good job. The quality of what is produced is very important. This method is also known as 'payment by results'.

> Definition – **deductions** are sums of money taken from salaries or wages before they are given to employees.

Activity

Look at the earnings of three friends, Mark, Luke and Sam.

- Sam is paid £5.10 an hour and works a 37.5 hour week.
- Luke is paid £180 a week.
- Mark is on piece rate, at £0.30 per piece.

i) How much does Sam earn a week?

ii) What is the difference between Sam's and Luke's weekly earnings?

iii) How many pieces would Mark have to produce to earn as much as Luke?

Salary

Salaried staff, particularly those at managerial level, are usually expected to work additional hours, if required, without being paid overtime. Professional people, such as teachers, journalists, solicitors, etc., are paid salaries.

Basic wage

This means the amount of money paid to a worker before adding any extra payments. In many jobs, the basic wage is all that a worker can earn, but in other jobs additional money can be earned through **overtime, bonuses, performance related pay** or **commission.**

Bonus

A bonus is a one-off extra payment. Some firms, like Ultra Electronics, pay all employees a bonus once a year. Others might give a bonus when the firm has done exceptionally well.

Overtime

Full-time workers working extra hours in any way are paid overtime rates. Overtime is paid at more than the standard hourly rate. Overtime is paid to operatives, not to management.

If the hourly rate is £5.00, overtime at time and half will be £7.50.

Performance related pay

This can be an additional payment which is made when workers have helped the company to achieve its targets and are then given a share of the profits. Some employees are employed individually on contracts which specify that if they do well they will receive an additional payment based on their performance.

Commission

Staff employed in selling can earn additional payments if they achieve above a certain amount of sales.

Definition – Simply put, **profit** is sales minus expenses. It is the main objective of private businesses. Profits belong to the owners of a business.

Figure 4.3.1 Payslip of a full-time senior administrator

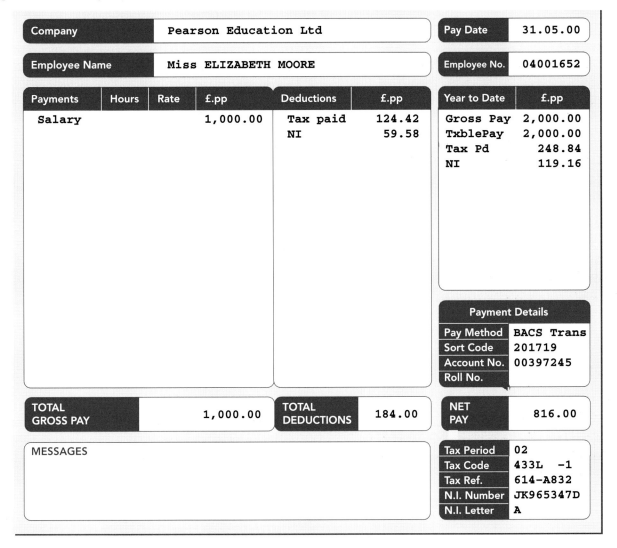

Company	Pearson Education Ltd			Pay Date	31.05.00
Employee Name	Miss ELIZABETH MOORE			Employee No.	04001652

Payments	Hours	Rate	£.pp	Deductions	£.pp	Year to Date	£.pp
Salary			1,000.00	Tax paid	124.42	Gross Pay	2,000.00
				NI	59.58	TxblePay	2,000.00
						Tax Pd	248.84
						NI	119.16

Payment Details

Pay Method	BACS Trans
Sort Code	201719
Account No.	00397245
Roll No.	

TOTAL GROSS PAY	1,000.00	TOTAL DEDUCTIONS	184.00	NET PAY	816.00

MESSAGES

Tax Period	02
Tax Code	433L −1
Tax Ref.	614−A832
N.I. Number	JK965347D
N.I. Letter	A

Figure 4.3.2 Payslip of a part-time dry-cleaning assistant

Pay No. BACS		Name DE CET		MR	B	ADJUSTMENTS BEFORE TAX		DRY CLEANING SERVICES
Pay Date 25/02/2000	Wk. 48	Tax Code 433L 1	NI A			Total adjustments	0.00	
						Taxable Gross	148.50	
NI Number JM148141B	Pay Point 25/5341							PAY ADVICE
Contract	Rate	Hours			Value			
00005290	4.500	14.00			63.00			
00005321	4.500	8.00			36.00	ADJUSTMENTS AFTER TAX		GROSS TO DATE 148.50
00005341	4.500	7.00			31.50			TAX TO DATE 0.00
00005364	4.500	4.00			18.00	Tax	0.00	PENS. TO DATE 0.00
						NI	1.65	EMPLOYEES NI TO DATE 1.65
						Total Deductions	1.65	EMPLOYERS NI TO DATE 0.00
								HOLIDAY PAY TO DATE 0.00
								SSP TO DATE 0.00
TOTAL HOURS	33.00			Basic Pay	148.50	NET PAY BACS 146.85		

Your normal hours are held as 20. If incorrect notify your Contract Manager

Methods of Payment
Cash

In the past, workers were paid in cash. The employer made up pay packets and these were given out to all employees at the end of each week. It was a big job for the employer who had to send someone to the bank to pick up the cash, and it was not very safe for the employees either. Nowadays, very few workers, apart from those working casually for a few hours, are paid in cash.

Cheque

The first change in the way in which people were paid was from cash to cheque. To be paid by cheque you must have a bank account, but some people were not very happy about that. Today, however, most people do use banks so there is no longer a problem. People who work part-time, or are on short contracts, are often, but not always, paid by cheque.

Credit transfer

The easiest way of payment is by credit transfer. This means that the payment is sent electronically from the employer's bank to the employee's bank account. It is easy for the employer because there is no need for pay packets to be made up or cheques to be written and signed. It is also easy for the employee who does not have to pay the money into an account. Very many people are now paid in this way and this includes most of those on salaries.

Benefits

In most cases, work benefits are received by full-time, permanent employees. Those given to part-time workers are considerably fewer. Benefits include the following:

- **shares** in the business (e.g. the workers at Ultra Electronics receive free shares and also can buy more at a reduced price);

- **discounts** – this means that workers can buy the products of the business at a discounted (lower) price. This benefit is enjoyed by employees of Marks & Spencer, for example;

- **subsidised meals** or **clothing** – this means that the business pays part of the cost of meals in a canteen, or of uniforms which must be worn.

The workers have to pay only a part of the actual cost. Subsidised canteens can usually be found in large business organisations and can be used by all employees. Uniforms and protective clothing are mostly for operatives;

- **company cars** – senior managers are often given a company car. In many cases the firm pays the road tax and insurance, and some also give a petrol allowance. This benefit is worth a large sum of money but is now usually taxed. Even after the tax is paid, however, it is still worth having.

- **Loans** – borrowing money is very expensive, so an employer who lends employees money cheaply is providing a very real benefit. Bank employees and those working in building societies can obtain loans to buy houses or flats (these loans are called mortgages) at special low rates.

Other benefits

Some employers provide other benefits for their workers, e.g.:

- **Health insurance;**

- **Pension schemes** – there are two kinds:
  i) a contributory scheme – the employee pays part of the cost, and the employer pays the rest;
  ii) a non-contributory scheme – the employer pays the whole amount;

- **Sports and social clubs.**

These benefits often make a lot of difference to the workers and enable them to have things which they would not have achieved by themselves. For example, health insurance, cheap but good meals at work, or nice cars are very popular with employees. The employers find that benefits are a good way to ensure that workers are happier and will stay loyal to the business.

It should also be remembered that although every employee works in order to earn a living, there are other aspects of work which also motivate people. Many individuals are ambitious and wish to progress in their chosen career. In order to do so, they are often prepared to take jobs which are not particularly well paid but which will give them the opportunity to gain experience and perhaps additional qualifications which, in the long run, will enable them to progress.

Revision

Questions

1   How are the following people likely to be paid?
    i)   Mr Green, managing director of a large company;
    ii) Jenny who is 15 and works as a Saturday girl at her local hairdresser's;
    iii) Amanda, secretary to Mr Green;
    iv) John and Greg, who work on the assembly line in a factory making door handles;
    v)   Peter, who has worked stocking shelves in the supermarket several evenings
         last week.   (10 marks)

2   Explain what a bonus is and when it is likely to be paid.   (1 mark)

3   How does credit transfer work and why is it now a popular method of payment?   (2 marks)

4   Give a definition of 'overtime', and explain why workers often like to work overtime
    hours.   (3 marks)

5   What are the advantages and the disadvantages of paying people piece rate?   (3 marks)

6   If you were working, which of the following benefits would you most like to have,
    and why:
    ● a subsidised canteen at work;
    ● a pension scheme to which your employer contributes;
    ● membership of a sports club;
    ● a company car.   (5 marks)

7   Give two examples of jobs in which piece rate payment is possible. Explain why.   (1 mark)

8   Give two examples of jobs which could not be paid at piece rate. Explain why.   (1 mark)

9   What deductions are taken from an employee's earnings?   (2 marks)

10 Explain what is meant by 'performance related pay'?   (2 marks)

11 John is a salesman. He earns 2.5% commission for every hundred pounds' worth of
    goods that he sells. Last week, John's sales were as follows:
    i)   £4,000
    ii) £ 210
    iii) £ 760
    iv) £ 930
    v)   £ 300
    How much commission did John earn last week?   (5 marks)

12 Some employers provide their employees with subsidised meals or other benefits.
    What does this mean?   (2 marks)

13 Company pension schemes can be contributory or non-contributory. What is the
    difference?   (2 marks)

14 Why, do you think, do many companies, such as Ultra Electronics, give their employees free company shares and also let them buy additional shares at a reduced price? How does this benefit:
   i)   the employee;
   ii) the employer? (8 marks)

15 What is the meaning of the term 'single status payments'? (2 marks)

16 What special benefits might be available to bank and building society workers? (2 marks)

CHAPTER 4

EMPLOYERS AND EMPLOYEES

Foundation and Intermediate

KEY TERMS:

job description   verbal warning

industrial action   compensation   unfair dismissal

In this chapter you will learn about the responsibilities of employers to their employees, and also the responsibilities of the employees. You will learn how important it is for everyone in a business organisation to work together as a team.

For a business to operate successfully, employers and employees must work together to achieve the aims of the organisation. Everyone understands this but, without clear guidelines, such co-operation would be impossible to achieve. The main rights and responsibilities of the employers and the employees are so important that they have been laid down in several Acts of Parliament. We will look at these later. First, it is necessary to examine the general principles regarding these rights and responsibilities.

As you know, most businesses must make a profit in order to survive. If a business makes losses, it will eventually close down. This would mean not only loss of profits for the owners, but loss of jobs for all employees. Therefore, all those involved in a business, from the chairman of the board to the junior clerks or operatives, have a common interest – to ensure that the business does well.

You can probably remember occasions when you were working in a group or team of people, maybe at school or college, when doing a part-time job or when taking part in sports events. If you do, then you will also remember whether the team worked well together or did not manage to co-operate. To work well together, every member of the team must know exactly what he or she should do, what they can expect from the team leaders and what the rules of the activity, sport or job are.

A business which fails to ensure that its employees work well together is very likely to get into difficulties. This is what management must do to prevent such a situation:

- provide the staff with a safe and healthy environment;

- treat all workers fairly;

- fulfil all legal requirements;

- create a friendly and supportive working environment.

The above are all the responsibilities of the management. The employees also have to contribute by recognising their own responsibilities.

The **contract of employment** is the document which gives details of the responsibilities of both the employer and the employee, with further details of what is required from the worker included in the **job description**.

Activity

A class of 24 GNVQ Business students has to prepare an important assignment. The students have to carry out some research into local firms, interview a number of employers and workers, and look up facts in textbooks. Then they must prepare a presentation which will include an OHP (overhead projector), informative handouts and posters.

All the students began to work individually and they soon found that it was very difficult to do everything required. Not only was it taking a great deal of time, but the local businessmen were not very happy to be asked for interviews by two dozen students. In the library, only a few students were able to get hold of the books they needed, and the others had to wait and were afraid that they would not be able to do their work in time.

Then one of them, Eddy, had an idea.

'Listen,' he said. 'Why don't we organise ourselves? After all, this is supposed to be a Business course, so let's be businesslike! Why don't we ...?'

What do you think was Eddy's idea?

How can the students organise themselves so that everyone is not doing exactly the same things and getting in everybody else's way?

Write a short report on how the students can organise their work as a team divided into smaller teams. Explain how this will be beneficial to all.

Contract of Employment
Happy Returns Ltd

Contract of Employment between Happy Returns Ltd and Amanda Lee

Happy Returns Ltd (the employer) and Amanda Lee (the employee) are the two parties to this contract.

Amanda Lee is employed as a senior supervisor by Happy Returns Ltd.

Duties: working in the main office of the employer, and supervision of the office staff.

Starting date: 1st January 2001

Hours of work: 37 hours per week, by arrangement (flexi-time is in operation)

Holidays: 20 working days per annum

Notice required: 2 weeks

Salary: £10,000 per annum, to be reviewed after one year

Pension scheme: non-contributory pension scheme.

The employer has grievance, sickness and injury procedures. If the employee needs help in any of the above matters, the Human Resources Manager will advise.

Employer's responsibilities to the employee

- to pay a fair wage;
- to treat all employees fairly and without discrimination;
- to provide a safe and healthy working environment;
- to provide reasonable conditions of work, such as holidays;
- to provide a contract of employment;
- to ensure that all employees are given an induction;
- to provide training on and off the job as necessary.

Employers should ensure also that each employee is given a **performance review** at least once a year. The purpose of the review is for both the employee and his or her line manager to look at the worker's performance together and see what has been done well and where, perhaps, there is room for improvement. The review can be very useful for deciding on a course of training that the employee might need. It is also an opportunity for the employee and the line manager to talk about the job, its requirements and how things are going generally. A performance review is *not* meant to be a test or to be used as a disciplinary procedure.

Performance Review Form

PERFORMANCE APPRAISAL

NAME ....

JOB TITLE ....

DATE OF APPRAISAL ....

APPRAISEE

This form provides you with an opportunity to:
  i.   Express your views about your job achievements.
  ii. Discuss ways in which further improvements can be made.
  iii. Discuss training needs and your own personal career plan.

Instructions: Fill in parts 1 and 2 and then pass the form to your supervisor. Your comments will form the basis of your appraisal interview.

1. Performance appraisal
Comment on your jobs and tasks. Identify those that you think went well, and those which could have gone better.

....
....
....

2. Improvement ideas
Identify aspects of your job where further imrovements could be made, either by yourself or with the co-operation of other people.

....
....
....

---

15. Appraiser's comments ....

....

16. Agreed action

Objective/Action ....   Timescale ....

17. For joint discussion:

i. Training and development (details and timescale) ....

ii. Additional comments ....

Print name of appraisee ....

Signed (*appraisee*) ....   Signed (*appraiser*) ....

Date ....

Grievance and Disciplinary Procedures

However carefully an organisation tries to do all that is necessary for the health and well-being of its employees, sometimes things do go wrong. Also, some employees, however carefully selected, do not behave at work as they should. This is why all businesses should have grievance and disciplinary procedures.

Disciplinary procedure

This is a way in which the employer can deal with an employee who breaks the rules or does not carry out his or her duties properly. Employers have to comply with the law when dealing with this sort of problem.

Activity

Try the following calculation: if a worker is ten minutes late four times a week for one year (take 48 weeks to be a year), how many working hours has he or she lost for the business?

For example, an employer cannot 'sack' a worker for coming late once or even twice. If an employee is late every day, the employer should, first of all, speak to the worker and try to find out the reason for this. If the lateness continues, the employee must be given a **verbal** warning. If things do not improve, **written** warnings must be given. Only if there seems no way out of the difficulty can the employer begin a procedure to end the worker's contract.

Definition – a **verbal warning** is the first stage of a disciplinary procedure taken by the employer against an employee.

There are many possible actions which can lead to a disciplinary procedure. You might think that lateness is not very important – do 10 minutes matter very much?

Disciplinary procedure might also be taken in cases of theft, fighting, cheating, drunkenness, etc.

Grievance procedure

Disciplinary procedure allows the employer to deal with unsatisfactory workers. For employees who think they have good cause to complain about their jobs, conditions, fellow workers or managers, there is the grievance procedure. Again, employment law lays down the rules, and employers should make sure that any employee with a complaint has the opportunity to explain their grievance, and the right to expect that it will be dealt with fairly.

If an employee is unhappy with the way in which his or her grievance has been dealt with, he or she can take the matter further, perhaps to an employment tribunal which is an independent body.

Employee's responsibilities to the employer
- to carry out the terms of the contract;
- to undertake such duties as can be described as reasonable;
- to be honest;
- to be punctual;
- to behave and dress as is appropriate.

Case Study: The receptionist and the kitchen worker

Lynn and Naomi both work in a large hotel. Lynn is a receptionist and Naomi works in the kitchen. Naomi dyes her hair a different colour every week and wears very colourful clothes. Her supervisor, Marianne, does not mind because, as she says, Naomi's hair is covered by a scarf and her clothes are under an overall while she is working.

Last week Lynn came to work with her hair dyed purple and several temporary tattoos on her arms. She was asked to go home and come back looking 'suitable for the job'. Lynn is very upset with her supervisor, Denise, and wants to know why the same rules do not apply to her as to Naomi.

We can say that the duties of the employer to the employee are the rights of the employee. Another important right of all workers is to belong to a trade union. Trade unions are associations of workers in different industries, and they exist to protect their members and to try and help them to get the best pay and working conditions. If a worker, or a group of workers, is in disagreement with an employer, a union representative will help the employees to solve the problem.

You are probably familiar with the term **strike**. A strike is a form of **industrial action** taken by workers in dispute with their employer; if a strike is called, the workers stop work and walk out. Although strikes do happen, they are not good for either the workers or the employer. Employers might lose a lot of business as a result of a strike, and might even go out of business. Employees lose pay and can lose their jobs. This is why nobody wants a strike. Most problems between employers and workers are usually solved by discussion and **negotiation,** frequently with the help of the trade union involved. Each union represents many workers and acts on behalf of them all. We can say that this collective approach is what gives trade unions their strength. In each negotiation, the union representatives speak for all the members, not just for themselves. Even those employers who would not listen to individual workers are likely to pay attention to what *all* their workers want or complain about.

Even when the employers and the unions cannot agree, it does not mean that the workers will immediately call a strike. There are a number of different ways in which employees can put pressure on their employers:

- **go slow** – the workers do not refuse to work, but work much more slowly than usual;

- **overtime ban** – the workers do not agree to work any additional shifts or hours;

- **working to rule** – when this happens, the employees refuse to do anything that is not in their job description or contract of employment.

Today fewer people belong to trade unions than used to be the case. The unions with the largest membership used to be those representing workers in manufacturing industries. As these industries have declined, so the numbers of people working in them have also decreased.

243

**Acts of Parliament
concerned with rights and responsibilities of
employers and employees**

- Employment Act 1990
- Citizens' Charter 1991
- Heath and Safety at Work Act (HASAWA) 1974
- Employment Protection (Consolidation) Act 1978
- Trade Union and Labour Relations Act 1992
- Trade Union Reform and Employment Rights Act 1993
- Wages Act 1986
- Sex Discrimination Act 1986
- Race Relations Act 1976
- Equal Pay Act 1970
- Minimum Wage Act 1998
- Employment Rights Act 1996
- Disability Discrimination Act 1995

As you can see, employers must be familiar with a large number of Acts of Parliament in order to make sure that their workers are treated as the law requires. For example:

- The **Employment Protection (Consolidation) Act 1978** states that: any employee working more than eight hours a week must receive a written statement of employment (not a contract, which gives all the conditions of work and must be signed) within two months of starting work.

- The **Health and Safety at Work Act 1974** states that all workers are entitled to:
  - i) a safe and healthy environment (this includes regulations regarding heating, lighting, air supply and noise);
  - ii) safe premises;
  - iii) safe materials and substances;
  - iv) safe equipment and machinery;
  - v) training, supervision and information as necessary.

- The **Wages Act 1986** gives the regulations regarding **deductions** which the employer may take from a worker's wage or salary – these include National Insurance (NI) contributions and income tax.

- The **Equal Pay Act, Race Relations Act** and **Sex Discrimination Act** state that everyone doing the same work in a business must be paid the same. Employers are not, for example, allowed to pay a woman less than a man if the work they do is the same or of equal value. The only reason why one employee may be paid more than another in the same work is because he or she has higher qualifications or greater experience.

Activity

If you have a part-time job you can find out what you need for this task yourself. If you have not, ask someone who is working to tell you about her or his workplace.

i) What safety equipment is there (e.g. fire extinguishers)?

ii) What information is there for workers on the use of such equipment?

iii) Are exits and entrances clearly marked?

iv) Are there any hazards to workers, such as flexes trailing across floors or doors that open outwards into busy corridors?

v) Do the employees have access to drinking water, toilets and cloakrooms?

Make a list of your findings. Write a short memo which could be sent to your supervisor, and include any suggestions for improvement if necessary.

HEALTH + SAFETY AT WORK!

Most employers are aware of their responsibilities and find the legislation helpful. Some employers, however, either do not take the trouble to find out what is required, or do not think that all the rules and regulations are necessary. This is where the law can help the employee. If an employee thinks that he or she has been unfairly treated, and if the matter cannot be sorted out at the workplace, perhaps with the help of the union representative, the employee can take the dispute to an **employment tribunal**. Employment tribunals are special independent courts which will look at all the facts of the dispute and decide who is right. If an employment tribunal decides that the employer is at fault, it might order the employer to pay **compensation** to the employee. If it is a case of **unfair dismissal**, the employer might also be ordered to give the worker his or her job back.

Definition – **unfair dismissal** is the sacking of an employee without following the correct legal procedure.

Revision

Questions

1 Why do people at work need protection? (2 marks)

2 Which Acts of Parliament were passed to make sure that all workers are treated fairly? (3 marks)

3 What are the main aims of trade unions? (2 marks)

4 Read carefully the three situations given below:
   i) Careen works in an office. Yesterday she tripped over a cable which had been left lying across the floor, and broke her ankle.
   ii) Pedro has just started working at the delicatessen counter of his local supermarket. He was shown how to use the bacon slicer and then left on his own. The guard of the slicer had not been replaced and when Pedro began to operate it he injured his hand quite badly.
   iii) Sidhu and Mary both started work in the same firm at the same time. Both have had good job appraisals but Mary has already been promoted twice while Sidhu has been passed over for promotion. Sidhu feels that her boss is treating her unfairly because she is of Pakistani origin.

   Explain which Act of Parliament is relevant to each of the cases, and advise Careen, Pedro and Sidhu what they should do. (12 marks)

5 Which Acts of Parliament deal with the following responsibilities of the employer:
   i) remuneration;
   ii) fair treatment of all employees;
   iii) adequate physical conditions at work;
   iv) the right of employees to join a trade union? (4 marks)

6 Why is it important for employers and employees to work well together, and what might be the outcome for the business if they fail to do so? (3 marks)

7 What details would you expect to be included in an employment contract? (4 marks)

8 Richard works as a warehouse manager for a large haulage company. He is reliable and punctual and enthusiastic in his approach to his job. He is in charge of five operatives and he was upset to learn from his line manager that three of his workers have complained about the way he runs the warehouse. They have said that Richard only issues orders and never discusses any new jobs with them. Two of them, Joan and Sunita, feel that he does not consider them as good as the men, and have said that they are paid less than some men who do the same job. Richard's line manager is worried that the women might 'cause trouble'. Finally, all the workers have signed a letter to management, complaining about conditions in the warehouse, particularly about lack of heating in the winter and the state of the bathroom.

   Richard does not understand what all the fuss is about. He knows that he is good at his job, reliable and efficient. He thinks that the workers have no cause for complaint as he always makes clear what he wants done and does not think that time should be wasted in discussions with the staff. He is not sure about rules and regulations regarding payment for the same work, and has no idea what the two women could do. In Richard's opinion, workers in a warehouse should not complain about cleanliness of bathrooms or low temperatures in the winter. 'It's a warehouse, not an office!' says Richard.

Richard's line manager has asked you to explain a number of points to Richard.

i) Why people should be paid the same wage for the same work.

ii) What steps he can take to make the employees feel part of a team.

iii) Why it is necessary to treat all workers fairly.

iv) What the legal requirements are about heating and sanitary arrangements at work.

v) What the workers can do if they are not satisfied with the management's response (and if it is fair of Richard's line manager to say that the two women are out to 'cause trouble').

In each explanation, refer to the relevant Act of Parliament. Present your answers in note form, and provide some suggestions as to how Richard himself can try to put things right, and why he should do so. (15 marks)

9 What is the difference between a 'go slow' and 'working to rule'? (2 marks)

10 Linda works as an administrative assistant in a busy office. She deals with customers and clients, answers the phone and keeps computerised records. She has a junior to help her. The junior normally collects the post and distributes it, makes tea and coffee, and operates the photocopier, as well as running messages. In the course of a typical day, Linda quite often helps the junior out if the girl has too much to do. Linda also frequently helps her other colleagues if she has some time to spare and they have a large amount of work to do.

Linda's union is now in dispute with the employers and has decided on industrial action.

i) What will Linda have to stop doing if the union decides on 'working to rule'? (2 marks)

ii) How will Linda's action affect other people? (2 marks)

iii) What would Linda have to do if the union decided on a 'go slow'? (2 marks)

iv) If everyone in the office started to work to rule, how might the customers, clients and the business itself be affected? (4 marks)

In your answers to Questions 11–14, you should:

i) state if there could be grounds for a grievance procedure or a disciplinary procedure;

ii) give reasons for your answer;

iii) state what the possible outcome of each situation might be.

11 Maya is an experienced accounts clerk. She has been in her present job for four years, and has always had excellent performance reviews. This year, her section supervisor retired. His place has been taken by Olaf, who has been heard on several occasions saying that he does not like working with women because they are 'slovenly and inefficient'. As the section is short-staffed, Olaf has been giving Maya more and more work, and has now given her a very poor performance appraisal. When she asked him why, he told her, 'You're incapable of doing your work properly.' (12 marks)

12 Julian works for a big marketing company. He went on holiday for two weeks, and was supposed to return in time for the start of a new advertising campaign. On the morning that he was due back, he telephoned his line manager to tell her that he had decided to stay on for two more days. Julian is very upset because when he got back, his manager warned him about his behaviour. The manager has said that she might start a disciplinary procedure. Julian is determined to start a grievance procedure against the manager.   (12 marks)

13 Jim and Stella work for the same company, doing the same job. Stella has more experience than Jim. She has just found out that Jim is paid quite a lot more than she is.   (10 marks)

14 Isabel is a receptionist in a large hotel. She has recently dyed her hair green and started wearing tracksuits to work. Her supervisor has told her that the hair colour and the clothes are unsuitable. Isabel is very annoyed, and has told everyone that she has no intention of dyeing her hair back to normal or dressing more formally.   (10 marks)

CHAPTER 5

TRAINING AND CAREER DEVELOPMENT

Foundation and Intermediate

KEY TERMS:

multiskilled   skills gap

In this chapter you will learn about how workers can gain additional qualifications and learn new skills while working in a business organisation.

First of all, we must be clear what is meant by the word 'training'. It is the process of developing the knowledge and skills of employees so that they become more efficient and better at their jobs.

Whether a business is large or small, it needs a flexible, **multiskilled** workforce. Here, flexible means able and willing to carry out a variety of tasks and to adjust to new conditions and situations within the workplace. 'Multiskilled' simply means 'with a number of skills'. A good example of a worker who must be flexible and multiskilled is the sole trader about whom you learned in Chapter 1. In larger organisations all employees should be trained not just when they arrive at the firm, but throughout their working lives. This is now widely accepted throughout industry but not so long ago this was not the view of senior management. Today, it is realised that training is of great importance to the business organisation and can help to:

- increase production levels;
- improve quality;
- avoid, or cut down, waste;
- reduce high staff turnover;
- prevent accidents;
- motivate staff.

All business organisations want to achieve these objectives and most now know that a well-constructed training programme is in itself a good motivator, giving workers the opportunity to update their skills or learn new ones, and making them feel that the employer cares about their progress and their future prospects. A well-motivated workforce is usually a happier workforce, and this is obviously a situation that any sensible management wants to encourage.

In the spring of 1996 almost 4 million people in the UK workforce had received job-related training in the previous four weeks.

At present, the categories of workers most likely to receive training are:

- those with higher level qualifications, i.e. beyond A Level and its equivalents;
- younger workers, in their first or second jobs.

The government has recognised for some time now that there is a considerable **skills gap** in the UK. This means the gap between what a person can do and what he or she should be able to do. The only way to fill the gap is through training.

Figure 4.5.1 Training fills the skills gap

The skills **GAP** can be filled by training

Skills a person has now

Skills a person should have

The skills gap also means that although in spring 1998 there were 1,766,000 unemployed people (6.1% of the workforce) in the UK (Office for National Statistics Labour Force Survey 1999), many of them did not have the skills that would have enabled them to fill vacancies in business organisations. The importance of filling the gap as quickly as possible cannot be overemphasised. Compared with other countries, the UK's record in training and education is very poor. Research in the mid-1990s put Britain near the bottom of the table of industrialised countries regarding the overall quality of its workforce. At present, the UK educates and trains fewer graduates, engineers and technologists than other countries in Western Europe and it is those countries that are our main competitors.

> Compared with Germany, France, Japan and the USA, British employers spend a much smaller percentage of their resources on training.

This unwillingness of employers to spend sufficient money on training programmes is shortsighted, as an improved workforce would bring greater productivity and profitability. On the other hand, in 1997 nearly 70% of employers stated that their businesses needed more skilled people, so they were actually aware of the need for a better-trained workforce.

Table 4.5.1 shows a breakdown of the costs of training provided by Panasonic. This very large Japanese manufacturer of electronic and electrical goods has worked out exactly how much it costs to train its employees, and how much more the company gains once the workers have achieved their qualifications.

Table 4.5.1 Breakdown of the costs of training

The costs and benefits of training	
Programme cost per Candidate	
Registration	£12.00
Module Assessment (£23.00 × 4)	£92.00
Final Assessment	£12.00
Delivery by external providers (£5600 × 12)	£467.00
Total	£583,00
Cost/Benefit analysis for programme to date	
Cost for 34 Candidates (34 × £583.00)	£19,822.00
Quantified saving from 34 projects	£2,244,358,00
Net saving	£2,224,536.00

Source: *Progress Magazine NEBS Management*, No. 20 Autumn 1998

Figure 4.5.2 Training notice board

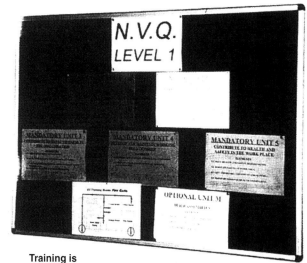

Training is an important part of the Panasonic strategy starting with NVQ Level 1 Performing Manufacturing Operations and going right up to post-graduate qualifications.

Matters have been improving in the UK, however, and the same report (see Figure 4.5.3) included the information that the majority of organisations said that they had both a training plan and a training budget, and, in addition, also provided the opportunity for their workers to have some off-the-job training.

Figure 4.5.3 Report on the benefits of training staff

TRAINING PAYS
The Panasonic experience

By David Pardey

Cost Benefit Analysis (CBA) is an important tool for any manager to use to assess a project or activity. Training is an important part of any organisation's strategy for achieving its goals. In this article, David Pardey finds out how Panasonic have used CBA to assess the contribution that one particular training programme in particular – their NEBS Management Certificate – has made to the company's success.

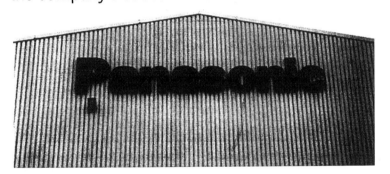

Recent research by UNiFI, the banking and finance union at Barclays, suggested that the lack of training opportunities was causing the bank to lose staff – at up to 20% per year! The problem was even greater with casual and contract staff (about one in five of the workforce), for whom little or no training is available, and where nearly one in three leave early.

At the same time, employers are experiencing severe skills shortages, with investment plans delayed and production limited by lack of appropriately skilled people. The IRS Employment Review in March this year described the situation as reaching a crisis', with higher labour turnover and difficulties in recruiting new staff causing problems for many firms. Further evidence has come from the Chartered Institute of Purchasing and Supply which has blamed skills shortages for an inability by suppliers to respond to new orders despite having unused capacity.

In the public sector, a shortfall in the numbers training for occupations like nursing and teaching are leading to forecasts of acute problems for the Government in meeting its pre-election pledges on waiting lists and class sizes. At a macro-economic level, the shortages in skilled people is leading to wage rises and consequent inflationary pressure, which has led in turn to higher interest rates being set by the Monetary Policy Committee, and fears of recession.

The difficulties for many firms in dealing with this situation are two-fold: training people to fill vacancies is often seen as:

- too time-consuming – the delay between the training and the return takes too long and is too uncertain, and

- too risky – people, once trained, may leave and give the benefits to other employers.

One company which has rejected this assessment and invested heavily in training is Panasonic, in Cardiff, and their experience of using NEBS Management and other qualifications, gives the lie to these objections. What's more, they are able to cost out the benefits from some of their training activities so clearly that it becomes obvious that far from costing them, training really does pay!

Source: *Progress Magazine NEBS Management*, No 20 Autumn 1998

Table 4.5.2 Employers' provision of training

Employers' provision of training, 1997

	Proportion of employers:				Involved in the last 12 months with:				
	Reporting an increase in skill needs	With a training plan	With a training budget	Providing off-the-job training in the last 12 months	NVQs/ SVQs	Youth training	Investors in people	Modern Appren-ticeship	Other nationally recognised vocational qualifi-cations
Great Britain	69	65	63	82	52	16	32	15	17
North East	71	71	64	84	66	27	38	19	23
North West (GOR) & Merseyside	63	67	64	78	60	14	43	19	15
North West (GOR)	64	70	69	79	61	14	45	19	16
Merseyside	56	54	43	74	56	14	35	17	13
Yorkshire and the Humber	65	66	64	84	64	24	35	24	21
East Midlands	68	64	58	78	43	13	26	12	24
West Midlands	67	63	58	89	64	17	37	16	17
Eastern	72	65	63	83	56	13	27	12	19
London	72	61	65	82	36	13	26	10	15
South East (GOR)	74	67	69	82	48	16	32	17	15
South West	69	64	58	81	50	13	32	13	16
England	69	65	63	82	52	16	33	15	17
Wales	68	62	54	75	56	21	36	10	18
Scotland	66	69	65	78	50	17	26	13	14

Percentages

Source: 'Skill needs in Britain 1997', IFF Research Limited for the Department for Education and Employment, in *Regional Trends 1998*

As you can see from Table 4.5.2, the provision of training varies from region to region. Merseyside, one of the most economically depressed regions in the UK, has the lowest proportion of employers with a training plan and a training budget.

Why does Merseyside have so few firms prepared to spend money and time on training?

We know that training is important, both to the employer and to the employee. Sometimes it is a way for people already working in the business to be able to progress to different and often better jobs. The important questions are: What kind of training? By whom? Where? In which areas?

Just as there are very many different jobs in many different industries, there are different kinds and methods of training. Different business organisations have varying needs and must select the right kind of training for their employees. There are, however, certain guidelines.

Induction Training

Happy Returns Ltd

New Employees' Induction Programme
Monday 14th January 2001

9.15 a.m.	Meet in the staff lounge for coffee
9.40 a.m.	Welcome by the Managing Director, who will introduce other members of senior staff
10.15 a.m.	Tour of the factory and offices
11.00 a.m.	Coffee
11.20 a.m.	Talk on Health & Safety
11.45 a.m.	The Human Resources Manager will explain contracts, grievance procedures and the appraisal system
12.30 p.m.	Lunch
2.00 p.m.	Meeting with supervisors
3.00 p.m.	Question and answer session
4.15 p.m.	Close

Induction training is given to new staff. It usually takes place soon after they join the company. During induction the new recruits are introduced to the company and given information about the business, the goods it makes, or the services which it provides. In particular, they must be told what their job involves and how, generally, it fits into the organisation. A typical induction in some firms may involve a half-day programme during which videos of the company are shown and the new staff are introduced to their supervisors, other managers, the team with whom they will be working, and other staff members such as the human resources manager. They will also be shown around the business, and arrangements about breaks etc. will be explained.

In some organisations, and in the case of more senior jobs, the induction programme might last much longer but normally employers want it to be efficient and concise so that the recruits can start working efficiently and with confidence as soon as possible.

Off-the-job Training

This type of training refers to skills that employees learn away from the workplace, e.g. at a further education college, or at the firm's training school. Some skills cannot be learnt while working, particularly the theory of a job, and this is why employers send employees on outside courses.

Jeanette began working as a Saturday girl at a hairdressing salon when she was still at school. When she left school, the salon owner offered her a full-time job which she has been doing for two years now. As Jeanette is ambitious and keen to learn, this year her employer has sent her on a hairdressing course at the local college, which she hopes to complete next year.

Large companies, like British Telecom, have their own training schools. You will also remember that the part-qualified nurses in the Young Veterinary Partnership attend Berkshire College of Agriculture on day release, in order to get their full qualification.

More and more frequently training for middle and senior management takes place at hotel conference centres. In these situations the point to note is that the skills to be learnt are delivered away from the workplace and the pressures of the daily routine, so that the participants are better able to concentrate and work together as a group.

On-the-job Training

People learn their new jobs at work by watching and copying the actions of other, more experienced employees. This type of training has its advantages and disadvantages.

Advantages	Disadvantages
• relatively cheap • easy to arrange	• only as good as the trainer • the trainer must also be trained

Some skills, e.g. how to use a certain piece of equipment, are better learnt on the job, while others, particularly those leading to formal qualifications, are more suitable for off-the-job training.

You will see from the Ultra Electronics case study that Ultra carries out much of its operator training in-house and on the job. Workers are placed in manufacturing cells (see page 198) and learn from each other under the direction of their supervisors and managers. In 1999 the Ultra training budget amounted to £160,000. This paid for an average of three and half days' training per operator per year. This is a little better than the national average of 2.3 days training per year (see Table 4.5.3). The engineers at Ultra receive a yearly average of five days' training.

In the Young Veterinary Partnership, a much smaller and very different type of business, only the veterinary nurses and some of the receptionists received on-the-job, in-house training.

The amount and type of job-related training varies in different workplaces and in different occupations. Those in the professions are most likely to receive training, with almost a quarter doing so, closely followed by skilled workers and those in technical occupations. Plant and machine operatives are the least likely to get any form of training, although this situation is changing slowly for the better. More employers such as Ultra Electronics are now providing training for all their worker.

Table 4.5.3 Job-related training opportunities

Employees[1] receiving job-related training[1]: by occupation and method of training, Spring 1996

United Kingdom   Percentages

	On-the-job training only	Off-the-job training only	Both on and off-the-job training	All methods of training
Professional	5.8	14.9	3.7	24.4
Associate professional and technical	5.0	13.8	5.3	24.2
Managers and administrators	3.7	10.2	2.6	16.4
Personal and protective service	4.8	8.2	2.9	15.9
Sales	3.6	8.8	1.5	13.9
Clerical and secretarial	3.9	8.0	1.8	13.7
Craft and related	3.3	4.7	2.5	10.4
Plant and machine operatives	2.3	2.8	0.8	5.9
Other occupations/no answer	1.9	3.9	0.7	6.5
All occupations	3.9	8.5	2.4	14.8

[1] Employees are those in employment excluding the self-employed, unpaid family workers and those on government schemes.

[2] Data are for people of working age (males aged 16 to 64 and females aged 16 to 59) receiving job-related training in the four weeks prior to interview.

Source: Department for Education and Employment, from the Labour Force Survey, in *Social Trends 1997*

Performance Reviews

Performance reviews play an important part in any training programme. They enable the employee to understand what skills he or she needs to learn, and give the employer the information needed to provide relevant training. As you learned in the last chapter, performance reviews are not tests or disciplinary measures. One of their main benefits is the opportunity for the employee to express his or her views and make requests for help or training.

Retraining

In the fast-changing world of business, skills can quite quickly become out of date. It is one of the important roles of management to organise refresher training courses. In the life of a business, and during an average employee's working life, many situations will occur in which the upgrading of skills and retraining will be needed.

Situations in which retraining is needed

- technological change;
- company reorganisation;
- preparation of workers for promotion;
- where skill shortages exist.

It should be clear that training is beneficial both to the employer and to the employee. Here are some of the major benefits:

For the employer

- improvement of the quality and motivation of staff;
- introduction of new ideas and skills into the organisation;
- raising of standards and reduction of accidents;
- better customer service;
- improved quality of the product or service;
- increase of productivity.

For the employee

- developing skills and knowledge;
- improving promotion prospects;
- greater job satisfaction;
- feeling valued by the employer;
- increase in effectiveness and confidence.

Motivation

To motivate means to provide a person with an interest in carrying out some activity. We all know that we like doing some things and are not at all keen on doing others. A person who is well motivated is willing to work very hard to achieve success. You only have to look at people in the world of sport to see that this is true. Without motivation, nobody would train in all weathers to run in the London marathon. Without motivation, people would give up anything that was difficult or time consuming. You are doing a GNVQ course to obtain a qualification, so we can say that you are motivated by your aim.

To do well, people have to want to do well, and they want to do well when their motivation is strong. It is very important that people in business are motivated, and employers are more and more aware of this.

You have probably heard people say that they only work because they need to earn money. It is true that we all must make a living, so our earnings are of great importance. It has been proved time and time again, however, that, important as money is, there are other things that are just as important to people as their weekly or monthly pay.

Here are some aspects of work which motivate people (although not every individual is interested in all of them):

- **working conditions** – these include health and safety, restrooms, staff canteen, etc.;
- **financial rewards** – including not only wage or salary but also dividends, bonuses, etc.;

- **job satisfaction** – this means knowing that the job is worthwhile, and feeling pleasure at doing it well;

- **additional benefits** – these could be private medical insurance, a company car or pension;

- **working arrangements** – for many people, as mentioned on page 211, the hours and flexibility of work are of great importance;

- **having responsibilities**;

- **possibility of promotion**;

- **being appreciated** by management;

- **training opportunities**.

As you already know, repetitive manual work can be very boring. Workers on assembly lines in factories, for example, have a high rate of illness and absenteeism. If you think about the reasons for this,

and refer to the motivating factors above, you will see that such workers:

- do not usually earn a lot of money;

- often work in conditions which are not particularly pleasant;

- rarely receive additional benefits;

- do not get much training;

- have very few prospects of promotion;

- often do not have much job satisfaction, as they deal with only one small part of the finished product.

This is why many employers now try to vary the jobs done by operatives, so that they can learn new skills. This gives them a new interest and makes them more interested in their jobs. Ultra Electronics has introduced worker cells for this purpose (see page 198).

Activity

i) Make a list of those aspects of work that would be most important to you if you were looking for a job now. Put them in order of importance, and briefly explain your **priorities**.

ii) Talk to three of your class members and ask them to give you their lists. Are they all the same? If they are not, why do you think they are different?

iii) Now talk to three people who are already in

full-time employment. Ask each one what motivates them at work. Make a note of their answers.

iv) Are the students' lists and the workers' lists the same? If not, why do you think they are different?

v) Write a short report on 'What motivates people at work', including your findings from the two groups of people with whom you have talked.

Revision

Questions

1. (Refer to the Ultra Electronics (page 196) and the Young Veterinary Partnership (page 195) case studies.)
   i) How much training per year do employees of Ultra receive on average? Do some receive more than others? (2 marks)
   ii) What kind of off-the-job training do some of the employees of the Young Veterinary Partnership receive? (1 mark)

2. Below is a list of various skills needed in different places of work. You should decide which type of training is suitable for which skill. Present your answer in two columns.
   a) using a fax machine
   b) producing a business letter
   c) NVQ in Office Technology
   d) GNVQ in Business
   e) operating a bacon slicer
   f) assembling a car
   g) leading a team
   h) washing and drying hair
   i) everyday care of sick animals
   j) learning about animal diseases (15 marks)

3. Explain the purpose of induction programmes. (2 marks)

4. What is on-the-job training? Give two examples. (3 marks)

5. What type of training is best done off the job? (2 marks)

6. What is retraining, and why is it necessary? (2 marks)

7. How does an employee benefit from training? (2 marks)

8. Which groups of workers generally receive least training? (1 mark)

9. Why should UK employers provide more training? (3 marks)

10. What is meant by the statement: 'On-the-job training is only as good as the trainer'? (2 marks)

11. You are working in the human resources department of a large manufacturing company. Your boss has asked you to look through all the requests for training that she has received and suggest how the training might be organised. In each case, state the type of training, and how and where it should take place.
    i) Two employees whose job appraisals show that they need to update their skills. (3 marks)
    ii) Twenty secretaries who are not confident enough to use all the new technology in the office. (3 marks)
    iii) Four new supervisors who have just been promoted but need to learn about managing people and keeping records. (4 marks)
    iv) An accounts clerk who is a capable and excellent worker, but lacks the qualifications needed for promotion. (3 marks)
    v) A note from the managing director, asking for something to be done about department heads who seem not to be able to work well together. (5 marks)

Revision Test

Part 1

Case Study

Joe and Marisa have just started work for Shop at Leisure plc, a large mail-order company. They have both completed their Intermediate GNVQ in Business and are delighted to be out in the world of work. Joe is working in the packing department, as assistant to the manager, Trevor Beck. Marisa has been given the job of administrative assistant in the general office of Shop at Leisure. Her line manager is Clare Curtis.

Joe and Marisa met for lunch one day last week and began to talk about their jobs. When they compared notes, they found that their conditions of service were very similar. The only difference was that the office workers are on flexi-time, while the packing department staff work from 8.30 a.m. to 5.00 p.m. from Monday to Friday, with an hour off for lunch. Joe was not very pleased about this, but Marisa reminded him that he was to be paid overtime if he had to work late but if she had to finish an urgent job she would not get any extra money for working a longer day.

Otherwise, they both were to be paid monthly, by credit transfer, both were to have four weeks' holiday a year, and both had been told they could enrol on a part-time Vocational A Level day course.

'I'm looking forward to getting my contract,' said Marisa.

'Yes,' said Joe. 'It's a pity we must wait till we have been here for three months!'

'I wonder,' said Marisa, 'how different our contracts are from Clare's and Trevor's.'

'Well,' said Joe, 'I can tell you that their contracts are quite a bit different, because I asked Trevor and he told me.'

'You mean they earn more money?'

'Of course they do – they both have more qualifications and experience, and have more responsible jobs! I meant other things.'

'Like what?'

'Trevor has five weeks' holiday because he has been with the firm for over five years. He also gets a bonus every year at Christmas if the packing department has done well during the year. Oh, and he, and all the other managers, belong to the company pension scheme which is non-contributory.'

'What does that mean?'

'It means that the firm pays every month into a pension fund for the employee, but the employee doesn't have to pay anything.'

Marisa sighed. 'I don't think that's very important,' she said. 'We're only seventeen, what's the point of having a pension fund?'

Joe disagreed with her. 'It's very important,' he said firmly. 'We're only seventeen now but time flies, and a pension is vital for the future. My father is very worried now because there is no such thing in his firm.'

'All right,' said Marisa. 'I think I see your point. But if Trevor gets a bonus and a pension scheme, he's doing very well. How much overtime is he paid? I know he often stays late when the work isn't finished.'

'He isn't paid any overtime,' replied Joe. 'None of the managers are. It's part of his job to be there and supervise us. He also has to be in first, and lock up at the end of the day. And sometimes he has to come in on a Saturday, or very early in the morning, if the managing director calls a meeting.'

'I know that,' said Marisa. 'Clare has to do that as well. She's always complaining about it, but she hasn't told us about the bonuses and the pension! She also complains about how much work she has to do to organise everybody in the office, and to make sure that everything is done properly and on time. She told me that I was lucky to be given the chance to go on day release. It's all right for her, she's got her qualifications!'

'Not necessarily,' said Joe. 'I don't know about Clare, but Trevor is doing an MBA course – he says he needs to learn more to be more efficient at his job and also if he wants promotion in the future.'

'And I suppose he gets time off for that?'

'No, as a matter of fact he doesn't, but he gets his fees paid.'

'Oh,' said Marisa. 'I didn't know that managers still had to learn things. I suppose I should have known, because Clare went to a training course in some hotel the other week.'

Joe was thinking of something else. 'Have you ever seen Miss Horshell, the MD?' he asked.

'Yes,' said Clare. 'She sometimes comes into the office on her way to a meeting or to collect some papers. She's really nice. I wonder how much she earns?'

'I've no idea,' said Joe, 'but I can tell you that she, and all the members of the board, have some company shares and a company car as well as a petrol allowance. If the company does well, she and the others also get a share of the profits.'

'How do you know all this?' asked Marisa, amazed.

'It's not a secret,' answered Joe. 'I'm very interested in how management jobs differ from those of ordinary employees like you and me, so I try to find out. This was easy, because Miss Horshell is new to the job, and somebody showed me the advertisement for her job that had been in the paper.'

'I see,' said Marisa. 'Well, all we have to do is to become heads of departments or managing directors, and then we'll get company cars and shares and things!'

'True,' said Joe, 'but it's not easy. You need experience and more qualifications and to prove that you are not just a good worker, but that you can manage people and keep them happy. There's another snag, as well – the managing director cannot work from 9 to 5, or whatever. Senior managers might earn a lot of money, but they have to put in a lot of time. Running a big business like Shop at Leisure is very difficult. They must make important decisions, look out for competition, and go to lots of meetings. If they make wrong decisions, the results might be disastrous for all of us. It's a great responsibility.'

'So,' said Marisa, 'would you like to be a senior manager one day? I don't think I would!'

'Maybe,' said Joe, 'maybe one day in the future.'

Answer the following questions as fully as you can.

1 What does the title 'line manager' mean? (1 mark)

2 Marisa is on flexi-time – explain how flexi-time works. (2 marks)

3 Joe and Marisa are to be paid by credit transfer. How does this work? (1 mark)

4 What other methods of payment are there? (2 marks)

5 Why do Marisa and Joe have to wait to get their written contracts? (2 marks)

6 Why does Trevor get five weeks' holiday a year? (1 mark)

7 What is a bonus? (1 mark)

8 What is a non-contributory pension scheme? (1 mark)

9 Why is Joe's father worried? (2 marks)

10 What is the difference between Joe and Marisa's working hours and the hours of the managers? (3 marks)

11 What additional benefits do the senior managers and members of the board at Shop at Leisure plc get? Can you think of some other benefits which an employee can receive? (6 marks)

12 Joe has told Marisa that if senior managers make wrong decisions the results might be 'disastrous for all of us'. What did he mean? Explain clearly. (3 marks)

13 Joe and Marisa have been given a day a week to go and study further. Explain how this should benefit them, and why it is also good for the company. (5 marks)

14 All the people you heard about in the case study work for the same employer, Shop at Leisure plc, but their jobs are very different. How does Trevor's job differ from Joe's? (3 marks)

15 As MD, Miss Horshell must make strategic decisions. Clare and Trevor make operational decisions. Both kinds of decisions are of great importance for a business. Explain the difference between them. (6 marks)

16 Here are some details of Joe's job:
   • working as an assistant to packing department manager;
   • must have at least GNVQ Foundation in Business;
   • salary: £8,000;
   • opportunity for further study;
   • paid overtime;
   • four weeks' holiday a year;
   • opportunity to learn on the job, and possibility of promotion;
   • must be computer literate.
   Draft an advertisement for Joe's job. (8 marks)

Part 2

Answer the following questions as fully as you can.

1 What are the main responsibilities of:
   i) a marketing manager;
   ii) a finance manager? (4 marks)

2 What are the main advantages and disadvantages of being a sole trader? (4 marks)

3 What do operatives do? (1 mark)

4 What are job roles? (1 mark)

5 What is the difference between a manager and a supervisor? (2 marks)

6 Why are some operatives' jobs boring? (1 mark)

7 How can an employer try and make such jobs more interesting? How is this done at Ultra Electronics? (5 marks)

8 What is meant by a 'flat' management structure? (1 mark)

9 Make a list of different working arrangements. (6 marks)

10   Explain how a job share works.   (4 marks)

11   Why are older workers sometimes better than younger ones?   (2 marks)

12   How do businesses recruit workers?   (6 marks)

13   What is meant by 'work of equal value'?   (1 mark)

14   What details must appear in a contract of employment?   (4 marks)

15   What is a disciplinary procedure?   (3 marks)

16   Name three Acts of Parliament which deal with people at work.   (3 marks)

17   What is the purpose of performance appraisal?   (2 marks)

18   Explain what happens when workers decide to 'work to rule'.   (1 mark)

19   What is 'off-the-job' training?   (1 mark)

20   What do some workers receive from their employers in addition to their wages or
     salary?   (2 marks)

21   Explain the difference between strategic and operational managers.   (5 marks)

22   Why is teamwork important to the success of a business?   (4 marks)

23   How does the job of the administrator at the Young Veterinary Partnership differ from
     similar jobs at Ultra Electronics, and why?   (6 marks)

24   The UK spends less on training than many other countries. Explain why it should
     spend more.   (4 marks)

Total marks: 110

UNIT 5

RETAILING

CHAPTER 1

TYPES OF RETAIL OUTLET

KEY TERMS:

retailing	chain store	multiples
department store	supermarket	hypermarket
convenience store	independents	cash and carry
symbol group	voluntary chain	concessions

In this chapter you will learn what retailing is and how it fits into the overall production process. You will also learn about the different types of retail outlet.

Introduction – What is Retailing?

> Definition – **retailing** is the sale of goods and services to consumers for their personal, family or household use.

When goods are manufactured (e.g. cars or fish fingers) they are not usually manufactured close to the people who want to buy them. It is the retailer who actually offers the goods to the consumer. If, as sometimes happens, manufacturers sell the goods directly to consumers, they are acting as retailers when they sell the goods. Examples include potters

who sell their own pottery on a market stall, and furniture manufactures who have a factory shop from which consumers can buy furniture. The traditional way that many goods reach the consumer is shown in the diagram below.

In some cases these functions may be combined, with producers or wholesalers acting as retailers as well. With other products, the wholesaler is cut out and the producers sell their products direct to the retailer.

Figure 5.1.1 Retail chain

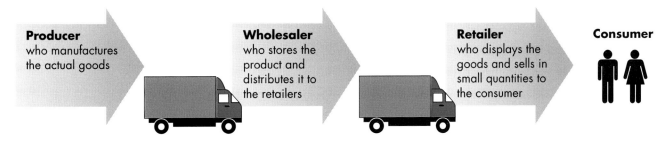

Producer
who manufactures the actual goods

Wholesaler
who stores the product and distributes it to the retailers

Retailer
who displays the goods and sells in small quantities to the consumer

Consumer

• Producer → consumer	e.g. mail-order firms, farm shops, factory door sales, craft products and double glazing sold door to door;
• Wholesaler → consumer	e.g. warehouse for furniture, some cash and carry stores and sales of golf equipment and computer equipment through what are called 'warehouse sales';
• Producer → retailer → consumer	e.g. most products in supermarkets.

Retailing is often thought of as just the selling of goods, but that is too narrow a definition. It also includes the selling of services if these are being sold to consumers. It is important to recognise that services are included. If you walk down any high street, or through a city or town centre shopping mall, it will not just be goods that are being offered to consumers, but also a very wide range of services. These are provided not only by banks, estate agents, travel agents, insurance companies, etc., but also by hairdressers, beauticians, chiropodists, sports centres, driving schools and cinemas. All are selling something to consumers and they are therefore retailing.

The Functions of Retailing

Most retailing is done by specialist retailers but, as we saw above, a producer or a wholesaler can be a retailer. It all depends on whether or not they are carrying out the functions of retailing. All retailers will provide some, if not all, of the following functions:

- They will sell goods or services to consumers. Businesses that sell only to other businesses are not retailing.

- They provide the good or service at a location that consumers can get to.

- They display goods, or advertise services, so that consumers can see what is being offered.

- They 'break bulk' so that the consumer can buy the products in small quantities. Very few individuals or even families want 200 tins of baked beans at one time.

- They usually offer a variety of the products in

which they specialise. For example, you will find a variety of different bicycles in Halfords.

- They will hold stocks of goods so that consumers can be fairly sure of finding what they want when they want it.

- They advertise the products on behalf of the producers. Usually this is done by displaying the goods or through in-store advertising, but it may be done as part of a general advertisement for the store, as with supermarkets advertising on national television.

- Many offer their own credit facilities either by allowing consumers to have an account and pay at the end of the month, or by offering their own credit card facilities.

- Most provide some kind of after sales service, such as acceptance of returned goods, delivery of purchased goods, or brochures on other services offered.

- They provide information to their customers about the products, and also feed information about sales and customers back to their suppliers.

Types of Retail Outlet

There are a great many different types of retail outlet, ranging from market stalls to hypermarkets, and from independently owned local shops to multinational chain stores. Nearly all of the well-known outlets, such as Tesco, Marks & Spencer, Thomas Cook and Abbey National, are very large companies with outlets in all UK cities and major towns. Other less well-known outlets are more difficult to classify without first finding out how many other shops are owned by the business, how big they are, etc. In this section we will look at the main types of retail outlet listed in the retailing unit and we will also note that there are other important retail outlets which have not been listed.

Local stores and convenience stores

Most sales of goods and services in the UK are made by a relatively small number of very big businesses. But huge numbers of shops are still owned by individuals or by just two people, often husband and wife. These businesses are called **independents** because the owners are not responsible to anyone else. They tend to be relatively small shops and usually the owners have only one store. Because of this they are also **local shops**.

> Definition – a **convenience store** is one that has under 3,000 square feet of sales area, and opens long hours seven days a week.

Typically, they will be found in small towns and villages, often placed on street corners, which is why these types of outlets are also called **corner shops**. They provide easy access for people living close by, however, and so they are also called **convenience stores**. Many of them sell products that people want regularly, such as newspapers, food and drink, or other household products, such as soap powder, that keep well and are needed from time to time.

> Definition – a **symbol group** is a voluntary group of wholesalers and independent retailers who act jointly to promote their businesses.

These small local shops do not have the power of the large national companies so many of them have joined what are called **voluntary chains** or **symbol groups**. These groups usually include wholesalers, so the individual shops can benefit from buying as a group and keeping their costs low. The retailers trade under a single name and this allows them to advertise jointly and to stock and sell products under a single name. Examples include:

- Londis, with 1,614 members, has depots in Andover and Erith (Kent);
- Mace, with 1,050 members, has depots in Bristol, Chelmsford, Maidstone, Norwich and Welshpool;
- Spar, with 1,600 members (and 2,652 outlets) across the UK;
- Nisa, with 306 members (and 3,000 outlets).

Case Study – The Happy Shopper

The Whitchurch Happy Shopper is an independent corner shop run as a partnership. The owners Mr B. Singh and his two sons, Mr K. Singh and Mr A. Singh-Jhutti, bought the convenience store in 1988.

Before they owned the store it had been operated as part of the VG voluntary chain and later as part of the Happy Shopper symbol group. The Singhs decided not to join the Happy Shopper group but continued to stock some of their products and to keep the name which was well known in the village.

Most grocery goods are chosen from the list of products stocked by Nurdin & Peacock (now Booker) in Eastleigh. Orders are sent via a modem. The goods are delivered to the store, for which a charge of £20 is made. Other goods, such as tobacco products, are collected. Wines are ordered through another contact and newspapers delivered from a local wholesaler on sale or return.

The three most important aims of the owners are to attract a large number of customers, maintain a healthy turnover and give customer satisfaction. Certain features help to meet each of these aims:

High number of customers — lottery, newspapers and groceries
High turnover — off licence, tobacco and lottery
High customer satisfaction — personal service
long opening hours
Monday to Sunday opening
wide range of products, especially in the off
licence

Some years ago a One Stop store was opened about $\frac{1}{4}$ mile down the road. Initially, the Singhs believed that this would have a significant effect on sales, but it has not. They put this down to the following factors:

- their location, close to Testbourne Secondary School and the housing in this area;

- an enlargement in the shop floor area, allowing them to stock a wider range of products;

- an increase in their range of alcoholic drinks. The One Stop store has a very limited range of alcoholic drinks and these have high prices;

- a corner location with off-road parking for passing traffic.

Chain stores/multiples

> Definition – **chain stores**, or **multiples**, are businesses that have more than 10 retail outlets.

Multiples now form the largest section of the retail market, with over 60% of all retail sales. They include most of the well-known retail names: Boots, Sainsbury, Tesco, River Island, Clarkes, W.H. Smith, Dixons, etc. Because of their size and their buying power, they have huge advantages over the small independent shops. These advantages include:

- being able to buy in bulk and get lower prices from producers;

- advertising all of their stores at the same time because they have the same name. This also makes expensive advertising, such as on national television, cost-effective;

- a standard range of products which means that customers will always know what to expect even if they are going to a branch that is not in their home town;

- the ability to raise finance more easily because large businesses tend to be treated better by banks and other financial institutions;

- the ability to keep their prices low which attracts more customers and makes it difficult for small competitors to stay in business;

- being able to afford to set up their shops in the best locations.

The term **multiple** simply means that a business has 10 or more retail outlets, so the term also includes all the main supermarkets, the main banks and building societies, many travel agents, betting offices, cinemas, fast-food outlets, and so on.

Some of the fast-food outlets and shops like The Body Shop are franchises. These are not strictly speaking real multiples because they are owned by independent owners. The owners are only buying the right to use the name of the franchiser. When you look at individual stores it is important to check who actually owns it. McDonald's, for example, owns some of the branches of the burger restaurants in the UK and these would be multiple stores. But many of the McDonald's restaurants are franchises, independently owned, and these are not multiples. They are, perhaps, best thought of as being like the voluntary chains mentioned above.

Case Study – Growth of a Multiple: 'The History of Dixons'

If you want a camera, a cam-corder, a hi-fi system, a PC or a TV one of the first high street shops that you are likely to visit will be Dixons. But the Dixons shops,

and there are now almost 350 of them, are part of a very much larger business empire called the Dixons Group plc. This short history of the company shows how a single shop has become a multinational retailing empire.

Dixons photographic studio was opened in Southend in 1937 by Charles Kalms. After the Second World War the company started to sell new and second-hand cameras, and had already established a mail-order section by the mid-1950s.

By 1957 the company had 60,000 mail-order customers and six retail outlets. When Dixons became a public company in 1962 it had 16 outlets and, through buying out its main competitors, Ascotts (1962) and Bennetts (1964), it continued to grow rapidly.

In the 1970s and 1980s new products were added, audio equipment and hi-fis, television and videos. It also continued to take over other chains of stores, notably the 613 Currys outlets in 1984, 337 Supersnaps outlets in 1986 and 106 Wigfalls shops in 1988.

In the 1990s PC World became part of the group and Dixons also set up the Links shops. By 1998 the Dixons Group could rightly claim to be the leading UK retailer of electronic products for the home. By then it had over 900 stores nationwide under one name or another.

Figure 5.1.2 Dixons retail outlets

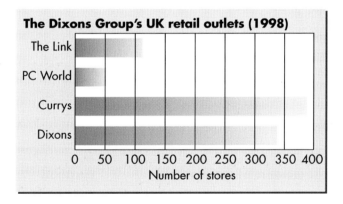

Full details of the Dixons Group's history and products can be found on **www.dixons.co.uk**.

Department stores

> Definition – a **department store** is a store divided into physically separated departments, selling at least four different classes of consumer goods, one of which must be women's and girls' clothing.

A department store, as the name suggests, is a retail outlet that is divided up into distinct departments. Many of the well-known department stores, such as Debenhams, British Home Stores and C&A, are also multiples. These are known as **multiple department stores**.

All department stores sell clothes (see definition) and the departments must be in one building. Department stores tend to have a more up-market reputation than supermarkets and this is because of the way in which they are normally run. Department stores have the following characteristics:

- Stores are divided into distinct departments selling different products, e.g. men's clothes, women's clothes, furnishings, kitchenware/china, cosmetics, and jewellery.

- Staff are trained to have expert knowledge about the goods being sold in their departments.

- Stores offer a wide range of customer services, including delivery of goods, credit facilities, accounts, in-store restaurants, and money-back guarantees.

- Stores are located in city and town centres, or in shopping malls.

- The layout of stores allows customers to walk around without pressure from sales staff and to decide what they might want to buy. When customers need assistance, sales staff are available within each department to provide expert advice.

Some department stores allow other retailers, and even producers, to set up their own departments within their stores. This arrangement is called a **concession**. It allows department stores to continue to provide a distinct variety of products in different parts of their stores but, at the same time, they escape the cost and responsibility of training expert staff who are buying in specialist products, e.g. Miss Selfridge operates 16 concessions in department stores including Cleary's, Keddies, Selfridges, Owen Owen, David Alders, The House of Fraser and Beales.

Case Study – the House of Fraser

The House of Fraser plc employs more than 7,000 staff, its shopping magazine is distributed to more than 1 million homes and it has a turnover of nearly £1 billion. Despite these facts, many people would not recognise it as a major trader in their own town or city in the UK. The reason is simple. Although the House of Fraser owns more than 50 department stores in the UK, only 14 of them use the Fraser name. The other names are well-known but most people do not realise that they are actually part of the House of Fraser group. They include:

Number of outlets	Name of the stores	Location
7	Army & Navy Stores	in the South East
3	Arnotts	in Scotland
4	Frasers	in Scotland
6	Binns	in Yorkshire/Humberside and the North
3	Dickins and Jones	in and around London
4	Dingles	in the South and South West
2	David Evans	in Wales
7	Rackhams	from Leeds to Cirencester
10	House of Fraser	from Carlisle to Swindon

Supermarkets, superstores and hypermarkets

> Definition – **a supermarket** is a self-service grocery with between 5,000 and 25,000 square feet of floor space.
>
> **a superstore** has a sales area of between 25,000 and 50,000 square feet.
>
> **a hypermarket** is a retail outlet with 50,000+ square feet of floor space.

When supermarkets first opened they sold only food, drink, tobacco and general household products. Today they sell newspapers, bake their own bread, have coffee shops, restaurants and petrol stations, and, in hypermarkets, they sell kitchenware, furniture and even garden mowers and mini-tractors. Most customers, however, still use supermarkets primarily to buy their weekly household shopping, and perhaps fill up with petrol, but the supermarket of the twenty-first century is a very different type of retail outlet to the supermarket of the 1960s.

Today most supermarkets, superstores and hypermarkets are located on the outskirts of town, although smaller town and city centre branches still exist. The major stores now tend to have most of the following facilities:

- extensive car parking space;

- in-store cafés or small restaurants;

- petrol service stations;

- a wide range of well-known foods, drinks and other grocery goods;

- a range of their own products, although these are made for them by other producers;

- in-store bakeries, fresh fish counters and delicatessens;

- electronic sales technology including scanners, EPOS, debit card facilities and, most recently, internet shopping;

- credit facilities, cash back and on-line banking;

- the National Lottery;

- newspapers, magazines and tobacco products.

Cash and carry, discount stores

> Definition – a **cash and carry** is a warehouse supplying trade customers with goods at wholesale prices.

Strictly speaking, cash and carry outlets are not part of the retail trade. They are wholesale outlets which buy their goods from the producers and then break the deliveries down into smaller quantities and sell them to the retailers. The original name comes from the fact that the customers would buy the goods they wanted with cash and take them away with them. Today cash and carry outlets operate just like other wholesalers and accept cheques, debit and credit cards and may deliver large orders.

Figure 5.1.3 Cash and carry outlets

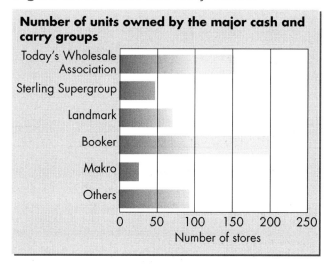

Some of these businesses specialise in certain goods, e.g. Hancock Cash and Carry Ltd (confectionery), Abacus Cash and Carry Ltd (toys) and Four Oaks Cash and Carry Ltd (plants for the horticultural trade). Others stock a wide range of goods, e.g. Booker Cash and Carry plc (now owners of Nurdin & Peacock plc) and Makro Ltd.

The main customers of the cash and carry outlets are the retailers. They get the benefits of the cash and carry wholesalers buying in bulk from the producers. This keeps the cost down. Individually, the retailers could not sell enough goods in their shops to get the same discount from the producers. By using wholesalers they can buy more cheaply than if they went direct to the producers as individuals.

The same, of course, is true of the final consumers, who buy even smaller quantities. Many businesses now recognise this and try to provide some of the benefits of the wholesaler direct to the consumer. This is done in all of the following ways:

- Supermarkets bulk-buy from producers and use their own warehouses (called **regional distribution centres**) to supply all their branches. High turnover and bulk-buying discounts keep the price low for the consumers.

- Some **discount stores** have been set up where goods are bought in bulk and then offered to consumers, almost as though they were buying

from a wholesaler. There is no special marketing or display and goods are often presented in the boxes in which they were delivered. This helps to keep costs low.

- Some wholesalers have become retailers. They display their products in warehouses but they now sell to the general public as well as to businesses. Staples, Reading Warehouses and MFI are all examples of this.

- Many cash and carry outlets that claim to serve only trade customers actually allow members of the general public to have cards and membership and to buy goods directly from them.

Case Study – Booker/Nurdin & Peacock branch integration completed

Following Booker's purchase of the Nurdin & Peacock cash and carry chain, it is now the leading food wholesaler in Britain, with an annual turnover of over £3.4 billion. In the past, these two companies competed strongly for customers and many of their warehouses were in the same areas. It has, therefore, been necessary to close some of the warehouses down.

The last of the 37 closures was made in June 1998, leaving a network of 176 branches across the country. All former Nurdin & Peacock branches have been brought up to the Booker standard to provide the best service for the customer.

Product, store and company details and the latest company news can be found at: http://www.booker-plc.com

Mail order and internet shopping

A study of retailing would not be complete unless the growing amount of direct selling from producers, wholesalers and retailers was also considered. The range of services now provided through the post, at the end of a telephone or via the internet is vast, and growing. Soon additional services will be available through cable links.

Mail order, or ordering goods by post, has been around for a long time. Catalogue companies such as Great Universal Stores (trading as Great

Universal, Choice, Kays, Burberrys and others) have a huge number of customers. GUS had profits of over £550 million in 1998. Most of these catalogue sales are for clothes, together with some general items, such as toys, garden equipment and electrical equipment. But there are a great many other companies which specialise in specific markets. Most computers are sold through computer magazines. Orders are made direct to companies such as Time which buys its computers from the producers, or direct to companies that actually produce computers themselves, such as Dell.

The *Retail Directory of the UK 1999* (Healey & Baker) lists over 500 mail-order firms, but there are also other mail-order businesses that are not listed. Many of these operate by putting advertisements into newspapers or magazines. Interested customers contact them, order by post or telephone and the goods are delivered by mail.

Internet shopping, or ordering goods and services from advertisements placed on internet web sites, is now widespread in the UK. Most of the major retail companies, including the supermarket chains, now have their own web sites which allow customers to order goods directly from them. The major mail-order companies also have web sites which allow customers to order using their computer links.

Some web sites offer access to a number of other businesses, for example Netscafé at **http://www.netscafe.co.uk/shop.htm** Other sites offer a range of products which the firm itself mainly provides, for example Shoppers Universe at **http://shoppersuniverse.com/** which offers 40,000 products.

On Saturday 5 June 1999 the *Daily Telegraph* reported that Tesco had succeeded in signing up $\frac{1}{4}$ million customers to its internet service in its first three months. That was still some way short of the market leader, Dixons' Freeserve with 1.3 million registered customers. But Dixons does have the attraction of a free internet service.

Most internet shoppers in the UK are men, but the new service offered by Tesco may change that. Most grocery purchases are made by women.

Tesco already has 10 million Club Card members and, with an expansion from 16 to over 100 stores offering home shopping, they may yet catch Dixons up.

Activity

The best way to learn about the variety of retailing that can be found in most towns and cities is to visit a range of retail outlets and see what they are doing.

Checking the functions of retailing

1 Choose one type of retail outlet to visit.
2 Make a check sheet so that you can record details when you make your visit. Your check sheet will need to cover all the points below.
3 Note down how the retail outlet meets the retailing functions of:
   a) being in the right location;
   b) advertising the products in the store;
   c) 'breaking-bulk'. Note the size of units being sold;
   d) offering a variety of the products in which the store specialises;
   e) the different methods of payment that they will accept.

Types of retail outlet

1 Choose an area of shops where there are at least 10 different retail outlets.
2 Put down the names of each of the outlets and decide what type of retail outlet it is, e.g. chain, department store, supermarket, discount store etc.
3 For each retail outlet explain why you have put it into a particular category.

Revision

Questions

Questions 1 to 3 are based on the following possible answers:

a) department store;

b) chain store;

c) convenience store;

d) supermarket.

These are types of retail outlet:

1   Which is being described when it is one of more than 10 outlets? (1 mark)

2   Which is likely to be found in a small village? (1 mark)

3   Which must sell women's or girls' clothing? (1 mark)

4   Name three of the major supermarket chains in the UK. (3 marks)

5   Give three examples of the types of product that are sold in **each** of the following situations:
    a) when a producer sells products direct to consumers;
    b) when a wholesaler sells products direct to consumers;
    c) when high street retailers sell services. (3 marks)

6   a) What is the difference between a convenience store, a supermarket and a hypermarket in terms of size? (2 marks)
    b) Give two other differences between convenience stores and supermarkets and explain why these differences occur. (4 marks)

7   Explain why most cash and carry businesses are not classified as retailers. (1 mark)

8   a) Explain what a **concession** arrangement is. (1 mark)
    b) Explain how this is of benefit to:
       i) the department store;
       ii) the firm being offered the concession. (2 marks)

9   How do symbol groups (voluntary chains) help local shops to compete against the supermarkets? (4 marks)

10 Which of the following statements are true and which are false? Explain your answers.
    a) 'Travel agents, banks and hairdressers are not retailers.'
    b) 'Independents are owned by the large supermarkets.'
    c) 'One role of the retailer is to break bulk.'
    d) 'Supermarkets only sell to customers who visit their stores.' (4 marks)

CHAPTER 2

FEATURES AND AMENITIES OF RETAIL OUTLETS

KEY TERMS:

location	high street	out-of-town
opening hours	Sunday trading	jobs in retailing
supervisor	range of products	store managers
window dressers	sales assistants	clerical workers
stock controllers	shelf fillers	checkout staff
methods of payment		

In this chapter you will learn why retail outlets locate where they do and what features and amenities they offer the consumers in order to attract them to their shops.

Locating Retail Outlets

The **location** of any business will depend upon a range of factors. These general factors are given in Unit 2, Chapter 3. Here we will look at factors that are particularly important for retail outlets.

Retail outlets must always be located where the consumer is prepared to visit and buy the products on sale. Twenty or thirty years ago this meant that most retail outlets were located in the centres of towns and cities. Today, the location of retail business shows a very different pattern.

> Definition – **high street** outlets are those located on the main streets in town and city centres. **Out-of-town** outlets are those located on the outskirts of towns or cities.

There is still a wide range of traditional 'high street' outlets in the centres of towns and cities (clothes shops, shoe shops, travel agents, banks, etc.) but many of the bigger outlets have moved. They are now to be found in either centre precincts (malls) or in out-of-town sites, many of which will have a variety of stores in the same location.

The businesses that have moved include the major supermarkets and the specialist chains. The new shopping malls will have many of the major chain names, e.g. Next, Boots, W.H. Smith, C&A, Dillons and Burger King.

Out-of-town centres tend to attract businesses that need large premises, e.g. supermarkets and firms selling furniture, DIY products, gardening products, electrical equipment and motoring accessories. Typical out-of-town outlets include Tesco, MFI, Homebase, PC World, Halfords, PETsMART and Tempo. These businesses have recognised that it is cheaper to locate outside the centre of town and that customers want to shop where they can take their purchases and put them straight into their cars.

Most stores expect the customers to visit them. Where this happens the stores consider all the following location factors:

- Where the customers are, and how many potential customers there are in the catchment area.

- What access the customers have in terms of parking, public transport, facilities for the disabled, etc.

- The availability of staff to run the store.

- What other shops and facilities are nearby? Will they attract customers? Are they competitors?

- What is the cost of buying or renting the premises and what are the rates?

- Transport links to their suppliers.

- What facilities are available in the store in terms of space, storage, gas, electricity, water and sewerage?

- How trade in the area has been changing in the last few years, e.g. is the area expanding or declining and how many shop premises in the area are empty?

Factors of particular importance to firms locating retail outlets in town/city centres

- Will the location be part of a shopping precinct/mall or on a main street?

- How many potential customers pass the shop?

- What stores are close by? Will they attract the right people? Are they potential competitors?

- Is there easy access for delivery lorries?

- Are there parking facilities for customers nearby?

- Is there good public transport to the shops?

- Is there general access for the disabled?

Factors of particular interest to firms locating retail outlets in out-of-town sites

- How will customers get to the site? By private car or by public transport?

- What land is available and will it allow for a big car and coach park?

- What other large stores are close by to help attract customers?

- Where is the major competition located?

- What is the catchment area? Will it attract customers from the whole town/city, from the surrounding villages and from other towns?

Factors of particular interest to firms locating retail outlets in villages

- How large is the village and will there be enough customers to make the shop profitable?

- Is there a similar retail outlet in the village and how will the competitor and customers react to a second shop selling similar products?

- Does the shop also provide accommodation or will a separate house have to be bought?

- Is the site on a major through-route so that it can benefit from passing trade?

- Does the village have other attractions that bring in potential customers, and is this all the year round or only seasonal?

- Is the village a place where the owners/managers want to live?

Case Study – Bluewater, the largest shopping centre in the UK

The Bluewater shopping, leisure and entertainment complex opened in March 1999. It is located between Dartford and Gravesend in Kent. With three shopping malls, and surrounded by seven lakes and woodland, it now claims to be the biggest of these multifunction complexes in the UK.

These complexes are not new. The Whitgift Centre in Croydon opened in 1969 and the Metro Centre in Gateshead in 1986. Bluewater boasts three leisure villages with restaurants, cafés and a multiplex cinema. But, again, this is not new. The Trafford Centre in Manchester, split into four interconnected areas, offers shoppers a 20-screen UCI Cinema and an 18-lane ten-pin bowling alley. There are also plans to develop 150 acres of land into a regional sports centre with, among other things, indoor and outdoor tennis courts, a golf course, a swimming pool and a rowing course on the Ship Canal.

So how does Bluewater measure up?

	Whitgift	Trafford	Metro	Bluewater
Retail units	160	280	326	320
Selling area (million sq. ft)	0.9	1.1	1.6	1.6
Catchment (million people)	1.8	5.3	3.0	1.5
Customers per year (million)	31.2	30.0	28.8	30.0
Parking for cars	2,400	10,000	12,000	13,000

Location of firms that sell direct to consumers

The other major change in retailing has been the growth of mail-order (and now e-mail order) shopping. Direct contact is made with the customers at their homes. Customers look at what is on offer and order by post or e-mail. The customer never visits the seller's premises in person and therefore it does not matter to the customer where the premises are located. This gives the seller a great deal of freedom. Mail-order firms tend to be located where there is good storage space, good transport links and where the cost of renting or building premises is low.

Features and Amenities of Retail Outlets

Retail outlets need to provide what the customers want if they are going to be successful. To do this they must not only provide the goods and services that customers want but provide them when they want them, where they want them, in the right quantities, with convenient methods of payment, etc. When retailers make choices about what to sell and how to sell, they are faced with a very large number of decisions. We will look at some of the main decisions below.

Figure 5.2.1 Retailers' decisions

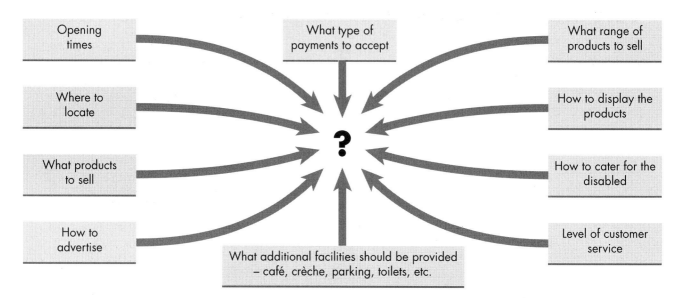

Opening hours

The traditional opening hours of 9.00 a.m. to 5.30 or 6.00 p.m. are still the norm for most town and city centre shops. Out-of-town supermarkets and large stores tend to open for longer hours: 8.00 or 9.00 a.m. to 7.00, 8.00 or even 9.00 p.m. Convenience stores need to compete with the large stores and tend to open early and close late. Many convenience stores open at 7.00 or 7.30 a.m. and do not close until 10 p.m.

Until 1994 it was illegal for most large stores to open for trading on a Sunday, but the Sunday Trading Act 1994 now allows all shops to trade on Sunday if they wish to. If the floor area is less than 280 square metres, the Act places no restrictions on small shops' opening hours. Larger shops may open on Sundays for any six continuous hours between 10 a.m. and 6 p.m. In Northern Ireland similar legislation was introduced in December 1997.

Retail outlets open on Sundays because:

- The law now allows them to open on Sundays.

- Customers expect Sunday opening.

- Many more women (who traditionally do the weekly shopping) now work, and Sunday opening is more convenient for them.

- Staff are willing to work on Sundays because they receive higher rates of pay.

- Competitors are opening on Sunday and if an individual store does not open, it will lose customers and sales.

Sunday opening is now a part of British life, as is late night shopping and, in some places, 24-hour shopping. It is mainly the out-of-town stores that have introduced Sunday shopping and most village stores and town and city centre stores remain closed on Sundays. In smaller towns and in villages, especially where the business is run by the owner, many shops still close during the week for an hour at lunchtime. Many also close for a half day on Wednesdays and/or Saturdays.

Many retail outlets, such as restaurants and public houses, will open at times when people wish to eat or relax, at lunchtimes and in the evenings. Cinemas tend to open in the afternoons and evenings. Newsagents are often open at 7.00 a.m. so that people can buy papers on the way to work, or in order that the paper boys and girls can deliver them to people's homes.

Overall, there are no set times for all retail outlets, and the times offered will generally be those that are most convenient for the customers.

Case Study – Opening hours in Winchester

Winchester has a city centre shopping area and two main out-of-town shopping zones. The city centre stores tend to open during traditional hours, mainly 9 a.m. to 5 p.m. Most stores are closed on Sunday although a few do open, including Dillons bookshop, British Home Stores and Games Workshop. The out-of-town stores open for much longer hours and are also open for the permitted six hours on Sundays. Figure 5.2.2 shows the contrast in hours for some selected stores.

Figure 5.2.2 Retailers' opening hours

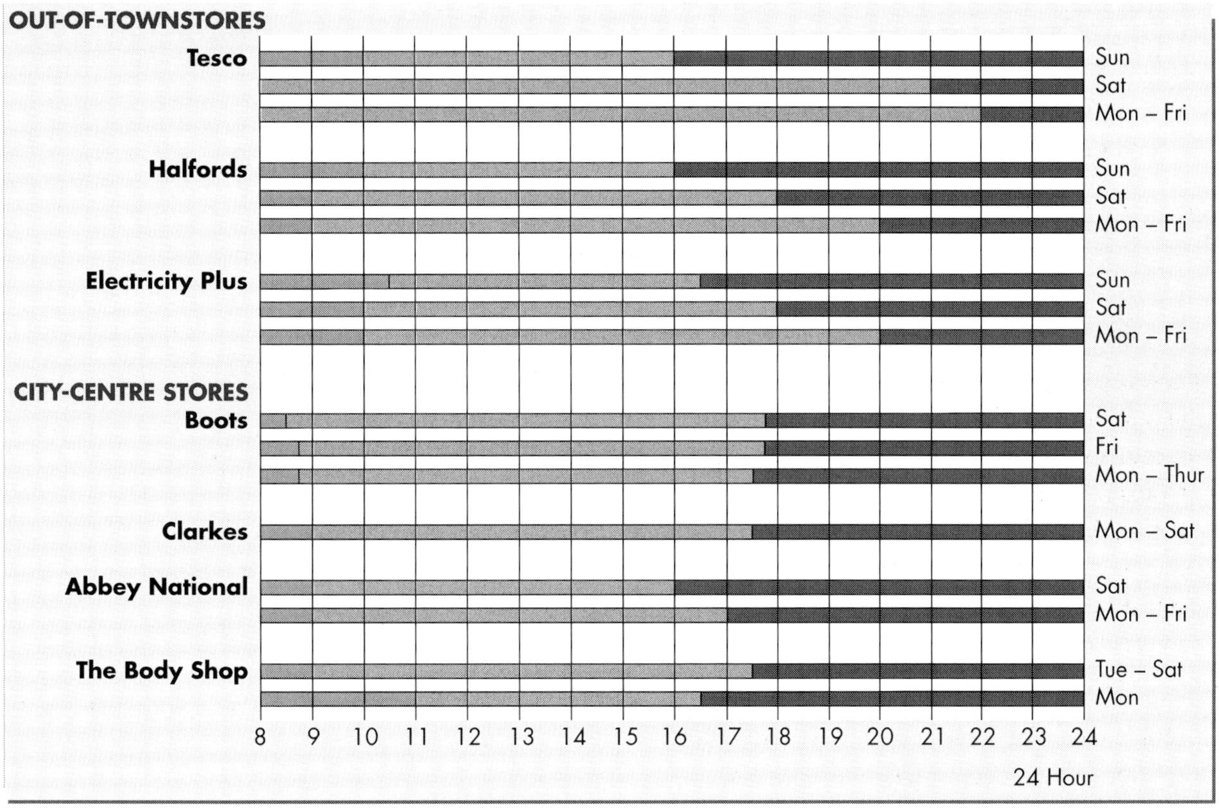

Methods of Payment Accepted by Retail Stores

- **Cash** is 'legal tender' and all stores must accept payment by cash if the customers choose to use cash. The only exception to this is when a customer tries to pay with coins which need to be accepted only up to a certain amount. Although cash must be accepted, people tend to use cash only for relatively small purchases. Retail outlets therefore need to offer customers a range of methods of payment. The following are the most common methods accepted by retailers.

- **Cheques** are orders from the customer telling their bank or building society to pass money from their account to the retailer's bank account. It takes about three days for the money to be passed across. There is also some risk that the cheque will not be honoured by the bank, so many retailers insist that customers use a 'bank guarantee card' when paying by cheque. This guarantees that the bank will pay, usually up to £50, if the customer has no money in his/her account.

- **Credit cards** allow customers to buy goods and services and pay for them when they receive their statements from the credit card companies, usually at the end of the month. When the customer uses a credit card to pay for something, the shop passes its claim for payment back to the credit card company which then pays the shop. Because the credit card companies must wait for payment from the customer, they usually charge the shop for the right to let customers use the credit card. This explains why the major supermarkets, and a growing number of major stores, are now offering their own credit cards (backed by high street banks).

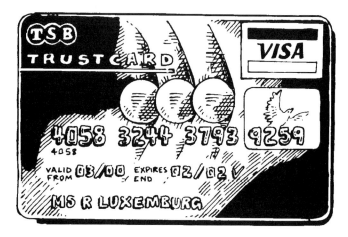

- **Debit cards** are rather like cheques. Using electronic connections, they tell the customers' banks or building societies to transfer money from the customers' accounts to the retailer's account. The transfer of funds is getting faster all the time, and is currently between one and three days.

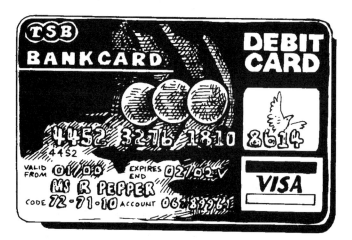

- **Customer accounts** are used by shops which have regular customers. The customers buy products through the month and are then sent a statement of account at the end of the month and must pay for the products then. This is not the same as a credit facility, although some stores do allow customers to pay only part of what is owed.

- **Hire purchase** allows customers to take the products now and pay for them over a period of months or years. This method of payment is used for buying consumer durables, such as washing machines, computers and cars. Customers are usually asked to pay part of the total price (a deposit), and the rest is then paid by a finance company with an agreement from the customer to make regular payments each month until the debt is paid off. Interest may or may not be charged on this loan. If it is, it is calculated as part of the monthly payment.

- **Coupons, vouchers,** and **tokens.** These can all be used to pay for goods or services in stores that agree to accept them. It used to be quite common for workers in offices to be given luncheon vouchers which they could then spend in certain pubs, restaurants and sandwich bars. Workers today prefer the money because they can choose where to spend it, or to save it if they do not want lunch.

Coupons are now widely used either by producers (e.g. 20p off the next packet of cereals purchased), or retailers (e.g. the supermarket loyalty schemes which allow customers to build up a monthly total of points which can then be exchanged for goods). Air miles also operate on this kind of points system.

Many retailers also offer vouchers which can be exchanged for products in the stores. W.H. Smith, Marks & Spencer and Dixons, among a great many others, offer gift vouchers which can be given as presents.

Further details of some of these methods of payment are given below under the **customer incentives** section.

Range of Products on Offer

Retailers need to strike a balance between offering customers a very limited range of products and offering them a wide range of products. A limited range of products will reduce costs for the business, but may not offer the customers what they want. A wide range of products will provide the customers with a good choice, but will cost the business more because it has to stock, display and provide advertising and information about many products. Some benefits of each are shown in Figure 5.2.3.

Figure 5.2.3 Benefits of offering more/fewer products

Limited range of products

- Retailers can specialise and give customers expert advice
- Bulk-buying keeps costs down
- Customers know what is being offered
- Only a few products have to be advertised
- Usually smaller premises are required, less display space, etc., all keeping costs low
- Concentration on a limited range should improve quality and the reputation of the firm

Benefits

Wide range of products

- Customers are given choice
- Products can all be found in one place
- Turnover tends to be higher and prices lower
- A wide range of products can be used as loss leaders
- When shopping for one product customers are often tempted to buy others
- The risk is spread so that if some products do not sell well others will still give the business profit

Retailers will choose to stock a limited range of products for a variety of reasons. There will be benefits, as shown above, but there are also other important reasons.

- They may have limited capital and will only be able to stock a limited range.

- Their shops may be small and that will also limit what they can sell.

- They may have experience in selling, or they may have been trained to sell, only one type of product.

- Many retailers want to specialise in one type of product because that is what interests them.

- Customers often want to go to shops that specialise and they may avoid a shop which is trying to sell too wide a range of products.

Some shops, such as those selling mobile phones, do have a very limited range of products, but others may only appear to have a limited range. Shops specialising in, say, fishing equipment may actually

stock a vast range of rods, hooks, flies, nets, books on fishing, waterproof clothing, etc., even though they sell only products related to fishing. Other shops, e.g. Tie Rack and Sock Shop, specialise in one type of product but actually stock a wide range of those kinds of products.

Supermarkets and hypermarkets are normally associated with selling a wide range of products. Many of the larger branches sell 4,000 to 6,000 different products, but they also sell very large numbers of the same sort of product and shelves may have up to 100 of the same item. Department stores also sell a wide range of products because they are split into departments, each with its own specialism.

Supermarkets, hypermarkets and department stores are all large-scale businesses and that is one reason why they stock such a wide range of products. They can afford to. There are, however, many smaller businesses that also stock a wide range of products. Local convenience stores are set up to provide customers with items that they have forgotten to shop for during the major weekly shopping trip, or items that they need quickly or just a few of. They are also there to supply people who find it difficult to travel far. Convenience stores, even relatively small ones, will therefore stock as many as 500 or 1,000 different items. Both the stock and the display of these goods will be in very much smaller quantities than those found in supermarkets.

Many discount stores will also offer a wide range of products. They buy these in from wholesalers and display them, usually in a single large open selling area. The goods are relatively cheap and usually of moderate quality. Essentially, the owners will try to sell whatever relatively small items they think customers will buy and so they are happy to offer a wide range of products. In these stores customers will find umbrellas, writing paper, Christmas decorations, sweets, indoor fireworks, shirts, teapots, picture frames, footballs, etc. The only goods that will not be for sale are ones which require a licence, such as alcohol, or special facilities, such as hot food.

> Definition – **own brands** are products that are sold under the retailer's own name or the retailer's trade name.

Most retailers buy in products from wholesalers and producers, display them and sell them. There are a large number of retailers who also sell **own-brand** products. Usually these are sold using the name of the retailer, (e.g. Tesco cola or Sainsbury toilet rolls). Sometimes the retailer uses a trade name which indicates that it is the store's own brand, (e.g. Marks & Spencer use the name St Michael for products).

Very few firms actually make their own-brand products themselves. They pay producers to make and package the products and the products are then sold by the retailers as their own. Using own-brand products allows retailers to advertise the store and the products at the same time. If the store has a good reputation, then no additional promotion is required for the individual products. This helps to keep the costs down and own brands tend to have a lower price than named products, such as Coca-Cola or Andrex. It also explains why nearly 30% of the sales of grocery products in the UK are own brand.

Case Study – Product differentiation in supermarkets

Most supermarkets offer a range of products that are basically the same, but they will be offered at different prices and will be of slightly different quality. The range will include value products which are very basic and have low prices and no fancy packaging. In Tesco these are called 'value line' items. In Sainsbury they are called 'economy' items.

They will also offer the brand leaders which are known to the public because of heavy advertising. These products include all the well-known names, such as Heinz, Cadbury, Walls, Colgate, and Robinson. Between these two extremes most supermarkets will also offer an up-market copy of the leading brand, and a mid-range product.

Offering all these different products allows the supermarkets to target different groups of people and to charge them different prices for what is essentially the same product. Examples are given in the table below.

Table 5.2.1   Price differences on selected items in Tesco (June 1999)

Cola (6 cans)	£	Toilet rolls – price/100 sheets	p	Cornflakes (500g)	100g
Value	0.95	Value	9.0	Value	9.6
Tesco own	1.59	Tesco mid-range	13.9	Tesco own	17.8
Virgin	1.89	Tesco luxury	15.0	Kellogg's	21.8
Coca-Cola	1.95	Andrex	15.8		
Pepsi Cola	1.99	Kleenex	19.4		
		Kleenex quilted	24.8		

The Role of Staff in Retail Outlets

The jobs that people carry out in different retail outlets vary a great deal. This is because retailing offers such a wide variety of goods and services. The examples overleaf show some of the differences in the range of jobs.

The job roles will also depend on how big the retail outlets are. In large supermarkets there will be check-out staff and shelf fillers, but also cleaners, supervisors, junior managers, separate department managers, deputy managers and branch managers, as well as accountants and, maybe, buyers, cooks, bakers, etc. In a small convenience store most, if not all, of these roles will be carried out by only two or three people.

Banks	Chemists
Tellers taking in and paying out cash	Sales staff
	Trained pharmacists
Receptionist	Shelf fillers
Advisers for:	In-store detectives
i) businesses	Supervisors
ii) investments	
iii) taxation	
iv) foreign currency	
Secretaries	
Cleaners	

Hairdressers	Butcher's Shops
Hairdressers	Butchers preparing food
Assistants	Sales staff serving customer
Receptionists	Assistants cleaning the shop

The range of jobs is vast and here we will examine a few that are fairly typical in retail outlets.

The store manager

In large retail chains the store manager will be responsible only for the individual store and many decisions, such as the range of goods to stock, the advertising policy and even pricing, will be decided by head office. In smaller businesses the individual store manager will make most of the important decisions about how the store is run. The manager will have all the following responsibilities:

- How the store is run day to day.

- What will be sold, how much, and for what price.

- Where the goods will be bought from and when they will be delivered.

- How the goods will be displayed and promoted.

- Which staff will be employed, how many, when, etc.

- How the premises will be equipped and maintained.

- Reporting details of performance back to head office or direct to the owners/directors.

In larger stores there will be managers for each of the departments. The human resources manager will be responsible for hiring and training staff. The buying manager will be responsible for choosing the goods to be sold and selecting the supplier. The store manager will, however, still have the responsibility of making sure that the other managers are doing their jobs properly.

Profile of a Checkout Manager in Tesco

A checkout manager is in charge of the checkout staff and customer service enquiries. They may work full-time or part-time.

The job role includes:
- managing the checkout staff and ensuring that the checkouts operate smoothly;
- managing staff on the customer service desk;
- recruitment and training of checkout staff and customer service assistants;
- monitoring the performance of checkout and customer service assistants;
- attending management team meetings;
- working on new initiatives in relation to checkouts and customer service.

Recruitment of checkout managers is usually from staff who are already working in Tesco as customer service assistants. They will have been checkout staff and may have worked elsewhere in the store as shelf fillers. Checkout managers:
- are responsible to the store manager;
- earn £14,500/year full-time;
- work a five-day week with late nights and Saturday and Sunday working every few weeks;
- get 22 days' holiday a year

Details of other job roles in Tesco can be found on the Tesco web site at www.tesco.co.uk/index.htm

---

Supervisors

Many larger retail stores will have supervisors whose main task is to ensure that the staff serving customers, stacking shelves, working on the checkouts, etc. are doing their jobs properly. In smaller stores this role is carried out by the managers. Where retail outlets are divided into departments, it will be the role of the department managers to supervise the staff working in their departments.

Sales assistants

The main role of the sales assistant is to serve customers and to ensure that goods and services are being sold. Their roles include:

- giving customers information and advice about the products on sale;

- packing goods into bags, boxes, etc. ready for customers to take away;

- taking payment for goods and services;

- advising customers about payment methods, credit facilities, guarantees, etc.;

- watching customers to see if they need help but also to ensure that they do not damage goods or fixtures and fittings and do not steal goods;

- presenting a good image for the business, including dressing appropriately, being polite and being positive about the products on sale.

The sales assistants are usually the first people that customers will see and talk to, so they are very important. Their exact roles will, of course, depend on what is being sold. In many supermarkets, the only member of staff with whom the customer has any contact is at the checkout. In banks it will be the cashier, in shoe shops it will be the sales assistant who brings the pair of shoes to be tried on, and in fast-food restaurants it will be the person taking the order and the payment.

Clerical workers

All businesses require the keeping of records, the writing of letters and the filing of data. All this 'paper work' is essentially the role of the clerical worker. Some of this clerical work is done by specialists, such as accountants, stock controllers and even lawyers, but much of it is done by secretaries, personal assistants and filing clerks.

Figure 5.2.4 Advertisement for course on office skills

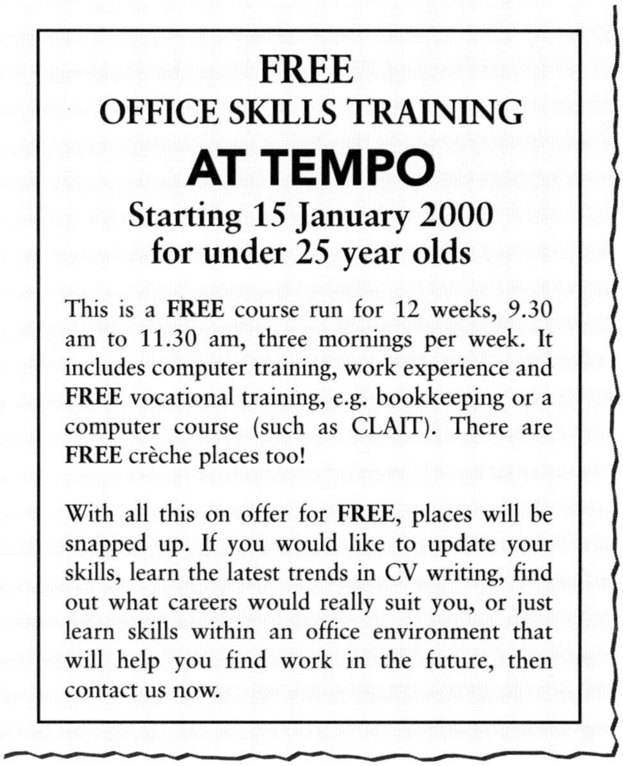

> ### FREE
> ### OFFICE SKILLS TRAINING
> ## AT TEMPO
> ### Starting 15 January 2000
> ### for under 25 year olds
>
> This is a **FREE** course run for 12 weeks, 9.30 am to 11.30 am, three mornings per week. It includes computer training, work experience and **FREE** vocational training, e.g. bookkeeping or a computer course (such as CLAIT). There are **FREE** crèche places too!
>
> With all this on offer for **FREE**, places will be snapped up. If you would like to update your skills, learn the latest trends in CV writing, find out what careers would really suit you, or just learn skills within an office environment that will help you find work in the future, then contact us now.

Large retail businesses are no different and will employ a range of clerical staff. In smaller businesses, it may be the owner, manager or assistant who carries out these duties. In many of the retail outlets which sell services, part of the clerical work will be done by the sales assistant because it is vital that all the details of what the customer wants and is buying are recorded.

Case Study – The clerical role of the sales staff in Thomas Cook

The role of the sales staff in Thomas Cook is not just to help customers find the holiday they want, but to record all the details, both for the customers and for the business.

The clerical duties will include:

- recording all details of the holiday on the standard forms;

- contacting the holiday company and transport company to confirm availability, book accommodation, flights, etc., and to confirm bookings;

- completing any paper work relating to travel insurance;

- communicating with customers when documents and details are received from the holiday and transport companies;

- dealing with any paper work that might arise from complaints, cancellations and alterations to the booking;

- completing any documentation relating to payments, deposits or refunds;

- passing all financial documentation through to the finance department.

Examples of Specific Roles in Retail Stores

Window dressers

Window dressers have a very special role to play in most retail outlets. It is the window display that people first see when they are passing or entering the shop. If it is eye-catching and appealing it may well encourage people to come into the shop and have a look around. Even if people have already decided to go into the shop the window display can say something about:

- what the shop has to sell;

- the quality of the products;

- the care and attention that the shop takes over its products and its customers;

- what is currently in fashion;

- which special offers are likely to be found inside;

- information such as opening hours and methods of payment.

In many shops, the window display is a major form of advertising and specialist window dressers are employed to decide what should be put in the window and how it can be made to attract customers. Many window dressers have been to art school or have taken courses in design. They may also have been trained in marketing or advertising.

Many displays will take hours or even days to construct and may then be left for a month or two before they are changed. Some stores bring in outside experts to design and create the displays.

Shelf fillers

Shelf fillers are found in stores where there is a high turnover of stock during the day. In shoe shops and clothes stores, where the turnover is lower, the shelves will be filled by the shop assistants.

Shelf filling in large supermarkets is a full-time job and the store will expect staff to carry out their jobs in a particular way. All of the following will be expected:

- that staff note which shelves are empty, or nearly empty;

- that they will collect stock from the storeroom and place it on the shelves;

- that new stock will be put behind old stock so that customers will take the old stock first;

- that when there is no replacement stock in the storeroom, other stock will be moved across to fill the space;

- that damaged stock is removed.

Someone, possibly the shelf filler, will also be responsible for checking stock that is close to its sell-by date and reducing it for a quick sale. Out-of-date stock will also need to be removed.

Checkout staff

Checkout staff in supermarkets have very specific and rather repetitive duties. Customers choose their own groceries, wheel them to the checkouts and then pay for them. Checkout staff normally have these duties:

- signing on to the checkout correctly so that they can be identified. Today most checkouts are automated with scanners and EPOS systems, so the performance of staff can be checked electronically;

- taking customers' purchases and scanning each one. Some items may need weighing and a code is then typed in for the type of good it is;

- calling a supervisor if anything is wrong and they cannot deal with it, such as an item having no bar code on it;

- taking payment from the customer, checking that notes are not forgeries and that credit and debit cards are not listed as stolen;

- offering services such as cash back;

- changing the rolls that record the till receipts;

- providing customers with bags;

- being polite and answering any queries.

In stores such as chemists, record shops and department stores, where consumers buy only a few items, it is now common to let the customers serve themselves and to have either a checkout or payment counter where the goods are paid for. Here the sales staff will be carrying out a very similar job to that of the checkout staff in a supermarket. Staff will, of course, be on hand to give advice about the goods on sale and, in chemists, there will be qualified pharmacists to make up prescriptions.

Security staff

Store detectives and security staff are increasingly important in self-service stores where people can pocket goods and walk out with them. Sometimes a store can lose over 10% of its stock through theft. Store detectives are dealt with in Chapter 7.

Stock controllers

Stock controllers are responsible for ensuring that the store has the right amount of stock. Getting the balance of stock just right is important.

If there is not enough stock:

- the shelves will be empty and customers will decide to shop elsewhere;

- possible sales will be lost and profits will be lower than they could be.

If there is too much stock:

- it will cost a lot to store it;

- it may go out of date and have to be thrown away;

- fashions may change or better products may be introduced which make the stock of little value.

Case Study – Staff roles in the Games Workshop

The Games Workshop is a store which sells games, miniatures and manuals for fantasy war games, but it is also a store that is run on quite different lines from most retail stores. Staff roles are also quite different.

The major task of the staff is to promote the games. Staff are recruited only from among enthusiasts, and often from people who have visited the store and shown a real keenness for the games, for collecting miniatures and for the whole fantasy world.

Each store has a manager who is responsible for the staff who are employed in the store, for staff rotas and for the general running of the store, but all the other roles are shared and staff will move from one job to another as required. The staff roles include:

- selling the games, miniatures, paints and manuals;
- running games in the store;
- running painting sessions in the store;
- painting miniatures for display;
- talking to customers and stirring up their enthusiasm for everything about the fantasy war game world;
- checking and ordering new stock;
- taking payments and checking cash at the end of the day.

Training is carried out both in the store and at regional centres. Store managers are expected to train their own staff and attend advanced training sessions themselves. As managers progress, they will visit other stores to help with training.

Activity

Retail outlets provide a wide range of features and amenities. Visiting different outlets in many places will help you to see how different these can be.

Location

1   Select one high street retail outlet and one local shop.
2   Draw a map to show where they are located in relation to other shops or houses.

List the factors which you feel have been most important in deciding where the two businesses are located.

Features

1   Select two or three different types of retail outlet shops in a town centre or a local arcade.

2   Note the following features for each:
   a) opening times;
   b) methods of payment accepted;
   c) range of goods or services for sale.
3   Explain how these differ between the outlets and why they are different.

Staff roles

From your own work experience or job, or from a visit to a small to medium-sized retail outlet:
1   List the different staff members.
2   Note their major job roles and what they have to do in order to meet these roles.
3   List any particular skills that you think are required for carrying out these job roles.

Revision

Questions

Questions 1 to 3 are based on the following answers.

These are all methods of paying for goods and services in retail outlets.

a) cash

b) cheque

c) credit card

d) voucher

1 Which method will allow a customer to buy only a particular product? (1 mark)

2 Which method will allow a customer to buy goods now and pay only part of what is owed at the end of the month? (1 mark)

3 Which method must be accepted as payment in all retail outlets? (1 mark)

4 Name three of the major supermarket chains in the UK. (3 marks)

5 a) State four factors of location that will be important for a business that wishes to open a new superstore on the outskirts of a large town. (4 marks)
   b) Explain why each of these factors is so important for the business. (4 marks)

6 Give two reasons why many large stores now open on Sundays. (2 marks)

7 Many retail businesses, such as banks, estate agents and travel agents, tend to locate their businesses very close to their competitors. Give two reasons why they do this. (2 marks)

8 For each of the following statements say if they are true or false and explain why.
   a) Both credit cards and debit cards allow customers to receive goods now but pay for them later.
   b) Credit cards can be used in any UK retail outlet.
   c) Debit cards can be used in major supermarkets to obtain 'cash back'. (3 marks)

9 Supermarkets sell a range of some goods that have different prices and are of slightly different quality. Toilet rolls are an example of this.
   a) Give four examples of other products for which supermarkets offer this kind of range. (4 marks)
   b) Explain why they offer their customers a range of the same product. (3 marks)

10 a) How do the opening hours of retail outlets (such as clothes shops and travel agents) in the centre of town, generally differ from the opening hours of stores (such as supermarkets and DIY stores) in shopping complexes on the outskirts of town? (3 marks)
    b) Explain why the hours are different. (4 marks)

11 Select two different job roles in retailing of which you have first-hand knowledge, then:
    a) List the main duties involved in carrying out each job.
    b) Note any differences between them.
    c) Explain why these differences occur. (10 marks)

CHAPTER 3

CUSTOMER INCENTIVES USED IN RETAIL OUTLETS

Intermediate

KEY TERMS:

pricing strategies	skimming	discounts
penetration pricing	loss leaders	sales
competitive pricing	multi-buys	free offers
samples	competitions	loyalty schemes
credit facilities	delivery	after sales service
warranty		

In this chapter you will learn about the different ways in which retailers attract customers to use their stores and how they decide on what price to sell their products at.

Introduction

Most retail outlets are in competition with other firms selling similar products. It is therefore very important for the retailers that they provide customers with incentives that will encourage them to shop at their stores rather than going to their competitors. Providing the right products at the right times and in the right places has already been looked at under marketing in Unit 1 Chapter 2, but there are many other factors that retailers need to take into consideration if their businesses are going to be successful. Some of these are covered in the following chapters. Here we will look at how price can be used as an incentive for customers and at other direct incentives such as delivery, credit and after sales service.

Figure 5.3.1 Customer incentives

Pricing Strategies

Retailers, like most businesses, use a wide variety of pricing policies, most of which are primarily designed to make profit for the business. In this section, however, we will be looking only at pricing strategies which act as an incentive to customers.

Competition-based pricing

> Definition – **competition-based pricing** is when businesses set the price of their products in line with the general price in the market.

When two identical products are on sale at different prices, nearly all consumers will go for the one at the lower price. Where it is easy for customers to shop at different stores there is likely to be a high level of competition and the store that can keep its prices lowest will be the one that gains the most customers.

This is why supermarkets are so successful. They buy in very large quantities, get the benefits of discounts for bulk buying and can then undercut all the smaller retailers. They are, however, very careful not to compete against each other, otherwise they would get into a price war and damage their own profits.

Many of the high street retailers are selling the same products. Dixons, W.H. Smith, Woolworths, MVC,

Figure 5.3.2 Low prices gain customers

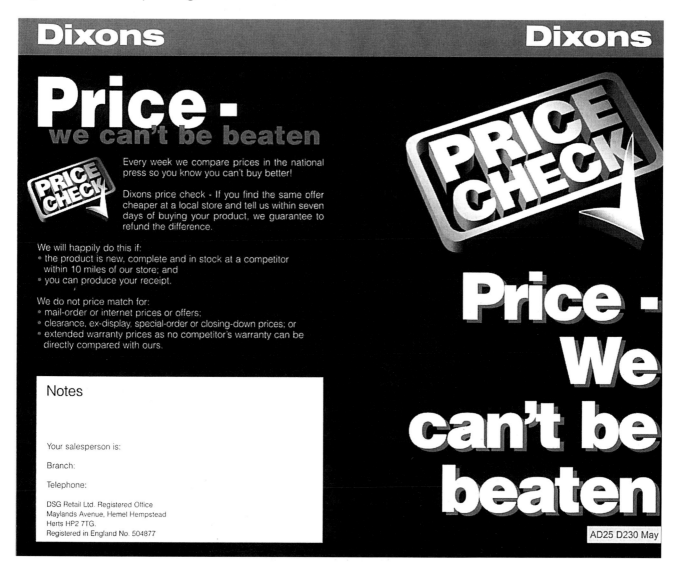

Game and many of the toy shops all sell Playstations and Playstation games and consoles, so it is easy for customers to compare prices. This encourages some stores to guarantee that they will not be undersold or 'we'll refund the difference'.

With clothes shops and shoe shops etc., each shop will have slightly different designs so it is harder for customers to make comparisons. The shops can, however, gain a reputation for value for money and, again, the shop that offers the best value for money will be the one that is likely to do best.

Penetration pricing

Definition – **penetration pricing** is setting the price of a product below the normal market price so that the product can enter the market.

Figure 5.3.3 Customers benefit from low introductory prices

NEW! RCI CRUISE EXCHANGE

with one SPACEBANK deposit you can...
Save up to 50% on a cruise

Take the 9 night "Autumn Isles" cruise and see how much you can save...

P&O Cruises Brochure Price **£1365**PP

RCI'S CRUISE SUPPLEMENT PRICE
£679pp

Penetration pricing is used by businesses to enter the market. The price is put below the price of competitors' products. This is done so that potential customers will try the product. After an introductory period the price will be put up to the normal market price but, hopefully, the customers now know that the product is good and will continue to buy it. Because this is done only to introduce a product to the market, and because the price is fairly quickly raised, competitors do not object to this pricing strategy.

A great many products are brought out at a low introductory price. This is very common with new magazines and with new food items. During this introductory period, when the price is low, the customers benefit, especially those customers who would have bought the product at the full price anyway.

Skimming

Definition – **skimming** is when the price of a new product is set high during its introduction to the market and is then lowered to gain additional customers.

Skimming is the opposite of penetration pricing. Here the price is set very high to start with. This allows the business to gain high profits from those customers who really want the product. Then, when those customers have bought the product, the price is lowered so that other people will be encouraged to buy it.

This is a common pricing policy with books where the hardback copy is brought out first, say, at £16 or £18, and then, seven months later, the paperback is brought out at, say, £5.99. It is also a common practice with console games. Many Playstation games are lowered in price after they have sold a certain amount, when they become 'platinum'.

Figure 5.3.4 Price of Tomb Raider Playstation games in Special Reserve's stores

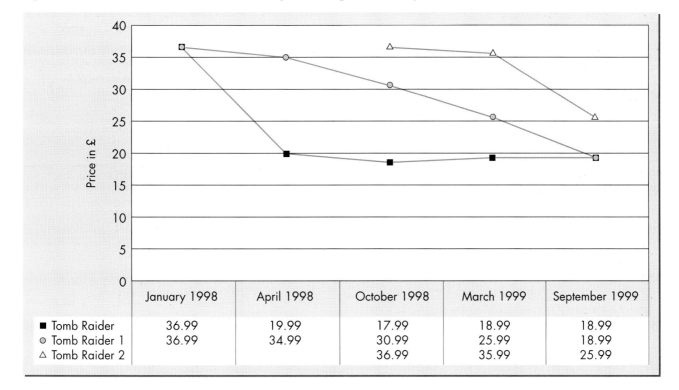

	January 1998	April 1998	October 1998	March 1999	September 1999
■ Tomb Raider	36.99	19.99	17.99	18.99	18.99
⊙ Tomb Raider 1	36.99	34.99	30.99	25.99	18.99
△ Tomb Raider 2			36.99	35.99	25.99

Sales

Definition – **sales** occur when the prices of products are lowered from their normal market prices.

Sales were traditionally used to clear old stock so that new stock could be brought in. The January sales marked the end of the Christmas buying period. With clothes shops in particular it was important to get rid of the winter range and bring in the spring and summer fashions. Today sales are held at any time of year, although sales just after Christmas are still common.

The reason for sales has also changed. Today this is just another marketing strategy, and when the sale is finished many products go back to their normal price. Sales are run for all of the following reasons:

- to clear old stock;

- to increase turnover;

- to improve the cash flow position;

- to capture market share;

- to respond to sales being run by competitors;

- to act as a loss leader (see below).

When items are offered for 'sale' strict conditions are laid down by law as to how this must be done. The previous price of the product must have been:

- the last price at which the product was available;

- the price of the product for at least 28 consecutive days before it was reduced;

- the price of the product in the actual shop where the sale is taking place.

Loss leaders

Definition – a **loss leader** is a product which is reduced in price in order to attract customers into a store to buy other products.

A loss leader is a product that is put down in price, therefore the business is losing profit. Sometimes the selling price is set *below* the cost price of the product and the business actually makes a loss when it sells the product. The aim of a loss leader, however, is not to sell the actual product that has been reduced in price but to persuade customers to come into the store and, hopefully, buy lots of other, fully priced products as well.

Every week the major supermarkets have **special offers** on a range of products. These products are carefully chosen so that they will appeal to a large number of people. Once the customers have been attracted to the supermarket to buy these special offers most of them will also do their weekly shopping there. What matters is getting the customers to the supermarket in the first place.

In public houses the **happy hour** is a form of loss leader. Customers are attracted in by drinks at half price in the hope that they will then stay for the rest of the evening and buy a great many more drinks at full price.

Discounts

Definition – a **discount** is a reduction in the normal price because of the way the customer buys the product.

Discounts are very common between manufacturers, wholesalers and retailers. If the retailers buy in sufficiently large quantities, they will get a discount from the suppliers. The price per unit will be lowered. Discounts may be given for a number of reasons:

- when customers buy more than a certain amount;

- when customers have been loyal to the businesses for a long period of time;

- when customers pay in cash rather than by cheque or credit card;

- when customers pay immediately or even in advance of receiving the product;

- when customers buy the product at a certain time, as with train or cinema tickets;

- when customers have a certain status, e.g. children, the unemployed or OAPs.

All of these kinds of discount will be offered by retailers to consumers in one business or another. The most common discount, however, is for buying large quantities, but not normally for buying large numbers of the same product. The way the discount usually works for the consumer is if they buy bigger packages. Generally a 200 gram jar of coffee costs less per 100 grams than a 100 gram jar, and the 50 gram jar is even more expensive.

Table 5.3.1 Buying in bulk benefits the consumer – Tesco (Winchester) June 1999

Milk price/pint in pence		**Persil** (Non-bio) price/100 grams		**Pepsi Cola** price/330 ml		**Kellogg's Corn Flakes** price/100 grams	
1 pint	47.7	1.35 kg	19.9	150 ml can	59.4	250 g packet	31.2
2 pints	45.9	2.70 kg	18.6	1 can	35.0	500 g packet	21.8
4 pints	39.2	4.50 kg	14.0	6 cans	33.2	750 g packet	21.2
6 pints	37.2	6.75 kg	13.3	12 cans	30.4	1000 g packet	17.9
				18 cans*	20.3		

* 18 cans of Pepsi were on special offer at the same price (£3.65) as 12 cans.

Discounts are also given for multiple purchases of products, e.g. packs of three pairs of briefs tend to be cheaper per item than a single pair of briefs; buying a box of 24 cans of Coke is considerably cheaper per can than buying one, four or eight cans. This is really an example of **multi-buying** (see below) but, because the products are packed in particular quantities, this is also known as **multi-packaging**.

Other Customer Incentives

The examples of incentives given above all relate directly to pricing. Many of the examples given below will also affect the prices of products in one way or another.

Multi-buys

> Definition – a **multi-buy** is any offer which involves the purchase of more than one product.

Retail stores have invented a huge range of multi-buy offers, the best known of which are found in supermarkets and grocery stores. However, the practice is actually found in most retail outlets in one form or another. When travel agents offer customers package deals which include flights, accommodation and excursions, they are offering a kind of multi-buy where the package is cheaper than the individual parts.

Some multi-deals are used as loss leaders, especially in supermarkets, but in some cases multi-deals actually give the retailers more profit if they persuade customers to buy more products than the customers originally intended. If a packet of cereal costs the retailers 70p and they normally sell the cereals for £1.60 they will make 90p profit per box. If they offer customers 'buy one, get a second at half price' it will cost them £1.40 and they will receive back £1.60 + 80p. This will give them £1.00 profit in total.

All of the following are examples of multi-buy offers:

- buy one get one free;
- buy one get a second at half price;
- get three for the price of two;
- buy one product and get a different product free or at a reduced price;
- buy one and get a coupon for your next purchase;
- discounts for buying large quantities of goods, e.g. a box of 24 cans of cola.

Free offers and samples

If new products are sold at the full market price many people will not bother to try them. That is why firms use **penetration pricing**. They may, alternatively give **samples** of the products away free. This allows potential customers to try them and, if they like them, they will then consider buying them at the full price.

This kind of incentive will be used only with products that people tend to buy over and over again, such as food, drink, cleaning products, etc., or with products where parts of them can be sold separately, as with demos of record albums or computer games.

Some wine merchants, such as Majestic, offer customers free wine tasting. Having tried a few wines, most customers are too embarrassed to walk out without buying some wine as well. Many computer software businesses produce demo disks to show customers what their software does, or how the games play. Often these are given away free in the hope that a taster will encourage the customers to buy the full version.

Competitions

Competitions are usually offered by the producers of products rather than by the retailers, but the competitions still help to increase sales for the retailers. Most competitions require the customers to buy the product and cut off part of the labelling to send in with the competition entry form. Alternatively, they must send a till receipt which has the purchase listed. Some competitions are free and do not require any purchase of the product at all. This is a form of public relations and helps to promote the image of the business and its products.

The prizes offered in these competitions vary widely, from holidays and cars to free samples of the products themselves. Some competitions expect answers to questions, others require the completion of some comment about the product, and yet others ask only for the customer's name and address. Some competitions insist that the entrant visits the shop in order to post the entry, and, once in the shop, it is hoped that the person will buy something.

Loyalty schemes

> Definition – a **loyalty scheme** is any incentive that makes a customer loyal to one business rather than another.

The loyalty cards offered by supermarkets and a growing number of other retailers are what immediately springs to mind when loyalty schemes are mentioned. They are certainly the schemes that are receiving most publicity as the economy enters the new century. In fact, there have been loyalty schemes for a very long time and these cards are only one of the latest ideas designed to tie customers to one retailer. Loyalty schemes include all of the following:

- offering discounts to loyal customers;

- offering customers credit facilities and accounts which encourage them to shop where they can buy now and pay later;

- giving air miles or premier points that can be spent at Argos, both of which require customers to shop at specific retail outlets if they are to build up a worthwhile level of points;

- vouchers that can be spent only in the store that issues them, e.g. £5.00 off your next purchase;

- vouchers that can be used in a different part of the retail outlet. Sainsbury's 2000 spring promotion gave vouchers for discounts on petrol bought at its petrol stations – 1p/litre discount for £25 spent in the store and up to 4p/litre discount for £100 spent in the store;

- tokens that can be used to benefit other people or organisations, e.g. 'Computers for schools' from Tesco and 'Free books for schools' from *The Times*, among others;

- savings stamps. These allow customers to buy stamps regularly over a period of time and then

spend them when they need to. Customers often use these to meet the increased expenditure needed at Christmas;

- loyalty cards which accumulate points that can be used for buying more goods in the store.

Many retail chains now offer customers special credit facilities and these help to tie the customer to the particular chain. This is explained below.

Loyalty cards are a very twenty-first century way of tying customers into a particular retail chain. Most of them operate in the same way.

1 Cards are issued only after a short questionnaire is completed. This gives the retail firm a profile of the customer which the firm can then match against what was actually bought by the customer. This provides valuable market research data for the business.

2 Points are given on the basis of how much is spent in the retail chain.

3 Points are then converted into a money equivalent which can be spent in the chain on future purchases.

4 Certain products on sale in the store attract bonus loyalty points.

5 Loyalty customers are sent special offers, coupons, etc. through the post.

Retailers have recognised that customers do not want to collect points simply so that they can reduce the cost of next month's grocery bill. The major retail chains are therefore offering their loyalty card customers alternatives to spend their points on.

Case Study – What can you do with your loyalty points?

At Sainsbury £1 spent equals 2 points. When 500 points are accumulated a reward voucher can be claimed. In 1999 each of these vouchers could be reclaimed against the following:

- £2.50 worth of goods purchased in Sainsbury's stores;
- £5.00 discount (for every £25 spent) in Burton Menswear, Dorothy Perkins, Evans, Hawkshead, Principles, Principles for Men, Racing Green, Topshop and Topman;
- 1 Whopper meal at Burger King;
- 1 free movie rental at Blockbusters;
- £5.00 off British/Scottish Gas quarterly bills;
- 1 haddock fillet and chips or 1 standard cod and chips at Harry Ramsden's;
- 40 air miles;
- 1 free UCI cinema admission;
- 1 half-price two-night break at over 250 UK hotels;
- £5.00 off two adult main course meals at Beefeater, TGI Friday's or Brewer's Fayre;
- 250 minutes of BT TalkTime;
- a donation of £2.50 to The Blue Cross or to NSPCC/Children 1st.

For further information on the Sainsbury's reward card check the internet at **www.sainsburys.co.uk**

Credit Terms

Allowing customers to buy products on credit is an important part of retailing. Most stores now provide some kind of credit facilities for their customers. Credit is important to retailers for all of the following reasons:

- It allows customers to buy things that they could not otherwise afford, e.g. cars, fitted kitchens and computers. It therefore increases sales of these kinds of products.

- If people are buying smaller items on credit and not paying for them until later, they are often tempted to buy more than they really need.

- With accounts, customers are likely to shop in the store regularly.

- Customers now expect credit facilities and if one store does not provide credit facilities they may well shop elsewhere.

- Credit facilities are often used as a way of promoting products or the store, especially if they are offered interest free.

In Chapter 2 (page 279) we looked at some of the ways of paying with credit, such as monthly accounts, hire purchase and credit cards. Here we will look at the credit terms.

All credit involves customers in paying for products some time after they have received them. In some cases the retailer will offer this as a free service. This happens with **monthly accounts** where the customer is sent a statement at the end of the month and then pays the amount owing. Most stores that offer this service make no additional charge but they will have terms, e.g.:

- Only regular customers may be offered the account.

- If the account is not paid in full at the end of the month interest may be charged.

- There may be a requirement that the customer is in full-time employment or has a regular income.

> Definition – **credit** is receiving a good or service now but paying for it in the future.

Other credit involves borrowing, either from the retailer or from a specialist lender. When borrowing takes place, terms will be laid down, as indicated in Figure 5.3.5.

Figure 5.3.5 Credit terms

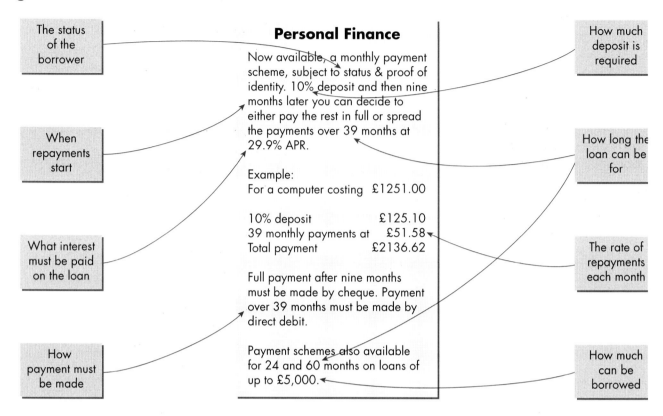

In the late 1990s retailers have been facing a great deal of competition and one way of attracting customers is to offer better credit packages than competitors. Actual details of credit terms have, therefore, become highly variable and it is now quite difficult for customers to know which provider is offering the best deal. All firms providing loans are required by law to publish the APR, and this does allow some basis for comparison.

> Definition – **APR** stands for **annual percentage rate of interest** and shows the actual rate of interest that borrowers must pay on average over the full period of the loan.

Delivery Terms

Many products sold by retailers are not taken home by the customers, but are delivered. This will tend to happen when:

- the products are very large, such as a bed or a washing machine;

- the products need to be ordered and will be delivered direct to the customer's home;

- the products are being ordered through mail order, over the phone, from newspapers and magazines or via the internet.

When retailers agree to deliver people's goods certain delivery terms will be involved. Common terms are:

- free delivery to homes within a certain distance;

- free delivery of goods above a certain value;

- delivery charges related to the number of items sent or how large/heavy they are;

- agreement to deliver within a certain time;

- agreement to deliver at a certain time of day, e.g. mornings, afternoons or evenings;

- delivery when full payment has been made.

After Sales Service

> Definition – **after sales services** are services provided to customers after they have bought the product.

After sales service, as the name suggests, is service given to customers after the sale of the product has been made. Providing credit facilities and delivery are both services that take place after the customer has been into the store to buy the goods. There is a wide range of after sales services that retailers can provide. The services include:

- credit facilities;

- delivery;

- warranties/guarantees;

- follow-up advice/helplines;

- servicing and maintenance of goods;

- refund and replacement services;

- discounts on replacing durable goods with a newer model, upgrades;

- information on new products being released.

> Definition – a **warranty** is an agreement made by the seller that if something is wrong with the product the customer will be compensated in some way. A **guarantee** is a statement that certain facts about the product are correct, and if they are not the customer will have a right to compensation.

Warranties/guarantees provide customers with a sense of security. They know that if something goes wrong with the good or service that they have bought there will be some way in which they will be compensated.

NETWORK Q

- **114 point service on all cars**
- **12 months/15,000 miles warranty**

With every car we sell included in the price is a minimum of 12 months' warranty covering both parts and labour.

- **12 months' Network Q Cover**
- **30 days' exchange pledge**

Should you not be entirely satisfied with your car, within 30 days, you may exchange it for a similar model, subject to conditions

- **AA assistance**
- **Guarantee cover during first 6 months/6,000 miles of clutch, brakes and battery**
- **HPI Autodata check**

Every used car which we have not owned from new is checked by a company called HPI, for damage claims, outstanding finance, police interest and hidden number plate transfers.

- **Vehicle mileage check**

The warranty itself will give details of what action the business will take to deal with any faults. These actions may include any of the following:

- replacing the product;

- repairing any faults, with goods repaired on site, or returned to the shop or manufacturer;

- paying the customer compensation, especially where a service such as a holiday, has been purchased.

Warranties will vary considerably depending on what product is being bought, and the best way to see the range of guarantees being offered is to collect in-store literature, and check what guarantees were given for durable goods in your own home.

Upgrades are very common with computer software and hardware, and customers are often offered new versions at a reduced price if they have bought earlier versions at the full price.

Refunds or **replacements** are common in many retail outlets, especially if there is something wrong with the products. In some clothes shops, such as Marks & Spencer, customers may return the clothes if they are not suitable, as long as they have not been damaged.

Servicing and **maintenance** is common with electrical equipment such as washing machines, but this is usually an additional service that has to be paid for. Sometimes it is included in the price. Stores selling bicycles usually offer a free service to tighten up all the nuts etc. two or three weeks after a new bike has been sold.

Activity

The customer incentives offered by retail stores vary widely. The best way to get an overview of these incentives is to check what individual retailers are doing. This can be done by checking magazines and papers, or the internet to see what incentives mail order firms offer. A visit to retail stores can also provide a wealth of information. These are tasks that will help you to collect a valuable range of data on the features covered in this chapter.

Pricing strategies

Some of these are difficult to identify but others can be spotted more easily.

1   Note down any products that you find that are first sold at a low price to penetrate the market. These will be examples of penetration pricing.
2   In your local supermarket note down the special offers placed on frequently bought items such as bread, butter, chicken portions. These may well be loss leaders.
3   Select two or three standard items that you know are being sold in at least three or four places. Note the prices. If they are very close they may well be examples of competition-based pricing.
4   Check advertisements for products in the press or from in-store posters and leaflets and note down what discounts are being offered.

Customer incentives

Data on these can be found by visiting retail outlets or by checking advertisements in the press or on the internet. Many leaflets, advertisements on television or mail shots also provide details.

1   In your local supermarket note down the different types of offer that involve multi-buys. Check multi-buy offers in other retail outlets such as department stores, clothes shops, and shops selling music CDs. Compare the types of multi-buy being offered.
2   Note any (i) free offers; (ii) competitions that are being run in retail outlets that you visit and note down the type of product that free offers/competitions are given on. Check both retail outlets selling goods and those selling services.
3   When you go to a supermarket, department store or other retail outlet, check if they have brochures or leaflets explaining what services they offer, and collect them. These should tell you about loyalty schemes, credit facilities, guarantees and after sales services.
4   Check advertisements in the press and on the internet to see what terms are offered for credit, delivery and prices. These may also be published as in-store literature and will always be provided if you ask for details in the store.

Conditions and terms for services such as credit, warranties and delivery vary with the firm involved. You need to get examples of agreements and offers so that you can see how they vary and what terms are fairly typical.

Revision

Questions

Questions 1 to 3 require one of the following answers.
These are all types of pricing strategy that a retail outlet might use:
   A competition-based pricing;
   B penetration pricing;
   C skimming;
   D using a loss leader.

1 Which pricing strategy would be used by a business when it reduces the price of one good in order to attract customers into its store to buy other goods?   (1 mark)

2 Which pricing strategy is being used when a business sets its price at the same level as other stores selling the same product?   (1 mark)

3 Which pricing strategy puts high prices on new products and then lowers the price?   (1 mark)

4 Give three reasons why a discount may be given to customers and explain what benefit there is for the business.   (4 marks)

5 Explain what a multi-buy is and give one example that is likely to be used by each of the following retail outlets:
   a) supermarket;
   b) greengrocer;
   c) clothes shop;
   d) fast-food restaurant.   (5 marks)

6 Explain what penetration pricing is and why the price starts off low and is then raised.   (4 marks)

7 Which good would you recommend that a supermarket should use as a loss leader? Explain why this would be the right good to use.   (4 marks)

8 Explain why businesses give customers free samples and explain which kinds of products would be most suitable.   (4 marks)

9 Give one example of a retail outlet that has promoted its products using a competition. What are the costs and benefits for a retailer of running the competition?   (5 marks)

10 In 1999 customers at Sainsbury's supermarkets could save over the summer using a savings card. The card had spaces for 75 £1 stamps which could be bought as customers do their shopping or from the customer services counter. For every £24 saved Sainsbury's gave a free £1 of savings, but this was only given if the card was used for making purchases in the month of December.
   a) Why was this savings card and the special offer of benefit to customers?
   b) What benefits did Sainsbury's gain from offering the savings card and the special offer?   (6 marks)

11 Explain what a loyalty card is and how it benefits both the customer and the
    business.   (6 marks)

12 a) List the main items that will be included in the credit terms offered by a retail
        business or a finance company when they allow customers to buy on credit.   (4 marks)
    b) What benefits do the customers and the retailers get from credit sales?   (4 marks)

13 a) Give four examples of products from different types of retail outlet that are likely to
        be delivered to a customer's home.
    b) Give three different reasons why delivery is offered.
    c) Give three different terms that the offer of delivery may depend on.   (10 marks)

14 List three examples of after sales services that are likely to be offered by a store selling
    hi-fi equipment. Explain how each service is of benefit to the customer.   (6 marks)

CHAPTER 4

IN-STORE ENVIRONMENT

KEY TERMS:

layout	flow	concessions
grid	merchandising	sales
checkout	counters	displays
corporate image	signposting	customer amenities
heating	lighting	in-store music

In this chapter you will learn about how and why retail stores create a particular atmosphere and image in their outlets.

Introduction

If you go into most branches of Boots, Dixons, Marks & Spencer or any of the major chain stores, each individual store will look similar to all the other branches. This is not chance. The chain stores make the environment in their outlets similar on purpose. They do this for a number of reasons.

- Each outlet is selling the same range of products so they will tend to look similar anyway.

- Making outlets the same means less expense on design because, once the inside of the store is designed for one outlet, it can simply be copied for all the others.

- The in-store environment is designed to create a particular atmosphere which makes a statement about the business. The owners will want to make the same statement in all their outlets.

- If all the stores look the same, each branch will advertise every other branch.

- If all the stores are the same, the customers will instantly recognise them and will feel comfortable shopping in them even if they go to other towns and cities.

- Customers know the layout in their local stores and will want the layout in the other stores to be the same so that they can find what they are looking for easily.

Retailers create a particular atmosphere and image for their stores in a number of ways. It is these ways that we will consider below.

Store Layout

The layout of the store is designed to do various things:

- give customers access to the goods or, where services are being sold (as in a travel agency), access to the sales staff;

- display the goods where they can be easily seen and selected;

- allow a free flow of customers around the store;

- use the space efficiently.

Figure 5.4.1 shows a very typical layout for a supermarket. The main layout is in a **grid** pattern with the shelves in straight lines and the aisles wide enough to allow customers to pass each other with their trolleys.

The thinking behind Tesco's layout

Meticulous planning goes into the layout of stores so that they are bright and welcoming and products are easy to find and select. Stores are designed to offer customers the widest possible choice of products in an environment which is spacious and attractive. Products must be easy to find and to take off the shelves, and aisles must be wide enough to allow the shelf fillers to top up products while not inconveniencing customers (including those in wheelchairs).
Source: Tesco's web site

The grid pattern is used because most customers will walk up and down every aisle and the grid pattern provides the most efficient use of space. The main concern of the supermarket management will be to work out which are the best products to put at the entrance so that customers will see them. The big supermarket chains tend to put fruit and vegetables near the entrance, or magazines and papers, but also special offers.

Figure 5.4.1 Typical supermarket grid layout

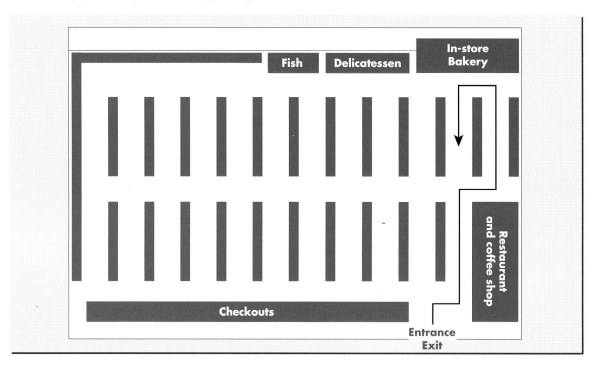

The line and arrow in Figure 5.4.1 shows the usual flow of customers through the supermarket. The restaurant is placed next to the entrance to encourage customers to use it either as they enter or after they have finished shopping and are about to leave. The checkouts are placed between the shelves and the exit so that customers find it easy to unload their shopping after they have collected everything, but also to make it more difficult for them to leave the store without paying.

Tobacco products are sold separately, partly because it is illegal to sell tobacco products to anyone under

the age of sixteen, but also because these are products that are easy to steal.

The benefits of a grid layout are:

- It is an efficient use of space.
- The flow of customers is fairly predictable so the retailer can choose where to put different goods for the greatest impact.
- Customers often walk up and down all the rows and hence pass all the products.
- The ends of rows stand out and are good places for special offers.

Figure 5.4.2 Free flow layout

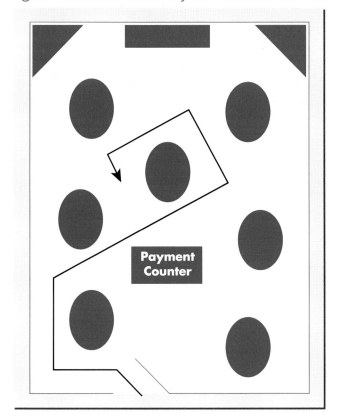

In some shops the layout appears to be very random. In many cases the goods have been set out in this way to encourage customers to wander about freely and look at all the products. This kind of layout is fairly common in large clothes stores.

The main benefits of a free flow layout are:

- It encourages people to wander about and see all the goods.

- There is a more relaxed atmosphere and people will want to stay longer.

- It is possible to see most of the store because there is usually little high shelving.

- Displays can be laid out to create attractive patterns which will encourage customers into the store.

With other stores the layout is used to create an image for the store. The Body Shop has a very open layout, which helps to create the impression of space and lets the customers browse and try out different testers.

The layout for retailers selling services tends to be quite different. That is because customers need to sit down and talk to the sales staff. The outlet will not need masses of shelving for goods. They may have leaflets or brochures but the main process of selling is talking to customers and giving them information and advice.

The layout for Toucan Travel in Andover (Figure 5.4.3) is very typical for this kind of service retailing. Here the desks are placed at an angle to help to separate each member of staff and their clients and give them some privacy. The wide space between the chairs and the stands holding brochures allows customers to browse even if they have to wait to be attended to.

Figure 5.4.3 Layout of Toucan Travel

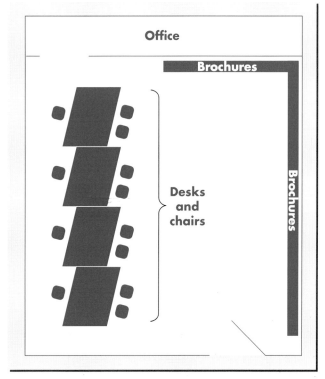

A visit to your local travel agent, estate agent or bank will show the variety of layouts for these kinds of businesses.

Hairdressers, betting shops, fast-food restaurants, etc. will tend to have their own specialist layouts. These reflect the need for customers to wait, to spend a long time there, to take what they have ordered and eat it, and so on.

In some stores, mainly department stores, concessions (see page 270) are given to other retailers to sell their goods in the store. The layout may then be very varied, with each separate retail firm deciding on a different layout for its part of the store.

Checkouts and Counters

> Definition – **checkouts** are payment desks placed at the exits of self-service retail stores.

As the name suggests, **checkouts** are placed next to the exits so that customers can pay as they check out. Many retail outlets now have self-service and customers fill trolleys or baskets with what they want and take them to the checkouts in order to pay. The reasons for placing the checkouts at the exit have been mentioned above but will include all of the following:

- This is the most convenient place for customers to pay because they are about to leave the store.

- It makes it more difficult for customers to leave the store without paying for goods because they have to pass the checkout to get out, and after they have paid they leave immediately.

- Checkout staff have no other major function except taking payment (although some may pack goods into bags). They can therefore scan goods and take payment rapidly and this means the checking process is very fast.

- Because checkout staff are not by the shelves they will not normally be asked questions such as where products are. This also helps them to do their jobs quickly.

Most stores now have scanners at the checkouts and some supermarkets have introduced hand-held scanners (see page 316) which means that the checkout staff need only to check the total and take payment.

> Definition – **counters** are staffed desks or service areas where staff take payment, serve or answer queries and give advice.

There are a great many different types of counters in retail outlets. Some of these serve the same function as a checkout and these are called **payment counters**. Customers will take their goods to these counters, have them checked, possibly packed, and pay for them.

In stores such as hi-fi and computer shops or shops selling CDs the goods on display will not be the ones that customers actually buy. New, often pre-packed, goods will be brought out of the storeroom. It therefore makes sense to place the counter near the storeroom. In music shops there is little worry about goods being stolen because all the cases are empty or have security attachments which set off an alarm if anyone leaves the shop with the good. The same is the case in many clothes shops.

With other goods, such as furniture or washing machines, the goods are likely to be delivered rather than taken away by the consumer. In this case the payment counter could be anywhere, but is likely to be placed where it is most convenient for the customers and where staff can keep an eye on what is going on in the store.

Counters will be available for all of the following purposes:

- for making payments;

- for inquiries and giving advice;

- for complaints, returned goods, refunds;

- for demonstrating how products work or can be used, as with electrical equipment or cosmetics counters in department stores;

- for serving food that needs some preparation, as with delicatessen and fresh fish counters in supermarkets.

Signposting

> Definition – **signposting** is the use of signs to tell customers where products and amenities are in the store.

In large stores **signposting** is a very important factor in keeping the customers happy. In supermarkets, where there are a great many goods placed on shelves in rows that all look much the same, signs are usually hung from the ceiling above the rows. This allows customers to see quickly where the products they are looking for have been placed.

In large department stores, which often have their departments on different floors, details will be put on notice boards at the entrance of the stores or near to the stairs or escalators. With open plan department stores, each floor will then have signposting above the separate departments.

Signposting is used in many different retail outlets to indicate where products are or what each section of the retail outlet is for. In banks, for example, it is common to have notices above the tills that tell customers if the service till is for normal money transactions, foreign exchange, general information or business banking.

Signposting should follow certain rules.

- It must be easy to see and placed where customers expect to see it.

- It should use contrasting colours so that the signs stand out.

- Comments should be short and clear.

- There should not be too much signposting, otherwise it becomes confusing.

Display of Goods

The way in which retailers display their goods has a very marked effect on how well the goods will sell. Goods should be displayed so that they attract customers and make them want to buy the goods. There are a great many display techniques that retailers use to persuade their customers to buy goods, e.g.:

- Clothes shops will display their clothes on slim dummy models to try to make their customers believe that if they buy the clothes they will look just like the models.

- Supermarkets used to place sweets next to the checkouts so that parents shopping with young children would be persuaded to buy the sweets while waiting at the checkouts in order to keep their children happy.

- Many stores display their special offers at the front of the store in order to attract customers in.

- Displays are made to stand out with bright colours so that customers will see them. At the same time the colours need to be appealing, otherwise customers will be put off.

- Displays show the best products in the store. This helps to convince the customers that all the products are of a similar high quality.

With the display of most goods there are general rules that will ensure that customers feel the retailer has their interests at heart.

1 Goods need to be displayed where customers have easy access to them.
2 Similar types of goods should be displayed next to each other.
3 Goods should be displayed with their prices so that customers know what they will be charged.
4 The goods on display should be the same as the goods that are taken out of the storeroom or from behind the counter and given to customers.
5 The display of goods should be attractive and make customers feel at ease in the store.
6 The best selling products should be displayed at eye level, because that is where customers look first. They then tend to look down and finally up. The worst selling products are usually put above eye level.
7 Damaged goods should be removed or they will give a bad image.
8 Displays should be carefully constructed so that they are not a danger to the customers or staff.
9 Stock on display should be regularly dusted to show that the product is still fit to buy and that the store is well maintained.
10 Gaps should be filled from the stock room or, if the product is out of stock, replaced with other similar products

Displays in retail outlets often reflect a wider pattern, where the retailer is using the display to get across a more general message. Examples include lifestyle, co-ordinated displays, theme and seasonal displays.

Lifestyle displays are ones which are trying to say something about the way people live their lives. They also reflect what people think is important in their lives.

Many more people now travel abroad for their holidays and they expect food retailers to stock and display more exotic foods. There is more concern about what we eat and wear and how production and packaging affects the environment. Retailers take these concerns seriously and display products to reflect our changing lifestyles.

There are many different aspects of lifestyle that retail outlets try to put across with their displays. Figure 5.4.4 shows some of the different characteristics that are behind people's lifestyles.

Figure 5.4.4 Lifestyle characteristics on which businesses base their displays

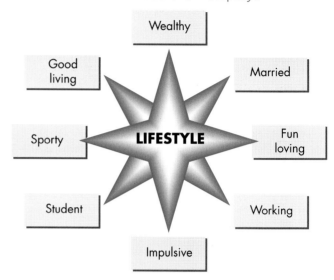

These will be taken into account when retailers decide how to display their products. For example, if they know that there are many students in the area and that students tend to be fairly hard-up they may stress value for money in their displays.

Case study – Catering for a lifestyle with little time to eat

In fast-food restaurants, like McDonald's or Burger King, every part of the service is designed to cater for a lifestyle in which people buy food, sit and eat it, and leave, all within 10 or 15 minutes. Fast-food restaurants provide food and drinks but they are selling a service, and each part of that service reflects a lifestyle where time must not be wasted.

How they cater for customers	**How that meets the lifestyle**
• There is one counter where everyone queues for food and drinks.	• Quicker than waiting at a table for someone to come and take the order.
• Food and drinks are served very quickly.	• Very little is cooked to order and best sellers are cooked in advance.
• Payment is made as the meal is ordered.	• Customers can then leave as soon as they have finished eating.
• All the plates, mugs, knives and forks are disposable.	• No washing up, little mess on the tables, the next customers can sit down and start eating.
• The chairs are relatively uncomfortable.	• Designed to discourage customers from staying too long.
• The rooms are far from peaceful.	• This creates an atmosphere of rushing that also encourages people to join the rush and leave.

Co-ordinated displays are ones where the products are all presented in the same way. They can be co-ordinated in a variety of ways, e.g.:

- by colour;

- by size, set out with small items at the front rising to large items at the back;

- by price, cheap items together, progressing to expensive items;

- by type, all the drinks together, all the cereals elsewhere.

Good co-ordinated displays will create an impact on the customers and make the products stand out. On the other hand, if they are too regimented, customers may be reluctant to take any products because this will spoil the display.

Theme displays concentrate on a particular theme to try to help sell the products. The Body Shop has an environmental theme in all its products and displays. At Hallowe'en many stores will have displays with witches, ghosts, etc. Many displays are related to themes from current films (see the example for merchandising below). When the football World Cup and European Cup competitions reach the finals stages, many stores suddenly have a football theme in their displays.

If the theme is popular with customers it will attract people into the store and they will then buy goods that have nothing to do with this theme. On the other hand, if they do not like the theme, or if something goes wrong (England get knocked out in the early rounds), then all the store's products might be adversely affected.

In **seasonal** displays goods or the stores themselves are decorated and packaged to reflect the season. In clothes stores, displays sometimes reflect the four seasons of spring, summer, autumn and winter. In most stores there is a Christmas display and often one for Easter and Hallowe'en.

Merchandising

> Definition – **merchandising** is the promotion of goods at the point of sale.

Merchandising is the name given to promoting products in the retail outlet where the products are being sold, i.e. at the **point of sale**. Merchandising is done in a variety of ways which include:

- advertising the products through:
  a) window displays;
  b) special display units with the products on show;
  c) the way in which they are stacked on shelves;
- placing the products where the customers will easily see them, often at the entrance or near the payment counter;
- creating the right atmosphere in the store, with heating, lighting and music. Record stores that wish to sell particular records may play them over the in-store speakers.

Merchandising is going on all the time but it is most noticeable when new products are being launched and stores allocate a great deal of space to just one range of goods. Many major films lead to a wide range of spin-off products which are then widely promoted in the shops as the film comes out.

It is a fairly common practice for stores to merchandise products by putting up **mass displays** of the same product. This draws attention to it and helps to increase sales considerably.

Promoting the Corporate Image

For many retail chains, creating a corporate image that makes them stand out from their competitors is very important. It must also be a corporate image that appeals to the customers. In 1998 and 1999 Marks & Spencer was seen by many commentators as having an old-fashioned, dull image and this damaged its sales and profits for those years.

The Body Shop is very keen to create a 'green' image and one that shows that it cares about the environment, animal welfare and low-paid workers in other countries. Its press releases, national advertising and web site give details of all of these concerns, but the stores themselves are also used to promote this corporate image.

- They tend to be decorated in green.

- They have in-store literature explaining their green policies.

- Their products also refer to elements of their green policy on the packaging.

Supermarkets are also very keen to promote an image of caring about the welfare of the consumer and will offer leaflets on healthy eating and provide toilets and changing facilities for babies; some now even provide crèche facilities. Most have listened to complaints from customers with children and now do not put sweets or small toys near the checkouts.

McDonald's insists that all its branches have a similar décor, although there is some local variation (e.g. Southampton's city centre branch has a nautical theme). The products for sale are very similar, all made from the same ingredients in the same way. The parent firm understands that it has created a reputation for a certain quality of food, service and environment. This has made McDonald's very rich and it wants to ensure that nothing happens to its image to damage that reputation.

Corporate image is created in a great many ways and all the individual parts build up to make the overall image. Other ways of creating the image are through:

- the layout of the stores;

- the way in which products are displayed;

- the quality of the products being sold;

- the uniforms the staff wear;

- the way that staff are trained and carry out their duties;

- the service and after sales service provided by the stores;

- even the lighting and background music used in the stores.

Case Study – Changing the corporate image

In 1997 and 1998 external surveys showed that customers' perception of Marks & Spencer stores had changed dramatically. Customers used to feel that the store and the products sold led the field in terms of quality, but the survey now showed that customers felt that the quality had fallen and that the clothes were dull and out of date.

More worrying perhaps was that internal research also showed that customers' perceptions were changing and this was confirmed as profits fell dramatically.

By the beginning of 1999 there was little evidence inside the stores that any major changes were being made to its image. There were, however, signs that the problems had been recognised.

Peter Salisbury, Chief Executive, said in the March 1999 interim report, 'We have already learnt from what went wrong, and identified much of what needs to be done to recover.'

Perhaps the change in image is already beginning as Marks & Spencer moves into e-commerce (selling goods on the internet). By July 1999 there were over 5 million hits/month on its web site. There is also a commitment to expand its financial services sector.

Customer Comfort and Amenities

If customers do not feel comfortable in a store they will not come back to shop there again. It is vital that retailers do as much as they can to provide the customers with the amenities they want and expect and to make the shopping experience as pleasant as possible.

Customer comfort is provided by means of all of the following:

- a reasonable temperature;
- good lighting;
- plenty of space to move about in;
- trolleys and baskets if more than one or two goods are required;
- easy access for the disabled;
- lifts or escalators between floors;
- somewhere to sit and wait where services are being sold if staff are occupied;
- enough staff to serve people quickly and prevent queues.

Good amenities also help to provide comfort for customers. Some amenities are mentioned above. Other common ones are:

- toilet facilities;
- parking;
- changing rooms and mirrors in clothes shops;
- help desks;
- trolleys with child seats;
- in-store cafés and restaurants;
- public telephones.

Heating, Lighting and Background Music

Heating and lighting help to provide a comfortable atmosphere for shoppers, but they also help to create part of the image of the store.

In winter, when there is a cold wind, rain or snow outside, a well-heated store provides comfort and also creates a feeling of caring and protection. On the other hand, when it is 30 degrees in the shade and hot and muggy outside, stores that provide air-conditioned premises keep their customers comfortable and also show them that the business is modern and concerned with customers' welfare.

Lighting is used to ensure that customers can see the products, move about easily, and read notices or prices, but it can also be used to create atmosphere. Lighting can make a store look bright and efficient or dark and mysterious. It can also be used to pick out particular features and products that the retailer wants to draw attention to.

An atmosphere can also be created by background music. In some stores 'canned music', i.e. pre-recorded music played through the in-store speakers, is played all the time. Other stores have recognised that this kind of music annoys customers and they have stopped playing it.

However, in some stores they do still use music to create a particular atmosphere. In Indian and Chinese restaurants the owners will play traditional Indian or Chinese music to create an ethnic atmosphere. In most clothes shops which sell clothes to teenagers and 20 to 30-year-olds, there is pop music, either canned or, more and more frequently, from the radio.

Activity

Every store has a slightly different in-store environment. The only way to see the variety of different environments is to visit stores and note down what is there. You should select different types of store and then record the data listed below.

Layout

1 Make a diagram of the layout.
2 Note what type of layout it is, where the counters and checkouts are.
3 Observe how most people circulate around the store and draw a main flow line on the diagram.
4 Note down why you think the layout is good, or how it could be improved.
5 Note down why you think the counters have been placed where they are.

Signposting

1 Note down what type of signposting, if any, is used and where it is placed.
2 Explain how the particular signposting used will help customers and suggest any improvements that could be made.

Displays

1 Note down what major displays are used in the store, including window displays.
2 Decide what type of displays they are (theme, co-ordinated, lifestyle, etc.).
3 Note what the theme or lifestyle is.

Merchandising and corporate image

1 List any merchandising that is used to promote products in the store.
2 Describe the image that you feel the store is trying to put across (modern, trendy, value for money, friendly, up-market, etc.).
3 List the features that you think help to create this image.

Amenities, heating, lighting and music

1 Make a list of all the special amenities (toilets, lifts, in-store restaurants, etc.) that are provided for the customers.
2 Note down whether there is any in-store music and what kind of music it is.
3 Note down what lighting is used and any special effects that this is designed to create.
4 Describe what atmosphere the store is trying to create with its music and lighting.
5 Note down what heating or air-conditioning/fans are used.

It may be possible to do all this in each store that you visit, but this will take some time and it may annoy the staff. Either explain what you are doing and ask for approval or note down these features over several visits or even in different shops.

Revision

Questions

Questions 1 to 3 require one of the following answers.

These are all parts of the in-store environment which form part of the image of the retail outlet:

A merchandising;
B signposting;
C corporate image;
D mass displays.

1 Which in-store environment will reflect the same image for all the stores in a chain?   (1 mark)

2 Which in-store environment promotes particular goods at the point of sale?   (1 mark)

3 Which in-store environment will help customers to locate particular goods in a supermarket?   (1 mark)

4 Draw the layout of a small store that you know well.   (2 marks)
   a) Explain what type of layout it has.   (2 marks)
   b) Explain how this layout will affect the flow of customers.   (2 marks)
   c) Indicate where the checkout or payment counter is.   (1 mark)
   d) Explain why the counter has been placed there.   (2 marks)

5 Explain how and why a shop selling clothes or music CDs and videos will have a different layout to an estate agent or a travel agent.   (6 marks)

6 a) Give two examples of retail outlets that do not have checkouts.   (2 marks)
   b) Explain why they do not use checkouts.   (4 marks)

7 a) Give three examples of how a department store is likely to use signposting.   (3 marks)
   b) Why is signposting necessary in a department store?   (2 marks)

8 a) Give one example of a store that you have seen which uses each of the following types of display:
      i) lifestyle;
      ii) co-ordinated;
      iii) theme.   (3 marks)
   b) For each of these explain how it helps to create or support a particular image that the store is trying to put across to its customers.   (6 marks)

9 a) Outline the corporate image that you think your local supermarket is trying to put across to its customers.   (2 marks)
   b) Give two examples of how the supermarket has supported this image through its in-store environment.   (2 marks)
   c) Explain why the two examples you have used help to support the corporate image.   (2 marks)

10 a) List the amenities provided in one of the last three stores you have visited.   (4 marks)

   b) For each of these amenities explain why it is important for this particular store to provide that amenity for customers.   (4 marks)

11 a) Describe the kind of (i) lighting and (ii) music that is used in a store that you know well.   (2 marks)

   b) For each, explain how it affects the atmosphere of the store.   (4 marks)

12 For any retail outlet you know well, explain how the in-store environment could be improved. Explain why the changes you suggest would improve the in-store environment for the customer.   (8 marks)

CHAPTER 5

RETAIL SELLING TECHNOLOGY

KEY TERMS:

electronic point of sale (EPOS)

electronic data interchange (EDI)

electronic funds transfer systems

bar codes

stock control

scanners

In this chapter you will learn about some of the technology that is now used in many retail outlets.

Introduction

A trip round a supermarket will show you just how extensively technology is now used as part of the selling process in retailing.

- All the goods on the shelves have bar codes on them.

- The checkouts use scanners to add up and record what you have purchased.

- Payment is frequently made with a debit or credit card and the information is passed electronically to your bank.

- Your loyalty card is scanned and points added automatically.

- The goods sold are recorded internally in the supermarket and will tell the management when to order more stock.

But it is not just supermarkets that use these systems. Most retail outlets that sell goods will have bar codes on their goods and will scan these to record what people have bought and how much they owe.

Service providers also use selling technology. They will generally accept credit and debit cards and they often have special computer software that allows them to access data very quickly. Travel agents, for example, will be able to check holiday details on-screen and will use telephone or e-mail links to confirm availability and book holidays with the holiday and travel companies.

Bar Codes and Scanners

Definition – a **bar code** is a way of giving something a unique code by using a series of bars that mean either numbers or letters.

A major part of electronic selling technology is based upon the use of bar codes. A bar code is a series of bars of different widths which refer to a number, letter or punctuation mark. With the most commonly used bar codes on goods each number is shown by using a pair of bars and the numbers 0 to 9 are distinguished by how thick the bars are and where they are placed.

Figure 5.5.1 shows the major type of bar code used in the UK and Europe. It is also used internationally. It is the European article number (EAN) and has 13 numbers. The bars are separated by two thin (and usually longer) bars so that the scanner knows where the bars start and end.

Figure 5.5.1 Tag and bar code

5 023084 175995

- The first numbers, one of which has no bars, show the country where the bar code was registered. In this case, 50 means it was registered in the UK.

- The next five numbers, in this case 23084, show the manufacturer's number, or if the retail outlet is selling its own products, it will be its number.

- The next five numbers, in this case 17599, identify the product. The number is unique to the manufacturer/retailer and will also identify the price, colour, size, pack size, etc. of the product.

- The last number, in this case 5, acts as a check to see that the whole bar code is correctly drawn.

As well as having the bars, most bar codes will have the number written on just in case the scanner is not working or the bars are damaged. Staff at the checkout can then type in the code and this will have the same effect as if the item was scanned.

> **www.adams1.com** is a site that provides a vast range of data on bar codes and has links to an even greater range of sites that show products, their uses and the latest news. It also shows that there is still a large number of different types of bar code in use around the world, not just the EAN with 13 numbers. Some of these use numbers, others use numbers and

Scanners read the bars by firing a laser beam at the bars and then matching the data to stored images. All the data on the bar code is read so the product is recognised and matched with details already in the computer system. The details in the computer will then show:

- what the product is;

- what the price is;

- if there is any offer so the price can be adjusted, or the second item not charged for;

- what quantities were bought, e.g. a pack of six cans of cola.

Scanners will also read customers' credit and debit cards and their loyalty and account cards. Sometimes the loyalty cards mean that customers are entitled to special treatment, e.g. discounts. The computer will note this and make the necessary adjustments to what customers are charged.

In most shops the scanners are built into the checkouts. Because laser technology and computers are used, scanning is a very fast way of checking the products, adding up what is owed and printing out receipts.

Some supermarkets now also have **hand-held scanners** which customers can pick up as they enter the store. The customers then scan each product they buy before it is put in the trolley. At the checkout they simply pass the hand-held scanner to the checkout staff. It is connected to the computer and gives the total owed. This process:

- saves time and cost for the business because the customer is doing one of the main jobs of the checkout staff;

- saves time for the customers because they do not have to wait at the checkout while all the goods are being scanned;

- is less effort for customers and staff because goods do not have to be taken out of the trolleys, scanned and then put back in the trolleys;

- gives customers a running total of what they are spending as they go round the supermarket;

- provides details of how the customers move around the store, which helps the business to plan where to display its goods.

It would be possible for people to put items into their trolleys without scanning them and thereby cheat the system, but random checks are made of some people's purchases. When this happens, all the items will be scanned again and anyone found with items that have not been scanned could be prosecuted for theft.

Electronic Point of Sale (EPOS)

> Definition – **electronic point of sale** means that electronic technology has been used where the goods are being sold in order to make this part of the selling process more efficient.

Electronic point of sale simply refers to introducing electronic technology where the goods are being sold and paid for. Scanning bar codes is part of this technology, but it also includes scanning loyalty cards, scanning credit and debit cards and sending messages to a customer's bank so that the retail outlet gets paid.

There is a huge range of possible EPOS systems for a retailer to choose from. The system that an individual retailer will select will be affected by the size of the business, how much the owners are willing to spend and what they want the EPOS system to do for the business. EPOS systems can provide all of the following facilities:

- creating bar code labels;

- scanning of bar codes;

- responding to keyboard instruction and pre-set keys for certain products;

- setting up prices, discounts, special offers, etc. that will register when the bar code is scanned;

- converting prices between different currencies, e.g. pounds and euros;

- identifying individual customers and treating them differently;

- creating a database on customers and what products they buy, when, how often, etc.;

- allowing payment by different methods, e.g. cash, cheque, credit and debit cards, and vouchers;

- updating stock records and checking what stock is available;

- recording all details from the checkouts, including who is operating it, what hours they work, how fast they work, and how much cash is taken.

Part of the EPOS system is to pass data back to the computers within the store, but also, via modem links:

- to computers at head office;

- to the business's own warehouses;

- to supplies so that more stock can be ordered;

- to banks to tell them that customers are spending money using credit cards and debit cards;

> Definition – **electronic data interchange** is using electronic connections between different sections of a business, or between one business and another, to transfer data to and from the centres.

All these electronic connections, which allow data to pass from one place to another, are part of what is called **electronic data interchange (EDI)**. EDI also covers internet shopping, where customers download catalogues of products and order electronically.

Using EPOS and EDI to manage stock and staff

When EPOS is used to manage stock, the checkout scanners are connected to a central computer. As the bar codes are scanned, the data is sent through to the central computer. As deliveries of new stock are received, details are also put on the computer database. Staff in the office can check all stock, order replacement stock automatically if required, change the prices, etc.

Hand-held scanners can be used by staff in the store to check details about stock on shelves, e.g. what the price should be if the price tag label has come off or if they want to check that stock is still available in the storeroom.

The systems will allow all the following stock control functions to take place:

- checking and recording what stock has been sold;

- identifying what stock needs to be reordered;

- showing the business which products sell best;

- identifying which products are slow sellers and may need to be reduced in price or withdrawn;

- printing out lists of stock that should be in the store so that they can be checked in the weekly or monthly stock-take;

- using hand-held scanners for the actual stock check;

- using the data from customers' hand-held scanners to see how they moved around the store and therefore where the best place is to put goods;

- preparing printed stock reports on what has sold, for how much, when.

As well as controlling stock the computer data can also be used to manage the checkout staff. The system will:

Figure 5.5.2 EPOS printout

```
          SAFEWAY
       lightening the load


       Customer Services Manager
            MIKE GODWIN

      Your checkout operator today was
                KATHY


   ABC NUMBER          6331250010239198862

                              £
     B/D SOUP CHKN+S/C
          REDUCED PRICE     0.64
     KEN DECAF/COFFEE       2.79
     HZ SOUP CHICKEN
          REDUCED PRICE     0.50
     S GRAPES SELECT        1.99
     S GRAPES SELECT        1.99
     * MULTISAVE *         -1.99
     S APPLES ROYAL GAL     1.69
     S SMALL BOUQUET
          REDUCED PRICE     0.99  a
     CARROTS                0.45
     S APPLES ROYAL GAL     1.69
     * MULTISAVE *         -1.69
     S LAMB WHOLE SHLDR     4.76
     CARROTS                0.45
     * MULTISAVE *         -0.45
     S CHKN THIGHS          2.26
     CUCUMBER WHOLE         0.49
     TUNA FLAKES/BRINE      0.38
     TUNA FLAKES/BRINE      0.38
     S DANISH BAR RASP
          REDUCED PRICE     1.67
     S SAVER WHT BREAD      0.17
     S SAV M/ROOM           1.59
   ABC 100 REWARD TENPIN

     ****              TOT     20.75
   15/09/99 17:49 7448 008 0834 149
            ANDOVER,SP10 1BG
        Telephone : 01264 363379
```

- record which member of staff is at which till and how long he or she has been working. This can be used to calculate their pay automatically and generate payslips, cheques, etc.;

- record how fast staff scan products and take payment for goods. If this is too slow it may lead to additional training, a cut in pay or even dismissal;

- record when tills are busiest and help to plan when to put on extra staff.

Electronic Funds Transfer (EFT) Systems

Definition – an **electronic funds transfer** system is any method through which payments are made or funds are transferred electronically.

Part of the purpose of the EPOS system is to allow customers to pay for their purchases using credit or debit cards. This is done by connecting the scanning facilities at retail outlets, via a computer and modem, to the banking system.

The connection is via the telephone system and is therefore electronic, which is why it gets its name of **electronic funds transfer system**. It is also know as EFTPOS (**electronic funds transfer at point of sale**). Because it involves the business sending details of payments to the banks and the bank confirming these, it is also part of EDI.

This system of electronic transfer of funds is not new. Automatic telling machines (cash points) have allowed customers to get cash outside banking hours for a long time. When the customer puts his/her card into the ATM it is scanned to check the personal identity number (PIN) and the account number and bank sort code. The customer confirms it is his/her card by keying in the PIN and then selects withdrawal of cash, payment in, bank balance, etc. All the data is then checked electronically in the bank system and, if approved, the customer's requests will be met.

Figure 5.5.3 Flow of ETFPOS

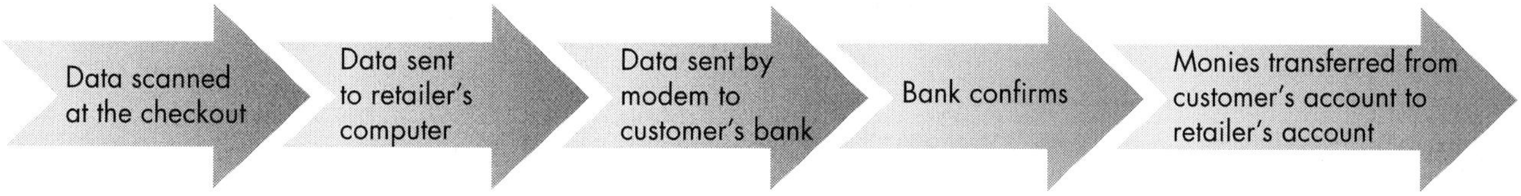

Data scanned at the checkout → Data sent to retailer's computer → Data sent by modem to customer's bank → Bank confirms → Monies transferred from customer's account to retailer's account

The EFT system in retail outlets is very similar and when customers' credit or debit cards are scanned a message is sent to the bank to ask for payment. The customers confirm that the cards are theirs, and that they want to pay, by signing the printed payment slips.

With the huge growth of sales of products via the internet, EFT systems are now common for this method of retailing as well. Customers can provide businesses with details of their credit or debit cards over the internet and businesses will use this to ask for payment, using EFT systems, from the customers' banks. Because the internet lacks security, however, there is always a risk that other people might get hold of your credit card or debit card number and use it for their own purchases.

Improving Customer Service

The introduction of the selling technologies described above has been of great help to businesses, but it has also been of benefit to customers. For customers, shopping and paying in retail stores has become quicker, easier and safer. Businesses use all these facilities to improve customer service and customers will benefit in the following ways:

- Stock control will be very much better so the goods that customers want should be available when and where they want them.

- The process of recording what is being bought is much more efficient so customers will be:
   i) served faster;

ii) find fewer mistakes in what they are being charged;

iii) have clear printed records of all transactions.

- As EFT is used customers will be able to pay using credit or debit cards instead of having to carry cash. This is easier and safer.

- Data can be provided for customers, e.g. on in-store till receipts, but general information and advice on products can also be downloaded from the internet.

Activity

Most retail outlets now have facilities that allow customers to buy products using credit cards and debit cards and most have the ability to scan bar codes at the till. The use that specific retail outlets will make of selling technology to control stock, staffing and record-keeping will, however, vary greatly from store to store.

Checking printed information

1 Collect copies of till receipts and records of the use of debit and credit cards.
2 Note down the basic information shown on these, e.g. time of purchase, quantity, location, loyalty points, member of staff.
3 Explain how each piece of information helps the business and the customer.

Checking on how individual businesses use selling technology

1 Arrange a visit to one outlet where you know retail technology is used. (**NB**: the bigger the outlet is, the more likely it is to use EPOS and EDI for managing stock and staff.)
2 By looking back at this chapter prepare a list of questions to ask. The questions should find out:
   a) What kinds of systems it uses.
   b) How it uses the systems for stock control.
   c) How it uses the systems to monitor and plan staffing.
   d) The benefits of the systems to the business.
   e) The benefits of the systems to the customers.

Revision

Questions

For questions 1 to 3 select one of the answers given.

1 When customers buy goods using debit cards the electronic funds transfer systems connect retail outlets with:

A their staff

B suppliers

C banks

D wholesalers. (1 mark)

2 Electronic data interchange (EDI) can be used only:

A if the retail outlet has a scanner

B if customers have debit or credit cards

C between retail outlets and their head office

D if the users are connected electronically. (1 mark)

3 EFTPOS stands for:

A electronic free transfer at point of sale

B electronic funds transfer at point of sale

C electronic funds transfer at place of sale

D electronics funds transport at place of sale. (1 mark)

4 List three reasons why hand-held scanners benefit: (6 marks)

a) the consumer

b) the business.

5 Five of the numbers of the 13-number EAN bar code are used to identify the product.

a) What do these numbers indicate?

i) the first two numbers

ii) the next five numbers

iii) the last number. (3 marks)

b) Manufacturers will encode their bar codes with details about their products, e.g. colour. Retailers will key in additional data for their EPOS systems, about details such as price.

i) Give two other details the manufacturers are likely to encode. (2 marks)

ii) Give two other details the retailers are likely to key in. (2 marks)

6 Explain why the use of bar codes and scanners is of benefit to:

a) the business; (4 marks)

b) the customers. (4 marks)

7 Explain how the electronic funds transfer system works and how this is of benefit to the business and to customers. (10 marks)

8 How do businesses use retail selling techniques to:

a) control stock; (5 marks)

b) control staffing? (5 marks)

CHAPTER 6

SELLING SKILLS IN RETAILING

KEY TERMS:

identifying customer needs	product knowledge
matching customers and products	opening the sale
closing the sale	explaining benefits
handling questions	offering alternatives
handling complaints	exchanging goods
capturing customer details	refunds

In this chapter you will learn about the selling skills that are required by staff in retail outlets and about how staff should handle complaints, refunds and exchange of goods. You will also learn how retail businesses collect customer details and how these help them improve services for customers.

Introduction

Before any business can sell its products successfully it must first of all establish what customers want. This is the purpose of market research and was covered in Unit 1, Chapter 2, page 28. In this chapter we will be looking at how staff serving in retail outlets should carry out their work so that goods and services are sold and customers are happy with what they have bought.

It must be remembered, however, that, before the sales staff can provide the right service for the customers, the business must have carried out good market research so that the store has:

- the right range of products available to attract customers;

- products offered at a price that customers will pay;

- an outlet located at a site where customers will want to come;

- an outlet open at times when customers will want to come;

- advertising and promotion so that customers know what is being offered.

Selling Skills for In-store Sales Staff

Some characteristics of sales staff are fairly general and will help to put customers at their ease and identify who the sales staff are. These include:

- being smartly dressed, often in uniform. This also tells customers who the sales staff are;

- being polite and helpful;

- being available to give information and advice;

- speaking clearly;

- concentrating on the selling process and noting such points as who is next to be served;

- following the procedures laid down by the particular retail outlet.

There will also be specific selling skills that staff should have in terms of selling the right products to customers.

Identifying customer needs

When customers enter a store, sales staff should generally try to find out what the customers want and try to provide it. How this is done will depend very much on what type of retail outlet is involved.

In supermarkets and self-service stores customers usually know what they want. Identifying customer needs has taken place through market research, goods are placed on shelves and signposted so that customers can find them easily. In these stores customers are usually left to find what they want by themselves. Sales staff will try to identify what customers want only if:

● customers ask for help;

● customers clearly need help;

● services are offered, such as delicatessen and fresh fish counters in a supermarket, or prescription and film processing counters in a chemist's shop.

In other stores, such as clothes shops or kitchen shops, customers may want to buy specific products and may need help finding or choosing them, but they may also wish just to browse. If it is clear that customers simply want to browse, they may be left to do this. A safer approach is for the sales staff to ask if they can be of assistance.

In yet other retail outlets, such as stores selling washing machines, hi-fi systems or cars, customers

"?"

usually require help in deciding what is the best product for them. Here, staff should approach customers and offer help. In many of these stores there will also be service counters where customers can go for information and advice.

Where services are being sold it is normal for sales staff to be seated at desks or behind counters and for the customers to approach them. Here it is expected that sales staff will discuss customers' needs and explain what alternative services could be provided.

When sales staff identify customer needs they should:

● listen carefully to what the customer says;

● ask questions so that they can find out what is best for the customer;

● match the product to the customer's needs.

Product knowledge

Customers expect sales staff to know what they are selling. Customers ask a great many detailed questions about products and if the sales staff cannot give them answers, the customers are likely to distrust the other details they are being given. That may well lead them to buy what they want elsewhere.

In supermarkets, staff who work on specialist counters, such as the delicatessen or the fresh fish counter, would be expected to have good knowledge of the products they are selling, and even ideas about how the foods should be prepared. Staff filling shelves are likely to know little more than where products are. Staff at the customer service desk will know more about the products if this has been part of their training.

In retail outlets where it is expected that staff have product knowledge, such as car showrooms, mobile phone stores, estate agents and banks, staff must make certain that they do know about the products. The exact information that customers want will depend on the type of product, but Figure 5.6.1 gives some examples for selling computers and houses.

Figure 5.6.1 Basic product knowledge

Basic product knowledge required for selling ...

... a computer

- Price
- Size of hard drive, RAM, Cache, etc.
- Speed of processor, modem, etc.
- Loaded software
- Compatibility with existing equipment
- What upgrades are possible
- Warranty/guarantee available
- Credit facilities
- Delivery terms

... a house

- Location
- Size and price
- Condition
- Facilities e.g. radiators, double glazing, etc.
- Reliable solicitors, surveyors, banks and building societies
- Legal procedure required to buy a house

Good product knowledge is important because:

- It makes the customers confident in the sales staff and they then trust any advice given.

- It allows the sales staff to advise customers on the best product for them.

- It allows sales staff to match the product to what the customers need and want. If customers are satisfied they will come back to the store again.

- If customers return products with faults it may be possible to correct them immediately or recognise that they are major faults and deal with them appropriately.

- When customers need after sales advice over the phone good product knowledge allows staff to give advice quickly and accurately.

Matching products to customers

If sales staff have identified what a customer wants and they know their products, they should be able to match the product to the customer's needs. This is not, however, just a case of giving the customer a product that will meet a basic need, but of taking into account all the customer's needs and circumstances. These needs and circumstances include:

- the type of product needed;

- the price range and the customer's income;

- the quality of the product;

- the age, size, height, etc. of the customer;

- how long the customer needs the product to last for;

- when the customer wants the product;

- catering for any special requirements, e.g. left-handedness and language difficulties;

- their needs in terms of credit, delivery and after sales service.

Selling the product

A product can be sold by using persuasive advertising and promotions and presenting products well. Customers can then be left to walk around the retail outlet, with no other pressure, choosing what they want. Alternatively, sales staff can put a lot of pressure on customers. With forceful salesmanship they can even get customers to buy products they do not need and probably do not want.

Good salesmanship will come somewhere in between these two extremes and should follow the kind of pattern shown below. This would be typical for stores and showrooms, where customers need to have products explained to them.

Opening the sale: ↓	When customers enter the shop sales staff should approach them and ask if they need help, but staff should not be pushy. This stage is known as the **opening of the sale.**
Identifying needs: ↓	Customers should be asked what they are looking for in terms of the type of product, its quality, price, what it is wanted for, etc. Good sales staff will also identify other characteristics of customers such as how knowledgeable they are, what value for money they expect, etc.
Explaining benefits: ↓	Having identified what customers want the sales staff should outline the benefits of the products that they feel most closely meet the customers' needs. The benefits need to be clearly explained because many customers have only limited knowledge about products, especially those using complicated technology.
Handling questions: ↓	When customers go to stores to buy products that they are not certain about they are likely to have a great many questions to ask. Staff need to know their products well, listen carefully to the questions and answer them appropriately. They should not talk down to customers and they should not tell them lies.
Offering alternatives: ↓	If customers are not happy with the products suggested, then sales staff should offer them alternatives, but again they should not be pushy. This might also be the right point at which to suggest alternatives that would be better, even if the customers have already indicated price and quality limits. If the products really are better, then the customers should know, the main reason being that they cannot complain later that they were not told.
Matching products to needs: ↓	This is the most important part of the selling process. By now the sales staff should know what is needed, what limitations the customer has in terms of income, size of family, etc. and what they really want. Success in matching the product to customer needs will bring the customer back next time they want a product that the store sells.
Closing the sale:	All sales are contracts, with the buyer offering to buy and the seller accepting the offer. The buyer will then pay for the products and the seller will give ownership of the product to the customers. The point at which this contract is agreed and the products paid for is called **closing the sale.**

These stages of selling will depend very much on what is being sold, how it is being sold and who the customers are. For example, in supermarkets:

- There is no real 'opening the sale' stage, except through advertising.

- 'Identifying customer needs' and 'matching the product to the customer' is done through market research.

- 'Explaining the benefits' is done through advertising.

- 'Offering alternatives' is achieved by displaying similar products next to each other.

- 'Closing the sale' happens when customers take their goods to the checkout to have them scanned and to pay for them.

Case Study – Selling products in the Games Workshop

The Games Workshop is set up and run quite differently from many other stores. (See also the case study on page 288.)

The approach of the staff to selling is to interact with the customers. Staff are aware of everyone entering the shop and will quickly approach them to offer help and inquire what they want. They will also ask customers what level of knowledge they have of the games and products. The support they provide to customers and the sales approach they take is then geared to the customers' needs and understanding.

Enthusiasm is the sales staff's key selling skill, but it comes from a sound knowledge of all the products on sale and full involvement in all aspects of the game itself. Sales staff will be players, readers of magazines and painters of models.

This approach to selling is not unique, but in most retail shops you will not be served by staff with this degree of enthusiasm and understanding of what they are selling.

Games Workshop management staff are currently being advertised for with the following person specifications:

STORE MANAGERS
THE IDEAL CANDIDATE:
- In a supervisory or management position already
- Able to lead and command staff
- Possesses drive and determination
- Has retail sales skills
- Can deliver quality customer service
- A good level of knowledge of the Games Workshop Hobby

TRAINEE MANAGERS
THE IDEAL CANDIDATE:
- Is energetic, enthusiastic, and ambitious
- Has a good level of knowledge of the Games Workshop Hobby
- Is possibly a graduate or looking for the first step on to the management level
- Has retail sales skills
- Can deliver quality customer service

Dealing with Customers' Complaints

Sometimes customers' complaints are genuine and sometimes customers complain just to be awkward or because they think they can gain some benefit from complaining. The sales staff must be able to distinguish between a genuine and a bogus complaint.

Genuine complaints are made for many reasons and would include situations where the product:

- was faulty;

- was damaged during manufacture, storage, retailing or transport;

- did not arrive on time;

- did not do what it was supposed to do;

- did not match the description given by the sales staff or on the package;

- went wrong fairly soon after it was bought;

- needed additions that the customer was not told about by the sales staff;

- was sold at the wrong price;

- caused injury to anyone.

Bogus complaints are also made for many reasons and would include situations where the customers:

- had changed their minds and did not now want the product;

- had broken or damaged the product and were pretending that it was already faulty when they bought it;

- had used the product for what they wanted and now no longer wanted it;

- wanted additional benefits, e.g. to get their money back and keep the product as well;

- just liked to make a fuss even though the product was perfectly all right.

Many complaints arise because the law has been broken. There is a large number of laws that try to protect the consumer. Some businesses do break the law occasionally, even though most of them try not to. Major consumers' laws include:

- **The Weights and Measures Act 1951** which makes it illegal to use faulty weighing equipment or to give short weights or short measures.

- **The Sale of Goods Act 1979** which states that products must be of merchantable quality (i.e. no serious defects), fit for the purpose they are intended for and as they have been described.

- **The Trade Descriptions Act 1968** which makes it illegal for businesses to give misleading descriptions of their products.

- **The Consumer Safety Act 1978** which makes it illegal to sell goods which may be harmful to customers.

- **The Food and Drugs Act 1955** and **The Food Act 1987** which insist that food is hygienically prepared and correctly labelled.

- **The Consumer Protection Act 1987** which makes it illegal, amongst other things, for a business to claim that its prices have been reduced when they have not. It also makes suppliers responsible for any injury that results from defective goods.

If the law has been broken, customers can take the business which is responsible to court. This may cost the business money and give it a bad reputation. Most businesses therefore try very hard to make certain that the products they provide will not break the law.

Many businesses also wish to make certain that customers are happy with the products they have bought even if the law has not been broken. It is common practice in reputable firms that if customers are not satisfied with a product, or find a fault with it, the business will take it back and either replace it or refund the money paid.

Case Study – Supermarkets' statements on product quality

SAINSBURY'S CARELINE: If you have any comments relating to our products or are not completely satisfied with your purchase please call this freephone number 0800 636262. Your statutory rights are not affected.

TESCO QUALITY: We are happy to refund or replace any Tesco product which falls below the high standard you expect. Just ask any member of staff. This does not affect your statutory rights.

SAFEWAY REFUND AND REPLACE: Safeway brand products are double guaranteed. If you are not totally satisfied with any item, please return it to a Safeway store for a refund *and* a replacement. This does not affect your statutory rights.

SOMERFIELD: Every Somerfield product has a quality guarantee. However if you are not entirely satisfied please return it to the store where it was purchased and your money will be refunded. This does not affect your statutory rights.

If this is the policy of the firm then most customers who complain about the condition or quality of the product will be given a refund and/or a replacement. It is, however, still important that the sales staff handle the complaint in the right way. Even if the customer has a genuine complaint about a product, the right approach by the sales staff will help to make certain that the customer buys products from the store in the future.

Many stores have special service desks for dealing with complaints, and also specially trained staff. When customers approach with a complaint it is important to:

- listen to them carefully;

- reassure them that their complaint is being taken seriously;

- decide on an appropriate action:
  - i) offer a refund and/or replacement;
  - ii) provide a credit note where refunds are not company policy;
  - iii) offer to have the product repaired, if this is appropriate;
  - iv) explain, carefully, why no action can be taken, if that is appropriate;

- apologise if the businesses is responsible;

"I want my money back now!"

- record the details of the complaint;

- record the action taken.

Capturing Customer Details

A great deal of information about how customers behave and what they think about the products is created through data gained from the selling process and from customers' complaints. If businesses want to understand their customers and produce better products for them they need to record all this data and act on it.

There are many ways in which businesses can capture this data.

Market research

This can be done by asking customers to answer, or fill in, a questionnaire or comment sheet. In many retail stores questionnaires or comment sheets are left on counters for customers to pick up and fill in if they wish to. Some stores have comment books or suggestion boxes for customers. The benefits of most of these are that:

- customers need to fill them out only if they want to;

- most sheets are very short and quick and easy to fill in;

- the questions are all the same so it is easy to build up an overall view of what people think;

- many comments sheets simply ask for general comments and customers can say exactly what they want and make complaints or suggestions, or give praise;

- if they know their comments will be kept confidential or if the businesses cannot know who has filled them out, customers may be prepared to say what they really think.

There are, however, also drawbacks because:

- many customers ignore them;

- people may only fill them out if they wish to complain;

- they tend to be short and so only a limited amount of information can be collected;

- most are confidential and it is impossible to match the comments to the type of buyer.

Some of these, as with the W. H. Smith customer comments card shown below, do ask for customer details. This allows businesses to tie the comments to specific types of buyer, but it also provides them with the names and addresses of people who they know have visited the store. This may be useful if the business wishes to carry out a mail shot about new products, or about changes that have taken place because of the customers' comments.

Figure 5.6.2 Customer comments card

Customer Comments

We would like to hear your comments so that we can continually improve our services for you.
You can call us on **01793 695195** (Monday to Friday 9am – 7pm, Saturday 9am – 5.30pm) or write to us completing the details below. E mail: customer.relations@whsmith.co.uk

Name: .... Date: ....

Address:... Telephone: ....

.... WHSmith Store: ....

Your comments:...

....

....

....

....

....

....

EAN 00403030

Thank you for taking the time to complete this card.

WHSmith

www.whsmith.co.uk

Using data from loyalty cards and store cards

When customers apply for loyalty cards or store cards, they have to fill out brief details about themselves. These details will include where they live and may ask about house ownership and income. These details allow the business to build up a profile of customers.

When customers use the cards, all the data is recorded against that person's profile. The business can then see all of the following buying patterns:

- What kind of products different people buy.

- How often they buy particular types of products.

- When they buy their products.

- How much they spend on each visit.

- How they react to advertising and special promotions on particular products.

- How they pay for their products.

Most regular shoppers have loyalty cards because there is no restriction as to who is allowed to have them. The stores can therefore build up a very good overall database on customers' shopping habits.

Using the EPOS system

The EPOS system (see page 317) will also capture data about sales, but for everyone, not just those with cards. It will record what has sold, when it was sold, the average amount spent by customers, etc. Where customers use hand-held scanners it can also record how customers move about the store.

Footfall counts and observation

It is often important to find out how many people come into a store and then leave without buying anything. This suggests that something is wrong with the products, with the way they are displayed and promoted, or with the customer service provided by the staff.

The number of people entering a store could be counted by a member of staff, but this would be time consuming. Some stores have pressure pads at the entrance and these record the number of people entering and leaving. The record can be compared to the number of sales made to find out, roughly, how many people come in but do not buy. On internet sites it is very easy to create counters that tell the firm how many times the site has been accessed.

Observation is also used to find out customers' reactions to goods, displays, etc. It is often quite easy to see from a person's body language and from the length of time they spend looking at a product, what they really think about it.

Customer complaints

Details of all customer complaints should be recorded. This should be done so that there is a record of what action was taken in case the customer wishes to take the complaint further.

Recording the data also allows staff and management to use it for capturing customer details. The nature of the complaint and the product involved will be recorded but quite often the name and address of the person complaining will also be recorded.

Why capture customer details?

The main reason for collecting this data is to enable businesses to work out what customers do, and why. The businesses will then be able to change their products and customer service to improve sales in the future.

What a business learns from capturing customer details will depend on exactly what data was collected.

- Data on when customers shop will help to decide staff rotas.

- Data on which promotions appeal most to customers will help businesses to decide about future promotions.

- Data on poor customer service may lead to extra staff training.

- Data on how many people enter and leave the store without buying may lead to a change in the range of products, the displays, the customer service, etc.

Activity

The ways in which individual retail firms choose to sell their products and handle complaints vary considerably. To gain a good overall picture of the range of approaches that retailers use, you should visit different types of store and record how they sell their products and handle complaints.

Observing selling skills

1 Prepare a record sheet that will allow you to record quickly all the points below.
2 Note down the type of retail outlet you are visiting (e.g. supermarket, clothes store, café, travel agent).
3 Think about how you were served and, when you have left the store, note down how the sales staff:
   a) opened the sale;
   b) identified what you wanted;
   c) asked and answered questions;
   d) demonstrated their knowledge of the products;
   e) explained the benefits of the products and introduced alternatives;
   f) closed the sale.

How complaints are dealt with

1 When you visit any retail outlet, collect any literature that refers to after sales services and to policies on returned goods/replacements/refunds.
2 Arrange to talk to the staff in charge of customer services and ask them how they handle complaints.
3 If you or your friends and family have to return goods or complain, note down how the staff in the store deal with this.

Capturing customer details

1 Pick up leaflets on loyalty cards and store cards and note down what information has to be given to the store in order to get the card.
2 Check the printouts of receipts and credit and debit payments etc. to see what information is being recorded, e.g. products, amount spent, time, loyalty card number and so on.
3 Check in-store to see if they carry out footfall counts, e.g. if they have pressure pads as you enter the store.
4 Ask customer services or the manager how they capture customer details.

Revision

Questions

1 When sales staff sell a product they go through certain stages from opening the sale to closing the sale. For two of the situations given below (i) list how sales staff will carry out each of the stages; (ii) explain, for each stage, why they will act in this way.
   a) Children go to their local convenience store to buy ice creams from the refrigerated cabinet.
   b) A customer is interested in buying the best car for her 18-year-old daughter.
   c) A computer fanatic visits a specialist computer shop to buy accessories for his computer.
   d) A customer goes to a travel agent to book a holiday in Ibiza.
   e) A customer goes to a restaurant to celebrate an anniversary.   (20 marks)

2 Explain why each of the following is important for sales staff:
   a) smart appearance;
   b) friendly approach;
   c) good product knowledge.   (10 marks)

3 How do sales staff normally identify customer needs in each of the following retail outlets?
   a) a supermarket;
   b) a bank;
   c) a shoe shop;
   d) a shop selling beds;
   e) a newsagent.   (10 marks)

4 Select one product the sales staff should have good knowledge of so that they can advise customers. List five main features of this product which they should know about.   (5 marks)

5 List the kinds of complaints that customers may make in the following situations:
   a) a customer who has bought bread from a baker's;
   b) a customer who has bought a pair of shorts from a clothes shop;
   c) a customer who has bought a holiday from a travel agent.   (10 marks)

6 a) Outline how good sales staff will deal with a customer who has been served a hot cup of coffee, has drunk half of it, and then complains that it is not hot enough.
   b) Explain why the sales staff should act in this way.
   c) Explain any possible drawbacks to your suggestions about how sales staff should deal with the complaint.   (10 marks)

7 Select one store you have studied in detail and outline how that store captures customer details. Explain why this is a good method of collecting the data.   (10 marks)

HEALTH, SAFETY AND SECURITY ISSUES

Intermediate

In this chapter you will learn about the health and safety issues involved in running a retail outlet and how businesses ensure that their outlets are safe for their customers and their employees. You will also learn how businesses create a secure environment so that their goods, money and premises are safe from loss, theft and deliberate damage.

Introduction

Health and safety

If a retail store is unsafe and there is a danger that people will be injured when they go to the store, they will avoid going there. Any retail business that does not provide a safe and healthy environment is likely to:

- lose customers as they decide to shop elsewhere;

- find recruiting employees difficult because they will not wish to work where it is unsafe;

- be breaking the law and may be fined, sued or be forced to close down;

- find that insurance companies are not prepared to insure them.

Figure 5.7.1 Injuries to retail staff

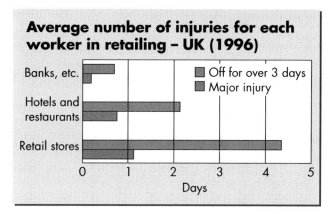

Average number of injuries for each worker in retailing – UK (1996)

Most people who use retail stores do, however, assume that the stores are safe. Some retailers take advantage of this and do not put in the necessary safety features. This is why there are laws to control the health and safety standards that must be met in retail outlets. Figure 5.7.1 shows that even in banks and building societies there are injuries. On average, each worker in general retail stores will suffer one major injury each year and will take at least three days off for injuries up to four times a year.

Security

Although theft is illegal there are no general laws which insist that retail outlets protect themselves against theft. Protecting the business is common sense and helps to ensure that the business will make as much profit as possible. Retail outlets can protect themselves against theft by ensuring that:

- goods cannot be removed from the store without the customers paying for them;

- goods or services cannot be stolen by the staff;

- money cannot be stolen, by customers or staff;

- goods or services cannot be paid for by cheque, credit card, etc. and taken away when there is no money in the bank account to pay for the goods or services;

- the premises cannot be broken into and goods or money stolen;

- the ideas of the store, e.g. the name it uses, how it advertises and presents its goods or services, cannot be copied.

The need for stores to protect themselves is shown in Figure 5.7.2. Over 26,000 cases of shoplifting were recorded by the police in 1997 and nearly 8,000 of these cases led to a prosecution in the courts. However, there were probably just as many that were never spotted.

Figure 5.7.2 Shoplifting statistics for 1997

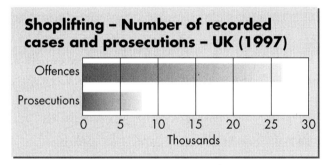

The way in which a store will protect itself will depend on what it sells, how big it is, the layout of the store, how the staff are trained and many other factors. The only way to find out how individual stores ensure their security is to visit them.

Health and Safety Hazards in Retail Outlets

Stores must provide a safe and healthy environment for their staff and for their customers. What is acceptable as safe and healthy is laid down by the law. The major UK law that deals with this is the

Health and Safety at Work Act 1974. Other, more recent Acts have added to these rules (particularly the health and safety legislation of 1992). When the Health and Safety at Work Act (HASAWA) was introduced, it recognised that both employers and employees had a duty to make certain that the working area was safe.

The main requirements of the law, as it relates to retail outlets, are:

The duties that the employers must meet

- to provide a safe and healthy environment for their staff to work in;

- to make certain that all equipment is safe to use and that staff are able to use all equipment in a way that will not endanger themselves or other staff;

- to provide information, instruction, training and supervision so that employees can work safely and without endangering the health of other staff or customers;

- to ensure that staff and customers are able to get out of the store without risk to themselves if they need to, e.g. if there is a fire or a bomb scare;

- to have a published health and safety policy which staff and customers can see if they need to.

The duties that the employees must meet

- to take reasonable care for the health and safety of themselves, other staff and customers;

- to follow the health and safety procedures laid down by the business;

- not to interfere with or misuse anything that has been provided to safeguard health or safety;

- to use equipment safely and to wear the required safety clothing;

- to undergo the required health and safety training.

The Role of the Health and Safety Executive

It is the role of the Health and Safety Executive (HSE) to ensure that risks to people's health and safety from work activities are properly controlled. This includes ensuring that the duties listed under the Health and Safety at Work Act are carried out so that employees and customers are protected.

Duties of the HSE include:
- inspecting workplaces;
- investigating accidents and cases of ill health;
- enforcing good standards, usually by advising people how to comply with the law, but sometimes by ordering them to make improvements and, if necessary, by prosecuting them;
- publishing guidance and advice;
- providing an information service;
- carrying out research.

The HSE also provides a very full and helpful web site at **www.open.gov.uk/hse/hsehome.htm**

If either the employer or the employee fails to follow the regulations laid down in the Act the inspectors have the right to:

- stop the business trading;

- insist that the business changes its procedure so that it will now be healthy and safe;

- take the business, or individual employees, to court if they have broken the law;

- take away any dangerous substances, machinery, etc. and either destroy it or make certain that it will be harmless in the future.

Health and safety issues and how they are identified, avoided and resolved

Most retail outlets have a wide range of facilities that could cause harm to someone. In an office, or even in a factory, it is usually only the staff who need to be protected against possible injury and they can be trained to avoid these dangers. In the case of a retail shop many customers also visit the premises. Most customers will not know what the dangers are and it is therefore vital that the staff and management in the store ensure that the risks of injury are kept to an absolute minimum.

The ways in which businesses can ensure that the risks of injury to staff or customers are kept to a minimum include:

- a clear understanding of what the dangers are;

- definite plans to identify dangers and to ensure that they are kept to a minimum;

- the appointment of a member, or members, of staff with the specific duty of ensuring high standards of health and safety in the business;

- regular checks to ensure that health and safety measures are being carried out;

- training of staff so that they know the dangers and how to minimise them;

- clearly written health and safety procedures which are given to all staff.

Even when all the points listed above are followed there are still dangers. The best way to find out what the possible dangers are is to visit different stores and look around to see which features could be dangerous. You should then write them down.

Below we will deal with a range of possible health and safety issues. This should help you to identify potentially dangerous features when you visit retail stores. Examples are given for each type of danger and also ways in which the store can avoid these dangers.

Dangers from fixtures and fittings

Store must have fixtures and fittings to display goods on, to provide desks for staff, and to provide facilities for customers such as mirrors, seats, heating and lighting. All these can cause health and safety problems.

Examples of dangers	How to avoid them
1 Sharp corners on furniture	1 Have rounded corners, padding or no furniture
2 Doors that could trap fingers	2 Either ensure doors are always open or that they have gaps when they are closed
3 Carpets that are frayed and may cause customers to trip up	3 Replace carpets regularly or make certain that they are properly tacked down and loose strands removed
4 Glass cabinets, counters, etc. that could get broken	4 Ensure that they are made of toughened glass
5 Glass doors that customers could walk into	5 Place notices, adverts etc. on the doors, or leave them open
6 Display racks that could fall over	6 Use solid racks and secure them properly to the floor, wall, etc.

Dangers from machinery and equipment

Dangers from machinery and equipment are most likely to affect staff working in the retail outlet, but some machinery or equipment could also be a danger to customers, e.g. equipment used by a dentist, an escalator in a department store, strobe lighting if customers suffer from epilepsy.

Examples of dangers	How to avoid them
1 Cutting equipment such as a meat slicer	1 Training in the use of the equipment and guards round the blades
2 Danger from vehicles used in large storerooms	2 Equip vehicles with flashing lights, horns, etc. and train staff to be careful. Do not allow customers into these areas
3 Electric shocks from faulty electrical equipment	3 Regular checks on electrical equipment for frayed wires, loose connections, etc. Ensure that no liquids are put near the equipment
4 Fumes from heating systems	4 Regular checks and servicing of the systems

Dangers from goods

The goods themselves can also create a danger. Some goods, such as fireworks and chemicals, are obviously dangerous and need to be stored securely. Other goods, which might be expected to be safe, can cause injury in certain circumstances.

Examples of dangers	How to avoid them
1 Danger from fireworks and chemicals	1 Store them where they can only be passed to customers as they buy them. Do not sell to children
2 Slippery floors caused by spilt liquids	2 Clean them up immediately and put out warning signs

3 Stacks of goods falling on customers	3 Make certain stacks are not too high and that they are stacked securely. Place displays away from customers	2 Food can go bad	2 Make sure that food is stored properly, at the right temperature, in protected areas, and is disposed of if it reaches its sell-by date
4 Goods with sharp edges	4 Ensure that they are properly stored and in protective packaging	3 Insects can spread germs	3 Cover the food and use appropriate methods to prevent insects getting near the food
5 Goods that can give off poisonous fumes if they catch fire	5 Store away from sources of fire and have ways of containing the fumes if a fire does start	4 Customers can contaminate food by handling it and putting it back	4 Get staff to serve customers or store foods in suitable packaging

Dangers from fire and explosives

(See emergency procedures on page 339.)

Dangers from unhygienic storage or preparation of food

Wherever food is stored, prepared or exposed to the open air, it can become contaminated and will then be a danger to customers. There are very strict rules about how food is prepared in retail outlets. The stores must also make certain that the food which they buy in is properly stored so that it does not get contaminated or go bad. The legal requirements about how foods must be prepared and stored are covered by the **Food Safety Act 1990**.

Examples of dangers	How to avoid them
1 Dirt and germs can get into the food	1 Make sure all surfaces are clean and that staff have clean hands or clothing that protects the food

The Food Safety Act 1990

This Act protects consumers against the production, storage or sale of food that could cause harm to the consumer. It covers a wide range of offences, including how food products are labelled and advertised. Measures include:

'*A person who sells, prepares for sale or packs any food that is unfit for human consumption or adulterated is guilty of an offence.*'

'*A person who sells, prepares for sale or packs any food that is damaged, deteriorated or perished is guilty of an offence.*'

'*A person who sells, prepares for sale or packs any food for which there is a prescribed food standard is guilty of an offence if the food does not comply with the prescribed food standard.*'

'*A person who packs or labels any food in a manner that is false or misleading in any particular, deceptive, otherwise contrary to, or not in compliance with the provisions of this Act is guilty of an offence.*'

Dangers from giving the wrong information about products

When customers buy products they expect them to be what they say they are and to do what they say they will do. If the products are something different or do not do what is claimed, they can be dangerous. Retail stores need to ensure that the goods or services that they sell are what they claim them to be. If the stores do not do this they can be sued under the **Sale of Goods Act** or the **Trade Descriptions Act**. More importantly, the goods or services may cause harm to their customers and, in some cases, even kill them.

Examples of dangers	How to avoid them
1 Customers choose products that are unsuitable	1 Staff should check that customers have what they **need**
2 Customers use products incorrectly and endanger themselves	2 Staff should check that customers know how to use products safely and provide clear instructions
3 Customers are given the wrong information	3 Staff should be trained and should ensure that they have good knowledge of all the products that they sell

Laws that apply to health and safety in the workplace

The main law that controls health and safety at work is the Health and Safety at Work Act (HASAWA) dealt with above. There are, however, many other laws and regulations that affect the way in which retail outlets must be run so that staff and customers will be protected. These include:

- Health and Safety (First Aid) Regulations 1981

- Food Safety Act 1990

- Management of Health and Safety at Work Regulations 1992

Figure 5.7.3 Fatal injuries sustained by employees and customers

Owners of retail outlets have a legal duty to provide a safe working and shopping environment for their employees and their customers. Despite this, accidents do occur. The number of fatal injuries between 1991 and 1997 is shown below. As well as these there were 7,483 major injuries for employees and 6,841 major injuries for customers.

How the injury was caused	Fatal injuries for employees	Fatal injuries for customers
Fell from a height	5	5
Struck by a vehicle	4	3
Hit aginst a fixed object	1	0
Hit by a flying object	1	0
Slipped or tripped	0	4
Other	0	3
Total	**11**	**15**
Where the injury occurred		
Food retail outlet	43%	44%
Specialist non-food outlet	21%	15%

- Workplace (Health, Safety & Welfare) Regulations 1992

- Provision and Use of Work Equipment Regulations (PUWER) 1992

- Health and Safety (Display Screen Equipment) Regulations 1992

- Manual Handling Operations Regulations 1992

- Personal Protective Equipment Regulations 1992

- COSHH (Control of Substances Hazardous to Health) Regulations 1994

- Health and Safety (Consultation with Employees) Regulations 1996

Many health and safety controls are now decided by the European Union (EU). These are issued as directives by the EU and the UK government then has to change our laws so that we are following EU law. This is why there are so many 'regulations'. It also means that new regulations are coming out all the time, and retailers must obey them.

Emergency Procedures

The only people who are normally in a factory or a school are people who work there. The workers, staff, students and managers know what to do in an emergency. In retail outlets, there are often many more customers than staff and the customers will not know what to do. It is therefore very important that the staff do know what to do and that there are clear emergency procedures.

Retail stores need to be prepared for all the following emergency procedures.

Evacuation of the premises

There must be a clear procedure for getting staff and customers out of the building, calmly and safely. Staff should be trained in what to do and where to go and details should be placed on a notice, displayed where it can be easily checked. These procedures will probably include:

- the sounding of an alarm;
- staff asking customers to leave;
- conducting customers to the nearest safe exit;
- checking the building to see that everyone is out;
- if there is a fire, calling the fire brigade, and tackling the fire with extinguishers etc. if it is safe for staff to do this;
- if it is a bomb alert, gas leak, etc. staff should not attempt to deal with it themselves and should inform the emergency services of their suspicions.

Preparing for emergencies

It is no good waiting until emergencies occur and then hoping that staff will be able to deal with them. Action needs to be carried out in advance.

- Staff should be trained in what to do in an emergency.

- There should be regular fire and evacuation drills.
- Exits and emergency exits should be clearly signposted.
- Direct links can be established with the fire brigade so that it is called as soon as the alarm goes off.
- Fire-fighting equipment should be in place and easy to access and use.
- All equipment, alarms, fire doors, emergency exits, etc. should be checked regularly and replaced if there are any faults.
- Details of emergency procedures must be displayed.

First aid

Most retail outlets have tens, hundreds and even thousands of people on the premises during a normal day. Some of these people will get injured and some will have medical problems. Stores need to be prepared for this and should have first aid procedures in place so that they can deal with any basic medical emergency.

- There should be staff who are trained in first aid.
- First aid kits should be easily available.
- There should be clear procedures for contacting the ambulance services when they are required.

Security in Retail Outlets

Security in retail outlets can be considered under three headings: goods, money and premises.

Making certain that goods are secure

When people think about goods being secure they usually think about the possibility of them being stolen. Figure 5.7.2 gave some idea of how often this occurs. Goods also need to be protected against vandalism and people deliberately damaging them or tampering with them in some way.

The goods in the store can be protected using all of the following methods:

- **Security cameras** so that customers can be observed from the counter or an office. This system can usually record customer movements on video. It is also known as **closed circuit TV (CCTV)**;

- **mirrors**, placed so that staff can see the store from the counters;

- **in-store detectives/security guards**;

- keeping goods in **locked cabinets**. This is very common for valuable items such as jewellery;

- placing counters and checkouts near the exits so that it is difficult for customers to leave without paying;

- placing **security tags** on goods which sound an alarm if they are taken out of the store. This is very common in clothes stores;

- **counter service** – giving customers products only when they ask for them, and pay for them, over the counter. This is the way which catalogue stores usually operate, but it is also common in bakers, butchers, fast-food restaurants and smaller stores where there is no self-service.

- regular **stock checks** will identify if goods are missing. They will also help to check if customers or staff are responsible. Staff can get round many of the other security checks by, for example, removing the security tags.

Where there is a danger that goods have been purposely tampered with, vigilance by staff, use of security cameras and regular checks on the goods themselves are the best ways to ensure that this does not happen again.

Making certain that money is secure

Money can be stolen from stores in two main ways. Customers or staff can steal money from tills or safes. Money can be lost if customers pay with, say, cheques when they have no money in the bank or when the cheque book or credit cards used have been stolen.

Protecting the cash should be done by:

- checking notes to see that they are not forgeries;

- putting all cash straight into a till, and making certain that the till is then kept shut;

- having staff at the till all the time or keeping it locked when there are no staff at the till;

- taking money from the till when a large number of payments have been made, and storing it somewhere more secure, e.g. a safe;

- depositing money daily in a bank;

- checking the money in the till against the till receipts to make certain that staff have not taken any money;

- ensuring that only authorised staff have access to money;

- using a panic button where there is a danger of armed robbery. Staff sometimes have a panic button which sends an alarm signal to another part of the store or to the police station. In banks and bureaux de change, where there is a great deal of money, the tills are behind toughened security glass.

Protecting against purchases by people who cannot pay or who have stolen credit cards should be done by:

- checking all cards and chequebooks against the lists of stolen cards that are sent to stores;

- accepting cheques only if they are supported by a bank card. This guarantees payment by the bank, up to a stated amount, even if the customer has no money;

- checking the signatures on the payment slips against the signature on the card;

- contacting the bank/building society if there is any doubt about the ability of the customer to pay. This is done automatically with debit cards.

Making certain that the premises are secure

During opening hours, staff are in the store and all the security measures mentioned above should be in operation. When the store is closed and the normal staff have left, special measures are needed to make the store secure. These measures include:

- **intruder alarms** which are set off by anyone entering the building. There are a great many different types of alarm, ranging from pressure pads on the floor to laser beams and electronic circuit breakers. When alarms go off at night they are usually connected to police stations as well as sounding outside the stores themselves;

- **access control systems** which are usually connected to the alarm system. These allow only authorised people to enter the premises and are usually turned on and off by a key, a punched-in code or a swipe card. They usually operate on a time switch as well;

- **security cameras** which record any break-ins and can identify the people involved. This may make thieves think twice about breaking into the store;

- **lighting** in the store means that anyone breaking in may be seen from outside;

- employing a **night watchman**. Often one watchman will patrol a number of shops to check that there have been no break-ins;

- using **anti-bandit glass**, which is strengthened to prevent the store windows being broken. In some stores, where 'ram raiders' have used vehicles to break through shop windows, owners have been forced to use steel bars and shutters to protect their premises;

- **smoke alarms** and **sprinkler systems** which are activated by the presence of smoke.

Activity

It is important that you visit retail outlets to see how they deal with health, safety and security issues, but this must be done in the right way. Many firms may object to you walking around their stores noting down what security systems they have or listing the possible causes of injury. It would be better to contact the store first and explain to the manager what you are studying. Alternatively, your teacher or lecturer may arrange this.

It is also possible simply to observe what the situation is in a store and then write down the details after you have left. If you have a part-time job in a retail outlet, you should know what the health, safety and security procedures are for your place of work. Note these down. Also ask your friends and other students on the course about their jobs. You will then have a wide range of examples.

Checking the law on health and safety

1 Look up the web sites referred to in this chapter. These will give you a good idea of just how wide these laws are. They will also give details of the kind of retail facilities and practices that are covered by the laws.

Safety issues in retail outlets

1 From the list of dangers given in this chapter, make a record sheet so that you can easily record any safety issues found in the store.

2 When you visit retail outlets note down the features in the store – doors, equipment, escalators, displays, etc. – that could cause injury or damage.

3 Next to each possible cause write down what the store has done to minimise the risk, or what it could do to minimise the risk.

Health issues in retail stores

1 Make a record sheet of possible health issues, such as food preparation, serving food, storage of food, dangerous chemicals, noxious fumes, so that you can easily record any health issues found in the store.

2 When you visit retail outlets note down any health features you see.

3 Next to each possible cause write down what the store has done to minimise the risk, or what it could do to minimise the risk.

4 If you have a chance to talk to staff or management, ask them what training staff are required to go through in order to ensure healthy practices.

Emergency procedures

1 When visiting retail stores note the obvious emergency features such as extinguishers, fire alarm points, emergency exits.

2 If you can, ask staff or management what training staff are given in emergency procedures and first aid.

3 If you are allowed to, check what is written on the emergency procedures notice or in any handbooks.

Security

Where security systems are involved, many businesses will not provide any details at all. You therefore need to be very tactful about how you carry out any survey work of real shops.

1 Observe what alarms are on the building, what type of shutters they use at night and what warnings they put on their doors or in the store about their security systems. These are put there for the customers, and potential thieves, to see, so the store should have no concerns about you making a note of them.

2 Note down which shops use different types of security to stop:
   a) the theft of goods, e.g. security tags, mirrors, and closed circuit TV;
   b) the theft of money, e.g. checking your identity or checking the banknotes;
   c) break-ins or damage to the premises, e.g. cameras, alarms, and smoke detectors.

3 Check the web sites of firms that provide security equipment and services. These will give you a good idea of the range of facilities that retail stores could use.

Revision

Questions

1 From your study of actual retail outlets list:
    a) four ways in which one retail outlet protects its goods from theft;
    b) three ways in which one retail outlet protects itself from losing money;
    c) three ways in which one retail outlet protects its premises from break-ins.   (10 marks)

2 State two requirements of the Health and Safety at Work Act for (i) employers; (ii) employees. For each of these requirements explain why they are important in a retail outlet.   (8 marks)

3 a) List six health and safety dangers which may be found in a fast-food restaurant:
       i) three which could affect the staff, and
      ii) three which could affect customers.   (6 marks)
    b) Explain how the restaurant can act to minimise the dangers which you have listed in question (a).   (6 marks)

4 For each of the following products explain how a retail store can minimise the risk to the customers who are buying them in the store:
    i) fireworks;
    ii) weed killer for the garden;
    iii) fresh meat products.   (6 marks)

5 Explain how a retail outlet can ensure that the following hazards are not a danger to customers or staff:
    i) wet floors from a water leak;
    ii) a sudden change of slope in the store;
    iii) a moving escalator;
    iv) electrical cables needed to run demonstration hi-fi systems.   (8 marks)

6 a) Draw the layout of a store that you have studied. On the diagram show where the emergency exits are and where the fire-fighting equipment is kept.
    b) Explain why the exits and equipment are placed where you have shown them.   (8 marks)

7 List the steps that members of staff should take if there is a fire in the store.   (5 marks)

8 a) Draw the layout of a store that you have studied which has security cameras and/or mirrors. On the diagram show where these cameras and/or mirrors have been placed.
    b) Explain why they have been placed where you have shown them.   (8 marks)

Revision test

This paper is longer than an external examination would normally be to allow students additional practice.

Time to complete the paper: 2 hours.

1   Explain why a store that is a member of a symbol group (Voluntary chain store) does not trade using its own name.   (3 marks)

2   a) List two functions which retailers carry out but which are not normally carried out by producers or wholesalers.   (2 marks)
    b) From your own studies give **one** example of a producer and **one** example of a wholesaler which carries out these functions and explain why they want to take on the role of the retailer.   (4 marks)

3   In the 1980s and early 1990s many supermarkets and major chains stores moved from town centre sites to out-of-town locations. Some supermarkets are now opening additional branches in back in the centres of towns.
    a) Explain why the stores moved out of the town centres   (4 marks)
    b) Explain why some of them are now re-opening additional branches in the centres of towns.   (4 marks)

4   Write down, in a table, the opening hours of a retail store that you have studied. Give full details for each day of the week.
    a) Explain how these opening hours affect (i) the business and (ii) the customers.   (4 marks)
    b) Give details of one retail business that has different opening hours and explain why the hours are different.   (4 marks)

5   a) Give examples of two different customer incentives used by a supermarket that you have studied.   (2 marks)
    b) Explain why they will help the supermarket to increase its profits.   (2 marks)
    c) Explain why one would be better than the other.   (1 mark)

6   Draw the shop layout of a small high street clothes or record store with which you are familiar and explain how and why this layout affects the flow of customers around the store.   (4 marks)

7   Explain why some stores have checkout counters at the exit point of their stores and why other stores put their counters in the centre of the store.   (4 marks)

8   If you were managing an estate agency what features would you provide to ensure that customers will be comfortable in the store? Explain clearly why the features would help to make the customers feel at ease.   (6 marks)

9   Toy sales tend to be very low in the summer months. Suggest a suitable theme display that a toy shop could use in order to increase its sales and explain why the theme you have chosen would be suitable.   (6 marks)

10 What is the difference between EPOS and EFTPOS?   (2 marks)

11 a) Give two pieces of information that are usually stored on a bar code. (2 marks)
   b) Explain how the use of bar codes in a store helps (i) the store and
      (ii) the customers. (6 marks)

12 How do loyalty cards help supermarkets to capture customer details and what use can
   the supermarkets make of this data? (6 marks)

13 State two different ways in which a clothes store can help customers who return goods
   that they do not want and explain why one way would be better than the other. (4 marks)

14 a) Describe how each of the following retailers usually "open the sale" for the products
      that they sell.
      i) A shop in a precinct that repairs shoes and cuts keys.
      ii) An out of town garden centre with a wide range of garden products.
      iii) A major internet company selling books. (3 marks)
   b) Explain why the three retailers open the sale in different ways. (3 marks)

15 Describe what steps a business that you have studied takes to identify its customers'
   needs. (4 marks)

16 a) Identify two health and safety hazards that are likely to be potential problems for a fish
      and chip shop. (2 marks)
   b) Explain what precautions the shop should be taking to ensure that each of these
      hazards does not become a problem. (2 marks)
   c) Explain why the fish and chip shop need to ensure that these hazards do not cause a
      problem. (4 marks)

17 Customers with disabilities can be at particular risk when they enter stores.
   a) Describe two different risks that a person in a wheelchair might face when shopping
      in a department store. (2 marks)
   b) What action does the law state that the business must take to ensure that such
      disabled people are not at risk? (4 marks)

18 With reference to a retail outlet which you have studied or of which you have personal
   knowledge, outline how the business prevents:
   i) shoplifting of goods
   ii) theft of money by staff
   iii) break-ins when the premises are empty.

Your answer should explain why the measures that the retail outlet has taken will help to
make the business more secure. (6 marks)

Total marks: 100

Index